MIGRATION
AND RESIDENTIAL MOBILITY
IN THE UNITED STATES

MIGRATION AND RESIDENTIAL MOBILITY IN THE UNITED STATES

Larry Long

for the
National Committee for Research
on the 1980 Census

RUSSELL SAGE FOUNDATION / NEW YORK

The Russell Sage Foundation

The Russell Sage Foundation, one of the oldest of America's general purpose foundations, was established in 1907 by Mrs. Margaret Olivia Sage for "the improvement of social and living conditions in the United States." The Foundation seeks to fulfill the mandate by fostering the development and dissemination of knowledge about the political, social, and economic problems of America. It conducts research in the social sciences and public policy, and publishes books and pamphlets that derive from the research.

The Board of Trustees is responsible for oversight and the general policies of the Foundation, while administrative direction of the program and staff is vested in the President, assisted by the officers and staff. The President bears final responsibility for the decision to publish a manuscript as a Russell Sage Foundation book. In reaching a judgment on the competence, accuracy, and objectivity of each study, the President is advised by the staff and selected expert readers. The conclusions and interpretations in Russell Sage Foundation publications are those of the authors and not of the Foundation, its Trustees, or its Staff. Publication by the Foundation, therefore, does not imply endorsement of the contents of the study.

Library of Congress Cataloging-in-Publication Data

Long, Larry E.
    Migration and residential mobility in the United States / by Larry Long.
        p.   cm.—(The Population of the United States in the 1980s)
    Bibliography: p.
    Includes index.
    ISBN 0-87154-555-1
    1. Migration, Internal—United States. 2. Residential mobility—United States.
I. Title. II. Series.
HB1965.L578   1988
304.8'0973—dc19   88-15758
                                           CIP

Cover and text design: HUGUETTE FRANCO

10 9 8 7 6 5 4 3 2 1

The National Committee for Research on the 1980 Census

The committee is sponsored by the Social Science Research Council, the Russell Sage Foundation, and the Alfred P. Sloan Foundation, in collaboration with the U.S. Bureau of the Census. The opinions, findings, and conclusions or recommendations expressed in the monographs supported by the committee are those of the author(s) and do not necessarily reflect the views of the committee or its sponsors.

Foreword

Migration and Residential Mobility in the United States is one of an ambitious series of volumes aimed at converting the vast statistical yield of the 1980 census into authoritative analyses of major changes and trends in American life. This series, "The Population of the United States in the 1980s," represents an important episode in social science research and revives a long tradition of independent census analysis. First in 1930, and then again in 1950 and 1960, teams of social scientists worked with the U.S. Bureau of the Census to investigate significant social, economic, and demographic developments revealed by the decennial censuses. These census projects produced three landmark series of studies, providing a firm foundation and setting a high standard for our present undertaking.

There is, in fact, more than a theoretical continuity between those earlier census projects and the present one. Like those previous efforts, this new census project has benefited from close cooperation between the Census Bureau and a distinguished, interdisciplinary group of scholars. Like the 1950 and 1960 research projects, research on the 1980 census was initiated by the Social Science Research Council and the Russell Sage Foundation. In deciding once again to promote a coordinated program of census analysis, Russell Sage and the Council were mindful not only of the severe budgetary restrictions imposed on the Census Bureau's own publishing and dissemination activities in the 1980s, but also of the extraordinary changes that have occurred in so many dimensions of American life over the past two decades.

The studies constituting "The Population of the United States in the 1980s" were planned, commissioned, and monitored by the National Committee for Research on the 1980 Census, a special committee appointed by the Social Science Research Council and sponsored by the Council, the Russell Sage Foundation, and the Alfred P. Sloan Foundation, with the collaboration of the U.S. Bureau of the Census. This committee includes leading social scientists from a broad range of fields—demography, economics, education, geography, history, political science, sociology, and statistics. It has been the committee's task to select the main topics for research, obtain highly qualified specialists to carry out that research, and provide the structure necessary to facilitate coordination among researchers and with the Census Bureau.

The topics treated in this series span virtually all the major features of American society—ethnic groups (blacks, Hispanics, foreign-born); spatial dimensions (migration, neighborhoods, housing, regional and metropolitan growth and decline); and status groups (income levels, families and households, women). Authors were encouraged to draw not only on the 1980 census but also on previous censuses and on subsequent national data. Each individual research project was assigned a special advisory panel made up of one committee member, one member nominated by the Census Bureau, one nominated by the National Science Foundation, and one or two other experts. These advisory panels were responsible for project liaison and review and for recommendations to the National Committee regarding the readiness of each manuscript for publication. With the final approval of the chairman of the National Committee, each report was released to the Russell Sage Foundation for publication and distribution.

The debts of gratitude incurred by a project of such scope and organizational complexity are necessarily large and numerous. The committee must thank, first, its sponsors—the Social Science Research Council, the Russell Sage Foundation, and the Alfred P. Sloan Foundation. The long-range vision and day-to-day persistence of these organizations and individuals sustained this research program over many years. The active and willing cooperation of the Bureau of the Census was clearly invaluable at all stages of this project, and the extra commitment of time and effort made by Bureau economist James R. Wetzel must be singled out for special recognition. A special tribute is also due to David L. Sills of the Social Science Research Council, staff member of the committee, whose organizational, administrative, and diplomatic skills kept this complicated project running smoothly.

The committee also wishes to thank those organizations that contributed additional funding to the 1980 census project—the Ford Foundation and its deputy vice president, Louis Winnick, the National Science Foundation, the National Institute on Aging, and the National Institute of Child Health and Human Development. Their support of the research program in general and of several particular studies is gratefully acknowledged.

The ultimate goal of the National Committee and its sponsors has been to produce a definitive, accurate, and comprehensive picture of the

U.S. population in the 1980s, a picture that would be primarily descriptive but also enriched by a historical perspective and a sense of the challenges for the future inherent in the trends of today. We hope our readers will agree that the present volume takes a significant step toward achieving that goal.

CHARLES F. WESTOFF

Chairman and Executive Director
National Committee for Research
on the 1980 Census

Acknowledgments

The major goal of this book is to integrate and communicate the trends and patterns of geographical mobility within the United States, as revealed by decennial censuses since 1940 and major national surveys conducted during those decades. Census questions on state of birth and residence five years earlier and survey questions on residence one year earlier provide overlapping images of the amount and major forms of geographical mobility in the United States from the late 1930s to the early 1980s. This book attempts to show where the picture is clear, where it is blurred, and where there are missing pieces that need to be filled in for policy or for research purposes.

Other studies have analyzed net migration for states and regions over longer periods of time, have undertaken more intensive analyses of the determinants of place-to-place migration flows, or have carried out more detailed research on particular types of mobility. This book was designed to give an overall perspective, highlighting relationships among the various forms and patterns of spatial mobility, as measured in censuses and surveys and describing what has changed and what has not over nearly the last half century.

With these goals in mind, I have drawn from many government publications, journal articles, and books and monographs about internal migration, and the extensive bibliography in this volume testifies to the vast expansion—perhaps it should be called proliferation—of research on the subject during the last twenty years or so. Until recently, demographers sometimes said that internal migration was the "stepchild of demography," but demographers, geographers, economists, and sociologists have contributed to the very rapid growth of publications that deal with internal migration. I have tried to concentrate on a few core questions that usually focus on trends and overlap academic disciplines. The book stresses what has been learned, and it tries to show how research and policy debates have influenced and been influenced by the availability of statistics on internal migration.

The work was supported by the Social Science Research Council and the consortium of organizations and experts that came together under SSRC's auspices. David L. Sills of SSRC, James R. Wetzel of the Census Bureau, and Charles F. Westoff of Princeton University were the visible presences behind the production of the series of analyses of the 1980 census. The advisory panel for this book was chaired by Sidney Goldstein of the Population Studies and Training Center at Brown University. The other members were Jacob Mincer of the Department of Economics at Columbia University, Julie DaVanzo of the Rand Corporation, and Diana DeAre of the Census Bureau's Population Division. Their comments were erudite, incisive, and offered in a way that gratifies and humbles an author. As chairperson of the National Committee for Research on the 1980 Census, Charles F. Westoff read the entire manuscript and provided comments that were as insightful as they were timely. These reviewers cannot be held responsible for the things I did badly or did not do.

The book was also made possible by the computer skills of several persons. In the Center for Demographic Studies, Mike Fortier designed the overall systems for computerized processing of data, text, and the bibliography. Ruth Breads programed many tabulations from microdata files maintained on mainframe computers. Tom Cochran did much of the manipulation of summary data on microcomputers, and Darlene Young and Pamela Smith prepared many computer-drawn charts and illustrations. Andrea Walter assisted in assembling the manuscript and verifying the tables in their final form.

Several chapters draw heavily upon work done over many years of collaboration with Kristin Hansen and Celia Boertlein of the Census Bureau's Population Division. They read and commented on the entire manuscript. Donald Dahmann of the Population Division also provided comments on the manuscript, and many other persons read portions of it. I tried to incorporate all the advice I received.

The manuscript benefited from careful and efficient work at the Russell Sage Foundation. Priscilla Lewis was in charge of making a book out of the text, tables, and figures, with the valuable editorial and production assistance of Charlotte Shelby and John Johnston. I am grateful for their expertise.

LARRY LONG

Contents

List of Tables

List of Figures

1

RESEARCH AND DATA ON GEOGRAPHICAL MOBILITY

NALYSIS of internal or international migration entails dealing with five questions: How much? Who? Where? Why? With what effect? Demographers are probably best at measuring how much migration occurs and who participates, at least in terms of characteristics of persons commonly measured in censuses and surveys. A geographer's skills help answer where migrants come from, where they go, and the spatial aspects of migration decision making. The last two questions are the most complex, for identifying why people move or stay and the effects of their mobility or stability requires the skills and insights of sociologists, economists, psychologists, and numerous other social scientists.

Though seemingly separate, these five questions become intertwined, for the dominant approach to answering the why of migration within the United States over the last two decades has been the application of econometric models that seek to infer the why by looking at the characteristics of areas migrants are moving to or from. Disaggregating such models by characteristics of migrants (for example, age) raises the further possibility of answering the who and with-what-effect questions. The with-what-effect question actually has many aspects: It can refer to the effects of migration on places, on people (those who do not migrate as well as those who do), and on more abstract concepts, such as occupational mobility of the labor force, the care of elderly persons whose children have moved far away, and the nature of participatory democracy and the role of voluntary activities in a society where individuals' commitment is to career and its advancement through migration rather than to places.[1]

Persons who analyze internal migration sometimes say that the subject of their research is complex because it subsumes so many questions and because users of the research seem to want answers to all of them at once. This inherent complexity is compounded by statistics that are expensive to collect, process, and analyze and are often inadequate to answer questions that arise in policy debates or are posed by sociological or economic theory. Moreover, the direct users of migration statistics are a diverse group with competing emphases and do not present a united front to the producers of migration statistics. Because of increased attention to the movement and distribution of population, research on internal migration has expanded enormously over the last two decades even if the resulting literature and public debate on the subject have been contentious over competing data, methods, and philosophical orientations.

With the curtailment of immigration in the 1920s, policy concerns and research attention began to shift to internal movements and the focus seemed to change from the somewhat heroic view of internal migration as the settling of the frontier in the nineteenth century to a more problem-oriented focus. The change in perspective reflected the economic difficulties experienced by agriculture in the 1920s and movement away from farms, and the Great Depression of the 1930s produced highly visible movements from the Great Plains states to the highways that led to California. The introduction of new migration questions on the 1940 census testified to renewed public concern with the measurement and analysis of long-distance movements, and suburbanization of the 1950s sparked interest in short-distance movements.

Several circumstances in the late 1960s and 1970s and new methodological developments combined to set off an explosive new round of research and policy debate on the causes and consequences of internal migration. One was the realization that the decline in fertility after the

---

[1] One of the strongest statements of the disadvantages that can accrue to a geographically mobile society was by Vance Packard in *A Nation of Strangers* (New York: McKay, 1972), which may be the only book on internal migration ever to make the best seller list. Its vignettes give many everyday examples of the effects of geographical mobility on people who do not move. In highly mobile Birmingham, Michigan, a housewife tells Packard that "many people prefer moving to staying around and saying good-by to everyone else." And Packard goes on to observe that "in such an environment millions of Americans who continue to live in one house might be called psychological nomads: they stay on but the turnover of people around them is so great that they can no longer enjoy a sense of place."

baby boom years was genuine and that low to moderate levels of fertility were likely to characterize the rest of the twentieth century. This recognition meant that in the eyes of many local public officials migration was coming to play a more visible and significant role in the growth or decline of local populations. It also meant that population projections came to be seen as more problematical, for migration flows for local areas change quickly, and better projection of population for subnational areas—states, metropolitan areas, cities, or various planning districts—required better migration data and theories of who moves where, why they move, and how they go about deciding to move or stay or pick one area rather than another.

Another development that spurred empirical and theoretical attention to migration was the sudden and unexpectedly large volume of migration to the Sunbelt, the loosely defined southern rim of the country. Migration to parts of the Sunbelt had been under way for a long time, but the rapidity of change and the numbers of people involved were not anticipated. The 1980 census counts caused more seats in the House of Representatives to shift from the Northeast and Midwest to the South and West than in any other decade in the country's history, providing a visible demonstration of the role of migration in quickly altering political constituencies.

Still another event that challenged existing theories of migration was the completely unexpected discovery of a shift of net migration balances toward nonmetropolitan territory around 1970. Since the industrial revolution urban areas had attracted migrants from rural areas, and a reversal of this pattern would challenge many economic theories of agglomeration and sociological ideas of the attractiveness of city lights. The net migration from metropolitan to nonmetropolitan territory from about 1970 to 1980 demonstrated new patterns and a need for better monitoring of internal population movements and a better conceptual scheme that could account for fluctuations in migration balances.

Migration research begins with definitions of what is to be analyzed. There are three critical aspects of defining what is and is not migration, and they need to be identified in order to understand the conventions that have been followed in censuses, surveys, and other sources of the raw materials of migration research. How these issues have been dealt with has strongly influenced the nature of migration research and the kinds of policy questions that can be adequately addressed with existing information sources. The rest of this chapter is devoted to definitional matters and how they have influenced the kinds of questions posed in migration research in the course of the increased attention to population movements over the last two or three decades.

Defining Usual Residence

One of the basic aspects of identifying what is to be considered migration is how residence is defined, for a critical aspect of the notion of migration or mobility is a change in residence.[2] With administrative records, like the population registers of many countries or information gathered as a consequence of participation in government programs, the definition of residence may be legally prescribed. A great deal of data on population movements within the United States are from censuses and surveys for which there is some leeway in how residence is to be interpreted. Censuses in the United States have more nearly followed a *de jure* than a *de facto* approach, in that the attempt at the time of the census is to establish each person's usual or customary (not necessarily legal) residence regardless of where the person may have been on the day of the census. This approach is desirable in that it eliminates many movements of very short duration, such as vacations, visits with relatives, employment at temporary or transitory worksites, and other circumstances that represent important forms of spatial movement but do not constitute a change of residence and therefore are not counted as migration. Admittedly, however, these kinds of movements may substitute for or be alternatives to the more permanent forms of movement that are to be called migration, and a complete theory of spatial mobility should specify these relationships.[3]

In U.S. censuses and surveys two groups of persons illustrate the complexity of defining usual residence as a first step toward later defining migration as a change of usual residence. One group consists of itinerant farm workers who may spend the winter in southern Texas or elsewhere in the Southwest and move northward in the spring and summer to harvest crops. The other group, of dramatically different socioeconomic status, consists of "snowbirds"—typically retired or semiretired persons who have two residences and may spend winters in Florida, Arizona, or elsewhere in the Sunbelt and spend the summer months in the cooler North, usually at what might be called their preretirement area of residence. When the census was taken in April 1980, many farm workers would already have left Texas, and some snowbirds

---

[2] A formal set of definitions of migration terms can be found in Henry S. Shryock, Jacob Siegel, and Associates, *The Methods and Materials of Demography*, vols. 1 and 2 (Washington, DC: U.S. Government Printing Office, 1971), pp. 616–672; and in United Nations, *Methods of Measuring Internal Migration*, Manual 6 (New York: United Nations, 1970), pp. 1–4 and 40–49.

[3] Michelle Behr and Patricia Gober, "When a Residence Is Not a House: Examining Residence-Based Migration Definitions," *Professional Geographer* 34, no. 2 (1982): 178–184.

would have gone North. If the farm workers reported Texas as their usual residence, they could have been recorded as nonmovers in the census if they said that their usual residence was the same in April 1975 as in April 1980. The snowbirds who were still in Florida in April 1980 and who reported a usual residence elsewhere would be assigned to their usual residence and likewise might appear in census tabulations as nonmovers.

Persons visiting relatives or staying temporarily in hotels or motels at the time of the 1980 census were asked to identify their usual residence and were assigned to it. Persons living in households received this instruction: "If everyone here is staying only temporarily and has a usual home elsewhere, please fill this circle." Over 300,000 households representing 547,000 persons filled the circle, and for some areas these nonpermanent residents were an important segment of the population. Households where everyone reported a usual residence different from that at the time of the 1980 census were most numerous in Florida, where they constituted about one household in 28.[4] The state most often reported as "home" was New York. The New York-to-Florida connection coincided with the largest stream of interstate migrants recorded in the 1980 census (discussed in Chapter 3), and if all of the seasonal snowbirds had been included, this migration stream would have been even larger. But most were not included because the approach in censuses has been to count only one "usual" residence. Almost certainly some persons who maintain two residences use seasonal movement between them as an alternative to permanent relocation.

College students who do not live with their parents are another group with somewhat ambiguous usual residence insofar as migration is concerned. In the 1940 census college students living in dormitories were assigned to their parents' residence; censuses since then have counted them where they lived while attending school. Census Bureau surveys, however, include college students as part of their parental household and probably understate the spatial mobility of college students relative to censuses. Regardless of where college students are counted, their movements between school and parental home are another illustration of the difficulty of distinguishing between seasonal movements and more permanent residential relocations.

There is no completely satisfactory way of overcoming the limitations of recognizing only one usual residence or of recording various seasonal or semipermanent movements as special forms of migration.

---

[4] U.S. Bureau of the Census, 1980 Census of Population, *Nonpermanent Residents by States and Selected Counties and Incorporated Places: 1980*, PC80-S1-6 (Washington, DC: U.S. Government Printing Office, 1982).

Theoretically pure but elaborate solutions could add to respondent burden or processing costs and impair the quality of migration data. Censuses and surveys probably never will record the full range of daily and seasonal movements that, with migration, constitute spatial mobility.

Defining the Length of the Migration Interval

The second issue in operationalizing the concept of migration is the period of time over which to measure movement. Using the concept of one and only one usual residence eliminates many daily or seasonal movements, for the idea is that migration should reflect residential relocation over some significant period of time. The earliest migration questions were for place of birth and did not ascertain migration over a specific period of time. In 1850 the U.S. census for the first time asked for state or country of birth, and by this time censuses in several European countries were asking respondents for their birthplace in terms of localities, areas smaller than a state or province.

Place-of-birth data provide useful insight into the geographical origins of the population of a country or region, but there are many shortcomings. Migration clearly characterizes a person whose place of usual residence at the census date was state A but who was born in state B. Missing, however, is knowledge of when the move occurred and the many invisible moves made by persons returning to their state of birth or engaging in other repeat movement.

After introducing the state-of-birth question in 1850, the U.S. census expanded it in 1870 to include state or country of birth of each parent.[5] This information added an additional dimension by allowing some inferences to be made about the birthplaces of two generations. The dual questions on state or country of birth of respondents and their parents were continued in decennial censuses from 1870 through 1930. From 1940 through 1970 parents' place of birth was asked only in terms of country of birth. In 1980 neither state nor country of birth of parents was asked, although the question on respondents' state or country of birth was retained.

The 1940 census is often said to be the first of the "modern" U.S. censuses. The Great Depression of the 1930s illustrated the need for statistics on the nature and extent of unemployment, and the 1940 census introduced many labor force concepts. The exodus from the Dust-

---

[5] Copies of each census questionnaire, from the first one in 1790 to the 1980 version, can be found in U.S. Bureau of the Census, *Twenty Censuses: Population and Housing Questions, 1790–1980* (Washington, DC: U.S. Bureau of the Census, 1978).

bowl states pointed to a need to measure migration over a specific period of time (rather than simply state of birth) and to obtain data on the characteristics of migrants, the places they were leaving, and the places they were going to. The Census Bureau in 1940 and in later censuses and surveys was faced with the problem of deciding the most useful interval over which to measure migration.

An interval that is too long is likely to introduce error through inability of respondents to remember and through nonresponse, as many persons may be intimidated by a long interval that refers to what to them seems like an arbitrary date far in the past. And if the migration interval is too long, it misses many intervening moves and the characteristics of migrants at the time of the census may be very different from the time of moving. In censuses taken every 10 years, as is the case in the United States, the temptation might have been to ask persons where they lived 10 years earlier, at the date of the last census. The designers of the 1940 census decided against this approach.

Although 10 years seemed too long, an interval that was too short would be equally unsatisfactory. An interval that is too short may blur the intended distinction between short-term, nonpermanent movements and the more permanent changes that characterize migration. Also, a very short interval may overlap with temporary events that are not characteristic of prevailing trends and produce a distorted view of migration patterns. The decision was made to include in the 1940 census a question on usual residence five years earlier. This was the first time a so-called fixed-period migration question was asked in the U.S. census, and a five-year interval is a convention that was followed in the censuses of 1960, 1970, and 1980 and also in censuses in a number of other countries.

In the 1950 census a one-year question rather than a five-year question was adopted because in 1945 many Americans were fighting in World War II or were at wartime residences in the United States. Unfortunately, however, the year preceding the 1950 census was a major postwar recession, so that migration data from the 1950 census are not representative of major migration trends around that time. Perhaps the most vivid example of how the 1949–50 migration data can be misleading is their portrayal of the South as having net inmigration in 1949–50, seeming to imply a striking reversal of the net outmigration that had characterized the region for decades. The South's net inmigration in 1949–50 seems, in retrospect, to have been the product of return movements, perhaps not unlike the return migration to many rural states in the early years of the 1930s, and other data soon showed the South to have substantial net outmigration. A census question on residence one year ago can be sensitive to cyclical disturbances of this type, and for small areas the one-year interval sometimes produced too few migrants for meaningful analysis.

There is no consensus as to the best or ideal interval over which to measure migration in censuses or surveys. A five-year interval, as does any relatively long interval, understates migration, for only the difference between current usual residence and that five years earlier is ascertained even though several intervening moves could have occurred. This feature of the question has some advantages, however, for it tends to obscure some short-duration moves that are "mistakes" undertaken with inadequate or erroneous information. DaVanzo's work with longitudinal data suggests that many moves of very short duration occur because of migrants' misperceptions of alternative opportunities and are quickly "corrected" through return or repeat migration.[6] The residential change over a five-year perspective may appear more in line with what are economically rational moves because it incorporates corrections to "bad" migration decisions made over shorter intervals.

In contrast to the practice adopted in censuses, surveys conducted by the Census Bureau have tended to use a one-year interval. Partly because the migration questions are asked once each year, the Current Population Survey began in 1948 to ask respondents about residence one year earlier.[7] A similar practice has been used in the American Housing Survey (formerly the Annual Housing Survey).

These decisions have led the United States to rely more on fixed-period migration questions than the alternative, a question on duration of residence.[8] The latter asks how long the respondent has lived continuously in the current locality and has the advantage of being able to

---

[6] Julie DaVanzo, "Repeat Migration, Information Costs, and Location-Specific Capital," *Population and Environment* 4 (Spring 1981): 45–73; Julie DaVanzo, "Repeat Migration in the United States: Who Moves Back and Who Moves On?" *Review of Economics and Statistics* 65, no. 4 (1983): 552–559.

[7] The use of a one-year mobility interval was interrupted in the early 1970s, when the mobility question was changed to adopt a varying interval so as to ask about residence in 1970; for example, the 1973 question used a three-year interval to ask about residence in 1970, the 1974 question used a four-year interval, and so on. In the late 1970s the question asked about residence in 1975. The reason for this change was that the Census Bureau was authorized to conduct a mid-decade census or other major statistical operation in 1975, and the decision was made to alter the format used in reporting surveys so as to report change since the last census or benchmark measure, which was assumed to be every five years. Integrating the CPS migration results more closely into the postcensal estimates of net migration for states and regions was also anticipated at that time. Funding for a mid-decade statistical program in 1975 was not approved, and beginning in 1981 the CPS resumed use of a one-year mobility interval.

[8] There are at least three exceptions. The decennial housing censuses and the American Housing Survey have included questions on duration of residence in current dwelling, the 1976 Survey of Income and Education had a question on length of residence in the state of residence at the survey date, and the 1970 and 1980 censuses had questions on year of immigration to the United States.

show the distribution of population by length of residence. A duration-of-residence question can also ask locality of previous residence and can include, but rarely does, a question on activity, occupation, or other characteristics at the time of the last move. The fixed-period migration questions used in U.S. censuses and surveys have at times asked about activity or status at the beginning of the migration interval.[9]

Defining Boundaries and Migration Distances

The third critical aspect of defining migration concerns the minimum distance or other method for distinguishing between migration and purely local moves. The basic idea is that a significant difference exists between migration and strictly local moving. The former is more disruptive, often entailing many other types of changes, like job relocations and alterations in networks of friends. Short-distance (local) moves may entail alterations in daily habits—commuting, shopping, and so forth—but not the more serious changes that are likely to accompany migration.

The analytical value in making a distinction between local moves and migration is often useful, for almost everyone agrees that a move from one apartment to another in the same building should not be considered migration.[10] A move down the block probably would not be considered migration by this reasoning, but what about a move across town? What about a move across a town the size of Los Angeles, which covers 465 square miles? Distance may be only part of the distinction between local moves and migration, and the degree to which distance reflects the disruptiveness of a move may decline over time with improvements in transportation and communication.

[9] The 1970 and 1980 censuses included questions on activity five years earlier (working at a job or business, in college, or in the armed forces). For those who reported working in 1965, the 1970 census also asked for occupation in 1965. The information on activity at the beginning of the census five-year migration intervals has shown that college students and members of the military represent a substantial proportion of interstate migrants; see John F. Long, "The Effects of College and Military Populations on Models of Interstate Migration," *Socio-Economic Planning Sciences* 17, no. 5–6 (1983): 281–290. The American Housing Survey has included a number of questions on characteristics of the previous housing unit for households that have moved in the 12 months preceding the survey.

[10] A really complete theory of spatial movements would include even the apartment-to-apartment moves, which were called "migration" by Everett Lee in "A Theory of Migration," *Demography* 3, no. 1 (1966): 47–57. Interviewers for the Current Population Survey are instructed to count apartment-to-apartment moves within the same building as a change of residence.

In practice, the distinction is typically made by conventions adopted by statistical bureaus or other data gatherers. Rarely are respondents asked to report the distance of a move. More common is to ask respondents the locality of previous residence, and in the United States the practice has been to ask for city and county. The 1940 census had no provision for recording the number of local movers but did record movement to and from counties or cities of 100,000 or greater population. The censuses of 1960, 1970, and 1980 asked respondents aged 5 and older whether their residence five years earlier was the same as at the time of the census and if not, the name of the city, county, and state five years earlier.[11]

A common practice in these censuses as well as in Census Bureau surveys has been to show the number of movers within counties, between counties within a state, and between states. Most other countries with fixed-period statistics on internal migration also report the number of moves or movers between localities that have some political or administrative function.[12]

The most obvious limitation of presenting U.S. statistics on internal migration on a county basis is that the more than 3,100 counties or county equivalents vary greatly in size and shape. The largest county in the 48 contiguous states[13] is San Bernardino, California, which covers over 20,000 square miles—an area larger than several states and larger than the Netherlands. San Bernardino County includes some of the eastern suburbs of Los Angeles and a considerable chunk of the Mohave desert. A move from the western end of the county to Needles, a community on the far eastern edge, would cover over 150 miles—hardly a local move but still intracounty. The nation's smallest county is Falls Church city, which covers two square miles and is a Virginia suburb of Washington, D.C. A move from Falls Church to neighboring Fairfax

[11] For the exact wording of the questions used in these censuses, see the questionnaires that are reproduced in U.S. Bureau of the Census, *Twenty Censuses: Population and Housing Inquiries, 1790–1980.*

[12] A useful compilation of publication practices and methods of collecting statistics on internal migration in a great many countries is the United Nations study, *Statistics of Internal Migration: A Technical Report*, Studies in Methods, series F, no. 23 (New York: United Nations, 1978). Several studies have compared survey practices in more developd and less developed countries, including Sally E. Findley, *Migration Survey Methodologies: A Review of Design Issues* (Liège, Belgium: International Union for the Scientific Study of Population, 1982); Sidney Goldstein and Alice Goldstein, *Surveys of Migration in Developing Countries: A Methodological Review* (Honolulu: East-West Population Institute, 1981); and Richard E. Bilsborrow, A. S. Oberai, and Guy Standing, eds., *Migration Surveys in Low Income Countries: Guidelines for Survey and Questionnaire Design* (London: Croom Helm, 1984).

[13] Some areas in Alaska are treated as counties for statistical purposes and are larger in area than San Bernardino County, but the Alaskan areas have had less stable boundaries and very few inhabitants.

County might cover only a few miles but would be *inter*county. These are the extreme cases in examining geographical movement on the basis of counties.

Counties have been used as a basis for producing migration statistics because their boundaries are relatively stable, they are recognizable areas for respondents to report, and they are used for many other statistical purposes, like establishing the boundaries of metropolitan areas outside of New England. The Census Bureau is often cited as "defining" migration on the basis of counties, and researchers readily note the conceptual inadequacies of such a definition, giving examples like those just discussed. Census Bureau publications may still sometimes seem to imply that the bureau has formally decided to define migration only in this way, but it is probably more correct to say that the bureau has adopted this convention for very practical considerations.

Since the 1960 census the Census Bureau has coded migration data in somewhat more detail to allow identification not only of moves within and between counties but also of moves within central cities of metropolitan areas, between central cities and the balance of metropolitan areas, and between metropolitan areas and nonmetropolitan territory. The county-based scheme has the advantage of continuity, whereas the latter may be more analytically useful for some types of questions. A disadvantage of the latter approach is that the number and boundaries of metropolitan areas change frequently as they grow outward and new metropolitan areas are carved out of what was formerly nonmetropolitan territory.

A universally better—and cost-effective—approach is not immediately evident. Persons changing residence could be asked distance of move and those moving some minimum distance thought to distinguish between local movers and migrants could be asked county, city, or postal code (ZIP) of previous residence. One precedent for this approach is the 1967 Survey of Economic Opportunity, which was conducted by the Census Bureau and asked respondents if they had ever lived more than 50 miles from their current residence. Those who answered yes were asked additional questions on previous places of residence. Respondents in the SEO who had moved more than 50 miles were not asked to report the actual distance of their last move, but other surveys conducted by the Census Bureau have asked respondents to report the distance of moves.[14] Numerous studies have inferred migration distances based on highway or airline mileage between cities of origin and destination, and the distribution of migration distances has been calcu-

---

[14] The Health Interview Surveys conducted by the Census Bureau for the U.S. Public Health Service have asked respondents to report the distance of their last move in miles.

lated by using the population centers of states or counties or origin and destination (discussed in Chapters 3 and 8). Data on distance moved would improve the analytical value of migration statistics, and although any minimum value—50 miles, 100 kilometers, or anything else—chosen to represent the dividing line between local mobility and migration would seem arbitrary, some convention along these lines might significantly improve the comparability of migration data from different sources or among countries.

The lack of consensus on the various aspects of identifying which moves to call migration has strongly influenced the nature of migration research and has impaired the cumulativeness of research findings. In the years following World War II, however, several landmark studies took approaches that have set the course for several lines of research that are most common today. They are important milestones in understanding the origins of current issues and debates in migration research.

Migration Research: The Postwar Years

Early work with the new fixed-period migration data from the 1940 and 1950 censuses continued to grapple with the problem of the appropriate geographical areas over which migration should be measured and analyzed. The new data offered the possibility of conceptualizing migration on a geographical basis other than conventional administrative and political areas even though the official publications focused on the production of migration and other statistics for states, counties, and cities because such areas use migration data to learn who is joining and who is leaving their constituencies. From an analytical point of view, however, individuals may or may not make decisions to move or stay on the basis of administrative boundaries, and early analysts worried over what were the proper geographical areas to use for the formulation of behavioral theories of spatial mobility. Since censuses appeared unlikely to ask respondents for actual distance moved or for precise location of previous residence (for example, street address), considerable effort in the early postwar years was devoted to finding ways of grouping counties into economically homogeneous aggregates that would constitute the geographical territory over which migration decisions were made and within which strictly "local" moves occurred. These territories might be metropolitan areas (or labor markets) or predominantly rural regions specializing in various forms of agriculture, mining, or resource extraction.

Bogue and colleagues developed a system of classification derived from grouping counties into metropolitan areas and nonmetropolitan regions, and the 1940 data were retabulated for these units.[15] Probably there is no permanent solution to the problem of establishing areas for migration research, for technology changes the location of economic activity and the meaning of "local" insofar as commuting is concerned; and much subsequent work has sought cumulativeness by using states or metropolitan areas even though the latter steadily become geographically larger.

The premier research effort to concentrate on migration at the state level was the three-volume work carried out at the University of Pennsylvania on population redistribution and economic growth from 1870 to 1950.[16] Several features have distinguished it as a lasting contribution. One is that it was the first to apply the survival-rate method to estimate net migration by age, sex, and race for all states over a long period of time. The study not only created a statistical data base, but also illustrated a method that has continued relevance to places and periods of time when no other source of information on internal migration is available. A second distinguishing feature was its empirical and ideologically neutral approach to the study of internal migration. Previous research undertakings often tended to take a crisis view of internal migration as a phenomenon of such cataclysmic events as economic depressions, natural disasters, and wars, or else took a "social problems" approach that dwelled on the potentially disruptive aspects of migration for individuals and communities. The historical perspective of the University of Pennsylvania study directed attention to internal migration as a continuing process—one that ebbs and flows with economic conditions—and not simply a product of extraordinary circumstances. The empirical nature of the study also shifted the focus of research away from a search for "laws" or universal regularities that could characterize internal migration for all places and all times.

[15] Donald J. Bogue, Henry S. Shryock, Jr., and Siegfried A. Hoermann, *Streams of Migration between Subregions: A Pilot Study of Migration Flows between Environments,* Subregional Migration in the United States, 1935–40, vol. 1 (Oxford, Ohio: Scripps Foundation, Miami University, 1957); and Donald J. Bogue and Margaret Jarman Hagood, *Differential Migration in the Corn and Cotton Belts: A Pilot Study of the Selectivity of Intrastate Migration to Cities from Nonmetropolian Areas,* Subregional Migration in the United States, 1935–40, vol. 2 (Oxford, Ohio: Scripps Foundation, Miami University, 1953). The system of "State Economic Areas," which formed the basis for many of the tabulations, was presented in Donald J. Bogue and Calvin L. Beale, *Economic Areas of the United States* (New York: Free Press, 1961).

[16] Everett S. Lee, Ann Ratner Miller, Carol P. Brainerd, and Richard A. Easterlin, *Methodological Considerations and Reference Tables;* Simon Kuznets, Ann Ratner Miller, and Richard A. Easterlin, *Analyses of Economic Change;* Hope T. Eldridge and Dorothy Swaine Thomas, *Demographic Analyses and Interrelations;* Population Redistribution and Economic Growth, United States, 1870–1950, vols. 1–3 (Philadelphia: American Philosophical Society, 1957).

Another landmark study was Shryock's *Population Mobility Within the United States*.[17] This work served to illustrate and publicize the use of censuses and national surveys of migration over fixed periods, and its attention to gross migration flows supplemented the focus on net migration that formed the basis of the University of Pennsylvania study. The Shryock book demonstrated the value of a continuing national data series on place-to-place flows that could measure the nature of migration differentials and selectivity of migration viewed from both the origins and destinations of migrants. Its textbook function of showing how to collect retrospective data and analyze the results served to guide subsequent research and data collection.

The work that more than any other introduced the behavioral approach of econometric modeling of place-to-place migration flows was Lowry's *Migration and Metropolitan Growth*.[18] Lowry's work dealt only with moves among metropolitan areas and focused on the metropolitan area rather than states or regions as the locus of migration decision making. It emphasized the interaction of conditions at origin and destination in influencing gross flows of migrants. The basic outline of his model is identified in Chapter 6 along with some subsequent refinements.

A major work that helped introduce survey approaches to analyzing internal migration was Lansing and Mueller's *The Geographic Mobility of Labor*.[19] Their work demonstrated the potential of national surveys that were too small to produce place-to-place migration flows or any other localized data but could include innovative questions on residential background, attitudes toward future moving, perceived barriers to moving, and other questions far too detailed ever to be included in censuses or routine surveys. Their work helped focus attention on migration as a general process rather than a fixed attribute of particular people and places.

These studies illustrate contrasting data (net migration, census data on place-to-place flows, and survey statistics on migration attitudes and intentions) and different research styles. But all had an essentially empirical orientation, with emphases on data development, fact-finding, and the testing of hypotheses. They set in motion orientations to migration research that have continued to the present.

---

[17] Henry S. Shryock, Jr., *Population Mobility Within the United States* (Chicago: Community and Family Study Center, University of Chicago, 1964).

[18] Ira S. Lowry, *Migration and Metropolitan Growth: Two Analytical Models* (San Francisco: Chandler, 1966).

[19] John B. Lansing and Eva Mueller, *The Geographic Mobility of Labor* (Ann Arbor: Institute for Social Research, University of Michigan, 1967).

Migration Research: The 1970s

Application of the alternative approaches outlined above caused research on internal migration to proliferate in the 1970s along with successive attempts to summarize and synthesize an explosion of empirical findings.[20] The bibliographical undertakings illustrate divergent producers of migration research and ways of describing, evaluating, and summarizing what they do.

Three major bibliographies appeared in 1975. Price and Sikes[21] provided an annotated listing and interpretative summary of over 1,200 studies of rural-to-urban migration in the United States and was used extensively by sociologists. Many of the studies they examined were conducted by individual researchers in rural outmigration counties and were typically undertaken for the purpose of ascertaining the characteristics of those who had left or were planning to leave. Such studies focus on the effects of migration on places of origin and express the fears of many rural counties that they were losing their "best" people (most highly educated, most intelligent, or with greatest leadership potential) and that the viability of rural communities was adversely affected by outmigration. Surveys conducted in places of destination—typically individual cities of the North or even specific neighborhoods—usually focused on migrants' adjustment, accommodation, and sources of information used in deciding to leave the rural area and choosing the destination (family and friends were frequently mentioned in this regard), often reflecting fears that inmigrants contributed appreciably to poverty, unemployment, crime, or other urban problems.

Price and Sikes also reviewed the results of the 1967 Survey of Economic Opportunity, one of the first U.S. government-sponsored surveys to probe migration background in depth, including questions on state of birth and type of residence at age 16 (rural, small town, big city, and so on) and place of last residence. From this source and many others Price and Sikes concluded that in the aggregate rural-to-urban migrants were better educated than the rural population from which they were drawn, and by the late 1960s the migrants were not materially less educated

---

[20] Prior to the burst of bibliographies in the mid-1970s the best-known efforts to catalogue research on internal migration were Dorothy Swaine Thomas's *Research Memorandum on Migration Differentials* (New York: Social Science Research Council, 1938) and J. J. Mangalam's *Human Migration: A Guide to Migration Literature in English, 1955–62* (Lexington: University of Kentucky Press, 1968).

[21] Daniel O. Price and Melanie M. Sikes, *Rural-Urban Migration Research in the United States: Annotated Bibliography and Synthesis* (Washington, DC: U.S. Government Printing Office, 1975).

than comparable populations at urban places of destination. Contrary to popular impressions, Price and Sikes could find little evidence to support notions that rural-to-urban migration was a primary cause of rising levels of crime, poverty, or welfare dependence in cities in the 1950s and 1960s. In terms of the effect of rural-to-urban migration on the migrants and their places of destination, Price and Sikes found that "the one conclusion that can be drawn from studies of the adjustment of rural-urban migrants is that there is no consistent pattern of failure of migrants to adjust to urban living and, thus, to pose problems for the urban areas in which they live."[22]

Greenwood's bibliography, which also appeared in 1975, was limited to work by economists to develop macro models along the lines of Lowry's. This limitation excluded virtually all of the studies in the Price-Sikes bibliography and concluded that ". . . relatively little research has focused on the consequences of migration."[23] The econometric approaches reviewed by Greenwood were intended to explore the determinants rather than the consequences or effects of migration. Greenwood's review pointed out a limitation of the census question on residence five years ago and a gap in U.S. statistics. For many of the models of migration to, from, or between geographical areas information was lacking on characteristics of the areas at the beginning of the five-year intervals (for example, 1955 or 1965), and many researchers had used end-of-period data or averaged data from successive censuses (for example, 1950 and 1960 or 1960 and 1970) to estimate mid-point measures. Such practices produce a simultaneity bias, for characteristics of areas after migration has occurred may reflect the effects of migration and do not accurately measure the determinants, as intended by the models. This source of error and aggregation biases (for example, using total migration flows rather than specific demographic or economic subgroups) led many migration models to produce "puzzling" results. For these and other reasons, many had failed to find the expected effects of characteristics at origin (rates of unemployment, rate of job growth, level of earnings, and so on) on migration.

The third bibliographical review to appear in 1975 was by Shaw, who, like Greenwood, focused on macro models of internal migration in

---

[22] Price and Sikes, *Rural-Urban Migration Research in the United States*, p. 27.

[23] Michael J. Greenwood, "Research on Internal Migration in the United States: A Survey," *Journal of Economic Literature* 13 (June 1975): 397–433. Ten years later, in another literature review, Greenwood again concluded that ". . . almost no attention has been paid to the consequences of migration of persons with different characteristics nor to many other important aspects of this relationship" (p. 526). Greenwood called for more extensive use of simultaneous-equations approaches in macro models and more use of microdata for theory development. Michael J. Greenwood, "Human Migration: Theory, Models, and Empirical Studies," *Journal of Regional Science* 25, no. 4 (1985): 521–544.

the United States but also included some findings from other countries.[24] Shaw noted many of the same specification problems observed by Greenwood and emphasized the failure of models to have predictive value in forecasting population movements. One reason might be the omission of variables to reflect the climate, amenities, or quality of life in addition to strictly economic characteristics, and an important research direction in recent years has been attempts to incorporate these attributes of areas (discussed in Chapter 6).

In 1976 Ritchey reviewed "explanations of migration" in a publication aimed mostly at sociologists, but specifically excluded studies of "the effects of migration on the individual and the impact of migration on society and communities."[25] Like Greenwood and Shaw, Ritchey concentrated on econometric approaches, identified numerous methodological problems in model design, and recommended a continuing national migration survey along the lines of the national fertility surveys or the World Fertility Survey.

The work of geographers on U.S. internal migration was reviewed by Bennett and Gade,[26] who considered analyses of both short-distance and long-distance movement. They recommended that future work show regard for how the two types of movement are related and may be changed by alterations in commuting fields. Like Ritchey, they called for better data, including the collection of more background information (more than just characteristics before and after a move, which is often simply the most recent move), and, like Shaw, they called for attention to a wider range of noneconomic variables and attributes of persons and areas and the ways that areal attributes are perceived and evaluated by migrants and potential migrants.

Migration Research: The 1980s and Beyond

The major literature reviews of the 1970s led to some new directions in migration research in the 1980s. One is a greater reliance on micro-level models based on individual characteristics as a basis for the-

[24] R. Paul Shaw, *Migration Theory and Fact: A Review and Bibliography of Current Literature* (Philadelphia: Regional Science Research Institute, 1975).

[25] P. Neal Ritchey, "Explanations of Migration," in Alex Inkeles, James Coleman, and Neil Smelser, eds., *Annual Review of Sociology* (Palo Alto, CA.: Annual Reviews, 1976).

[26] D. Gordon Bennett and Ole Gade, *Geographic Perspectives in Migration Research: A Bibliographical Survey* (Chapel Hill: Department of Geography, University of North Carolina, 1979). A more recent synthesis of the migration literature summarized by a geographer—but not limited to the work of geographers—is W. A. V. Clark's *Human Migration* (Beverly Hills, CA: Sage, 1986).

ory development and exploring the behaviorial bases for why migration occurs.[27] Primary data sources for such approaches have included computer-readable microdata from censuses and longitudinal surveys that develop migration data as a consequence of tracking individuals from year to year.[28] The longitudinal surveys offer the possibility of exact comparisons of characteristics of persons before and after moving and allow for the inclusion of areal characteristics to investigate individual-areal interactions in decisions to move or stay or pick one destination over another. When continued long enough, the longitudinal surveys allow the study of migration sequences, like return and repeat movements, and how the timing of migration in the life cycle affects other characteristics of persons and families. This general approach focuses attention on migration as a process rather than an attribute of specific areas.

Another new thrust is to use migration information from censuses and administrative records to develop migration models that work—that is, can be used, in the context of various assumptions about economic change, to improve projections of population of subnational areas.[29] What the literature reviews of the 1970s and early 1980s consistently showed was a plethora of explanations of migration and its causes with relatively few applications. Improved population projections are one of the clearest applications of migration research.

This book attempts to use migration data from censuses and continuing national surveys to do some of the things they do best and for

[27] See Julie DaVanzo, "Microeconomic Approaches to Studying Migration Decisions"; John L. Goodman, Jr., "Information, Uncertainty, and the Microeconomic Model of Migration Decision Making"; and other chapters in Gordon F. DeJong and Robert W. Gardner, eds., *Migration Decision Making* (New York: Pergamon Press, 1981).

[28] The most frequently used longitudinal surveys for migration research are the National Longitudinal Surveys and the Panel Study of Income Dynamics, which are compared in Richard E. Bilsborrow and John S. Akin, "Data Availability versus Data Needs for Analyzing the Determinants and Consequences of Internal Migration: An Evaluation of U.S. Survey Data," *Review of Public Data Use* 10 (December 1982): 261–284.

[29] The prospects for developing annual interstate migration data from administrative records are discussed in R. A. Engels and Mary K. Healy, "Measuring Interstate Migration Flows: An Origin-Destination Network Based on Internal Revenue Service Records," *Environment and Planning A* 13 (November 1981): 1345–1360. The shortcomings of current data and some new approaches to forecasting migration are identified in Andrew M. Isserman, David A. Plane, and David B. McMillen, "Internal Migration in the United States: An Evaluation of Federal Data," *Review of Public Data Use* 10 (December 1982): 285–311; Andrew A. Isserman, David A. Plane, Peter A. Rogerson, and Paul A. Beaumont, "Forecasting Interstate Migration with Limited Data: A Demographic-Economic Approach," *Journal of the American Statistical Association* 80 (June 1985): 277–285; A. M. Isserman, "Economic-Demographic Modeling with Endogenously Determined Birth and Migration Rates: Theory and Prospects," *Environment and Planning A* 17 (1985): 25–45; and D. A. Plane and P. A. Rogerson, "Economic-Demographic Models for Forecasting Interregional Migration," *Environment and Planning A* 17 (1985): 185–198.

which there is no substitute in administrative records or longitudinal or local surveys. The very broad goal is to identify major trends in the amount and direction of spatial movement of population within the United States and some of the major identifiable consequences, as shown by censuses of 1940, 1960, 1970, and 1980 and other relevant sources of information. The focus is upon change and continuity in gross rather than net movements over nearly the last half century.

Chapter 2 compares alternative measures of the volume of movement within the country for long periods of time and shows how different observers have explained and evaluated the significance of this mobility. The chapter also identifies some major migration differentials for the purpose of assessing their effect on the amount and rate of moving within the United States.

Chapter 3 concentrates on where major migration streams have originated and terminated since the 1930s, using states for this purpose because they represent the smallest and most stable geographical areas for which information over long periods can be compiled and because of their relevance to many policy concerns. The chapter focuses on changing propensities to move to and from several Great Lakes industrialized states which experienced substantial growth in jobs for many decades before being dubbed the "rustbowl" as many of their jobs moved to the Sunbelt or abroad in the 1970s.

Chapter 4 continues the analysis of major interstate and interregional migration streams by disaggregating recent flows according to an additional characteristic—the migrants' place of birth—in order to give an idea of the representation of return and repeat movement.

Chapter 5 considers the effects—or potential effects—of migration on areas, especially at the regional level. It looks at the racial composition of migration streams and examines some alleged consequences of migration, particularly the effects of population movements on regional levels of education, poverty, and some other characteristics. The chapter highlights changing policy issues and proposals for dealing with some of the presumed effects of internal migration.

Chapter 6 directs attention away from regions to a metropolitan and nonmetropolitan perspective, which was the focus of renewed research and policy analysis over the last decade and a half as migration shifted from favoring metropolitan territory to favoring nonmetropolitan territory and then changed again about 1980 to favor metropolitan areas. The chapter attempts to explain why people move to, from, or between metropolitan and nonmetropolitan environments.

Chapter 7 further evaluates why people move but uses a different approach—by looking at self-reported reasons for moving. The chapter points out the shortcomings of inferring migration's causes by asking individuals, but it illustrates some kinds of questions that are uniquely answerable by asking movers why they leave some areas and how they pick new ones.

Chapter 8 analyzes census and survey statistics for the purpose of comparing nations according to the spatial mobility of their populations. It compares countries and some of their major metropolitan areas according to rates of residential mobility.

This arrangement of chapters is intended to summarize and integrate what censuses since 1940 and major national surveys inaugurated since World War II tell us about the how much, who, where, why, and with-what-effect questions that are subsumed in a reasonably full analysis of migration. The emphasis of the book is upon what has been learned about trends and where to look for more detailed analyses of specific questions.

NATIONAL RATES
OF GEOGRAPHICAL MOBILITY

THIS CHAPTER investigates two deceptively simple questions. First, how much geographical mobility, over short distances and long distances, exists in the United States as a whole? Second, how have levels changed over long periods of time as well as in the recent past? Why these questions are deceptively simple will be made clear later.

Why they are important seems self-evident in that attention to demographic variables most often begins by focusing on levels and rates, whether numbers of births or deaths, changes in birth or death rates, or other measures of volume, quantity, or incidence. The major thrusts of research on migration within the United States over the last two decades or so have been directed at questions of where, why, and with what effect rather than of how much. The reasons for this focus of attention may be simply the conceptualization of migration as a change of residence involving an origin and a destination. Analyzing the origin-destination aspects of migration has been greatly facilitated and expanded by the application of complex statistical models whose philosophical underpinning is to infer the why of migration by examining the where.

Over long periods of time, however, many persons have volunteered theories and speculations of the causes and consequences of geographical mobility when viewed at a national level. This chapter reviews some of these interpretations of national mobility, and then it seeks to quantify rates of short- and long-distance moving for the United States for as far back as statistically possible. The chapter identifies some major migration differentials and looks to changes in population composition as intermediate explanations for changes in rates of geographical mobility for the United States as a whole.

Thinking About and Researching the National Mobility Level

Concern with trends in the overall level of internal migration can be traced at least as far back as Ravenstein, whose statistical analyses of internal migration were published in the 1880s and are still widely cited. The first of his two famous essays on "laws" of migration was devoted mostly to statistics on county or country of birth, as recorded in the 1871 and 1881 censuses of England, Wales, Scotland, and Ireland, and the second was expanded to similar information from censuses of other European and North American countries.[1] The second essay concluded with a review whose last point was: "Does migration increase? I believe so!"[2] For the preceding two or three censuses, he noted that the percentage of population living outside their locality of birth increased in every country he examined, except for England between 1871 and 1881. He suggested why migration increased and what it meant:

> Wherever I was able to make a comparison I found that an increase in the means of locomotion and a development of manufactures and commerce have led to an increase of migration. In fact you need only seek out those provinces of a country within which migration is proceeding most actively, and you will either find yourself in the great centres of human industry, or in a part of the country whose resources have only recently become available. Migration means life and progress; a sedentary population stagnation.[3]

Ravenstein concluded that the level of migration in the United States was higher than in Europe. The basis for this conclusion was that the percentage of the U.S. population living outside their state of birth was higher than the percentage of population living outside their local-

---

[1]E. G. Ravenstein, "The Laws of Migration," *Journal of the Royal Statistical Society* 48 (June 1885): 167–235; and "The Laws of Migration," *Journal of the Royal Statistical Society* 52 (June 1889): 241–305. Although the titles of his two papers refer to "laws" of migration, Ravenstein took great care to state that they were only statistical regularities. He undertook his work to demonstrate that internal migration was not a random process, as a colleague had asserted.

[2]Ravenstein, "The Laws of Migration" (1889), p. 288.

[3]Ravenstein, "The Laws of Migration" (1889), p. 288.

ity of birth in the European countries he studied, and in every case the American states were much larger in size than the localities in the other countries. Ravenstein proclaimed "the great mobility of the native Americans," adding that "they are greater wanderers, less tied to home associations, than are the inhabitants of Europe."[4] He offered an explanation: "This fact is sufficiently accounted for by the vast extent of unoccupied land, and the great natural resources of the country, which have as yet hardly been touched."[5] This last statement seems to imply that U.S. mobility levels would decline with the settlement of the country and exploitation of natural resources, at least until the United States could develop the "means of locomotion" and manufacturing and commerce which Ravenstein said fueled migration within Europe.

These conclusions were not without precedent. The 1850 census of the United States was the first to include a question on state or country of birth, and in what might have been an early census monograph, the Superintendent of the Census for 1850 explained some of the main findings and interpreted the data on state of birth to mean that

> the roving tendency of our people is incident to the peculiar condition of their country, and each succeeding Census will prove that it is diminishing. When the fertile plains of the West shall have been filled up, and men of scanty means cannot by a mere change of location acquire a homestead, the inhabitants of each State will become comparatively stationary, and our countrymen will exhibit that attachment to the homes of their childhood, the want of which is sometimes cited as an unfavorable trait in our national character.[6]

This account of census results contains an observation, a prediction, and an editorial. But it was essentially the same conclusion later suggested by Ravenstein's statistical analysis: internal migration was high in the United States but might decline with the disappearance of the frontier.

Even earlier Alexis de Tocqueville had sensed that high rates of internal migration were distinctive traits of Americans and offered an interpretation that need not imply declining national rates of internal movement. In *Democracy in America*, published in 1834, de Tocqueville observed that

> in the United States a man builds a house in which to spend his old age, and he sells it before the roof is on; he plants a garden and lets it just as the trees are coming into bearing; he brings a field into tillage and leaves other men to gather the crops; he settles in a place, which

[4]Ravenstein, "The Laws of Migration" (1889), p. 280.
[5]Ravenstein, "The Laws of Migration" (1889), pp. 280–281.
[6]Joseph Kennedy, *Report of the Superintendent of the Census for December 1, 1852* (Washington, DC: Robert Armstrong, Printer, 1853), p. 15.

he soon afterwards leaves to carry his changeable longings elsewhere. . . .[7]

He offered an interpretation that linked national rates of moving less to
technological factors and more to values and attitudes. In the chapter
entitled "Why the Americans Are So Restless in the Midst of Their Prosperity," he said that in the presence of material abundance and without
a hereditary class structure, Americans believed that economic advancement was open to all who would work hard and be ready to move about
and take advantage of opportunities wherever they might occur. These
traits were related to other characteristics that de Tocqueville identified
with Americans in the 1830s, including a desire for change, a readiness
to accept innovations, and a pragmatic disposition. Hence, Americans'
high rate of migration might very well be preserved through prosperity,
an open class structure, and a belief in individual opportunity.

By the close of the nineteenth century, however, the evidence
seemed to support Ravenstein. Adna Weber's classic study of internal
migration and urbanization, *The Growth of Cities in the Nineteenth
Century*, updated some of Ravenstein's earlier work with place-of-birth
statistics.[8] Weber found that Americans were still more geographically
mobile than Europeans since Americans were more likely to leave their
state of birth than Europeans to leave the much smaller municipality or
other locality of birth. "Within the last quarter of a century, however,
internal migration in the United States has declined," concluded Weber
in 1899 from place-of-birth statistics from decennial censuses and state-
sponsored mid-decade censuses taken in New York, Massachusetts, and
Rhode Island. The mid-decade censuses in these states included questions on county of birth and showed modest increases between 1855 and
1885 in the percentage of population living in their county of birth. For
most European countries Weber found modest decreases in the latter
half of the nineteenth century in the percentage of population living in
their locality of birth, implying an increased rate of internal migration.

Ravenstein and Weber were both writing as the industrial revolution was transforming Europe and beginning to transform the United
States. With industrialization came rapid urbanization, improved transportation and communication, and great economic rewards for migra-

---

[7]Alexis de Tocqueville, *Democracy in America*, vol. 2 (New York: Vintage Books,
1945 [1834]), pp. 144–145. Many statesmen, diplomats, and informal observers of American life in the nineteenth century made similar observations. A South American states-
man in 1847 observed that "if God were suddenly to call the world to judgment He would
surprise two-thirds of the American population on the road" (p. 8). This and many other
anecdotal, literary, and historical observations on the level and significance of Americans'
mobility have been collected and presented in a very readable fashion in George W. Pierson, *The Moving American* (New York: Knopf, 1973).

[8]Adna Ferrin Weber, *The Growth of Cities in the Nineteenth Century* (Ithaca, NY:
Cornell University Press, 1962 [1899]), pp. 250–251.

tion to and between cities. In retrospect, it hardly seems surprising that both Ravenstein and Weber found increases in the percentage of European populations living outside the locality of their birth. Neither Ravenstein nor Weber, however, attempted to formulate an explicit theory, and their lasting contribution is that they were the first to document for a large number of countries the increased level of internal migration that accompanied the industrial revolution.

Dynamic, Nonlinear Theories of National Mobility

The work of Ravenstein and others in the late nineteenth century suggested linear theories of migration. Migration seemed explainable by the existence of new lands to be settled and by industrial expansion which drew residents of settled areas to "urban frontiers." The total amount of migration might decrease if there were no unsettled frontier to move to, but it might increase with improvements in transportation and communication. In the United States, the Great Depression of the 1930s upset such linear conceptualizations, for in the very early years of the depression there occurred a movement back to the land, and more intensive analysis of extant census materials on state of birth or net intercensal migration found shifting flows of migrants as some areas came to offer slightly greater economic advantage than others or possessed appealing climates or other amenities.[9] Such work suggested that

---

[9]There was comparatively little empirical attention given to migration within the United States between the publication of Weber's book in 1899 and the early 1930s. International migration was at its peak during this period and may have overshadowed interest in internal movements. The Great Depression gave rise to four monographs on internal migration. C. Warren Thornthwaite's *Internal Migration in the United States* (Philadelphia: University of Pennsylvania Press, 1934) analyzed up to 1930 the state-of-birth data that Weber concentrated on and illustrated the application of survival-rate methods of estimating net intercensal migration. Carter Goodrich's *Migration and Economic Opportunity* (Philadelphia: University of Pennsylvania Press, 1936) empirically developed ideas of migration flows being determined largely (but by no means entirely) by the shifting economic advantages of different areas. The Thornthwaite and Goodrich studies set the stage for the massive University of Pennsylvania study, Population Redistribution and Economic Growth, which is identified in Chapter 1. Then in 1937 Warren Thompson's *Research Memorandum on Internal Migration in the Depression* (New York: Social Science Research Council) sought to document a net city-to-farm movement in the early 1930s as industrial jobs suddenly disappeared. All three works suggested that the quantity of internal migration was probably increasing as a result of improvements in transportation and communication (mostly cheaper cars and more roads) but not necessarily linearly, for all stressed variable and shifting determinants of movements. All suggested that migration did not always go to the "right" locations and policy intervention might be useful in this regard. Their attention to the "where" of migration was complemented by Dorothy Thomas's focus on who moves in her *Research Memorandum on Migration Differentials* (New York: Social Science Research Council, 1938). Published over a four-year span, these four books stressed the need for better data to improve knowledge about domestic population movements, and they served to justify and guide the inclusion of a new question on the 1940 census to measure the volume and direction of migration over a five-year period.

the direction of migration flows, and possibly the volume as well, did not follow linear patterns. Since then, most theoretical attention has been directed at the changing determinants of migration flows rather than the total amount of migration.

A few contemporary studies, however, have gone back to some of the same kinds of place-of-birth data available to Ravenstein and Weber and have developed theories of a "mobility transition" along the lines of the demographic transition.[10] The well-known demographic transition postulates that in the course of modernization mortality declines first and birth rates decline later; rapid population growth occurs until both fertility and mortality decline to low levels and may fluctuate thereafter. The idea of a mobility transition that parallels the demographic transition asserts that with the onset of modernization, the overall level (rate) of migration increases and migration is primarily in the form of rural-to-urban moves. As industrialization and modernization spread to more regions, migration may continue to increase as improved transportation and communication increase the amount of information available and decrease the uncertainty of moving. During this stage cities may compete for new industries and migrants, and interurban moves become more important and at some point become a majority of all moves. Finally, at advanced stages when level-of-living differences among areas have diminished, there may be more urban-to-rural movement and more "consumer-oriented" migration toward warm climates or locations with other amenities. The implication is that internal migration reaches a high level and thereafter may fluctuate, partly—but not entirely—with business cycles.

For "superadvanced societies" the type of mobility may change if commuting can substitute for residential relocation or there are changes in the nature of work allowing more persons to work at home and make fewer daily trips to work.[11] For example, telecommuting (working at home via computer hookups) or more "cottage industries" carried out in one's home might mean fewer trips (though possibly greater workplace-residence separations) and fewer residential adjustments. Such specula-

---

[10]The most explicit attempts to formulate and test notions of a mobility transition are Wilber Zelinsky, "The Hypothesis of the Mobility Transition," *Geographical Review* 41 (April 1971): 219–249; and William L. Parish, Jr., "Internal Migration and Modernization: The European Case," *Economic Development and Cultural Change* 24 (July 1973): 591–609.

[11]Zelinsky updated his earlier work to incorporate criticisms and add new ideas about "superadvanced" societies. Wilbur Zelinsky, "The Demographic Transition: Changing Patterns of Migration," in Conference on Science in the Service of Life, *Population Science in the Service of Mankind* (Liège, Belgium: International Union for the Scientific Study of Population, 1979).

tive views of a high-tech future usually seem to imply fewer residential relocations.

To evaluate the hypothesis of a mobility transition one can update the state-of-birth data that formed the basis of Ravenstein's and Weber's work in the latter half of the nineteenth century. A better test, to be presented later, comes from examining rates of interstate migration over five-year intervals from 1935 to 1980. And since World War II one can further complete the picture with data on year-to-year changes in both short-distance and long-distance moving.

State of Birth as a Measure of Migration

The 1850 decennial census in the United States first asked respondents to report their state or country of birth, and a similar question has been included in each census since then. The data from these questions constitute the longest series of migration statistics for the United States. Not until 1940 did the U.S. censuses begin to ask migration over a fixed period—residence five years before the census.

Data on state of birth have many obvious limitations. At best they are said to measure "lifetime" migration, in the sense that a person born in state A and living in state B at the census date clearly had made an interstate move, but exactly when the move was made cannot be inferred. Many return and repeat moves never get counted; for example, some persons will cancel their moves by leaving and then returning to their state of birth. Others will move from state A to B and then to state C and a census state-of-birth question will record these persons as moving from A to C. And the data are subject to misreporting. A few persons will not know where they were born; others will be confused by changing boundaries of states—an important problem in nineteenth-century data. The instructions since 1950 have asked persons to report their mother's usual place of residence rather than the hospital or other location where the birth actually occurred, but many persons still misreport and give a *de facto* rather than a *de jure* answer. This last problem is especially serious when one asks for birthplace in terms of small localities (say, counties instead of states) or in countries where many women go to big-city hospitals to give birth. The decennial censuses of the United States have asked for birthplace in terms of state or country and never in terms of counties or cities.

Another problem with this series is nonresponse, which has become more serious in recent censuses. What appears as nonresponse in the final data can represent persons who did not answer the question on place of birth or errors made in processing the data. Until 1960 nonresponse to the place of birth question was 1 percent or less of the total population; in 1960 it was 2.7 percent and then rose to 4.6 percent in 1970 and 4.9 percent in 1980. A rising nonresponse rate to the place-of-birth question is part of a general tendency for recent censuses to fail to collect complete information for a growing proportion of persons, as discussed more fully in Appendix A. Still another problem with U.S. data on state of birth is that variations in the precise way the question is worded may seriously affect the statistics. As discussed in Appendix A, the wording of the question in 1970 seems to have resulted in too many persons reporting that they were living in their state of birth.

In spite of difficulties in interpreting the data, Table 2.1 shows the 130-year series on place of birth. Using the total U.S. population reporting place of birth as the base, Table 2.1 first shows the percentage born in their state of residence at the date of each census, the percentage born in other states, the percentage who were other natives (mostly persons born in U.S. territories or possessions or born abroad to American parents), and the percentage who were foreign-born (born outside the United States to foreign parents). The last two columns limit the universe to persons born in the United States and show the percentage living in their state of birth and the percentage living in another state. This table is essentially an extension of the data analyzed by Ravenstein, Weber, and others.

The decline in U.S. mobility noted by Weber beginning after the middle of the nineteenth century was based on the kind of data shown in column 2 or column 6, both of which reveal that the decline continued until about 1900. Column 2 shows that the proportion of the U.S. population *not* born in the state where they were living at the census date declined from 21.3 percent in 1850 to 17.8 percent in 1890 and 1900. Column 6 limits the denominator to persons born in the United States and shows that for U.S.-born persons over 24 percent were living outside their state of birth in 1850 and 1860 but under 21 percent by 1900. By these measures, proportionately fewer Americans were living outside their area of birth at the beginning of the twentieth century than 50 years earlier.[12]

On the one hand, this apparent decline in mobility is surprising

[12]Trends in such measures can be influenced by many factors that are impossible to control for. For example, if inmigration occurs in bursts or is quickly reduced as immigration was reduced in the 1920s, the proportion of an area's population born somewhere else may begin to decline because of the aging and dying of former inmigrants. Fertility also influences the measure. High fertility may tend to reduce the percentage of population born somewhere else if a large proportion of an area's population consists of children, for children are more likely than adults to be living in their area of birth.

TABLE 2.1

Percentage of U.S. Population Living in State of Birth, Living Outside State of Birth, or Born Outside United States: 1850–1980

	Total U.S. Population Reporting Place of Birth				U.S.-Born	
	Living in State of Birth	Not Living in State of Birth	Other Natives[a]	Foreign-Born	Living in State of Birth	Not Living in State of Birth
1850	67.4%	21.3%	0.0%	11.2%	76.0%	24.0%
1860	63.9	21.0	0.0	15.1	75.2	24.8
1870	65.7	19.9	0.0	14.4	76.8	23.2
1880	67.6	19.1	0.0	13.3	77.9	22.1
1890	67.3	17.8	0.0	14.9	79.1	20.9
1900	68.5	17.8	0.1	13.6	79.4	20.6
1910	66.7	18.4	0.1	14.7	78.3	21.7
1920	67.4	19.2	0.1	13.2	77.8	22.2
1930	67.5	20.7	0.2	11.6	76.5	23.5
1940	70.5	20.5	0.2	8.8	77.5	22.5
1950	69.1	23.7	0.3	7.0	74.4	25.6
1960	68.3	25.6	0.6	5.6	72.7	27.3
1970	67.8	26.1	1.2	5.0	72.2	27.8
1980[b]	64.0	29.0	0.9	6.1	68.8	31.2

SOURCES: Data for 1960 and earlier are from U.S. Bureau of the Census, *State of Birth*, PC(2)-2A, (Washington, DC: U.S. Government Printing Office, 1963), table 1. Data for 1970 are from the 15 percent sample questionnaire.

[a]Includes persons born in Puerto Rico, in outlying areas, or born abroad of American parents.

[b]1980 data are before allocation of nonresponse. Nonresponse was not allocated before 1980; see Appendix A.

because U.S. territory was expanding and new lands were being opened for settlement. After 1850 and especially after the Civil War much of the Great Plains came to be organized into states as well as the Rocky Mountain region out to California, which became a state in 1850. By 1900 all of this territory was organized into states, except for Oklahoma, which became a state in 1907, and Arizona and New Mexico, which were admitted as states in 1912. In 1959 Alaska and Hawaii were admitted as states. As successive territory was opened for settlement, one might have expected an increase in the proportion of population living outside their state of birth. On the other hand, of course, as areas for settlement became settled and the frontier closed, one might expect some decline in the proportion of Americans leaving their state of birth. If one accepts 1890 as the closing of the frontier, the proportion of Americans leaving their state of birth had already begun to decline slightly.[13]

After 1900 the percentage of population living outside their state of birth began to increase until the depression decade of the 1930s. In 1900 under 18 percent of the American population were living in their state of birth; by 1930 it had risen to over 20 percent, and then it declined by 1940. The early years of the depression appear to have been a time of return migration of young persons who had left farms for cities in the 1920s and had no place to go but "back home" as jobs disappeared and new jobs did not emerge.[14]

After the Depression the percentage living outside their state of birth resumed its rise. As shown in column 2, this percentage rose to 23.7 in 1950, 25.6 in 1960, 26.1 in 1970, and 29.0 in 1980. The percentage of U.S.-born population living outside their state of birth (column 6) shows a parallel rise. The largest increases were between 1940 and 1950 and between 1970 and 1980, although the latter increase may be overstated if the 1970 question assigned too many persons as living in their state of birth.

In addition to the reasons already mentioned, the series can be affected by changes in the underlying age distribution. Because of the large increase in births after World War II, the apparent increase in the percentage of population living outside their state of birth is understated somewhat between 1950 and 1970 and overstated between 1970 and

[13]The reason for accepting this date as the closing of the frontier is that the official in charge of the 1890 census said that no clear line of settlement where density fell below two persons per square mile could be discerned in the 1890 census results and hence he could not draw a line representing the nation's frontier. This otherwise obscure observation was read by Frederick Jackson Turner who used it as the basis for writing "The Significance of the Frontier in American History."

[14]Thompson, *Research on Internal Migration in the Depression*, pp. 19–30.

1980. The reason is that the proportion of persons living in their state of birth is high among persons under age 20 or so, rises rapidly by age 30, and then levels off or slowly drifts upward. From 1950 to 1970 the percentage of the U.S. population under age 20 was unusually high because births were high, exerting a downward influence on state-of-birth measures of mobility. The subsequent decline in births and the aging of many members of the baby boom beyond age 20 by 1980 would tend to overstate the increase in the percentage of population living outside their state of birth. Age-standardization can correct for this effect, although sufficient age details are not available for the entire series. To illustrate, however, if the age-specific probabilities of the U.S.-born population living outside their state of birth in 1970 were applied to the 1980 age distribution, the figure in column 6 for 1980 would have been 29.0 instead of 31.2. Hence, the apparent increase between 1970 and 1980 in the percentage of population living outside their state of birth can be attributed partly to changes in age composition. At almost every age group the percentage living outside their state of birth was higher in 1980 than 1970; only among persons aged 5–9, 20–24, and 25–29 did the percentage living outside their state of birth fail to increase between 1970 and 1980. The inference is that the state-of-birth data show a decline in mobility of persons in their 20s (and their children) between 1970 and 1980; as shown later, such a change conforms with period rates of moving. Otherwise, the state-of-birth data suggest increasing mobility since World War II.

Between 1970 and 1980 the percentage of the U.S. population born abroad to foreign-born parents reversed a decline of several decades. Back in 1850 about 11 percent of the U.S. population was foreign-born. The figure fluctuated between 13 and 14 percent between 1870 and 1920, and then it declined with the passage of laws curtailing immigration in the 1920s. It declined sharply between 1930 and 1940 because of mortality of an aging immigrant population and because the 1930s was the only decade in which the United States has had net emigration. Thereafter, the proportion of the population that was foreign-born continued to drift downward, to 5.0 percent in 1970. It rose to 6.1 percent in 1980 as a result of increased immigration.

About the only other source of data on American mobility over long periods is from matching information in successive city directories or manuscript censuses. The method is to trace individuals from one city directory to the next or from one census to the next and, after adjusting for mortality, inferring migration from the nonmatches. These studies have produced what seem like high rates of migration to, from, and within nineteenth century cities and have tended to debunk images of a high degree of residential stability of urbanites before the twentieth century. One study attempted to synthesize these materials and compare them with five-year migration rates from recent censuses.[15] The general conclusion was that rates of urban mobility seemed to be rising in the early 1800s and attained a level that persisted for a century before dropping to a historic low in the 1930s and then rising again in the 1950s and 1960s.

Period Rates of Interstate Migration

As discussed in Chapter 1, the 1940 census was the first to measure migration over specific intervals rather than the lifetime approach based on state-of-birth information. The censuses of 1940, 1960, 1970, and 1980 asked respondents where they lived five years earlier (the 1950 census asked about residence one year earlier because many Americans were abroad or at wartime residences in 1945). The only type of migration strictly comparable in the 1940, 1960, 1970, and 1980 censuses is between states. Compared with state-of-birth data, the data on state of residence five years before the census more accurately measure when movement occurred and allow one to relate migrants' characteristics closer to the time of migration.

Fixed-period migration data can be subject to errors similar to the state-of-birth data because some respondents may have as much or more difficulty recalling where they lived five years earlier as where they were born. In 1940 residence five years earlier was reported for all but about 1 percent of persons aged 5 and over; this nonresponse rate rose to 1.6 percent in 1960, to 6 percent in 1970, and to about 8 percent in 1980, when it was allocated by computer prior to publication. Rising nonresponse over this period of time and the introduction of new processing procedures in 1980 obviously mean that precise inferences about stability or change over this period should be made cautiously.[16]

The percentage of the U.S. population moving between states is presented in Table 2.2 for 1935–40, 1955–60, 1965–70, and 1975–80 on both an observed and age-standardized basis, the latter according to the 1980 U.S. age distribution. The age-standardized values show the overall

[15]James P. Allen, "Changes in the American Propensity to Migrate," *Annals of the Association of American Geographers* 67 (December 1977): 577–587.

[16]Nonresponse was only partially allocated in 1960 and 1970, leaving publication categories labeled "moved, residence five years ago not reported." For Chapter 2 persons in this category in 1960 and 1970 were assigned a mobility status in accordance with the distribution of movers who reported previous residence elsewhere in the same county, in another county in the same state, in another state, or abroad. Appendix A discusses how the computer assigned mobility status for such persons in 1980.

TABLE 2.2

Percentage of Population Aged 5 and Over Moving Between States:
1935–40, 1955–60, 1965–70, and 1975–80

	Moving Between States				Percentage Change		
					1935–40 to 1955–60	1955–60 to 1965–70	1965–70 to 1975–80
	1935–40	1955–60	1965–70	1975–80			
Observed	5.4%	9.3%	9.9%	9.9%	71.8%	6.3%	−0.2%
Age-Standardized	5.3	9.9	10.3	9.9	87.3	3.9	−3.9

NOTES: Base population is the end-of-period population minus movers from abroad. Persons who in 1960 and 1970 were reported as "moved, residence five years earlier not reported" were assigned a mobility status proportionate to the numbers reporting moving within counties, between counties within a state, between states or from abroad. Age-standardization is based on the 1980 age distribution. Percentage change is computed from unrounded numbers.

rates that would have been observed in the earlier years if the age-specific rates in those years were applied to the 1980 distribution of the population by age. The base for the percentages is the end-of-period population, minus movers from abroad. The values may be interpreted as rates since they represent interstate migrants as a proportion of the surviving beginning-of-period population (less emigration). Rates of change are also shown.

As expected from the state-of-birth series, the interstate migration rate increased greatly between 1935–40 and 1955–60. About 5.4 percent of the "surviving" 1935 population of the United States moved between states in the following five years; for 1955–60 the comparable figure was 9.3 percent. This change represented a 72 percent increase–87 percent on an age-standardized basis. The interstate migration rate then rose again—but more moderately—between 1955–60 and 1965–70, as would be expected from the state-of-birth data. Every state participated in this rise in the propensity to move to other states, as shown in Chapter 3.

Unlike the state-of birth measure, however, the five-year interstate migration rate failed to increase between 1965–70 and 1975–80. On an age-standardized basis, it decreased slightly, from 10.3 to 9.9 percent. For the reasons mentioned earlier, one should avoid overinterpreting small differences, but the two series—state of birth and residence five years ago—clearly show different trends. The state-of-birth data showed a continuing increase in the proportion of population living outside their state of birth after World War II; the five-year migration data show the percentage of population moving between states reaching a peak in the 1950s and 1960s and then declining.

Reconciling these two series for the post–World War II period is difficult. Logically speaking, one might hypothesize a decline in repeat moving. That is, maybe the proportion of persons moving from their state of birth continued to rise (except, as noted, at ages 5–9 and 20–29), but the tendency to engage in successive interstate moves may have decreased between 1970 and 1980. Such a pattern would cause the state-of-birth measure to go up and the five-year migration rates to go down. Chapter 4 suggests little support for this hypothesis, however. There appears to be no obvious way to fully account for what seem to be different directions in the rate of mobility as measured by state-of-birth and five-year interstate migration data in the 1970 and 1980 censuses.

Countervailing Influences on Period Rates of Migration

There are numerous demographic, economic, and social trends that might have countervailing effects on the level of interstate migration as measured by five-year rates of moving. Comparing and contrasting them is a way of evaluating and explaining the apparent decline in period rates of interstate migration between the late 1960s and the late 1970s. What follows identifies some possible sources of change as a prelude to testing some of them for clues to which demographic groups may have done more moving or less in the late 1970s than in earlier decades. Some trends that would tend to *decrease* the rate of migration as measured over fairly short fixed periods, like one or five years, might include the following.

First, generally slower economic growth in the late 1970s compared with the 1960s may have dammed interstate migration, particularly among the young.[17]

Second, several social changes might produce the same effect. For example, much has been written about increased labor force participation of women and the growth of two-earner families. When there are two careers in one decision-making unit (household), some job offers or other alternative opportunities will be foregone if the benefit to one spouse will not offset the household loss if the other spouse cannot obtain employment (or comparable earnings) in the new location. The ef-

---

[17]"There is a strong positive correlation between swings in economic activity and in net interstate migration" (pp. 318–319), wrote Dorothy Thomas in "Age and Economic Differentials in Interstate Migration," *Population Index* 24 (October 1958): 313–325. A more detailed analysis appears in Hope T. Eldridge and Dorothy Swaine Thomas, *Demographic Analyses and Interrelations*, Population Redistribution and Economic Growth, United States, 1870–1950, vol. 3 (Philadelphia: American Philosophical Society, 1964).

fect of rising labor force participation rates of women is to increase the proportion of earners in two-career households, and such households tend to have lower rates of long-distance migration than otherwise similar households with only one earner.[18] But these trends predate the 1970s, and they did not lower five-year rates of interstate migration in the 1950s or 1960s. Of course, it is possible that "threshold effects" exist and that the threshold was passed by 1980. Also, the 1975–80 period may be qualitatively different because of much greater commitment of women to careers and career advancement and not just to participating in the labor force. Censuses measure labor force participation but not the degree of dedication to career.

Third, housing conditions in the 1970s could have had a depressing effect on interstate migration. Homeownership grew rapidly after World War II and was still rising at the time of the 1980 census, and even though homeowners have lower migration rates than renters, the rising homeownership rate did not depress migration rates in the 1950s or 1960s. But mortgage interest rates were much higher in the 1970s than in the 1950s or 1960s, and housing prices tended to rise faster than average family income in the 1970s. Inflation of housing prices was especially rapid in some fast-growing parts of the Sunbelt and below average in outmigration regions of the Frostbelt. Ostensibly such circumstances inhibit migration from Frostbelt to Sunbelt and will cause others to forego job opportunities if the potential increase in salary is exceeded by the costs of a much larger, more expensive mortgage at the new location. But other homeowners can capitalize on the appreciation of housing values and, in effect, finance a move and higher interest rates through appreciation of their existing residence. The effects on migration are likely to be especially great when interest rates are high and housing values are not appreciating—a condition more characteristic of the early 1980s

[18]The theoretical rationale was developed by Jacob Mincer, "Family Migration Decisions," *Journal of Political Economy* 86 (October 1978): 749–773. Empirical studies of the migration of two-career couples include Larry Long, "Women's Labor Force Participation and the Residential Mobility of Families," *Social Forces* 52 (March 1974): 342–348; Julie DaVanzo, *Why Families Move: A Model of the Geographic Mobility of Married Couples* (Washington, DC: U.S. Department of Labor, 1977); Steven Sandell, "Women and the Economics of Family Migration," *Review of Economics and Statistics* 59 (November 1977): 406–414; Daniel T. Lichter, "Household Migration and the Labor Market Position of Married Women," *Social Science Research* 9 (March 1980): pp. 83–97; and Daniel T. Lichter, "The Migration of Dual-Worker Families: Does the Wife's Job Matter?" *Social Science Quarterly* 63 (March 1982): 40–57. These studies focused on the effects of employment of husbands and wives on subsequent migration. The effect of migration on subsequent earnings of husbands and wives is the focus of Daniel T. Lichter, "Socioeconomic Returns to Migration among Married Women," *Social Forces* 62 (December 1983): 487–503; and Glenna Spitze, "The Effect of Family Migration on Wives' Employment: How Long Does It Last?" *Social Science Quarterly* 65 (March 1984): 21–36.

than of the 1970–80 decade. Nevertheless, it is possible that a high rate of homeownership, high mortgage interest rates, and geographical variability in new construction and appreciation of housing values interacted to increase costs and create stronger barriers to interstate migration in the 1970s than in the 1950s or 1960s.

A fourth factor that might lower rates of interstate migration is suggested by a number of studies (reviewed in Chapter 6) on residential and environment preferences. These studies showed a long-standing preference of a wide segment of the population for living in rural locations and in smaller, cleaner, and more environmentally pleasant metropolitan areas. In fact, migration flows shifted toward such areas during the 1970–80 decade, suggesting that more persons were able to achieve their residential preferences. The implication is these persons would be reluctant to engage in subsequent migration. An increased ability to achieve residential preferences in the late 1960s or early 1970s might, therefore, have lowered migration rates in the late 1970s.

In a contrast to these migration-reducing effects are some trends that could increase migration rates. First, the age composition shifted to put more persons in the 20–30 age range, which would increase the all-ages rate of moving, other things being equal. This effect is removed, however, by standardizing for age, as is done in Table 2.2.

Another compositional effect is educational level. For a long time reseachers have observed a positive association between level of education and the propensity to engage in interstate migration and inferred that rates of interstate migration would rise as a consequence of rising levels of education.[19] Educational levels have risen greatly since World War II and might be expected to steadily increase the rate of interstate migration.

Still another compositional effect might be changes in households. During the period of study, more persons came to live in two-career families, a situation that would tend to decrease migration rates. But at the same time, married couples were increasingly likely to split up—a situation ostensibly favoring the severing of ties with an area and the freedom to migrate. In other words, alternative job opportunities could decrease migration for some (two-career) married couples and increase

---

[19]Most analyses of the education-migration relationship date from the introduction of a fixed-period question in the 1940 census or the incorporation of such questions in later surveys. The earliest forecast of rising interstate migration as a consequence of rising educational levels may have been in 1930. A study in that year employed partial correlation techniques to analyze educational measures and state-of-birth data and concluded: "Illiteracy in the United States is decreasing. Concomitantly with it, and represented by it, educational status is rising. Hence it is to be expected, other conditions remaining the same, that mobility to other states will increase" (p 385). Sanford R. Winston, "The Relation of Educational Status to Interstate Mobility," *Social Forces* 8 (March 1930): 380–385.

divorce—and subsequent migration—for others. Other changes in households and living arrangements, such as more one-person households and fewer children, probably reduce ties to an area and thereby facilitate migration.

Some work force changes since World War II probably have acted to increase rates of interstate migration. A decline in self-employment in local enterprises and a growing proportion of persons employed by national or multinational corporations that have a habit of transferring employees would tend to raise national rates of long-distance migration. Such effects, however, were probably more pronounced in the 1950s and 1960s than in the late 1970s. Of course, a few types of self-employment, like consulting and freelance writing, may allow the freedom to live wherever one wishes, but the implication is that if such persons live wherever they want to, they have no incentive to move thereafter.

A comprehensive test of these competing migration-reducing and migration-increasing scenarios is not possible here, but it is possible to examine some of the considerations mentioned, especially the demographic ones. The most direct tests are for the effects of changes in population composition by age and educational level. Simply controlling for one influence at a time is no substitute for a multivariate approach that might examine the interactive effects of many variables. An intermediate approach is simply to examine if the most basic migration differentials have changed in ways that might increase or decrease the total amount of interstate migration.

Migration Differentials by Age

Demographers have carried out a great many studies of migration differentials, and the characteristic of persons that is most consistently associated with a high likelihood of moving long distances is simply age. Almost always and almost everywhere, rates of long-distance migration reach their peak among persons at the young-adult ages and decline rather sharply thereafter, sometimes increasing slightly around the age of retirement.[20] Since this single characteristic is so strongly associated with the probability of migration, a logical first step in accounting for the substantial rise in the interstate migration rate between

---

[20]For model migration schedules that describe the typical shape of migration age curves observed in a number of countries, see Luis J. Castro and Andrei Rogers, "What the Age Composition of Migrants Can Tell Us," *Population Bulletin of the United Nations*, no. 15 (1983): 63–79; and "Patterns of Family Migration," *Environment and Planning A* 15 (February 1983): 237–254.

1935–40 and 1955–60 and the modest decline between 1965–70 and 1975–80 is to ask which age groups accounted for (or "caused") the observed changes. Specifically, was participation in these changes the same for all age groups?

The explanations for the typical age curve of migration usually emphasize the obvious: Young adults include persons going away to college, leaving school for full-time employment, joining or leaving the military, changing jobs frequently until they find a career orientation, getting married and setting up households, and engaging in activities or making changes in living arrangements that are likely to be associated with migration. A human capital approach suggests that young adults are more likely to "invest" in migration because they have a longer time over which to recover the costs of migration and their investment in it.[21] Almost no attention has been given to how the average age profile typically associated with a nation's internal migration might change over time. One clue, however, comes from the University of Pennsylvania study of rates of net migration by age for intercensal decades from 1870 to 1950. Rates of net migration showed a strong tendency to peak at ages 20–24 in prosperous decades but somewhat later during depressed decades; Eldridge described this as "the phenomenon of postponement, or, more properly a deferred response resulting from a deferral of the stimulus of prosperity" (p. 219).[22] As migration increased during or after World War II, one would probably expect greater-than-average increases among young adults. Comparing migration rates of young and old in 1935–40 and 1955–60 provides a test of this hypothesis. Table 2.3 presents interstate migration rates for age groups comparable in all four censuses. The age groups shown reflect age at the census date—after migration—and migrants were slightly younger at the time they moved (or last moved).

As hypothesized, the increase in the rate of interstate migration between 1935–40 and 1955–60 was far greater for persons in their 20s than for older age groups. The propensity to move between states rose by 156

---

[21]The human capital approach has been used to account for the age selectivity of migration in many studies, including Aba Schwartz, "Migration, Age, and Education," *Journal of Political Economy* 84, no. 4 (1976): 701–719; W. Cris Lewis, "The Role of Age in the Decision to Migrate," *Annals of Regional Science* 11 (November 1977): 51–60; and James N. Morgan and Edward H. Robb, "The Impact of Age upon Interregional Migration," *Annals of Regional Science* 15 (November 1981): 31–45. For a study that specifically relates age, interstate migration, and change in occupation and industry over the 1965–70 period, see Alan M. Schlottmann and Henry W. Herzog, Jr., "Career and Geographic Mobility Interactions: Implications for the Age Selectivity of Migration," *Journal of Human Resources* 19 (Winter 1984): 72–86.

[22]Hope T. Eldridge, "A Cohort Approach to the Analysis of Migration Differentials," *Demography* 1 (1964): 212–219.

TABLE 2.3

Percentage of Population Moving Between States, for Selected Age Groups:
1935–40, 1955–60, 1965–70, and 1975–80

| | Moving Between States | | | | Percentage Change | | |
| | | | | | 1935–40 to 1955–60 | 1955–60 to 1965–70 | 1965–70 to 1975–80 |
Age	1935–40	1955–60	1965–70	1975–80	1935–40 to 1955–60	1955–60 to 1965–70	1965–70 to 1975–80
20–24 Years	8.0%	20.5%	20.2%	16.0%	156.3%	−1.7%	−20.9%
25–29 Years	8.9	18.8	19.6	17.6	120.2	4.4	−10.6
30–34 Years	7.8	11.6	14.1	14.2	61.7	12.2	0.2
35–44 Years	5.8	8.7	9.2	9.8	49.8	5.7	7.0
45–54 Years	4.0	5.3	5.4	5.6	32.8	1.0	4.8
55–64 Years	3.2	4.3	4.2	4.9	34.3	−2.2	16.9
65 Years and Over	2.5	4.2	4.5	4.4	78.5	6.8	−1.4

NOTE: See NOTES for Table 2.2.

percent for persons aged 20–24 and 120 percent for persons aged 25–29. The rate of increase was less for older age groups, and among persons aged 45–54 it increased by only 33 percent. For persons aged 65 and over the rate of increase was higher—79 percent, an increase faster than any other age group except persons in their 20s. Presumably, the very rapid increases among persons in their 20s represent the "damming" effect of the depression on migration of the young and the return in the 1950s to normal rates of interstate migration of persons in their 20s.

There could be some biases in comparing 1935–40 migration with 1955–60 migration because of changes in census enumeration procedures. In the 1940 census, for example, college students were enumerated as part of their parents' household, but beginning in 1950 they were counted where they went to school. The effect of this change would probably inflate migration rates of college students in 1960 relative to 1940. But a very large increase in migration rates characterizes not only persons aged 20–24 but also those aged 25–29, and even those aged 30–34 had a greater increase in interstate migration rates between 1935–40 and 1955–60 than older persons (up to age 65). The increase in migration propensity for persons in their 20s is probably overstated by the data in Table 2.3, but it still seems valid to assume support for the hypothesis that difficult economic times in the 1930s caused postponement of normal migration of young persons.

From 1955–60 to 1965–70 interstate migration rates continued to rise, but in an erratic fashion. Rates for persons in their 20s rose by less than 2 percent, and rates rose for all other age groups except 55–64. No pattern in these changes is immediately evident.

Between 1965–70 and 1975–80 something surprising happened: Rates declined among persons in their 20s. Rates of moving between states declined by nearly 21 percent for persons aged 20–24 and by nearly 11 percent for persons aged 25–29. Interstate migration rates rose between ages 30 and 65. The baby boom cohort experienced less interstate migration at ages where migration normally peaks than the generation that preceded it. The decline in the age-adjusted rate of interstate migration observed in Table 2.2 was accounted for almost entirely by declines in migration among members of the baby boom generation.

Table 2.3 shows the small changes in the precise ages when interstate migration peaks. The University of Pennsylvania study suggested that migration would peak early in prosperous decades and relatively late in depressed decades. In 1935–40 migration rates peak at ages 25–29. In the relatively prosperous 1950s and 1960s interstate migration rates peak at ages 20–24. In the less prosperous 1970s the rates show a late peak—ages 25–29. The inferences drawn from the University of Pennsylvania are borne out for the 1940–80 period.

Although these results regarding the effects of relative economic conditions on the peak ages of migration were suggested by the University of Pennsylvania study, only one study anticipated the decline in migration rates for the baby boom generation. Wilson deduced that the generational crowding experienced by the baby boom cohort because it is so much larger than preceding cohorts would, in the context of slowed economic growth, result in less migration.[23] His expectation seems to have been borne out, for members of the baby boom generation were less likely than their parents to migrate in their young-adult years. A conclusion is that future anticipations regarding changes in migration diffentials should be analyzed in the context of age, period, and cohort effects.[24]

Migration Differentials by Level of Education

Apart from age, the characteristic of individuals that most strongly indicates the likelihood of migrating is level of education. This generalization applies to men and women. Other socioeconomic measures tend not to be as efficient as educational attainment in discriminating

[23]Franklin D. Wilson, "Cohort Size Effects and Migration," *International Migration Review* 17 (Autumn 1983): 485–504.

[24]For an application of age-period-cohort models to migration data, see Brian L. Pitcher, William F. Stinner, and Michael B. Toney, "Patterns of Migration Propensity for Black and White American Men: Evidence from a Cohort Analysis," *Research on Aging* 7 (March 1985): 94–120.

between who is likely to move long distances and who is not. Occupational categories often encompass persons with vastly different migration probabilities. For example, many white collar professional workers have high rates of migration—but not if they are doctors, lawyers, or others who have local clienteles or are locally licensed. Some salaried sales workers have very high migration rates, but not those in retail sales, who have very low rates. And changes in occupational categories make comparisons over long periods of time difficult or impossible. Income, too, is not by itself a very good indicator of who is likely to move. The chronically poor have low rates of migration because they cannot finance a long-distance move, and many are tied to areas through locally administered welfare programs. Many high-income people also have low rates of migration because they have location-specific capital, like businesses or local professional practices. Furthermore, income and occupation at the census date may be quite different from what they were five years earlier, at the beginning of the migration interval used in U.S. censuses. Compared with other socioeconomic or family or household measure, education is a more enduring characteristic and a more parsimonious indicator of who is likely to move long distances.[25]

A problem with using educational level to gauge trends in migration differentials is that "we do not know whether it is the absolute level of education itself that is significant or the level relative to the average for the population."[26] Those who argue in favor of the absolute level would observe that going to college has typically entailed migration, perhaps more so for private than public colleges, but in either case college attendance often exposes one to a new area or to persons from different areas. And college education is supposed to expand one's horizons and emphasize universal knowledge rather than localized skills. A college education is an investment in human capital, which should improve one's competitive advantage and open up opportunities for a variety of jobs in many geographical areas. Those who would argue that educational level is a relative measure that should be adjusted over time would observe that since World War II there has been a proliferation of

[25]This point of view is argued in Larry H. Long, "Migration Differentials by Education and Occupation: Trends and Variations," *Demography* 10 (May 1973): 243–258. The use of educational qualifications in a more general framework for analyzing internal migration is given in Leon F. Bouvier, John J. Macisco, Jr., and Alvan Zarate, "Toward a Framework for the Analysis of Differential Migration: The Case of Education," in Anthony H. Richmond and Daniel Kubat, eds., *Internal Migration: The New World and the Third World* (Beverly Hills, CA: Sage, 1976); and Leszek A. Kosinski, "Education and Internal Migration," in Helmut V. Muhsam, ed., *Education and Population: Mutual Impacts* (Liège, Belgium: Ordina Editions, 1975).

[26]Ann R. Miller, "Interstate Migrants in the United States: Some Social-Economic Differences by Type of Move," *Demography* 14 (February 1977): 6.

four-year colleges so that fewer people need leave home to get a college degree. They would also argue that in the competition for jobs one's salability is relative and that a college education becomes less significant if all the other applicants have it.

In evaluating migration differentials over time, one can treat educational attainment as either an absolute or a relative measure. Adjusting it can be quite complex since one would probably want to take into account educational level relative to one's age peers as well as the size of one's generation relative to other generations. On an absolute basis, one would probably anticipate declines in the selectivity of migration for the most recent period, at least for members of the baby boom generation. The reason is that diminished returns to schooling experienced by the baby boom generation have been felt especially by those with the most education.[27] The payoffs of additional schooling over merely a high school education have declined for the baby boom generation, perhaps implying a lower return to an "investment" in interstate migration. Table 2.4 is intended to offer a simple test of this hypothesis. It shows interstate migration rates by age and years of school completed for 1935–40, 1955–60, 1965–70, and 1975–80. The age and education categories represent "least common denominators"—those common to all four censuses.

First, observe that rates of interstate migration vary considerably by years of school completed. In 1940, only 6.3 percent of persons at ages 25–34 who had less than a high school education (that is, less than 12 years of school completed) had moved between states in the preceding five years. Interstate migration rates successively rise with increasing educational attainment, to 19 percent for those with a college degree (that is, 16 or more years of school completed). Hence, for the 25–34 age group, persons with a college degree were three times as likely to engage in interstate migration in 1935–40 as those who failed to complete high school.

Data are not available for other age groups for the 1935–40 period, but for the other migration intervals the relationship between years of school completed and migration probabilities is seen to remain positive but is attenuated. That is, the differences in migration rates between the poorly educated and the highly educated decrease with age.

Educational levels were rising rapidly over the period covered by Table 2.4. In 1940 nearly two thirds of persons aged 25–34 were without a high school diploma; only 6 percent had college degrees. By 1960 more

[27]See Wilson, "Cohort Size Effects and Migration"; and James P. Smith and Finis Welch, "No Time to Be Young: The Economic Prospects for Large Cohorts in the United States," *Population and Development Review* 7 (March 1981): 71–83.

TABLE 2.4

Percentage of Population Moving Between States, by Age and Level of Education: 1935–40, 1955–60, 1965–70, and 1975–80

Age and Years of School Completed	Moving Between States				Percentage Change		
					1935–40 to 1955–60	1955–60 to 1965–70	1965–70 to 1975–80
	1935–40	1955–60	1965–70	1975–80			
25–34 Years							
Less than 12 Years	6.3%	11.2%	10.5%	9.2%	77.4%	−6.1%	−12.8%
12 Years	9.7	14.1	13.8	12.0	45.0	−2.3	−12.7
13–15 Years	14.3	21.3	21.1	17.1	49.5	−0.9	−18.8
16 or More Years	19.0	30.9	34.0	25.9	62.8	10.0	−24.0
35–44 Years							
Less than 12 Years	NA	6.4	6.2	6.1	NA	−3.2	−0.6
12 Years	NA	8.6	8.4	8.0	NA	−2.5	−3.7
13–15 Years	NA	13.0	12.5	12.0	NA	−4.2	−3.5
16 or More Years	NA	16.9	17.0	15.8	NA	0.7	−7.1
45–64 Years							
Less than 12 Years	NA	4.0	3.5	3.8	NA	−11.5	7.4
12 Years	NA	5.8	5.1	5.2	NA	−12.5	2.2
13–15 Years	NA	7.0	7.2	7.2	NA	2.8	1.6
16 or More Years	NA	8.9	9.0	8.3	NA	1.6	−8.0
65 Years and Over							
Less than 12 Years	NA	3.7	3.8	3.6	NA	1.5	−4.2
12 Years	NA	6.0	6.0	5.5	NA	0.6	−8.5
13–15 Years	NA	6.3	6.6	6.1	NA	3.4	−7.5
16 or More Years	NA	7.7	7.8	6.8	NA	0.3	−12.5

NOTES: NA means "not available." The age and educational categories shown are those common to tabulations from the four censuses. NOTES for Table 2.2 apply to this table.

than a majority of this age group had a high school diploma, and 11 percent had college degrees. In 1970, 7 in 10 had completed at least high school, and 15 percent had college degrees. By 1980, 23 percent had college degrees.

Persons at all educational levels participated in the increased propensity to move between states between 1935–40 and 1955–60, but at ages 25–34 increases were greatest at the educational extremes. The above-average increases for persons with less than a high school education perhaps reflect industrial transformations at that time. The 1950s were a period of extensive mechanization of agriculture, substituting machinery for unskilled labor and quickly generating a pool of surplus farm workers with very low levels of education. It was also a time of accelerated and massive migration of blacks from the South, and their lack of access to educational opportunities meant an exodus of persons with few educational credentials. So perhaps it is not surprising that interstate migration rates increased more for persons without a high school diploma than for others between 1935–40 and 1955–60.

Persons aged 25–34 with four or more years of college also had above-average rates of increase in interstate migration between the late 1930s and the late 1950s. Part of this increase could be changed enumeration procedures (college students were counted at their parents' address in 1940 but at their school address thereafter), but it may also reflect the unique position of the parents of the baby boom generation. Being depression-era babies, persons who reached young adulthood after World War II or in the 1950s were not only smaller in number than the generation that preceded them, but also better educated, and their skills were in demand by an expanding economy shifting toward managerial and professional occupations.

This explanation also seems to account for the continuing increase in interstate migration rates of persons with college degrees between 1955–60 and 1965–70, whereas rates declined for persons with less education. As Table 2.4 shows, at ages 25–34 the rate of interstate migration rose by 10 percent between 1955–60 and 1965–70 for persons with a college degree, but rates declined for each of the groups with less education. The demand for persons with college degrees rose more rapidly than demand for others, and rates of interstate migration appear to have changed accordingly. Migration differentials by education widened between 1955–60 and 1965–70.

Between 1965–70 and 1975–80 rates of interstate migration declined for each of the four educational levels, but more for persons with four or more years of college than for the others aged 25–34. The rate for persons with four or more years of college fell by 24.0 percent, whereas the rate for persons with less than a high school education fell by only 12.8 percent. Perhaps as the earnings payoff to obtaining a college degree fell for the baby boom generation, rates of interstate migration adjusted and fell more for the college educated than for persons with less education. Other circumstances may also account for the above-average decrease in interstate migration among young, well-educated persons. For them, the growth of two-career couples was very great and the migration-inhibiting effects of equal commitment to two careers in one household may have been especially pronounced. Finally, some decline in interstate migration rates for this group might be due to more young persons defraying the rising cost of college by attending an in-state institution that offers tuition benefits to state residents. Attending a local college, and perhaps even living with one's parents while doing so, rather than going to another state for a college education could negate some of the migration-increasing effects of college attendance. All of these are ad hoc explanations which cannot be fully tested. They all seem to point consistently to explaining why one might expect above-average declines in interstate migration of young persons with four or more years of college.

An especially interesting feature of Table 2.4 is the demonstration that even at older ages interstate migration rates fell more for persons with four or more years of college than for others. For example, at ages 35–44, interstate migration rates declined by only 0.6 percent between 1965–70 and 1975–80 for those with less than a high school education, but the decline was 3.7 percent for those with a high school diploma, 3.5 percent for those with one to three years of college, and 7.1 percent for those with four or more years of college. At ages 45–64, interstate migration rates rose for all education levels except the highest, and even among persons aged 65 and over interstate migration rates declined more for the top educational level than for others. Considering educational level in absolute rather than relative terms, migration differentials according to education decreased at every age group between the 1965–70 and 1975–80 intervals, primarily as a result of a lowering of rates among the college educated.

The general conclusion seems to be that migration differentials by age and level of education have changed since World War II roughly in line with changes in economic returns to education.[28] The well-educated at every age group experienced high returns to schooling in the 1950s and 1960s and interstate migration rates increased more for college graduates than others during this period. As the returns to a college education fell, college graduates became less likely to "invest" in interstate migration in the late 1970s, and migration rates fell more for them than for others.

This assessment is intended merely to point out that migration differentials in highly industrialized societies need not follow linear trends, but appear to respond to age, period, and cohort effects and their interaction with broader social and economic trends. This perspective seems to offer a more analytically useful framework for accounting for changes in migration rates and differentials since World War II than the earlier listing of migration-increasing versus migration-decreasing social trends.

This last point suggests a modification and extension of one aspect of the general notion of a "mobility transition" mentioned earlier in this

---

[28]The declining-returns-to-education thesis is presented in Richard B. Freeman, "Overinvestment in College Training?" *Journal of Human Resources* 10 (Summer 1975): 287–311; R. B. Freeman, "The Decline in the Economic Rewards to College Education," *Review of Economics and Statistics* 59 (February 1977): 18–29; and Finis Welch, "Effects of Cohort Size on Earnings: The Baby Boomers' Financial Bust," *Journal of Political Economy* 87, pt. 2 (October 1979): S65–S97.

chapter. Several studies have noted that not only does the general level of migration increase with industrialization and economic development, but migration tends to become less selective over time.[29] The basic idea is that the earliest migrants are engaging in path-breaking behavior and are highly selected according to measured variables like schooling and unmeasured variables like risk-taking, innovativeness, and foresight. Over time, however, uncertainty is reduced as the earlier migrants assist (or even subsidize) the migration of other family members and friends and relatives. As knowledge of alternative opportunities becomes more widespread, a wider variety of persons participate in the now well-worn migration paths, and selectivity decreases. The results just presented demonstrate what in retrospect seems obvious: Migration selectivity does not decrease indefinitely and on a national level may fluctuate in economically developed countries in accordance with the unique experiences of different cohorts.

Short-Distance Moving

Up to now attention has been focused entirely on long-distance, interstate migration. Most changes in residence, however, cover short distances. Relatively little attention has been given to trends in the volume or rate of short-distance moving, for almost all research on short-distance moves has been directed at identifying how families and households go about deciding whether to move or stay and, if the former, how they choose a new residence or a new neighborhood. Nevertheless, there are perhaps two bases for expecting declines in the rate of short-distance moving since World War II.

The first was stated by Hawley in 1950 in the context of a theory of human ecology:

> Motor vehicle transportation seems to have introduced a new resistance to migration. The lengthening commuting radius afforded by the automobile has reduced the amount of migration necessary, at least within

---

[29]"Migration is likely to become less selective as economic development proceeds" (p. 8). Jeffrey G. Williamson, "Regional Inequality and the Process of National Development: A Description of the Patterns," *Economic Development and Cultural Change* 13 (July 1965): 3–84. A fuller discussion with examples is given by Harley L. Browning, "Migrant Selectivity and the Growth of Large Cities in Developing Societies," in National Academy of Sciences, *Rapid Population Growth: Consequences and Policy Implications* (Baltimore: Johns Hopkins University Press, 1971). An interesting case study is readably presented in Jorge Balan, Harley L. Browning, and Elizabeth Jelin, *Men in a Developing Society: Geographic and Social Mobility in Monterrey, Mexico* (Austin: University of Texas Press, 1973).

local areas. . . . Thus he [the worker] has acquired a wider area in which he may seek employment without having to move his residence. . . . The full effect of the increasing commuting radius on the amount of migration, however, has yet to be felt.[30]

In other words, more extensive automobile ownership or improvements in public transit that increase commuting radii might reduce the need to move locally in response to changes in location of work. Since automobile ownership was increasing rapidly after World War II, the implication might be a lessened need to move locally. In the context of the hypothesis of the mobility transition in advanced societies, commuting might substitute for some types of more permanent spatial relocation.[31]

The other reason for expecting less local moving derives from linking local mobility and longer-distance migration. Several studies, discussed in Chapter 6, have reported a positive correlation between inmigration to cities or metropolitan areas and local moving. The reason for this association seems to be that many inmigrants to an area will subsequently move within the area as their knowledge of housing markets increases and they are able to attain housing and a neighborhood more in line with their preferences. Their influx may disrupt existing housing markets, sometimes in the "invasion-and-succession" process described by early urban sociologists. The inference is that if there were less long-distance migration, there might be less short-distance moving.[32]

There are few differentials associated with local mobility in such a way that their change might imply a corresponding change in the amount or rate of local mobility. Most research on local mobility identifies residential changes with life cycle events, like setting up households independent of one's parents, getting married, having children, and so on. A growing proportion of the nation's population in their late teens or in their 20s might, other things being equal, increase the amount of local mobility. Declining fertility should mean fewer adjustments of housing in response to the birth of children, but more marital instability should increase local mobility as spouses or partners split and go their separate ways. The housing developments discussed earlier

[30]Amos Hawley, *Human Ecology: A Theory of Community Structure* (New York: Ronald Press, 1950), p. 337. The same point was repeated in Hawley's *Urban Society: An Ecological Approach* (New York: Ronald Press, 1971), p. 177, and in his review of Vance Packard's *A Nation of Strangers*: "The widening radius of daily mobility has reduced the need for residential relocation as an adjustment to job and other role changes"; *American Journal of Sociology* 79 (July 1973), 167.

[31]Zelinsky, "The Demographic Transition."

[32]John L. Goodman, Jr., "Linking Local Mobility Rates to Migration Rates: Repeat Movers and Place Effects," in W. A. V. Clark, ed., *Modelling Housing Market Search* (New York: St. Martin's Press, 1982).

in the context of long-distance migration probably act to reduce local mobility.

All things considered, there seem to be more reasons for expecting a decline than an increase in the amount of local moving. As discussed in Chapter 1, the Census Bureau since 1948 has used a one-year interval in surveys to measure movement within and between counties and states and a five-year interval in the censuses of 1960, 1970, and 1980. In recent years, the Bureau has expanded the survey questions on mobility to measure geographical movements within and between metropolitan areas as well. Exactly how one should define a "local" move for research purposes has never been specified, and the available data force one to concentrate on moves within and between counties and states even though many city-to-suburb or other intrametropolitan moves might more properly be considered strictly local moves. From the two series (surveys and censuses) two questions can be asked. First, how much geographical mobility occurs within counties and between counties and states? Second, how has the propensity to move within and between counties changed since World War II? Table 2.5 addresses the first question.

Most residential changes occur within rather than between counties, but the proportion of all moves that are intracounty has clearly declined since World War II. From the one-year mobility data, one can see that in the late 1940s about 67 or 68 percent of all changes of residence were within a county; since the late 1960s, however, about 60 or 61 percent of all moves were within a county. The five-year mobility question shows a lower proportion of total moves to be intracounty because the longer interval counts only the "net" change over the period and some persons who moved within a county later moved again and crossed a county boundary. The proportion of all moves occurring within a county fell from 62.0 percent in 1955–60 to 55.7 percent in 1965–70 and then to 54.0 percent in 1975–80. As will be pointed out shortly, the proportion of all moves that are within a county has fallen simply because the propensity to move short distances has declined more than the propensity to move longer distances.

Table 2.5 also shows that the representation of moves of intermediate distance—between counties within a state—has tended to increase. Over one-year periods from 1948 to 1976 the proportion of all moves that were between counties within a state was close to—usually slightly higher than but sometimes lower than—the proportion of moves that were interstate. Beginning in 1976, however, the proportion of moves that were between counties within a state appears to have increased. The five-year data from censuses also show an increase in the proportion of moves that are between counties within a state. As rates

TABLE 2.5

Distribution of All Persons Changing Residence During One- or Five-Year Intervals, According to Location of Previous Residence: 1948–84

	Persons Changing Residence (thousands)	Moved Within a County	Moved Between Counties Within a State	Moved Between States	Moved from Abroad
12-Month Intervals[a] Ending					
April 1948	28,672	67.0%	16.2%	15.2%	1.6%
April 1949	27,603	68.1	14.5	15.7	1.7
March 1950	28,017	68.8	15.6	13.9	1.8
April 1951	31,464	65.8	16.8	16.5	1.0
April 1952	30,478	65.2	15.9	16.8	2.1
April 1953	31,526	65.5	14.7	17.5	2.3
April 1954	30,025	63.4	16.5	16.8	3.3
April 1955	32,419	65.0	17.0	15.1	2.9
April 1956	34,040	67.0	17.2	14.8	2.8
April 1957	32,723	65.9	15.9	15.5	2.7
April 1958	34,103	64.6	16.6	16.4	2.5
April 1959	33,640	66.3	16.1	15.1	2.5
March 1960	34,685	65.1	16.5	15.9	2.5
March 1961	36,533	66.5	15.0	15.7	2.7
April 1962	35,218	66.3	15.5	15.8	2.4
March 1963	36,432	63.3	15.7	18.2	2.8
March 1964	37,186	64.8	16.6	16.3	2.3
March 1965	38,844	64.7	17.0	15.8	2.5
March 1966	37,586	64.3	16.7	16.7	2.3
March 1967	36,523	61.2	17.3	17.9	3.6
March 1968	37,886	60.6	17.4	18.6	3.4
March 1969	37,332	61.6	16.9	17.7	3.7
March 1970	38,095	61.0	16.4	18.5	4.1
March 1971	37,705	61.0	16.4	18.4	4.1
March 1976	36,793	60.9	19.3	16.7	3.1
March 1981	38,200	60.5	19.9	16.2	3.4
March 1982	38,127	60.5	19.2	17.4	2.9
March 1983	37,408	61.1	19.8	16.5	2.6
March 1984	39,380	60.0	20.8	16.4	2.7
5-Year Intervals[b]					
1955–60	79,607	62.0	17.1	18.3	2.6
1965–70	87,531	55.7	20.1	20.7	3.5
1975–80	97,628	54.0	21.1	20.9	4.0

[a]From Current Population Surveys for persons aged 1 and over at the survey date. Data are not available for 1972–75 or 1977–80.

[b]From decennial censuses for persons aged 5 and over at the census date.

of intracounty and interstate migration have fallen, moves of intermediate distance have increased as a proportion of all moves.

Finally, Table 2.5 shows the proportion of movers who originate outside the United States. In the late 1940s and early 1950s movers from abroad were less than 2 percent of all persons who had changed residence in the preceding 12 months. Movers from abroad reached their maximum proportion of all movers during the years of the Vietnam war, when they exceeded 4 percent of all persons changing residence. In the early 1980s movers from abroad were less than 3 percent of all persons changing residence.

Table 2.5 shows the different groups of movers as a proportion of all movers. Table 2.6 shows the proportion of the population engaging in the different forms of mobility; it simply divides each of the mover groups by the total population at the survey or census date. The data in Table 2.6 are sometimes said to represent "status" rates of mobility since they show the mobility status of the population; the data in Tables 2.2, 2.3, and 2.4 represent "at risk" rates of moving because movers from abroad were excluded from the base so as to represent the population "at risk" of moving internally.

The proportion of the U.S. population who had moved within a county in the 12 months preceding the survey exceeded 13 percent in every year but two between 1948 and 1965. The percentage was between 11 and 12 between 1967 and 1971 and below 11 for each year since then for which data are available. The apparent year-to-year changes usually are not statistically significant, but the average value for the early 1980s appears to be about 2 percentage points below the average level of intracounty moving that prevailed from the late 1940s to the mid-1960s. Similar changes are shown by the census data. Between 1955 and 1960 about 31 percent of the U.S. population moved within a county. Between 1965 and 1970 about 26 percent moved within a county, and by 1975–80 the percentage was 25. Both sets of data show intracounty mobility rates declining by the late 1960s.[33]

The survey data for a one-year interval show no perceptible change in the percentage of population moving between counties within a state. For all but one of the 29 years for which data are available persons moving between counties within a state exceeded 3 percent of the population. The census data for 1955–60, 1965–70, and 1975–80 show successive increases.

One might summarize these findings in light of earlier examination

---

[33]Five-year rates of moving are almost never five times the one-year rates because simply comparing residence at the beginning and end of a five-year period misses the intervening moves picked up by annual measurements.

TABLE 2.6

Percentage of U.S. Population Changing Residence During One- or Five-Year Intervals, According to Location of Previous Residence: 1948–84

	Changed Residence at Least Once	Moved Within a County	Moved Between Counties Within a State	Moved Between States	Moved from Abroad
12-Month Intervals[a]					
Ending					
April 1948	20.2%	13.6%	3.3%	3.1%	0.3%
April 1949	19.1	13.0	2.8	3.0	0.3
March 1950	19.0	13.1	3.0	2.6	0.3
April 1951	21.2	13.9	3.6	3.5	0.2
April 1952	20.2	13.2	3.2	3.4	0.4
April 1953	20.4	13.5	3.0	3.6	0.3
April 1954	19.2	12.2	3.2	3.2	0.6
April 1955	20.5	13.3	3.5	3.1	0.6
March 1956	21.1	13.7	3.6	3.1	0.6
April 1957	19.9	13.1	3.2	3.1	0.5
March 1958	20.3	13.1	3.4	3.3	0.5
April 1959	19.7	13.1	3.2	3.0	0.5
March 1960	19.9	12.9	3.3	3.2	0.5
March 1961	20.7	13.7	3.1	3.2	0.6
April 1962	19.6	13.0	3.0	3.1	0.5
March 1963	20.0	12.6	3.1	3.6	0.6
March 1964	20.1	13.0	3.3	3.3	0.5
March 1965	20.6	13.4	3.5	3.3	0.5
March 1966	19.8	12.7	3.3	3.3	0.5
March 1967	19.0	11.6	3.3	3.4	0.7
March 1968	19.5	11.8	3.4	3.6	0.7
March 1969	19.0	11.7	3.2	3.4	0.7
March 1970	19.2	11.7	3.1	3.6	0.8
March 1971	18.7	11.4	3.1	3.4	0.8
March 1976	17.7	10.8	3.4	3.0	0.6
March 1981	17.2	10.4	3.4	2.8	0.6
March 1982	17.0	10.3	3.3	3.0	0.5
March 1983	16.6	10.2	3.3	2.7	0.4
March 1984	17.3	10.4	3.6	2.8	0.5
5-Year Intervals[b]					
1955–60	50.1	31.4	8.6	9.2	1.2
1965–70	47.1	26.2	9.5	9.7	1.6
1975–80	46.4	25.1	9.8	9.7	1.9

[a]From Current Population Surveys for persons aged 1 and over at the survey date. Data are not available for 1972–75 or 1977–80.

[b]From decennial censuses for persons aged 5 and over at the census date.

of interstate migration changes since World War II. First, between the late 1960s and 1980 the propensity of the U.S. population to move within counties declined by 15 to 20 percent (the exact figure depends on whether or not one standardizes for age and whether one uses the one-year or the five-year rates). Second, the rate of interstate migration, as reported earlier, declined more modestly, by no more than 5 or 10 percent (again depending on the series and whether there is standardization for age) between the late 1960s and the early 1980s. Third, the rate of moving between counties within a state may not have gone up on an annual basis but may have done so over a five-year period.

Why, then, have rates of movement over intermediate distances—between counties within a state—been maintained while movement over shorter and longer distances diminished? Part of the reason may be simply the continued outward movement of jobs from cities to suburbs, exurbs, or areas even farther out; such a centrifugal movement of employment centers across county lines may facilitate more housing adjustments across county boundaries. Part of the reason for maintaining the rate of intrastate moving across county boundaries may have to do with Hawley's observation that transportation and commuting improvements—namely, extensive automobile ownership and vast public expenditure on freeways, expressways, and commuter roads—may have diminished the amount of movement within cities but increased movement out of them, and movers from cities to suburbs or to farther-out exurbs are likely to cross a county boundary.[34]

It is difficult to quantify how commuting distances in the United States have increased during the post–World War II period that has been the focus of this chapter. During this period of time, however, the percentage of workers living and working in different counties has drifted upward. Commuting distances may change as a result of prices and the values that people put on their time spent commuting or the advantages that derive from living near or far from workplaces. A widening commuting radius (or potential for commuting) may expand our notion and perception of what is a local move. Movement over distances that once were local may diminish, but movement within the expanded notion of "local" may increase. These considerations suggest that there may be no strict solution to demographers' long-standing search for how to define

---

[34]The use of commuting as an alternative or substitute for migration appears to account for decreased migration rates in eastern Europe since World War II, according to Roland J. Fuchs and George J. Demko, "The Postwar Mobility Transition in Eastern Europe," *Geographical Review* 68 (April 1978): 171–182. They report that movement between localities fell by one third from a peak in the 1950s in the German Democratic Republic and by nearly one half in Poland, Czechoslovakia, and Hungary.

"local" moving and distinguish it from true "migration." What is genuine migration may be simply movement that exceeds distances too far to commute under existing costs, technology, and infrastructure. In this sense, the difference between local moving and migration can vary from place to place and time to time.

Age and Short-Distance Moving

As with interstate migration, one can get a more detailed look at who is doing less local moving by examining age-specific data. Figure 2.1 shows rates of moving by age (five-year intervals) and type of move for 1955–60, 1965–70, and 1975–80. Figure 2.2 is based on one-year rates of moving from surveys of 1971 and 1983.

Both sets of data tell essentially the same story. Rates of within-county moving are down for almost all age groups. For persons in their 20s, the evidence seems somewhat clearer for the one-year data than for the five-year data. Much local moving at these ages is necessitated by setting up independent households, getting married, and so forth, and what could be happening is that the likelihood of moving at least once over a five-year period for these reasons may not change much although the likelihood of doing so more than once in five years could decline. If this description is accurate, then the five-year rate would change less than the one-year rate.

Beyond age 40 the five-year rates of intracounty moving show sustained and substantial declines from 1955–60 to 1965–70 and again in 1975–80. For most of the age groups between 45 and 65, the rate of intracounty moving fell by about one third between 1955–60 and 1975–80. Rates also fell for persons over age 65. Since the decline began in the 1960s, it is unlikely that high mortgage rates and rapid escalation of housing prices in the last 10 to 15 years constitute an adequate explanation.

The incontrovertible conclusion is that from the late 1950s to the early 1980s persons in their middle years have come to experience increasing residential stability. On the one hand, this could be good news, implying that increasingly households have been able to acquire at relatively early ages satisfactory housing that reduces the need for later housing-related moves that typically characterize intracounty moving. On the other hand, it could, in the more recent period, mean greater difficulty in upgrading housing by moving to a newer, bigger, or better home. Both descriptions could apply—the former to the 1950s and 1960s

FIGURE 2.1

*Percentage of U.S. Population Moving Within Counties,
Between Counties Within a State, and Between States,
by Five-Year Age Groups: 1955–60, 1965–70, and 1975–80*

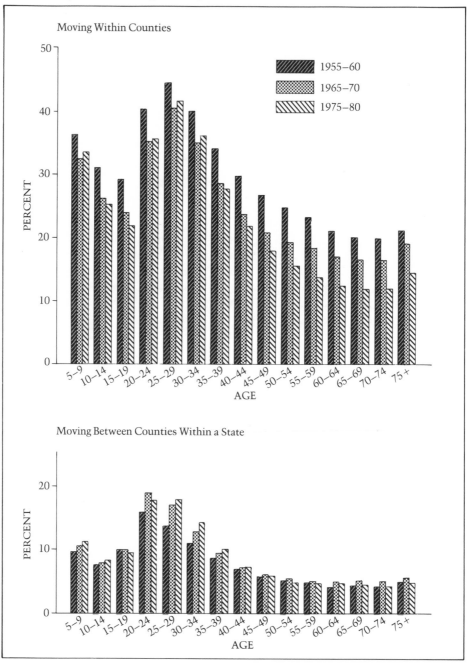

FIGURE 2.1 *(continued)*

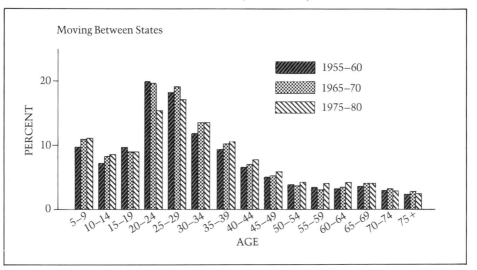

and the latter to the 1970s. From available data and research there is no completely satisfactory explanation of why intracounty rates of moving have declined for persons aged 40 and over for the period covered.

The relative stability in post–World War II rates of moving between counties within a state seems to exist at every age group. The five-year data may imply some increase among persons in their late 20s or early 30s, but the one-year data do not.

The one-year rates of interstate migration imply the same pattern described earlier from the five-year rates from censuses. Interstate migration rates declined for persons in their 20s and perhaps early 30s (and, of course, the children of these persons) but not at older ages.

Summary and Conclusion

As noted in Chapter 1, the dominant themes of migration research in the United States over the last two decades or so have been the determinants of migration. What determines where migrants go has been asked far more often than how many migrants there are or how the total number of migrants changes. Comparatively little theoretical or empirical attention has been directed at what determines the amount, volume, or quantity of migration within the United States.

Many writers of the late nineteenth and early twentieth centuries

FIGURE 2.2

Percentage of U.S. Population Moving Within Counties, Between Counties Within a State, and Between States, by Single Years of Age: March 1970–March 1971 and March 1982–March 1983

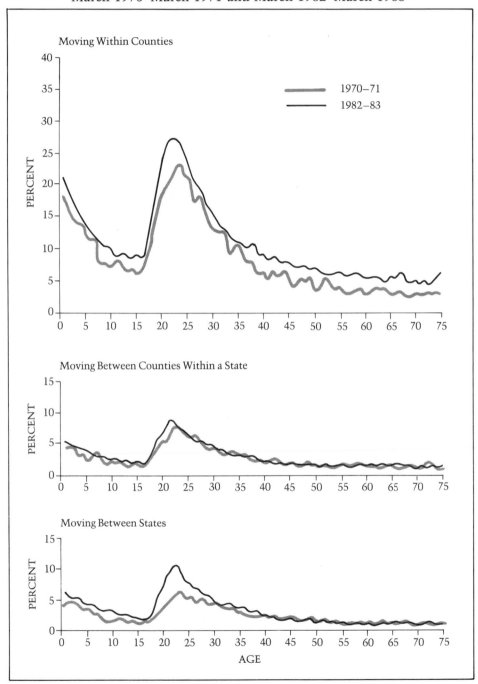

seemed to imply that the major directions of population movements were rather straightforward—toward unsettled areas, and, after the onset of industrialization, toward centers of commerce—and that the total volume of movement might decline without new frontiers to move to but might increase if industrialization and technological developments lowered the costs and uncertainties of moving.

In the United States the Great Depression of the 1930s challenged linear concepts and simple explanations of the volume and direction of internal migration and demonstrated a need for current information. The 1930s represented a decade of unanticipated movements that at the time seemed to imply more moving around. In retrospect, however, it appears that there was less total migration in the 1930–40 decade than in the immediately preceding or succeeding decades. The rise in the nation's rate of interstate migration during or just after World War II was led by young, highly educated persons who found their skills in demand by an expanding economy.

The decline in interstate migration, evident when comparing the 1980 census results with the 1970 results, seems also to have been led by young, well-educated baby boomers holding on to jobs in a slow economy. The determinants of the national rate and its changes probably entail more than just age, period, and cohort effects. Also involved are changes in families, living arrangements, and career orientations of men and women. Available data from earlier censuses and surveys tended not to focus on these topics, and it is not now possible to disentangle their separate effects on changes in the total amount of long- and short-distance moving.

Short-distance moving was at a higher level from the late 1940s to the early 1960s than it has been since then. Its decline may be related to changes in the amount of long-distance movement, and recent declines in short-distance moving may be uniquely related to new conditions in housing markets and home finance. Short-distance moving may be reduced by forces that deconcentrate jobs and residences and expand commuting fields. The rate of moving over intermediate distances—measured, perhaps poorly, by moves between counties within a state—seems not to have changed much since the late 1940s.

Like the better-known demographic transition, there almost certainly is a mobility transition that sets in motion major new migration currents with the onset of modernization and increases the total volume of movement. In advanced societies, however, the various forms of spatial mobility may become substitutable and blurred. Their nature and relationships have not been well conceptualized or measured.

3

MIGRATION FOR STATES

T HE PREVIOUS chapter directed attention at how much migration occurs within the United States, whereas this chapter concentrates on streams and flows that highlight where migrants come from and where they go. More specifically, this chapter identifies major interstate migration streams over the 40 years from the late 1930s to the late 1970s. The reasons for this focus are that only the censuses of 1940, 1960, 1970, and 1980 asked questions on state or country of residence five years earlier, and information from them constitutes the longest series of data on migration streams over specific intervals of time. The 1950 census used a one-year interval rather than a five-year interval because a great many Americans were overseas or at wartime residences in 1945. Results from the 1950 census are not included because the 1949–50 migration interval corresponded to a major postwar recession and migration patterns for that 12-month period do not conform to general postwar trends.

One of the goals is the purely empirical one of documenting and describing the changing origins and destinations of major interstate migration streams during the latter half of the 1930–40, 1950–60, 1960–70, and 1970–80 decades. These materials have not previously been brought together in this way. From the depression of the 1930s to the economic dislocations of the late 1970s the largest migration streams have sometimes originated in states experiencing extremely high rates of outmigration but at other times have simply represented flows among populous or contiguous states. The chapter seeks to track how migration streams and rates for individual states have changed over this period of time.

An analytical function is served by summarizing such data to answer elementary—but fundamental—questions about the changing nature of interstate migration. On average, have interstate migration flows successively covered longer distances since the depression years of the 1930s, or has a limit been reached? Have states become more alike or less alike in the rates at which they send and receive migrants? Has migration become more efficient or less efficient in bringing about population redistribution at the state level? Has the tendency of migrants to gravitate to high-income states strengthened or weakened since the 1930s? Do such measures exhibit steady trends or sharp fluctuations in response to changing economic and social conditions over this 40-year period? Answering these specific questions and identifying their implications can provide an initial response to the more general question, "How has migration in the United States changed over the last half century?"

For a few highly industrialized states that belong to what came to be called the Frostbelt or Rustbelt, this chapter takes a somewhat more detailed look at migration by age and level of education—the two variables that were identified in the last chapter as being among the most consistent in differentiating between migrants and nonmigrants. The purpose is to illustrate some features of the migration of young and old and the representation of the poorly educated and the well educated in states' inmigration and outmigration.

The focus on outmigration from industrialized states is in response to policy concerns over whom the Frostbelt states were losing and, by inference, whom the Sunbelt states were gaining. Much has already been written about movers to a number of individual states in the Sunbelt, for one of the ironies of migration research is that it is easier and cheaper to study areas of inmigration than areas of outmigration. The reason is that it is fairly simple to draw samples of local populations and develop questionnaires that ask about the mobility status of current residents. Or one can examine successive phone books, city directories, utility hookups, or other administrative records of local areas to identify recent inmigrants. But methods for surveying who has left an area are less well developed and are much more expensive. The result is that between censuses more is likely to be known about inmigrants to areas of net inmigration than outmigrants from specific origins. Censuses are particularly well suited to correcting for this bias in migration research. The perspective of a wider number of areas and a wider variety of characteristics (including race) is presented in Chapter 5 in the context of shifting policy concerns.

As discussed in Chapter 1, the data come from asking about state of residence five years earlier for all persons aged 5 and over at the census date. Such an approach misses intervening moves within the interval. For example, a person who lived in state A throughout 1975 and then moved to state B in 1976 and moved back to state A in 1977 and continued to live in state A would not be counted as in interstate migrant by the 1980 census. A person who was living in state A in 1975 but moved to state B in 1976 and then to state C in 1977 and continued to reside in state C would be counted as having moved directly from A to C by the 1980 census.

Migration Streams

There are many reasons for supposing that potential migrants make decisions to move or stay and that migrants choose their destinations on the basis of social or economic areas other than states. These reasons include the obvious fact that states vary greatly in size (and the District of Columbia is typically treated as a state); they exhibit considerable heterogeneity in the amount of their territory that is urban and rural; they sometimes encompass a variety of climates and subregions of vastly different levels of economic activity; and they typically have a great many local governments capable of enacting programs and policies that can influence the migration decisions of individuals and firms.

Nevertheless, states have been a major focus of migration research for many reasons. One overriding reason is that they present stable geographical boundaries that serve as the basis for producing statistics, including migration statistics. Another reason is that some state-wide policies and programs, particularly tax or economic development programs, may influence the locational decisions of individuals or firms. Finally, there is always the possibility that potential migrants may, because of strong ties to state of residence, actually think in terms of states, choosing an in-state location rather than moving to another state, when other things are equal. With regard to the last point, state boundaries may distort individual perceptions of distance, so that another location within the same state may be viewed as closer (physically or psychologically) than an otherwise similar location in another state.

Regardless of whether states are or are not the appropriate areas for analyzing migration, the fact is that states are the smallest geographical areas for which comparable data on migration streams can be obtained from each of the censuses of 1940, 1960, 1970, and 1980. Moreover, because of the stability of their boundaries, states have figured prominently in historical studies of internal migration and population redistribution. The classic study in this regard is the three-volume work produced at the University of Pennsylvania in the late 1950s.[1]

This study was the first to apply the census-survival-ratio method to develop estimates of net migration by age, sex, and race for each state from 1870–80 to 1940–50.[2] It was the first to systematically relate the redistribution of population through migration to changing economic activity, especially the location of manufacturing and changing income levels of states over eight decades. It is the definitive analysis of interstate population redistribution brought about by internal and international migration from the end of the Civil War up to the era of "modern" censuses that have directly produced data on gross migration flows from questions on residence one or five years earlier.

Many of the findings from the University of Pennsylvania study are so basic that reseachers now take them for granted. For example, the study was among the earliest to demonstrate and the most thorough to document that (1) internal migration was far more important than areal differentials in fertility in redistributing population during the period studied; (2) for virtually all states young adults were typically responsible for a disproportionately large part of a state's total net migration; (3) net migration balances of states represented not simply a drift toward less settled, frontier areas of the country but were systematically related to changing relative economic conditions even among industrialized states, (4) the amount of population redistributed through migration was positively related to long swings in business cycles, with more net redistribution taking place in prosperous than depressed decades.

---

[1]Everett S. Lee, Ann Ratner Miller, Carol P. Brainerd, and Richard A. Easterlin, *Methodological Considerations and Reference Tables*; Simon Kuznets, Ann Ratner Miller, and Richard A. Easterlin, *Analyses of Economic Change*; Hope T. Eldridge and Dorothy Swaine Thomas, *Demographic Analyses and Interrelations* (Philadelphia: American Philosophical Society, 1957).

[2]The census-survival-ratio method was later modified and used to develop estimates of net intercensal migration for counties by age, sex, and race for 1950–60 and 1960–70. See Gladys K. Bowles and James D. Tarver, *States, Counties, Economic Areas, and Metropolitan Areas* (pts. 1–6) and *Analytical Groupings of Counties*, Net Migration of the Population, 1950–60, by Age, Sex, and Color, vols. 1 and 2 (Washington, DC: U.S. Government Printing Office, 1965). See also Gladys K. Bowles, Calvin L. Beale, and Everett S. Lee, *Net Migration of the Population, 1960-70, by Age, Sex, and Color* (pts. 1–7) (Athens: University of Georgia, 1975). Comparable estimates of net migration for counties for 1970–80 are not now available because the higher rate of coverage in the 1980 census than in the 1970 census means that census survival rates cannot be formed with the same methods used for 1950–60 and 1960–70, when differences in coverage between censuses was less.

Besides estimating net migration for states, the University of Pennsylvania study also sought to examine migration streams by using census data on state of birth cross-classified with state of residence at the census date, for successive censuses from 1870 to 1950.[3] Such data show net lifetime state-to-state redistribution of population, but from it one cannot deduce gross flows over specific periods of time. Census data on residence five years earlier can overcome this shortcoming, and the maps presented in Figure 3.1 show the five largest interstate migration streams in 1935–40, 1955–60, 1965–70, and 1975–80. The five largest streams are obviously not a representative sample of all the 2,550 streams to and from each of the 50 states (after Alaska and Hawaii became states in 1959) and the District of Columbia. As will be shown, concentrating on the five largest streams illustrates how a large volume of migration between areas sometimes derives from very high rates of exodus at the origin but at other times is largely the product of large populations in contiguous states.

What one sees in these maps is the development of a truly national system of migration flows sometime after World War II. In the latter half of the depression decade of the 1930s, interstate migration streams clearly define two intraregional systems, one joining the northeastern states of Pennsylvania, New York, and New Jersey, and the other connecting Oklahoma, Texas, and California. In the northeastern one Pennsylvania sends many persons to New York, which itself sends many persons to New Jersey. In the southwestern one, Oklahoma sends many people to California and Texas, and Texas sends many people to California.

The largest interstate migration stream was from Oklahoma to California, precisely the route described by novels, folksongs, and newspaper articles which chronicled the exodus from the Dustbowl states in the 1930s. Prior to that time no other interstate migration stream had been so thoroughly depicted in literature and song, except possibly for accounts of the settling of the West, which most often seemed to portray migration positively or at least optimistically and occasionally presented the migrants in heroic or mythic terms. The Oklahoma-to-California stream in the 1930s may have been the first to generate distinctly negative views of the causes and consequences of interstate migration. It may have helped change the view of migrants from that of strong pioneers to disadvantaged families forced to relocate over great distances.

The nation's second largest migration stream in the late 1930s—

---

[3]The use of state-of-birth data to study migration streams can be found in Eldridge and Thomas, *Demographic Analyses and Interrelations*, pp. 108–130.

only slightly smaller than the one from Oklahoma to California—covered the much shorter distance from New York to New Jersey. The third largest was again from Oklahoma, this time terminating in Texas; the fourth largest was the movement from Pennsylvania to New York, and the fifth largest was from Texas to California.

Data on migration streams for the immediate postwar period would be useful, for by the late 1950s the picture had changed dramatically. What one sees in the map for 1955–60 is longer arrows depicting what looks like a more nearly national migration system that connects widely dispersed states. In 1955–60 New York and California prominently feature in cross-country migration streams. The two largest streams both originate in New York, with one terminating in New Jersey and the other in Florida. The nation's largest migration stream, from New York to New Jersey, almost certainly represents the growth of suburban communities built across the river from New York City and offering single-family homes, backyards for the baby boom children to play in, and lower taxes for parents to pay. The New York-to-Florida stream represents another postwar phenomenon—a tendency to retire from the labor force at earlier ages and the cumulated affluence that allowed more persons to spend their active retirement wherever they wanted to but particularly in states with warm climates and recreational opportunities.

The other three of the five largest migration streams of the late 1950s all terminated in California. One originated in Texas, another in Illinois, and the third in New York. They illustrate the attractiveness of California over a wide geographical area, to residents in the Southwest, the Midwest, and the Northeast. They depict migration streams covering vast distances. They probably represent essentially labor-force migration, although obviously lifestyle, environmental amenities, and many factors other than simply California's growing economy in the 1950s attracted many new residents.

The map of interstate migration in the late 1960s bears considerable similarity to the one for the late 1950s: the largest stream from New York to New Jersey and the second largest from New York to Florida. The Texas-to-California stream retained its third-place ranking, and the New York-to-California stream was still among the top five. But the stream from Illinois to California dropped out of the top five and was replaced by a stream from California to Washington state. This map suggests that California lost some of its attractiveness, both in terms of its ability to pull in people from other states and in terms of retention of its own population.

The map of interstate migration streams in the late 1970s bears some similarity to the one for the late 1960s but with several important exceptions. Three of the top five interstate migration streams still orig-

FIGURE 3.1

The Five Largest Interstate Migration Streams: 1935–40, 1955–60, 1965–70, and 1975–80

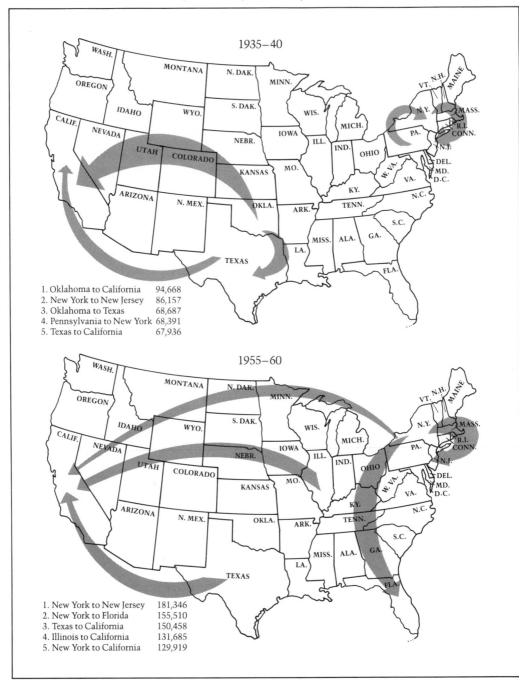

1935–40

1. Oklahoma to California 94,668
2. New York to New Jersey 86,157
3. Oklahoma to Texas   68,687
4. Pennsylvania to New York 68,391
5. Texas to California   67,936

1955–60

1. New York to New Jersey 181,346
2. New York to Florida   155,510
3. Texas to California   150,458
4. Illinois to California 131,685
5. New York to California 129,919

FIGURE 3.1 *(continued)*

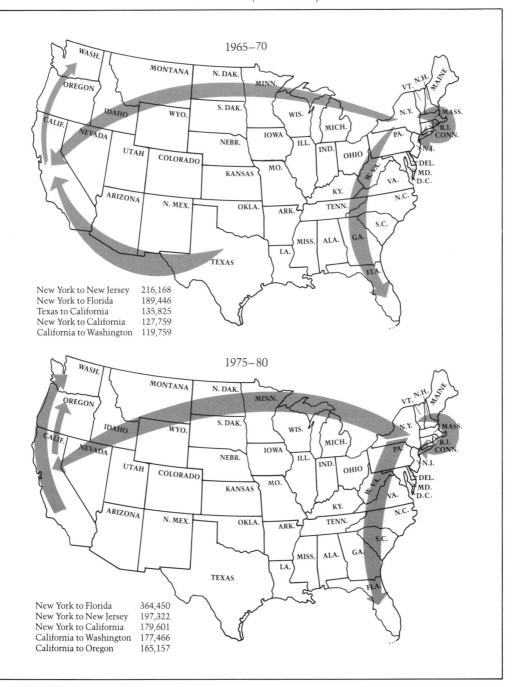

1965–70

New York to New Jersey	216,168
New York to Florida	189,446
Texas to California	135,825
New York to California	127,759
California to Washington	119,759

1975–80

New York to Florida	364,450
New York to New Jersey	197,322
New York to California	179,601
California to Washington	177,466
California to Oregon	165,157

inated in New York, but the New York-to-Florida stream replaced the New York-to-New Jersey stream as the nation's largest. One should not conclude that retirement had in some sense become demographically more important than suburbanization, but the map does testify to the shift of migration streams southward as Florida's economic growth probably exerted increased attractiveness for New Yorkers, of both retirement and preretirement ages.

The other major change reflected in the map of 1975–80 migration streams is further evidence of decreased attractiveness of California. The Texas-to-California stream dropped out of the top five and was replaced by a second stream from California, this time to Oregon. The arrows from California to Oregon and to Washington state testify to the attractiveness of the Pacific Northwest to residents of California.

Though highly visible and widely publicized, the top five migration streams represented less than 6 percent of interstate migrants in each of the four migration intervals. They constituted 5.9 percent of the nation's interstate migrants in 1935–40, 5.3 percent in 1955–60, 4.6 percent in 1965–70, and 5.3 percent in 1975–80. The maps that display major migration streams are a useful way of illustrating which states have been the origin or destination of the largest of the 2,550 interstate migration streams, and the maps seem to illustrate a changed nature of interstate migration from a system of intraregional flows to a more nearly national system. But the gross flows themselves tell one nothing about the extent to which large migration streams derive, on the one hand, from high rates of outmigration at origin and, on the other, from large populations. This shortcoming can be overcome simply by developing rates of inmigration and outmigration.

Migration Rates

A great deal of attention has been devoted to the proper methods for constructing rates of inmigration, outmigration, and net migration.[4] A rate should represent a value between 0 and 1, but this rule is not always adhered to. In the case of outmigration, it is a fairly straightforward procedure to construct rates on this basis. To get the base for such a rate using census data from questions on residence five years earlier, one takes the population aged 5 and over at the census date (the end-of-period population), subtracts the inmigrants, and adds the outmigrants.

[4]Ralph Thomlinson, "The Determination of a Base Population for Computing Migration Rates," *Milbank Memorial Fund Quarterly* 40 (July 1962): 356–366.

When the number of outmigrants is divided by this base, the result represents the proportion of the beginning-of-period population who moved to another state (and, of course, survived to be counted in the census). This type of rate is sometimes referred to as being on an "at risk" basis because it depicts outmigrants as a proportion of a state's population "at risk" of outmigration. The resulting rates are sometimes said to represent migrants as a proportion of the "surviving" beginning-of-period population. This approach is used in computing rates of migration between metropolitan and nonmetropolitan residential categories, discussed in Chapter 6.

The population at risk of migrating *to* a state is the total U.S. population (or even the rest of the world) living outside the state at the beginning of the migration interval and surviving to be counted in the census. If one excludes international migration, one could compute the base of an at-risk rate of inmigration to a state by taking the entire U.S. population living outside the state at the census date, adding inmigrants to the state (that is, outmigrants from the rest of the United States), and subtracting the state's outmigrants (that is, inmigrants as seen from the perspective of the rest of the United States). This approach would be conceptually analogous to at-risk rates of outmigration, but the base is extremely large and the resulting rates appear quite small when compared with outmigration rates computed on an at-risk basis. Computing at-risk rates of inmigration is seldom done. Most researchers simply take inmigrants over the migration interval and divide by the end-of-period population.

For purposes of comparing migration rates for states for 1935–40, 1955–60, 1965–70, and 1975–80, outmigration rates were computed on an at-risk basis and the number of inmigrants was divided by the end-of-period population. Both sets of results were multiplied by 100 and referred to as rates. Figure 3.2 shows the states with the highest and lowest rates of outmigration during each of the four migration intervals. Figure 3.3 displays the states with the highest and lowest rates of inmigration. The purpose here is to quickly and easily show where migration has been most and least intense from the late 1930s to the late 1970s. However, data for every state and the District of Columbia and Puerto Rico are given in Appendix C. For the purposes of Figures 3.2 and 3.3 the District of Columbia was not treated as a state.

In the late 1930s the states where the propensity to leave was greatest included the Dustbowl states of Oklahoma and South Dakota and the Rocky Mountain states of Wyoming, Arizona, and Nevada. It comes as no surprise to find that the rate of exodus from the Dustbowl was high during the depression, but it may be surprising to find that the rate of exodus from Arizona and Nevada was also great even though both

FIGURE 3.2

The Five Highest and Five Lowest Outmigration Rates, for States:
1935–40, 1955–60, 1965–70, and 1975–80

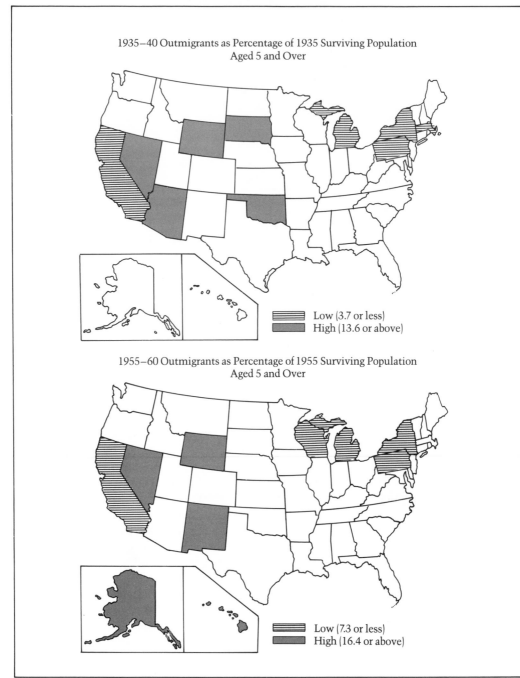

1935–40 Outmigrants as Percentage of 1935 Surviving Population
Aged 5 and Over

Low (3.7 or less)
High (13.6 or above)

1955–60 Outmigrants as Percentage of 1955 Surviving Population
Aged 5 and Over

Low (7.3 or less)
High (16.4 or above)

FIGURE 3.2 *(continued)*

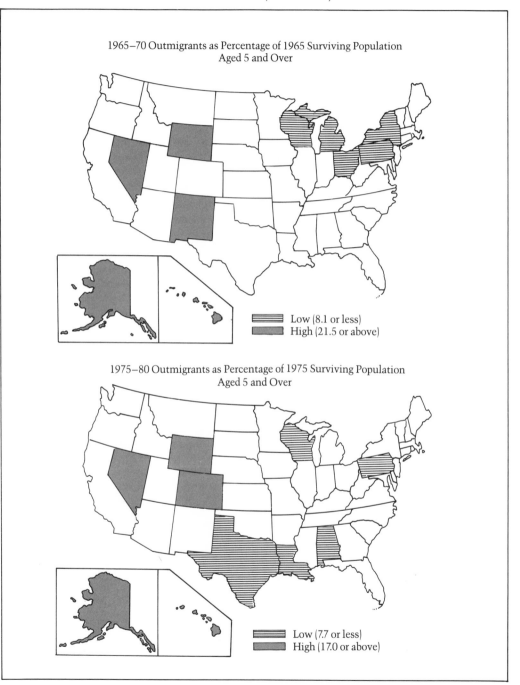

1965–70 Outmigrants as Percentage of 1965 Surviving Population
Aged 5 and Over

Low (8.1 or less)
High (21.5 or above)

1975–80 Outmigrants as Percentage of 1975 Surviving Population
Aged 5 and Over

Low (7.7 or less)
High (17.0 or above)

FIGURE 3.3

The Five Highest and Five Lowest Inmigration Rates, for States:
1935–40, 1955–60, 1965–70, and 1975–80

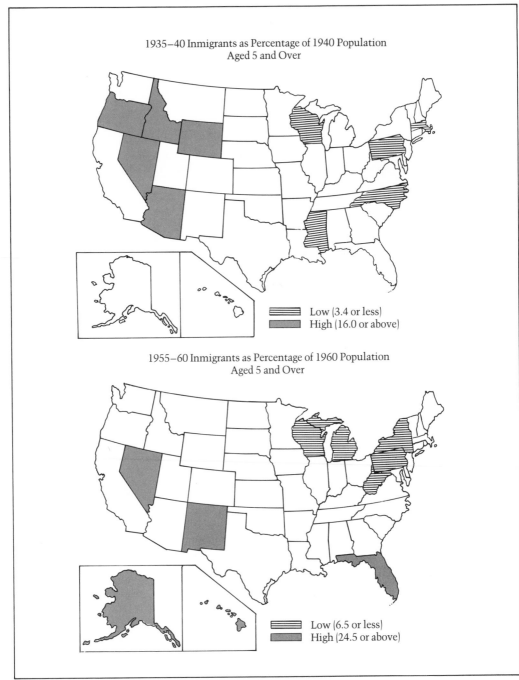

1935–40 Inmigrants as Percentage of 1940 Population
Aged 5 and Over

Low (3.4 or less)
High (16.0 or above)

1955–60 Inmigrants as Percentage of 1960 Population
Aged 5 and Over

Low (6.5 or less)
High (24.5 or above)

FIGURE 3.3 (continued)

1965–70 Inmigrants as Percentage of 1970 Population
Aged 5 and Over

Low (7.7 or less)
High (23.5 or above)

1975–80 Inmigrants as Percentage of 1980 Population
Aged 5 and Over

Low (7.3 or less)
High (22.8 or above)

states were growing rapidly and attracting inmigrants. This point will be returned to later.

The states with the lowest rates of outmigration in 1935–40 were California and four northern industrialized states (Massachusetts, New York, Pennsylvania, and Michigan). Finding that residents of these states had low rates of outmigration during the depression is hardly surprising. What the outmigration rates illustrate is simply that the large migration stream originating in New York reflected a large population base, whereas the two large streams from Oklahoma represented a high rate of exodus (though not the nation's highest).

California remained among the lowest five states in rates of outmigration until 1965–70, when it began to contribute to one of the five largest interstate migration streams (Figure 3.1). From 1935–40 to 1965–70 the low-outmigration states show an increasing tendency to cluster around the Great Lakes, but by 1975–80 this clustering was weakened. In 1975–80 the five states with the lowest rates of outmigration were Texas, Louisiana, Alabama, Wisconsin, and Pennsylvania—states that are seldom grouped on any other demographic measure. It is, of course, easy to rationalize the low outmigration rates from Texas and Louisiana by noting that they had strong economic growth and extensive development of oil and gas resources after the oil embargo of 1973–74. But in fact their rates of outmigration were only modestly lower than those for Pennsylvania, Wisconsin, and some other Rustbelt states with net outmigration and sluggish economic growth.

The clustering of low-outmigration states around the Great Lakes was broken up because a few experienced increasing rates of departure. The rate of outmigration from New York increased by 28 percent between 1965–70 and 1975–80, and no state experienced a greater increase in the rate of outmigration. New York's increasing exodus probably represented continued suburbanization to neighboring New Jersey and Connecticut and loss of job seekers to Sunbelt areas. Ohio and Michigan also experienced increases in outmigration rates between 1965–70 and 1975–80. Ohio's rate rose 11.7 percent and Michigan's rose 11.4 percent; their rising rate of exodus presumably reflects primarily a Frostbelt-to-Sunbelt shift of job seekers. Even with these increases in outmigration rates, the Great Lakes states still had below-average rates of outmigration during the extensive dislocations that occurred in the late 1970s in the automobile, steel, and other heavy industries concentrated in the area. This is not to say that the populations of these states are unresponsive to alternative economic opportunities, but their populations have been characterized by below-average outmigration rates for at least the last 40 years.

The five states with highest outmigration rates have included

Alaska, Hawaii, Nevada, and Wyoming since the 1950s, and New Mexico in 1955–60 and 1965–70 and Colorado in 1975–80. Outmigration from these states is heavily represented by return and repeat migrants, as analyzed in the next chapter, which for the most recent period disaggregates total outmigrants and inmigrants by place of birth. For outmigration in general, one can summarize by saying that many high-growth states in recent decades have been characterized by above-average rates of outmigration, just as many low-growth states have had below-average rates of outmigration.

The Perspective of Areas of Inmigration

The other side of migration—the inmigration rates—is shown in Figure 3.3. One of the most distinctive features of these four maps is the increasing clustering of low-inmigration states around the Great Lakes. In 1935–40 the low-inmigration states were quite scattered (Massachusetts, Pennsylvania, North Carolina, Mississippi, and Wisconsin), but by 1965–70 the lowest inmigration rates were found in a tight cluster around the Great Lakes (New York, Pennsylvania, Ohio, Michigan, and Wisconsin). The same five states continued to have the lowest inmigration rates in 1975–80. In other words, the distinctly low rates of migration to Rustbelt states developed long before the economic dislocations of the late 1970s.

The states with high inmigration rates often have high outmigration rates. Since the late 1950s the states with the highest inmigration rates have been Alaska, Hawaii, and Nevada (rounding out the top five were New Mexico and Florida in 1955–60, Arizona and Florida in 1965–70, and Arizona and Wyoming in 1975–80). Alaska, Hawaii, and Nevada were also in the top five states in outmigration rates in 1955–60, 1965–70, and 1975–80. Clearly, these three states stand out as having high turnover of population, with migrants flowing in and flowing out at rates far exceeding the national average. Their populations have grown rapidly not so much because they are able to hold on to the people they attract, but because they continue to attract more people then they lose through migration.

The high rates of inmigration and outmigration for Alaska, Hawaii, Nevada, and some of the Rocky Mountain states are probably attributable partly to the boom-and-bust cycles of their economies and to military populations that come and go. Some locations in these states have industries that expand or contract much more rapidly than general business cycles, and some areas depend heavily on military or other big contracts (like aircraft purchases) and may very quickly hire or fire large numbers of workers as contracts are won or lost. Some workers who move to such areas may be employed by firms in highly competitive industries where birth and death rates of individual companies are quite high. Conceivably these states attract restless persons who do not settle down but prefer a lifestyle of changing environments; one often hears such folksy explanations of migration to these areas as, "People don't come here so much as they leave somewhere else."

Whatever the explanation, the outcome is vast differences in the proportions of state populations that consist of "natives." Only 23 percent of Nevadans in 1980 were born in Nevada; only about 33 percent of Alaskans were born in Alaska, and only 35 percent of Floridians and Arizonans were natives. At the other extreme were Pennsylvania (84 percent of whose population in 1980 was born in Pennsylvania), New York (80 percent of its population was born there), and West Virginia and Kentucky (both have populations where 80 percent are natives).

Such information helps make understandable what appear to be low outmigration rates from northeastern and midwestern states with deteriorating economic conditions in the 1970s. They had low outmigration to some degree as a result of a low proportion of residents who had previously moved. Persons who have moved once are likely to move again, and persons most sensitive to changing economic conditions are probably those who have moved before.

The inmigration rates shown in Figure 3.3 include movers from outside the United States. Excluding them would have a large effect for some states in the 1975–80 interval, as shown by data presented in Appendix C. The state most dependent on migrants from abroad was New York; 41.8 percent of persons moving to New York state between 1975 and 1980 were moving from abroad (which includes Puerto Rico). California received 35.2 percent of its inmigrants from abroad, primarily from Latin America and Asia. Hawaii received 25.8 percent of its 1975–80 inmigrants from abroad, mostly from Asia. States least dependent on movers from abroad were New Hampshire, Arkansas, and West Virginia; each had under 5 percent of inmigrants coming from abroad in 1975–80. The heavy representation of movers from abroad among migrants to New York has existed for quite some time. In the late 1930s 25 percent of migrants to New York state came from outside the United States, in 1955–60 about 36 percent came from abroad, as did 39 percent in 1965–70.

Most movers from abroad in 1975–80 were not Americans returning home. Only about 27 percent of 1975–80 movers to the United States were born in the 50 states or the District of Columbia. Another 2.8 percent were persons born abroad to American parents. The other 70 percent were persons born abroad to foreign-born parents. The figures are even higher for New York and California. Nearly 87 percent of movers from abroad to New York in 1975–80 were foreign-born; for California the figure was 84 percent. These data mean that 36 percent of all inmigrants to New York in the 1975–80 period were foreign-born, and nearly 30 percent of California's inmigrants were foreign-born.

To sum up: What one finds from rates of inmigration and outmigration is a clustering of states around the Great Lakes which since the 1930s have had below-average rates of both inmigration and outmigration. This cluster was broken up somewhat by above-average increases in outmigration rates in some Great Lakes states between the late 1960s and the late 1970s. One finds another, somewhat looser cluster of western states with consistently above-average rates of inmigration and outmigraton. A few hypermobile people may account for a disproportionate amount of internal migration,[5] and for the 1975–80 period the next chapter directly asks how much of the nation's migration and how many movers to and from each state were by persons leaving their state of birth, returning to it, or making repeat (nonreturn) moves. The maps in Figures 3.2 and 3.3 show the states where migration was most active and least active from the late 1930s to the late 1970s.

Net Migration and Its Efficiency

Neither inmigration rates nor outmigration rates are, taken separately, good predictors of whether a state has net gain or loss of population through migration. Moreover, since there seems to be a positive association between the two rates,[6] net movements may appear inefficient in bringing about population redistribution. Almost always an

[5]Sidney Goldstein, "Repeated Migration as a Factor in High Mobility Rates," *American Sociological Review* 19 (October 1984): 536–541; Sidney Goldstein, "The Extent of Repeated Migration: An Analysis Based on the Danish Population Register," *Journal of the American Statistical Association* 59 (December 1964): 1121–1132; and Peter Morrison, "Chronic Movers and the Future Redistribution of Population: A Longitudinal Analysis," *Demography* 8 (May 1971): 171–184.

[6]Studies have consistently found high correlations between inmigrants and outmigrants as well as migration rates for metropolitan areas, even when the migration data are disaggregated by age, race, and occupation. For the U.S. case, see Ann R. Miller, "The Migration of Employed Persons to and from Metropolitan Areas of the United States," *Journal of the American Statistical Association* 62 (December, 1967): 1418–1432; and Celia A. Morgan, "A Note on a Perennial Question in Migration Analysis," *Growth and Change* 5 (October, 1974): 43–47. For Canadian metropolitan areas, see Leroy O. Stone, "On the Correlation between Metropolitan Area In- and Out-Migration by Occupation," *Journal of the American Statistical Association* 66 (December 1971): 693–701. The contribution of these studies is to show that the inability to predict net migration from either gross inmigration or outmigration derives not simply from differences in the inmigration and outmigration streams but exists even when the gross streams are disaggregated by age and occupation.

area's net migration is only a small percentage of the total movement in and out, and considerable research attention has been devoted to measuring and explaining just how small a percentage net migration is of total inmigration and outmigration and why it varies among areas. The degree to which movements cancel one another can be expressed as the ratio of an area's net migration to total inmigration and outmigration. The ratio is typically multiplied by 100 and has been labeled migration's "efficiency."

Attention to migration's efficiency (sometimes called effectiveness) may derive from Ravenstein, one of whose "laws" of migration was that streams tend to generate counterstreams, implying considerable inefficiency as flows counteracted one another.[7] Dorothy Thomas noted that over a long period of time migration within Sweden tended to become "quantitatively less effective; that is, for compensated migration to assume a relatively more important role in comparison with net or uncompensated migration" (p. 292).[8] Working with U.S. census data, Shryock found what seemed like low efficiency ratios for the 1935–40 and 1949–50 intervals and concluded: "It could be hypothesized that a great deal of milling about that had but little effect on population . . . would involve social and economic costs that were disproportionate to the benefits gained by the national or regional economy, or by the migrants themselves."[9]

Schwartz studied U.S. interregional migration for 1955–60 and found efficiency of streams to be negatively related to the degree of similarity in earnings at origin and destination; that is, the greater the overlap in the distribution of earnings at origin and destination, the lower the efficiency of migration.[10] He argued that since past migration had been from low-wage to high-wage regions and had acted to equalize interregional earnings differences, what looked like current inefficient migration really represented efficient migration in the past. According to

---

[7]". . . with each main stream or current of migrants there runs a counter-current, which more or less compensates for the losses sustained by emigration," wrote E. G. Ravenstein in "The Laws of Migration," *Journal of the Royal Statistical Society*, 47, pt. 2 (1885): 187.

[8]Dorothy Swaine Thomas, *Social and Economic Aspects of Swedish Population Movements, 1750–1933* (New York: Macmillan, 1941).

[9]Henry S. Shryock, *Population Mobility Within the United States* (Chicago: Community and Family Study Center, University of Chicago, 1964), p. 285.

[10]Aba Schwartz, "On Efficiency of Migration," *Journal of Human Resources* 6 (Spring 1971): 193–205. A conceptually similar approach was employed in a study of interregional migration of black men in 1955–60; see Eui Hang Shin, "Trends and Variations in Efficiency of Black Interregional Migration Streams," *Sociology and Social Research* 62 (January 1978): 228–245. Schwartz disaggregated his results according to age and educational level in "Migration, Age, and Education," *Journal of Political Economy* 84 (August 1976): 701–719.

this view, migration might be expected to become less efficient over time as long as areal earnings differentiation decreased.[11]

The concern over migration's efficiency is with the redistribution of the total population. Even when opposing streams completely cancel one another, they may differ vastly in their composition so that even if an area's net migration is zero its population composition may be changed by the inflow and outflow of different groups. Researchers sometimes use the word "efficiency" to refer to the degree to which migration goes to the "right" places—that is, from areas of surplus workers or limited opportunity to areas with a shortage of workers or offering higher wages. The focus here is simply with the degree to which migration brings about net redistribution of the total population.

Where migration is most and least efficient in redistributing population is shown in Table 3.1, which ranks states according to the efficiency measure for each of the four intervals. Efficiency is net migration (excluding movers from abroad) divided by gross migration (inmigrants plus outmigrants), multiplied by 100. An index of 100 is indicative of perfect efficiency. The table also shows net migration rates, which are usually expressed as net migration divided by the beginning-of-period population. But since there is no official beginning-of-period population, the practice adopted for Table 3.1 was to divide each state's net migration by the surviving beginning-of-period population—the same base as used for the outmigration rates.

The most efficient migration in the late 1930s was to California and Florida and *from* North Dakota, South Dakota, and other states of the Great Plains. The value of 61.1 for California means that net migration was 61.1 percent of gross inmigration and outmigration. Or, alternatively, 38.9 percent of moves in and out were offsetting.

During the Great Depression migration was as efficient in removing population from North Dakota as it was in adding people to California. The efficiency of North Dakota's outmigration is shown in Table 3.1 to be 62.2, about the same efficiency rating as California's net inmigration. For every person who moved to North Dakota in 1935–40, four left. For every person who moved from California, four moved in.

By the late 1950s the efficiency of migration to California had declined, but the efficiency of migration to Florida rose. These two states were still the most efficient gainers of population through migration.

---

[11]Decreasing migration efficiency has also been forecast for the 1980s on the expectation that consolidation and integration of the new metropolitan areas that grew rapidly in the Sunbelt in the 1970s will result in future streams that are more often accompanied by strong counterstreams. See David A. Plane, "A Systemic Demographic Efficiency Analysis of U.S. Interstate Population Exchange, 1935–1980," *Economic Geography* 60 (October 1984): 294–312.

TABLE 3.1

*States' Net Migration, Rate of Net Migration, and Ranking
According to Efficiency of Migration for Persons Aged 5 and Over:
1935–40, 1955–60, 1965–70, and 1975–80*

1935–40	Net Migration	Rate of Net Migration	Efficiency
Net Inmigration States			
California	664,866	11.7	61.1
Florida	146,849	9.4	42.0
Oregon	77,445	8.4	32.0
Maryland	61,318	3.8	28.8
Delaware	10,325	4.4	28.2
Washington	80,351	5.3	27.3
Arizona	37,771	9.4	25.7
Michigan	76,006	1.6	19.6
Nevada	8,014	8.8	17.6
Connecticut	24,885	1.6	16.5
Virginia	43,950	1.9	14.7
Idaho	16,376	3.6	12.5
New Mexico	13,785	3.1	11.2
District of Columbia	22,487	6.4	10.2
New Hampshire	6,118	1.4	9.9
Indiana	26,282	0.8	8.3
New Jersey	29,381	0.8	8.2
Louisiana	8,638	0.4	4.7
Colorado	9,112	0.9	4.0
Wyoming	2,741	1.2	3.7
Rhode Island	411	0.1	0.7
Net Outmigration States			
North Dakota	− 66,481	− 10.4	− 62.2
South Dakota	− 61,212	− 9.6	− 52.5
Nebraska	− 106,648	− 8.1	− 47.6
Oklahoma	− 183,899	− 8.1	− 42.4
Kansas	− 111,050	− 6.3	− 35.4
Alabama	− 72,978	− 2.8	− 32.9
Arkansas	− 75,463	− 4.2	− 26.7
Kentucky	− 54,813	− 2.1	− 22.6
Iowa	− 60,883	− 2.6	− 22.3
Pennsylvania	− 103,673	− 1.1	− 20.0
Missouri	− 85,489	− 2.4	− 17.8
Mississippi	− 28,430	− 1.5	− 17.8
Utah	− 12,392	− 2.5	− 16.7
West Virginia	− 27,242	− 1.6	− 16.5
Wisconsin	− 31,776	− 1.1	− 15.1
Maine	− 8,627	− 1.1	− 14.0
Tennessee	− 38,750	− 1.5	− 13.6
Vermont	− 5,731	− 1.7	− 13.1
Massachusetts	− 32,242	− 0.8	− 12.8

TABLE 3.1 *(continued)*

1935–40	Net Migration	Rate of Net Migration	Efficiency
Georgia	− 33,245	− 1.2	− 11.7
South Carolina	− 15,987	− 0.9	− 10.9
Montana	− 11,129	− 2.2	− 10.8
New York	− 57,150	− 0.5	− 7.3
Minnesota	− 17,944	− 0.7	− 7.2
North Carolina	− 14,940	− 0.5	− 6.6
Texas	− 20,131	− 0.3	− 3.7
Illinois	− 19,055	− 0.3	− 2.8
Ohio	− 9,751	− 0.2	− 2.0
1955–60			
Net Inmigration States			
Florida	776,796	22.5	50.5
California	1,122,204	9.2	40.7
Arizona	162,310	17.6	35.1
Delaware	16,980	4.7	16.8
Nevada	21,132	9.6	15.5
Maryland	86,533	3.4	14.3
New Mexico	42,700	5.7	13.2
New Jersey	111,724	2.2	12.6
Colorado	59,149	4.1	11.8
Connecticut	35,827	1.7	9.6
Alaska	11,530	6.9	7.7
New Hampshire	8,202	1.6	6.7
Hawaii	10,028	1.9	5.6
Virginia	43,294	1.3	5.0
Washington	29,045	1.2	4.7
Utah	5,475	0.7	3.2
Net Outmigration States			
West Virginia	− 137,179	− 7.7	− 42.7
North Dakota	− 37,073	− 6.4	− 30.6
District of Columbia	− 82,173	− 11.4	− 27.0
South Dakota	− 37,951	− 6.0	− 26.4
Pennsylvania	− 280,252	− 2.7	− 26.0
New York	− 402,819	− 2.7	− 25.5
Iowa	− 96,378	− 3.8	− 24.4
Kentucky	− 107,601	− 3.9	− 22.4
Nebraska	− 61,453	− 4.8	− 21.6
Mississippi	− 71,090	− 3.6	− 20.5
Michigan	− 165,252	− 2.4	− 19.6
Arkansas	− 66,042	− 4.0	− 17.8
Kansas	− 79,889	− 4.1	− 15.2

TABLE 3.1 *(continued)*

1955–60	Net Migration	Rate of Net Migration	Efficiency
Maine	−23,472	−2.7	−15.0
Oklahoma	−73,393	−3.5	−14.2
Tennessee	−80,402	−2.5	−13.7
North Carolina	−76,535	−1.9	−12.3
South Carolina	−44,870	−2.1	−11.8
Vermont	−8,605	−2.5	−11.5
Montana	−16,988	−2.8	−11.1
Alabama	−51,674	−1.8	−10.9
Massachusetts	−64,513	−1.4	−10.5
Rhode Island	−15,507	−2.0	−9.9
Illinois	−125,683	−1.4	−9.3
Missouri	−65,941	−1.7	−9.2
Indiana	−51,522	−1.3	−7.5
Minnesota	−29,904	−1.0	−7.0
Wisconsin	−29,569	−0.9	−6.9
Georgia	−42,501	−1.2	−6.7
Wyoming	−6,372	−2.2	−5.4
Idaho	−9,390	−1.6	−5.2
Ohio	−61,721	−0.7	−5.1
Texas	−28,055	−0.3	−2.0
Louisiana	−6,564	−0.2	−1.6
Oregon	−4,596	−0.3	−1.1

1965–70			
Net Inmigration States			
Florida	573,505	10.4	30.9
Washington	183,993	6.4	23.7
Arizona	110,085	7.5	18.3
Maryland	122,238	3.6	14.7
New Hampshire	24,828	3.9	13.8
Vermont	13,228	3.4	13.8
Colorado	81,701	4.3	12.2
Oregon	56,815	3.1	11.8
California	369,992	2.1	11.6
Nevada	21,603	5.3	10.3
Delaware	12,106	2.5	9.0
Georgia	73,850	1.8	8.8
Texas	138,842	1.4	8.2
Virginia	66,046	1.6	5.9
Alaska	8,354	3.3	4.4
Connecticut	21,611	0.8	4.1
New Jersey	40,398	0.6	3.5
North Carolina	21,428	0.5	2.7
South Carolina	12,417	0.5	2.7
Oklahoma	3,294	0.1	0.6

TABLE 3.1 *(continued)*

1965–70	Net Migration	Rate of Net Migration	Efficiency
Missouri	3,571	0.1	0.4
Tennessee	2,883	0.1	0.4
Rhode Island	795	0.1	0.4
Net Outmigration States			
District of Columbia	−82,383	−10.9	−31.4
North Dakota	−50,953	−8.3	−31.4
South Dakota	−46,831	−7.1	−29.8
New York	−567,910	−3.4	−29.7
West Virginia	−80,470	−4.8	−25.8
Montana	−34,527	−5.2	−18.7
New Mexico	−56,234	−5.8	−16.9
Iowa	−73,062	−2.8	−16.5
Wyoming	−20,058	−6.2	−16.1
Pennsylvania	−190,997	−1.7	−15.1
Nebraska	−41,155	−3.0	−13.3
Alabama	−72,646	−2.3	−13.0
Mississippi	−49,051	−2.4	−12.8
Illinois	−197,904	−1.9	−12.4
Maine	−21,313	−2.3	−12.1
Kentucky	−48,014	−1.6	−9.3
Kansas	−47,426	−2.3	−8.6
Louisiana	−38,753	−1.2	−7.6
Ohio	−83,123	−0.9	−6.0
Massachusetts	−42,921	−0.8	−5.4
Indiana	−42,135	−0.9	−5.3
Idaho	−11,012	−1.7	−5.2
Utah	−11,820	−1.3	−5.0
Wisconsin	−19,305	−0.5	−3.6
Arkansas	−12,802	−0.7	−3.4
Minnesota	−14,087	−0.4	−2.7
Hawaii	−4,003	−0.6	−1.5
Michigan	−2,688	0.0	−0.3
1975–80			
Net Inmigration States			
Nevada	112,689	18.4	31.6
Florida	823,227	10.1	29.6
Washington	280,417	8.1	29.2
Arizona	245,688	11.1	25.8
Oregon	166,856	7.5	25.3
Texas	574,007	4.7	25.0
Wyoming	47,358	12.7	24.5
Utah	66,398	5.6	19.5
Oklahoma	116,818	4.4	18.0
New Hampshire	44,765	5.6	16.4

TABLE 3.1 *(continued)*

1975–80	Net Migration	Rate of Net Migration	Efficiency
Idaho	44,378	5.6	15.0
Colorado	128,685	5.2	13.2
Tennessee	102,986	2.5	12.9
Georgia	131,123	2.7	12.7
Arkansas	56,140	2.7	12.0
South Carolina	66,674	2.4	11.2
North Carolina	87,244	1.6	8.8
Alabama	47,240	1.3	8.0
New Mexico	30,080	2.6	7.8
Louisiana	46,550	1.2	7.7
Vermont	7,459	1.6	5.8
Virginia	64,438	1.3	4.9
Kentucky	22,938	0.7	3.9
Maine	6,250	0.6	2.9
California	94,458	0.5	2.6
West Virginia	5,289	0.3	1.7
Montana	1,518	0.2	0.7
Net Outmigration States			
New York	−1,097,197	−6.4	−46.8
District of Columbia	−72,493	−11.0	−27.0
Illinois	−453,337	−4.2	−26.1
Ohio	−361,080	−3.5	−24.1
Michigan	−246,954	−2.8	−21.9
Pennsylvania	−264,183	−2.3	−18.7
Massachusetts	−166,984	−3.1	−18.2
New Jersey	−225,305	−3.2	−17.3
Iowa	−59,678	−2.2	−12.3
South Dakota	−19,515	−3.0	−12.2
Connecticut	−74,452	−2.5	−12.1
Indiana	−82,807	−1.6	−9.7
Rhode Island	−15,048	−1.7	−8.8
Nebraska	−28,473	−1.9	−8.5
Maryland	−74,753	−1.9	−8.3
Hawaii	−23,822	−2.8	−7.4
Minnesota	−43,358	−1.1	−7.3
Alaska	−16,080	−4.3	−7.1
North Dakota	−10,711	−1.8	−6.6
Wisconsin	−37,978	−0.9	−6.1
Delaware	−9,221	−1.7	−5.9
Missouri	−23,377	−0.5	−2.7
Kansas	−12,657	−0.6	−2.2
Mississippi	−2,210	−0.1	−0.5

NOTES: Net migration excludes movers from abroad. The rate of net migration is net migration divided by the beginning-of-period surviving population, multiplied by 100. Efficiency is net migration divided by gross migration, multiplied by 100.

The states with the most efficient *out*migration in 1955–60 were West Virginia and North Dakota.

A decade later, in the late 1960s, interstate migration generally seems to have declined in the efficiency with which population was redistributed. The states with the most efficient net inmigration were not gaining population through migration as efficiently as were the gaining states in 1935–40 or 1955–60. And states with net outmigration were not losing population as efficiently as those with net outmigration in 1935–40 or 1955–60.

In the late 1970s, however, net migration for many losing states as well as gaining states increased. The nation's most efficient migration flow in 1975–80 was from New York state. Internal migration removed population from New York state in 1975–80 more efficiently than it removed population from West Virginia in the 1950s or from Oklahoma in the 1930s. For every 100 persons who moved to New York state between 1975 and 1980 from elsewhere in the United States, 276 left.

For a number of states net inmigration was also more efficient in 1975–80 than in 1965–70. For example, the efficiency of net inmigration to Nevada and Texas increased markedly between the late 1960s and the late 1970s. The Great Lakes states, which were earlier observed to have had below-average rates of inmigration and outmigration in 1975–80, had above-average efficiency ratings. Michigan's net outmigration was only slightly less efficient than Texas's net inmigration.

Finally, observe that fewer states had net outmigration in 1975–80 than any of the other migration intervals. Twenty-two states (counting the District of Columbia as a state) had net outmigration in 1975–80 compared with 28 in 1965–70, 35 in 1955–60, and 28 in 1935–40. The declining number of states with net outmigration was part of the general diffusion of population growth that marked the 1970–80 decade.[12] Never before in the twentieth century did so many counties grow in population, and, according to Table 3.2, not since the Great Depression had so many states experienced net inmigration.

Summarizing Changes in Interstate Migration

Although it is common to focus on interstate migration on a state-by-state basis, as has been done up to this point, there is also a need to summarize to express the national experience. A way of summarizing

---

[12]Larry Long and Diana DeAre, "Repopulating the Countryside: A 1980 Census Trend," *Science* September 17, 1982, pp. 1111–1116.

TABLE 3.2

Summary Measures of Interstate Migration for Persons
Aged 5 and Over: 1935–40, 1955–60, 1965–70, and 1975–80

	1935–40	1955–60	1965–70	1975–80
Interstate Migration Rate[a]				
Observed	5.4	9.3	9.9	9.9
Age-standardized[b]	5.3	9.9	10.3	9.9
Mean Distance Moved (miles)[c]	606	756	767	804
Efficiency[d]	21.0	18.0	11.6	16.8
Coefficient of Variation[e]				
Inmigration rates	.73	.56	.41	.48
Outmigration rates	.55	.35	.34	.28
Percentage Moving to State with				
Higher per Capita Income	60%	55%	53%	44%

[a]Percentage of U.S. population aged 5 and over at the census date who were living in a different state five years earlier. Persons abroad five years earlier were removed from the numerator and denominator. Persons not reporting residence five years earlier (1940, 1960, and 1970 censuses) were assigned a mobility status in the same proportions as persons reporting residence five years earlier.

[b]Age-standardization is based on the 1980 U.S. age distribution.

[c]Excludes Alaska and Hawaii.

[d]Efficiency is the sum of net inmigration to states having net inmigration (or net outmigration from states having net outmigration) divided by total interstate migration; the result is multiplied by 100. The efficiency measure excludes movers from abroad.

[e]Inmigration rates exclude movers from abroad. Alaska, Hawaii, and the District of Columbia are excluded for both inmigration and outmigration rates.

the migration streams displayed in Figure 3.1 is to ask if their average distance has changed. The most likely hypothesis is that since the 1930s the friction of distance has been reduced through continued improvements in transportation and communication, and so the average distance moved by interstate migrants should increase. But there is an upper limit, and the chart of the largest streams in 1975–80 shows fewer cross-country arrows and greater representation of intraregional arrows. Neither the censuses nor the major surveys that collect migration data (the Current Population Survey and the American Housing Survey) have asked migrants to report distance moved, but distances can be inferred from information on state-to-state flows and distances between states, based on their population centers.[13] This method provides a basis for

[13]The method was first used by Tarver and McLeod to analyze migration distances for the 1935–40 and 1955–60 intervals. See James D. Tarver and R. Douglas McLeod, "Trends in Distances Moved by Interstate Migrants," *Rural Sociology* 35 (December 1970): 523–533; and "Trends in the Distance of Movement of Interstate Migrants," *Rural Sociology* 41 (Spring 1976): 119–226.

determining whether the average distance covered by interstate moves has changed over the 40 years from the late 1930s to the late 1970s. Since the method assumes that migration is between the population centers of states, it tends to overstate actual distances moved by interstate migrants.

The average distance covered by interstate moves is shown in Table 3.2, along with four other measures intended to summarize the experiences of individual states. One is simply the national interstate migration rate, adapted from Chapter 2. Another is the coefficient of variation of states' inmigration and outmigration rates, calculated from the type of data mapped in Figures 3.2 and 3.3 and intended to show whether states have become more alike or less alike in the rates at which they send and receive migrants. The efficiency of interstate migration is summarized from data developed for Table 3.1. Finally, Table 3.2 shows the proportion of interstate migrants whose state of destination had a higher per capita income than their state of origin, intended to reflect the degree to which interstate population movements represent a drift from low- to high-income states. These materials suggest seven ways of summarizing interstate migration trends and patterns from the late 1930s to the late 1970s.

First, as noted in Chapter 2, the percentage of the U.S. population engaging in interstate migration increased greatly between the late 1930s and the late 1950s and on an age-standardized basis has declined somewhat since then. Virtually all states participated in this increase. The greatest increases in outmigration rates between 1935–40 and 1955–60 were in Rhode Island (161 percent increase) and West Virginia (130 percent increase), but even Oklahoma and the Dustbowl states of the Great Plains had higher rates of outmigration in the 1950s than in the 1930s; each of these states also had higher rates of inmigration. For the more recent migration intervals one finds a mixed pattern, with many states experiencing increases in inmigration or outmigration rates and other states having decreases; the overall result, without standardizing for age, is approximate stability in the percentage of the U.S. population engaging in interstate migration over three five-year intervals from the 1950s to 1980.

Second, interstate migration streams have come to cover successively longer distances, from an average of 606 miles moved by 1935–40 migrants to 804 miles moved by 1975–80 migrants. Most of this increase was between the 1930s and the 1950s, when the average distance moved increased by 150 miles, or 25 percent. There was virtually no change in distance moved between 1955–60 and 1965–70 and a comparatively small increase by 1975–80. For each of the four migration intervals the average distance moved is a summary of 2,352 migration streams (Alaska and Hawaii are excluded). Such a measure illustrates that over the 40-year interval the average interstate migrant came to travel farther from where he or she started out. The distance moved will not increase forever, and the limit may soon be reached, if it has not already been attained.

Third, the efficiency with which migration brings about redistribution of population among the states decreased from the 1930s to the 1960s but increased by the late 1970s. The measure of efficiency shown in Table 3.2 is obtained either by summing net inmigration to states having net inmigration or by summing net outmigration from states having net outmigration; disregarding the sign, the two values are equal since migration from outside the United States is excluded. When this value is divided by total interstate migration and multiplied by 100, it represents the net interstate redistribution of population for each 100 interstate moves. In 1935–40 the figure was 21.0, meaning that each 100 moves brought about a net redistribution of 21 persons, or, alternatively, that 79 out of every 100 moves canceled each other. By 1955–60 the efficiency of interstate migration was down to 18.0, and by 1965–70 it had declined to 11.6. By 1975–80 it was up to 16.8. Migration in the late 1970s therefore represented a break in the past pattern and was more efficient in shifting population among the states, particularly toward Sunbelt states. Declining efficiency of internal migration means an increased importance of counterstreams (flows against the path of net redistribution) and suggests growing heterogeneity of motivations for migration, so that more people have reasons to go to places where others are leaving. The theory that declining efficiency results from increasing heterogeneity of motives and decreasing areal differences in income suggests that the slight rise in efficiency in the 1970s may be temporary.

Fourth, states differ less in the rate at which they send migrants than in the rate at which they receive migrants. The coefficient of variation (the ratio of the standard deviation to the mean) was higher for inmigration rates than outmigration rates for each of the four migration intervals. In other words, states form a tighter cluster around the mean rate of outmigration than the mean rate of inmigration. What this may mean is that states differ less in terms of the forces which impel migration to occur than in the criteria by which migrants choose among potential destinations. If migration is thought of in the classic push-pull terms, this finding suggests that states differ more in the pull than the push. Table 3.2 shows that this pattern has existed for quite some time, even during the Great Depression.

Moreover, states have become increasingly alike in the rates at which they send migrants to other states. The coefficient of variation in outmigration rates declined consistently from .55 in 1935–40 to .28 in

1975–80, meaning that states were coming to form a tighter cluster around the mean rate of outmigration. In spite of news stories in the late 1970s about declining economic opportunities in industrialized states around the Great Lakes and increased rates of exodus to the Sunbelt, the result of such changes was to make states more alike in rates of outmigration. As mentioned earlier, the rates of outmigration from the Great Lakes states generally increased between 1965–70 and 1975–80, but since these states had had below-average rates of outmigration previously, the outcome was to make them more like other states in rates of outmigration.

States were also becoming more alike in inmigration rates until the 1975–80 migration interval. The coefficient of variation of inmigration rates fell from .73 in 1935–40, to .56 in 1955–60, to .41 in 1965–70, but increased to .48 in 1975–80. Migration streams were somewhat more concentrated in a few destinations, as suggested earlier when it was noted that the five largest interstate migration streams shown in Figure 3.1 represented a declining proportion of total migration from 1935–40 to 1965–70 but increased slightly in 1975–80. This is another measure of how 1975–80 migration was a break from past patterns. The increased concentration of migration flows to a few states helps account for raising the overall efficiency of migration in the 1975–80 period.

The final generalization about how migration has changed since the Great Depression concerns a declining tendency of migrants to move in the direction of higher income. Many factors interact in influencing migration decisions, and this simple comparison is not intended to suggest causality but merely to summarize a single aspect of interstate migration. The only income measure available at the beginning of each of the migration intervals was per capita income. Quite clearly, the tendency to move from low-income to high-income states has weakened considerably. About 60 percent of interstate migrants in 1935–40 were moving to a state where per capita income was higher than the state they left. In 1955–60, 55 percent were moving in the direction of higher income; in 1965–70 the figure dropped to 53 percent; and by 1975–80 a majority of migrants were going to a state where per capita income was *lower* than the state they left. Of course, many of these low-income states were rapidly growing states in the Sunbelt where incomes were relatively low but where jobs were growing and prospects for future growth of earnings were good. To a considerable extent this statistic is simply a reflection of the faster-than-average growth of income in traditionally low-income areas and the diminishing of areal differences in income. But it can effectively illustrate the inaccuracy of trying to describe internal migration as a consistent drift of population to high-wage areas. The statistic suggests a growing complexity of migration patterns, where migration streams tend often to be canceling and many persons of different demographic or economic characteristics have cause to move to areas where others are leaving.

To sum up, the 1975–80 migration interval continued some patterns evident in earlier decades, including a tendency for migration distances to increase, for more persons to move to low-income states, and for states to become more alike in outmigration rates. The 1975–80 period differed from other postwar periods in that interstate migration became a more efficient mechanism for redistributing population, as states became more dissimilar in inmigration rates and migration streams were somewhat more strongly directed to a few fast-growing states.

Age of Interstate Migrants

It is, of course, possible that variability among the states in the rates of inmigration and outmigration shown in Figures 3.2 and 3.3 is affected by compositional factors. For example, a state's overall low rate of outmigration may be due partly to its having a comparatively old population, perhaps as a result of past high rates of outmigration among the young. Or inmigration may be selective of one age group and outmigration selective of another. The high concentration of interstate migration that occurs over a short age range (typically age 20 to 30 or 35) is illustrated in Chapter 2 and in Appendix B. In order to control for age differences among states and to see to what extent the "typical" age profile illustrated in Chapter 2 applies to each state, rates of inmigration and outmigration by five-year age groups were computed for each state.

The ranking of states according to migration rates does vary somewhat by age. During the 1975–80 interval, Alaska had the highest rate of outmigration at every age group. Nevada had the second highest rates of outmigration among persons under age 20 and over age 55, suggesting that Nevada may have comparatively less holding power for families with children and some persons of retirement age. However, Nevada had the highest *in*migration rates at most age groups, and differences in rankings are based on very small differences in rates of migration.

Some of the most significant changes in rankings occur around the retirement ages. New York state generally has below-average rates of outmigration at preretirement ages, but at ages 60–64 New York had the fourth highest rate of outmigration. And at ages 65–69 New York moved into the number three spot, behind only Alaska and Nevada in the propensity of its residents to move to other states. After age 70 New York state's ranking dropped slightly.

In general, however, states that have high rates of outmigration tend to have comparatively high rates at most age groups. And states with overall low rates of outmigration tend to have relatively low rates at most ages (New York state's high elderly outmigration seems to be the major exception to this rule). Conversely, states with high rates of inmigration tend to have comparatively high rates at most ages.

An age pattern that bears closer investigation is that associated with migration out of America's "industrial heartland." The economy of this region was built around heavy industry including steel, coal, automobiles, and many other traditional manufacturing enterprises. The severe economic dislocations in this region in the late 1970s caused it to be dubbed the Rustbelt, in contrast to the gleaming image conveyed earlier in the decade by designating the growing southern rim the Sunbelt. America's industrial heartland-turned-Rustbelt would, at the minimum, include New York state, Pennsylvania, Ohio, and Michigan. As would be expected, these four states had above-average increases in their overall outmigration rates between 1965–70 and 1975–80, although they still had below-average rates of outmigration—a characteristic they have shared since at least the 1930s. Even though the deterioration of the area's economic base did not bring outmigration rates up to the national average, it might have upset the "normal" age pattern of migration. Specifically, deteriorating economic conditions might prolong migration beyond the usual ages when rates are high. Hence, migration from an area may be disruptive not only in terms of its level but the range of ages it affects.

A simple test of this proposition for states of the industrial heartland is to compare age-specific rates of outmigration with the national average. This comparison is presented in Figure 3.4, which shows the age curves of outmigration rates from the four states and the national average and the ratio of each state's outmigration rate to the national average.

Figure 3.4 shows that the below-average rates of outmigration from these four states cannot be attributed to their underlying age distributions. At most ages under 50 or so these four "industrial heartland" states had outmigration rates below the national average for 1975–80. Quite simply, residents of New York, Pennsylvania, Ohio, and Michigan were at most ages under 50 less likely to engage in interstate migration than was the national average for 1975–80.

The profile of age-specific rates of outmigration from each of these four states bears considerable similarity to the classic shape described in Chapter 2, at least up to age 50. Rates are relatively high among children under age 10, then decline among persons in their early to mid-teens, and then rise rapidly to a peak among persons in their 20s. These

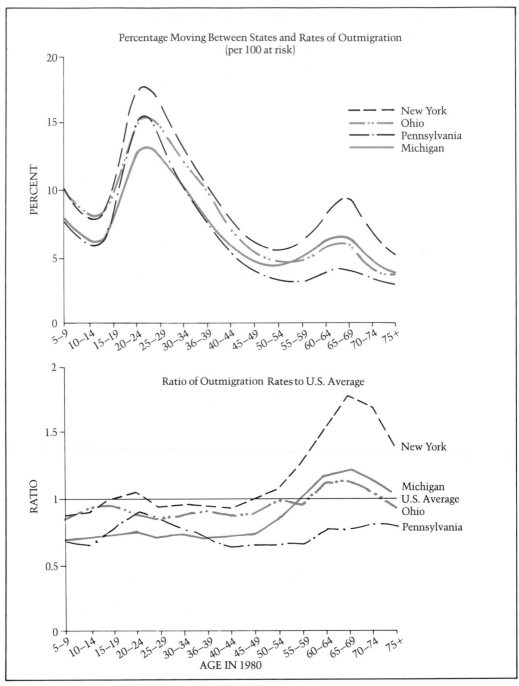

FIGURE 3.4

How Outmigration Rates for Four "Industrial Heartland" States Compare With U.S. Average, by Age: 1975–80

Percentage Moving Between States and Rates of Outmigration
(per 100 at risk)

New York
Ohio
Pennsylvania
Michigan

PERCENT

Ratio of Outmigration Rates to U.S. Average

RATIO

New York

Michigan
U.S. Average
Ohio

Pennsylvania

AGE IN 1980

are ages in 1980, after moving; migrants were younger, perhaps two and a half years younger, at the time of moving. There is no support for the hypothesis that economic adversity of the late 1970s prolonged outmigration beyond the "normal" age range.

Up to about age 50 outmigration rates are consistently below the national average. The only exception is that outmigration from New York State was at or above the national average at ages 15–19 and 20–24. Hence, outmigration from America's industrial heartland in the late 1970s may have been disruptive in the sense that it raised overall rates of outmigration, but not in the sense that it prolonged outmigration beyond a "normal" age range. Unfavorable economic conditions in the region may certainly have caused many people to move to the Sunbelt who had not expected and did not want to move, but their "unexpected" outmigration simply brought them closer to the national experience of migration.

The major difference between rates of outmigration from these four heavily industrialized states and the rest of the nation begins around age 50 and increases until around age 65. All four states show some increase in outmigration rates around age 65, and New York, Michigan, and Ohio rise above the national average. New York is the most extreme case among all the states in this regard. The probability of leaving New York reaches its peak among persons in their mid-20s and then begins to decline, only to begin another rise after age 50 and reach another, secondary peak just before age 65. The probability of a 35-year-old New Yorker engaging in interstate migration is below the national average; the probability of a 45-year-old New Yorker moving to another state approximately equals the national average. But the probability of a 65-year-old New Yorker moving to another state is 81 percent above the national average. No other state shows so great an increase in the propensity to migrate after the customary low among persons somewhere in middle age. The connection of retirement with interstate migration is obviously high in New York.

An examination of each state's inmigration and outmigration rates by age showed that states are much more alike in the migration of persons in their 20s than any other age group. The coefficient of variation for states' outmigration rates is .40 at ages 5–9, drops to .30 at ages 20–24, and then rises gradually to .67 at ages 60–64.[14] These figures show that the clustering of states around the average rate of outmigration is

---

[14]These age-specific coefficients of variation of inmigration and outmigration rates are larger than the values reported in Table 3.2 because Table 3.2 excludes the District of Columbia, Alaska, and Hawaii in order to maintain comparability with the earliest period when Alaska and Hawaii were not yet states. The age-specific data mentioned in the text include all states and the District of Columbia.

much tighter at the ages when migration is at its peak. A similar pattern characterizes inmigration rates. The coefficient of variation is .45 at ages 5–9, reaches a low of .41 at ages 25–29 and 30–34, and then rises to .93 at ages 65–69. This information demonstrates that at every age group states are more variable in terms of inmigration than outmigration. These results suggest that the forces that cause migration among young adults are less geographically variable than the forces that produce migration among persons nearing retirement.

The efficiency measure shows a somewhat similar age pattern. Interstate migration is least efficient among persons aged 30–34 and reaches maximum efficiency at ages 65–69 (these are ages in 1980, after migrating). Every 100 interstate moves among persons aged 30–34 brought about a net redistribution of only 11 persons; every 100 moves of persons aged 65–69 produced net redistribution of 48 persons. This information suggests that the reasons for migration of persons at or just beyond the peak ages of migration may be more numerous and geographically variable, producing relatively more counterstreams than at other age groups. At retirement ages, however, migration streams tend more nearly to be unidirectional and less likely to be offset by counterstreams.

Education of Interstate Migrants

Even though adverse economic conditions in the four industrial heartland states just examined did not seem to prolong outmigration beyond a "normal" age range, another important aspect of migration from this region concerns educational level. Did these states lose their best-educated persons or those with the least education in the late 1970s? While many other characteristics of migrants from these states might be examined, education is an enduring characteristic, which does not change over the migration interval. Unlike the 1970 census, the 1980 census did not ask a question on occupation at the beginning of the migration interval, so it is impossible to accurately assess occupational mobility over the 1975–80 interval.

Educational level of inmigrants and outmigrants should be a guide to these states' gains and losses of human capital. Since educational attainment is strongly related to age, it is often necessary to control for age in order to measure net gains and losses according to migrants' level of schooling. Table 3.3 shows gross and net migration by years of school completed for four age groups—25–29, 30–34, 35–39, 40–44, and 45–49—for the four industrial heartland states examined earlier. These four

TABLE 3.3

Inmigrants, Outmigrants, and Rates of Outmigration and Net Migration,
for New York State, Pennsylvania, Ohio, and Michigan,
by Five-Year Age Groups (25–49) and Years of School Completed: 1975–80

Age and Years of School	Inmigrants	Outmigrants	Net Migration	Outmigrants per 100 at Risk	Outmigration Rate Relative to U.S. Average	Net Migration Rate (per 100 at Risk)
NEW YORK						
25–29 Years						
Less than 12 Years	8,102	17,564	−9,462	7.2	70.0	−3.9
12 Years	27,299	59,474	−32,175	11.0	82.2	−5.9
13–15 Years	29,163	59,759	−30,596	15.8	84.1	−8.1
16 Years	38,487	57,228	−18,741	24.2	90.7	−7.9
17 or More Years	38,273	50,278	−12,005	25.7	78.1	−6.1
30–34 Years						
Less than 12 Years	5,572	17,098	−11,526	6.7	83.5	−4.5
12 Years	18,023	48,556	−30,533	9.1	86.9	−5.7
13–15 Years	16,729	44,211	−27,482	14.1	92.3	−8.8
16 Years	17,891	35,611	−17,720	18.8	92.2	−9.3
17 or More Years	27,360	49,670	−22,310	20.4	81.2	−9.2
35–39 Years						
Less than 12 Years	5,010	15,409	−10,399	5.9	85.7	−4.0
12 Years	10,723	36,593	−25,870	8.0	91.6	−5.7
13–15 Years	8,701	24,737	−16,036	11.9	91.3	−7.7
16 Years	7,860	18,402	−10,542	14.8	89.6	−8.5
17 or More Years	12,229	27,322	−15,093	16.3	85.9	−9.0
40–44 Years						
Less than 12 Years	3,721	13,900	−10,179	5.1	93.6	−3.7
12 Years	6,834	24,451	−17,617	6.4	88.5	−4.6
13–15 Years	4,634	14,340	−9,706	9.4	88.1	−6.4
16 Years	3,663	10,171	−6,508	11.2	89.7	−7.2
17 or More Years	5,639	13,280	−7,641	11.3	83.2	−6.5
45–49 Years						
Less than 12 Years	3,038	12,765	−9,727	4.4	103.4	−3.4
12 Years	4,781	20,460	−15,679	5.5	100.7	−4.2
13–15 Years	3,125	10,750	−7,625	8.2	97.2	−5.8
16 Years	2,347	7,142	−4,795	9.1	92.6	−6.1
17 or More Years	3,859	7,636	−3,777	7.7	74.6	−3.8
PENNSYLVANIA						
25–29 Years						
Less than 12 Years	6,918	7,834	−916	6.7	65.2	−0.8

TABLE 3.3 (continued)

Age and Years of School	Inmigrants	Outmigrants	Net Migration	Outmigrants per 100 at Risk	Outmigration Rate Relative to U.S. Average	Net Migration Rate (per 100 at Risk)
PENNSYLVANIA (continued)						
12 Years	28,707	34,541	−5,834	7.5	56.2	−1.3
13–15 Years	20,318	28,482	−8,164	15.6	83.3	−4.5
16 Years	21,256	39,027	−17,771	26.2	98.2	−11.9
17 or More Years	19,148	30,587	−11,439	32.7	99.3	−12.2
30–34 Years						
Less than 12 Years	5,297	6,634	−1,337	5.5	68.6	−1.1
12 Years	20,028	26,149	−6,121	6.3	60.1	−1.5
13–15 Years	14,910	18,765	−3,855	12.9	84.4	−2.7
16 Years	13,858	18,494	−4,636	18.0	88.3	−4.5
17 or More Years	17,359	22,353	−4,994	21.8	86.7	−4.9
35–39 Years						
Less than 12 Years	4,746	5,677	−931	4.2	61.4	−0.7
12 Years	14,052	18,634	−4,582	5.4	61.7	−1.3
13–15 Years	8,511	9,843	−1,332	11.0	84.2	−1.5
16 Years	7,063	8,101	−1,038	13.7	83.2	−1.8
17 or More Years	9,297	12,270	−2,973	17.2	90.7	−4.2
40–44 Years						
Less than 12 Years	3,804	5,247	−1,443	3.5	64.5	−1.0
12 Years	9,096	11,895	−2,799	4.0	55.6	−0.9
13–15 Years	4,675	5,749	−1,074	8.8	82.7	−1.7
16 Years	4,005	4,711	−706	10.7	85.8	−1.6
17 or More Years	5,095	5,053	42	11.1	81.7	0.1
45–49 Years						
Less than 12 Years	3,500	4,634	−1,134	2.6	60.6	−0.6
12 Years	6,273	9,360	−3,087	3.2	58.3	−1.1
13–15 Years	3,144	4,229	−1,085	7.3	87.0	−1.9
16 Years	2,713	3,669	−956	8.9	90.7	−2.3
17 or More Years	3,094	3,660	−566	9.4	91.0	−1.5
OHIO						
25–29 Years						
Less than 12 Years	9,895	11,295	−1,400	8.5	83.2	−1.1
12 Years	31,677	39,794	−8,117	9.2	69.0	−1.9
13–15 Years	22,532	31,809	−9,277	16.6	88.5	−4.8
16 Years	20,170	31,399	−11,229	25.3	94.8	−9.1
17 or More Years	17,225	25,149	−7,924	33.1	100.4	−10.4

TABLE 3.3 *(continued)*

Age and Years of School	Inmigrants	Outmigrants	Net Migration	Outmigrants per 100 at Risk	Outmigration Rate Relative to U.S. Average	Net Migration Rate (per 100 at Risk)
OHIO *(continued)*						
30–34 Years						
Less than 12 Years	7,096	10,700	−3,604	8.2	101.7	−2.8
12 Years	19,857	31,337	−11,480	8.2	77.7	−3.0
13–15 Years	14,969	22,989	−8,020	14.2	92.6	−4.9
16–36 Years	13,995	18,851	−4,856	18.8	92.3	−4.8
17 or More Years	16,044	21,587	−5,543	24.7	98.1	−6.3
35–39 Years						
Less than 12 Years	5,669	9,507	−3,838	6.8	99.5	−2.8
12 Years	13,305	21,699	−8,394	7.0	79.8	−2.7
13–15 Years	8,148	12,946	−4,798	12.9	98.9	−4.8
16 Years	6,918	10,582	−3,664	18.2	110.1	−6.3
17 or More Years	8,188	11,934	−3,746	19.6	103.6	−6.2
40–44 Years						
Less than 12 Years	4,660	8,305	−3,645	5.4	99.1	−2.4
12 Years	9,636	14,693	−5,057	5.5	76.8	−1.9
13–15 Years	5,416	7,506	−2,090	10.3	96.3	−2.9
16 Years	4,018	5,789	−1,771	13.8	110.8	−4.2
17 or More Years	4,484	5,845	−1,361	14.0	103.4	−3.3
45–49 Years						
Less than 12 Years	3,960	7,588	−3,628	4.4	102.2	−2.1
12 Years	5,633	10,651	−5,018	4.3	78.9	−2.0
13–15 Years	3,163	5,500	−2,337	9.0	106.5	−3.8
16 Years	2,531	3,465	−934	9.6	98.4	−2.6
17 or More Years	2,820	3,943	−1,123	11.1	107.4	−3.2
MICHIGAN						
25–29 Years						
Less than 12 Years	7,921	8,784	−863	7.6	74.0	−0.7
12 Years	25,514	28,560	−3,046	8.2	61.1	−0.9
13–15 Years	20,753	24,952	−4,199	12.1	64.6	−2.0
16 Years	14,911	21,968	−7,057	22.6	84.7	−7.3
17 or More Years	13,035	19,882	−6,847	26.8	81.3	−9.2
30–34 Years						
Less than 12 Years	5,333	6,994	−1,661	6.9	84.9	−1.6
12 Years	14,814	20,078	−5,264	6.7	63.8	−1.8

95

TABLE 3.3 *(continued)*

Age and Years of School	Inmigrants	Outmigrants	Net Migration	Outmigrants per 100 at Risk	Outmigration Rate Relative to U.S. Average	Net Migration Rate (per 100 at Risk)
MICHIGAN *(continued)*						
13–15 Years	12,877	18,116	−5,239	10.6	69.0	−3.1
16 Years	10,208	13,477	−3,269	16.4	80.4	−4.0
17 or More Years	12,036	18,144	−6,108	20.7	82.1	−7.0
35–39 Years						
Less than 12 Years	4,581	5,552	−971	5.4	79.4	−1.0
12 Years	9,958	14,033	−4,075	5.5	63.2	−1.6
13–15 Years	6,215	10,059	−3,844	8.9	67.9	−3.4
16 Years	5,275	6,724	−1,449	13.1	79.7	−2.8
17 or More Years	6,657	9,400	−2,743	14.8	78.2	−4.3
40–44 Years						
Less than 12 Years	3,308	5,074	−1,766	4.5	82.6	−1.6
12 Years	6,099	10,011	−3,912	4.7	65.4	−1.8
13–15 Years	3,783	5,841	−2,058	7.6	71.5	−2.7
16 Years	2,892	3,312	−420	10.1	80.6	−1.3
17 or More Years	3,057	4,676	−1,619	11.2	82.3	−3.9
45–49 Years						
Less than 12 Years	2,749	4,943	−2,194	3.7	85.7	−1.6
12 Years	4,389	7,961	−3,572	4.1	73.7	−1.8
13–15 Years	2,502	3,660	−1,158	6.0	71.0	−1.9
16 Years	1,551	2,533	−982	8.4	85.8	−3.3
17 or More Years	2,069	2,464	−395	7.3	70.8	−1.2

NOTE: Inmigrants exclude movers from abroad.

states typically had rates of outmigration below the national average at these ages but above-average rates at older ages. Looking at educational patterns for ages 25 and over misses some moves of persons leaving high school by age 18 to look for work but has the advantage of eliminating most moves associated with college enrollment. Previous censuses were not consistently tabulated to show inmigrants and outmigrants for states, but Chapter 5 analyzes the effects of migration on educational levels of persons aged 25–34 over the 1940–80 period for nine regions of the country. Chapter 5 also examines the effects of some other characteristics of interregional migrants, particularly race and poverty status.

Table 3.3 shows, first, that the four states almost always had net outmigration at each of the five educational levels. Hence, their net outmigration was widespread and not concentrated among, say, high school dropouts or college graduates. With one minor exception, this generalization applies at each age group for each state.

Second, outmigration from each state was almost always positively related to educational level. At ages 25–29 and 30–34, rates of outmigration are typically three to four times greater for persons with 17 or more years of school (implying education beyond the usual four-year baccalaureate degree) than among persons with less than 12 years of school completed. Differences in outmigration according to educational level are somewhat less at ages 35–39, 40–44, and 45–49. These patterns simply duplicate the national experience, as discussed in Chapter 2. At each of the age-education categories, however, the four states typically had lower rates of outmigration than the national average. The lower-than-average rates of outmigration from these states cannot, therefore, be attributed to either the age or educational distributions of their populations.

However, the ratios of their outmigration rates to the national average are usually higher (New York is most often the exception) for the upper end than the lower end of the educational distribution. This means that for these states the propensity to engage in interstate migration was closer to the national average for the well-educated than for the poorly educated. These four industrial heartland states were somewhat more likely to be losing their better-educated persons.

This relationship is also seen in the net migration rates, which are formed by dividing net migration by the 1975 "at risk" population, the same base for the outmigration rates. The net migration losses are usually slightly greater for persons with 16 or 17 or more years of school completed than for persons with only a high school education or less schooling (again, New York is less consistent than the other states). The differences do not seem great, but the rates at which these states lost population through migration were slightly greater for college-educated persons. For example, at ages 25–29, Pennsylvania lost 0.8 percent of its 1975 "at risk" population with less than a high school education; but net outmigration in 1975–80 of persons with 17 or more years of school completed was 12.2 percent of its 1975 "at risk" population at this educational level. Of course, for these and many other northeastern states education has been something of an export industry, and they might be expected to be losing college graduates. But they also tended to lose college graduates more rapidly than other persons at ages beyond those normally associated with college graduation. There are numerous exceptions to this generalization, but the data suggest that net outmigration from this region more strongly removed college graduates than persons with no more than a high school education.

Summary and Conclusion

Migration patterns of states are often described in terms of net movement. Prior to the 1940 census, net migration was about the only way to describe migration for states, and even in recent years considerable media attention has been focused on net movements because intercensal population data are usually estimates of total population change and its components—natural increase and net (but not gross) migration. During the 1970s extensive media attention was directed at the redistribution of population from a number of Frostbelt states (especially the Rustbelt segment) to many Sunbelt states. Underlying the net movements, however, are far more extensive gross flows, and net migration is typically only a small percentage of the total in and out movements. The net outmigration states of the Northeast and Midwest are not distinguished by high rates of departure among their residents; on the contrary, they typically had below-average rates of outmigration among persons at the prime migration ages. Their below-average rates of outmigration were accompanied by rates of inmigration that were even further below the national average.

High-growth states in the West and South typically have above-average rates of both inmigration and outmigration. They grow rapidly because they continue to attract more people than they lose through migration. At any given moment, their populations have a high proportion of persons born elsewhere; in seven states (Nevada, Alaska, Florida, Arizona, Wyoming, Oregon, and Colorado) a majority of the 1980 population was born somewhere else. They have high outmigration rates partly because persons who have moved once are likely to move again and a large proportion of their population has moved at least once.

The greatest rates of increase in outmigration rates between 1965–70 and 1975–80 were in states of the Northeast and Midwest—areas which since the Great Depression of the 1930s had typically had below-average rates of outmigration. An increase in the propensity of their residents to depart made these states more like other states.

Migration in the 1970–80 decade seemed surprising in many ways. The amount of migration gain experienced by many southern and western states was not forecast, nor was the loss to many of the more heavily industrialized states in the North. Modeling state migration has sought to statistically explain such movements in some ways illustrated in Chapter 6 with respect to metropolitan areas, but econometric approaches to state-level migration have seldom been evaluated in terms of their ability to forecast.[15] Future attempts at modeling interstate migration are likely to be judged at least in part by their predictive ability.

Migration out of four Rustbelt states was found to follow an age pattern similar to the national average, at least up to around age 50. The four states were used to illustrate that industrial, high-income states of the Northeast and Midwest show almost a bimodal pattern of outmigration with the peak rate occurring among persons in their 20s and a secondary (but still pronounced) peak around age 65. There was a modest tendency for the Rustbelt region to have greater net losses among college-trained persons than persons with no more than a high school education.

Interstate migration in 1975–80 may have been surprising in terms of the rapid and unanticipated changes in net flows. It continued some trends established by the 1930s: The average distance of migration streams continued to increase and states came increasingly to resemble one another in outmigration rates. Some trends evident in 1935–40, 1955–60, and 1965–70 were altered: Migration efficiency increased slightly and states became somewhat less similar in the rates at which they attracted migrants from other states in 1975–80. All states participated in the increase in the national rate of interstate migration between the 1930s and the 1950s.

[15]The prospects for developing an interstate migration model that can forecast are discussed in Andrew M. Isserman, David A. Plane, Peter A. Rogerson, and Paul M. Beaumont, "Forecasting Interstate Migration with Limited Data: A Demographic-Economic Approach," *Journal of the American Statistical Association* 80 (June 1985): 277–285.

RETURN AND REPEAT
INTERSTATE MIGRATION

A MAJOR ADVANCE in migration research over the last two decades has been the development of a conceptualization of migration as something much more than a one-time, once-and-for-all event. Partly because of data limitations, prior theory and research often seemed to be based on a dichotomous view of migration, with the population neatly classified as migrants *or* nonmigrants as if the two were always clearly distinct. Conceptual advances since then have begun with the premise that migration experience is rather widely distributed in the population at large since almost everyone changes residence at some point in life and almost no one is truly a lifetime "nonmigrant." The new approaches emphasize the degree to which individuals have been exposed to migration, as measured by the number of previous moves, the time since the last move, or the relationship of prior moves to various life-cycle events.[1]

---

[1]An inverse association between duration of residence and probability of moving was demonstrated by a number of studies in the late 1960s, including John B. Lansing and Eva Mueller, *The Geographical Mobility of Labor* (Ann Arbor: Institute for Social Research, University of Michigan, 1967); George Myers, Robert McGinnis, and George Masnick, "The Duration of Residence Approach to a Dynamic Stochastic Model of Internal Migration: A Test of the Axiom of Cumulative Inertia," *Eugenics Quarterly* 14 (June 1967):

The empirical basis for the new approaches has often come from ad hoc local surveys and from national longitudinal surveys, especially the Panel Study of Income Dynamics and the National Longitudinal Surveys, both of which were identified in Chapter 1. These and other longitudinal surveys generate migration data because they follow the same individuals over time regardless of where they may be living; comparing current residence with residence at the last round of interviews yields migration data. Such information gathered over a sufficiently long period of time creates the possibility of identifying each move in relation to previous moves or periods of nonmovement.[2] Cross-sectional surveys that ask individuals about previous places of residence can produce abbreviated migration histories. Censuses and cross-sectional surveys like the Current Population Survey capture only the most recent move in what is actually a succession of moves differentiated by timing and intervening episodes of nonmovement.

Census data will never offer the rich opportunities for conceptualization and theory development that are afforded by the longitudinal sur-

---

121–126; Peter A. Morrison, "Duration of Residence and Prospective Migration: The Evaluation of a Stochastic Model," *Demography* 4 (1967): 553–561; and Kenneth Land, "Duration of Residence and Prospective Migration: Further Evidence," *Demography* 6 (May 1969): 133–140. These studies were based on radically different sources of data: the Lansing-Mueller study came from a national sample of the U.S. population with questions on places of previous residence; the Myers et al. study was based on questionnaires distributed to high school students in the state of Washington; the Morrison study was derived from the 1967 Survey of Economic Opportunity; and the Land study used data from the population registration system of the Netherlands. Over a period of about two years these studies demonstrated a seemingly universal property of migration that was invisible in most censuses and surveys.

[2]The analytical opportunities offered by longitudinal surveys and the ways of conceptualizing migration sequences are best illustrated in work by DaVanzo and Morrison and by Sandefur. See Julie DaVanzo and Peter A. Morrison, "Return and Other Sequences of Migration in the United States," *Demography* 18 (February 1981): 85–101; Julie DaVanzo, "Repeat Migration, Information Costs, and Location-Specific Capital," *Population and Environment* 4 (Spring 1981): 45–73; Julie DaVanzo, "Repeat Migration in the United States: Who Moves Back and Who Moves On?" *Review of Economics and Statistics* 65, no. 4 (1983): 552–559; and Peter A. Morrison and Julie DaVanzo, "The Prism of Migration: Dissimilarities between Return and Onward Movers," *Social Science Quarterly* 67 (September 1986): 1–13. The DaVanzo-Morrison studies attempted to estimate the number of annual moves that are missed by census questions on residence five years earlier. Sandefur's work has focused on the ordering of current and previous moves in relation to other life-cycle events: Gary D. Sandefur, and Wilbur J. Scott, "A Dynamic Analysis of Migration: An Assessment of the Effects of Age, Family and Career Variables," *Demography* 18 (August 1981): 355–368; and Gary Sandefur, "Variations in Interstate Migration of Men across the Early Stages of the Life Cycle," *Demography* 22 (August 1985): 353–366.

veys.[3] With census data the researcher typically trades some degree of conceptual fuzziness for geographical focus. The use of longitudinal surveys to analyze return and repeat migration tends to direct attention to migration as an attribute of persons and its influence on other individual characteristics, whereas censuses are probably best used to focus on migration as an attribute of areas and a linkage among them. In this way, census data can offer a spatial perspective not available from extant longitudinal surveys.

This chapter concentrates first on what can be said about national trends in the rate and volume of each of three types of moves representing persons (1) leaving their state of birth, (2) returning to their state of birth, or (3) making repeat moves that are neither to nor from state of birth. The chapter then examines the importance of each of the three types of movement for individual states for the 1975–80 period—somewhat like the attention to rates and streams of interstate migration featured in Chapter 3. How the three types of gross migration change so as to alter net migration is illustrated for regions from the late 1950s to the late 1970s. The chapter concludes by analyzing the age and educational composition of the three groups of migrants.

Numbers and Rates: The National View

At a minimum, then, how much interstate migration consists of persons who have moved before and are either returnees or persons making other types of repeat moves? The answer to such a question obviously depends on how one defines return migration: Does it mean

[3]Behavioral theories of migration have been formulated and tested, however, using microdata files from censuses to compare state of birth, residence five years before the census, and residence at the census date. The 1970 data have been particularly important because only in that census were respondents asked their occupation and industry of employment five years earlier. In 1980 respondents were asked if in 1975 they were on active duty in the armed forces, attending college, or working at a job or business. Persons giving the last response were asked if they worked full or part time but were not asked to report industry or occupation. Insightful analyses of these data are presented in Henry W. Herzog, Jr., and Alan M. Schlottmann, "Moving Back vs. Moving On: The Concept of Home in the Decision to Remigrate," *Journal of Regional Science* 22, no. 1 (1982): 73–82; Henry W. Herzog, Jr., and Alan M. Schlottmann, "Migrant Information, Job Search and the Remigration Decision," *Southern Economic Journal* 50 (July 1983): 43–56; Henry W. Herzog, Jr., and Alan M. Schlottmann, "Labor Force Mobility in the United States: Migration, Unemployment, and Remigration," *International Regional Science Review* 9, no. 1 (1984): 43–58; Henry W. Herzog, Jr., Richard A. Hofler, and Alan M. Schlottmann, "Life on the Frontier: Migrant Information, Earnings, and Past Mobility," *Review of Economics and Statistics* 67 (August 1985): 373–382; and Alan M. Schlottmann and Henry W. Herzog, Jr., "Career and Geographic Mobility Interactions: Implications for the Age Selectivity of Migration," *Journal of Human Resources* 19 (Winter 1984): 72–86.

going back to one's birthplace or simply any place or area of previous residence? If the former, does "origin" mean where one was born, graduated from (or attended) high school, or some other indicator of where one spent one's formative years? All of these approaches are logical possibilities.

Census data measure only returns to state of birth, but even this measure is sufficient to show that at least since the late 1950s most interstate migrants are persons who have moved before.[4] Table 4.1 shows how many interstate migrants who were born in the United States were (1) leaving their state of birth, (2) returning to their state of birth, and (3) making repeat, nonreturn interstate moves. Excluded from this table are interstate migrants who were born outside the United States.

In 1955–60 just under 50 percent of U.S.-born interstate migrants were leaving their state of birth. About 17 percent were moving back to their state of birth, and 33 percent were moving between states but not to or from their state of birth. Interstate migrants who were born outside the United States clearly have had prior migration experience, and including them reinforces the assertion that at least as early as the 1950s most interstate migrants had prior exposure to migration. Persons born outside the United States represented close to 5 percent of interstate migrants in the 1950s and 1960s.

Because of changes in census procedures, precise evaluation of

---

[4]The series begins with 1955–60 because the 1940 census, which first asked the residence-five-years-ago question, did not publish any tabulations of 1935–40 migrants disaggregated according to birthplace. Microdata tapes from the 1940 census create the possibility of extending comparisons to 1935–40. The first of the three-way tabulations (birthplace, residence five years before the census, and residence at the census date) were produced in the 1960 census reports and duplicated in the 1970 publications. Several peculiarities of the published data from the 1960 and 1970 censuses on residence at the three points in time have hindered their use. For example, the tabulations showed five-year inmigrants to each state according to whether the migrants were moving from their state of birth, back to it, or making a repeat (nonreturn) move, but parallel tabulations were not prepared for outmigrants. No tabulations on residence at the three points in time were prepared as part of the publication program of the 1980 decennial census.

The published data from the 1960 and 1970 censuses led to several important conclusions about the national incidence and rates of return and repeat interstate migration: (1) return migrants were by no means retirees "going home," for their average age tended to be in the late 20s compared with an average age in the early 20s for interstate migrants who were leaving their state of birth, (2) the lower period rates of interstate migration among blacks than whites could be attributed in substantial part to less return and repeat migration among blacks, and (3) chronic movers consisted disproportionately of the highly educated. Hope T. Eldridge, "Primary, Secondary, and Return Migration in the United States, 1955–60," *Demography* 2 (1965): 444–455; Anne S. Lee, "Return Migration in the United States," *International Migration Review* 8 (Summer 1974): 283–300; and Ann R. Miller, "Interstate Migrants in the United States: Some Social-Economic Differences by Type of Move," *Demography* 14 (February 1977): 1–17.

TABLE 4.1

Number of Migrants and Rates of Leaving State of Birth,
Returning to State of Birth, and Making Repeat Interstate Moves
for Persons Aged 5 and Over: 1955–60, 1965–70, and 1975–80

	Total Interstate Migrants[a]	Leaving State of Birth	Returning to State of Birth	Other U.S.-born Interstate Migrants
Number of Migrants				
1955–60	13,390,427	6,675,068	2,291,746	4,423,613
1965–70	15,816,156	7,127,367	3,144,388	5,544,401
1975–80	19,109,483	8,021,132	3,679,815	7,408,536
Percentage Distribution				
1955–60	100.0%	49.9%	17.1%	33.0%
1965–70	100.0	45.1	19.9	35.0
1975–80	100.0	42.0	19.2	38.8
Migrants per 100 Persons at Risk[b]				
Observed				
1955–60	9.4	6.3	6.1	11.8
1965–70	9.8	6.0	7.3	12.9
1975–80	9.9	5.9	6.2	12.6
Age-standardized[c]				
1955–60	10.3	6.9	6.3	12.0
1965–70	10.6	6.4	7.3	13.0
1975–80	9.9	5.9	6.2	12.6

[a]Excludes persons born outside the United States. Data from the 1960 and 1970 censuses also exclude persons not reporting birthplace or residence five years earlier; in 1980 these types of nonresponse were allocated.

[b]See text for specification of base populations.

[c]Obtained by applying 1955–60 and 1965–70 age-specific rates to 1975–80 base populations.

trends in these measures is difficult. As discussed in Appendix A, the handling of the state-of-birth question in 1970 probably resulted in an overstatement of persons who were reported as living in their state of birth. This means that in Table 4.1 the number of interstate migrants classified as return migrants is overstated in 1970 compared with 1960 and 1980. Nevertheless, it appears that between the late 1950s and late 1970s persons leaving their state of birth represented a declining proportion of interstate migrants and persons making return and repeat (nonreturn) moves increased as a proportion of interstate migrants. As can be seen in Table 4.1, the proportion of U.S.-born interstate migrants who were leaving their state of birth is shown to have declined from nearly 50 percent in 1955–60 to 45 percent in 1965–70 and to 42 percent in

1975–80. Repeat (nonreturn) migrants are shown to have risen from 33 percent of the total in 1955–60, to 35 percent in 1965–70, and to nearly 39 percent in 1975–80. Return migrants are shown to have been 17.1 percent of interstate migrants in 1955–60, 19.9 percent in 1965–70, and 19.2 percent in 1975–80.

Further interpretation requires information on changes in the propensity to make each of the three types of moves, as is given in the bottom part of Table 4.1. The rates represent the actual movers as a percentage of the population eligible to make each move. The base for the rate of moving away from state of birth is simply the total number of U.S.-born persons aged 5 and over living in their state of birth at the beginning of each of the five-year migration intervals. The base for rates of return and repeat migration is the total number of persons aged 5 and over living outside their state of birth at the beginning of the five-year migration intervals used in the censuses.[5] Rates are shown as observed and standardized for age, using the age distributions of the respective at-risk populations over the 1975–80 interval.

On an age-standardized basis, about 6.9 percent of all persons living in their state of birth in 1955 moved to another state by 1960. By 1965–70 this rate declined to 6.4, and by 1975–80 it was 5.9. The propensity of the general population to leave their state of birth seems, therefore, to have declined rather steadily over this 20-year period.

For persons living outside their state of birth at the beginning of each of the migration intervals, the age-standardized rate of return is shown to be 6.3 in 1955–60, 7.3 in 1965–70, and 6.2 in 1975–80. Since the number of migrants classified as returnees was overstated in 1970, the return migration rate for 1965–70 is spuriously high. A clear trend is not evident, and the most conservative conclusion may be that the rate of return to state of birth was about the same in the late 1970s and the late 1950s.

The last column shows that persons living outside their state of birth were nearly twice as likely to move onward than back to their state of birth. The rate of repeat migration is shown to have been 12.0 in 1955–60, 13.0 in 1965–70, and 12.6 in 1975–80. Perhaps it is significant that the rate of onward migration is only twice the rate of return movement. If persons living outside their state of birth picked their next

---

[5]For 1955–60 and 1965–70 these bases were reconstructed from data provided in published census reports. For 1975–80 they were reconstructed from a combination of two computer files, one representing a sample of 5 percent of the total U.S. population (used to identify persons who did not move between 1975 and 1980) and another of all persons who moved from one state to another between 1975 and 1980. The reconstructed beginning-of-period populations, like the migrants, reflect only survivors to the end of the five-year migration intervals.

state of residence at random, the rate of onward migration would be 49 times the rate of return since there are 49 possible destinations (including the District of Columbia with the 50 states). In general, persons living outside their state of birth were about three times as likely to move between states in the five-year intervals than persons living in their state of birth.

Trend comparisons are affected not only by the overassignment of persons as living in their state of birth in 1970, but also by the introduction of extensive allocation procedures in 1980. In 1960 and 1970 persons not reporting state of birth or residence five years earlier were excluded in developing the data in Table 4.1 for 1955–60 and 1965–70, whereas in 1980 persons not reporting a place of birth or residence in 1975 were assigned responses by the computer algorithm described in Appendix A. Persons not answering these questions are more likely than the general population to be migrants, and the allocation of nonresponse seems to raise the numerator of the rates shown in Table 4.1 for 1975–80 more than the denominator. The rates for 1975–80 are probably a better estimate of the "true" rates than those for 1955–60 and 1965–70, which probably understate migration propensities. For these reasons, the propensity of the population to leave their state of birth probably declined more than is implied by the figures in Table 4.1. The total number of interstate migrants can be doubly affected because a declining rate of departure from state of birth puts fewer persons at risk of making return or repeat moves.

This interpretation seems to be consonant with the conclusion of Chapter 2 that period rates of interstate migration have declined in the United States since the late 1960s. The present results suggest that the factors identified as hindering migration since then probably act to keep more persons in their "home" state and reduce somewhat the number of persons who are likely to become frequent movers. The countervailing factors which intuitively would seem to raise migration rates—for example, increasing numbers of smaller households—may mean that of those who do move, the likelihood of moving again may not be very different from that of earlier decades.

Major Streams

The spatial view afforded by census data is perhaps best illustrated by disaggregating the major interstate migration streams featured in Chapter 3 according to migrants' prior mobility experience. Figure 4.1 does this for the five largest interstate migration streams in 1975–80,

shown as the last map in Figure 3.1. Figure 4.1 also shows three additional maps that display the five largest streams of persons who are (1)
leaving their state of birth, (2) returning to it, or (3) making a repeat
(nonreturn) interstate move in 1975–80.

Since Figure 3.1 included interstate migrants in 1975–80 who were
born outside the United States, so does the first map in Figure 4.1. Of
the total interstate migrants in 1975–80, 6.1 percent were born outside
the United States, 39.4 percent were leaving their state of birth, 18.1
percent were returning to their state of birth from elsewhere in the
United States, and 36.4 percent were U.S-born but were moving between states other than their state of birth. Persons leaving their state
of birth—labeled "primary migrants" in Figure 4.1—tend to be overrepresented in the nation's largest interstate migration streams.[6]

By 1975–80 the five largest interstate migration streams originated
in New York and California, the two most populous states. Persons
leaving their state of birth represented 63.1 percent of migrants in the
largest stream, from New York to Florida. They were 55.3 percent of the
migrants from New York to New Jersey and 55.9 percent of the migrants from New York to California. Clearly, the largest migration
streams originating in New York consisted disproportionately of native
New Yorkers who may have been leaving for retirement or a job in Florida, housing or a suburban lifestyle in New Jersey, and the jobs, climate,
or lifestyle of California.

But what of the other two very large streams—those originating in
California and terminating in Washington and Oregon? Are they made
up of disenchanted Californians who in the late 1970s were said to be
fleeing from smog, crowding, and congestion in California for cleaner
air and a better quality of life in the Pacific Northwest? Obviously census data do not answer such questions, but they do show that native
Californians were moderately overrepresented in these two streams. Nationwide, 39.4 percent of interstate migrants were leaving their state of
birth compared with 40.2 percent of California-to-Washington migrants
and 46.0 percent of California-to-Oregon migrants. Still, native Californians' overrepresentation in these two streams is far below the proportionate representation of native New Yorkers in major streams from
New York. Return migrants were underrepresented and repeat migrants
were overrepresented in the streams from California to Washington and
Oregon.

In absolute numbers, however, Oregon and Washington were recip-

---

[6]Researchers have tended to follow Eldridge ("Primary, Secondary, and Return Migration in the United States, 1955–60") in referring to persons leaving their state of birth as
"primary" migrants.

FIGURE 4.1

The Representation of Primary, Return, and Repeat Migrants in the Nation's Largest Interstate Migration Streams and the Largest Streams of Primary, Return, and Repeat Migrants: 1975–80

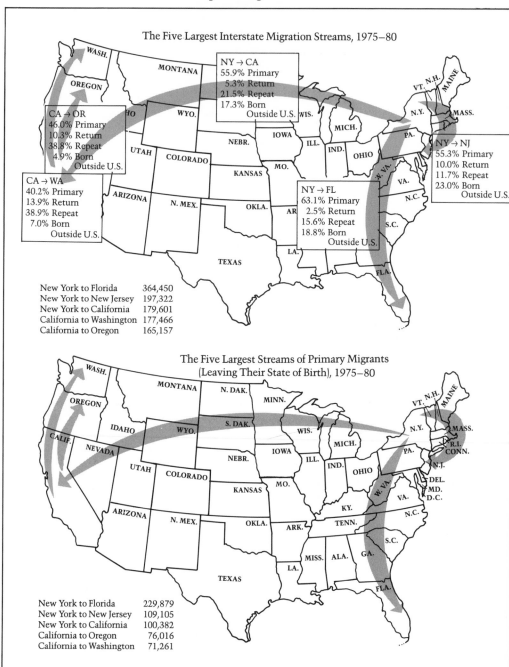

The Five Largest Interstate Migration Streams, 1975–80

NY → CA
55.9% Primary
5.3% Return
21.5% Repeat
17.3% Born
    Outside U.S.

CA → OR
46.0% Primary
10.3% Return
38.8% Repeat
4.9% Born
    Outside U.S.

CA → WA
40.2% Primary
13.9% Return
38.9% Repeat
7.0% Born
    Outside U.S.

NY → NJ
55.3% Primary
10.0% Return
11.7% Repeat
23.0% Born
    Outside U.S.

NY → FL
63.1% Primary
2.5% Return
15.6% Repeat
18.8% Born
    Outside U.S.

New York to Florida   364,450
New York to New Jersey   197,322
New York to California   179,601
California to Washington 177,466
California to Oregon   165,157

The Five Largest Streams of Primary Migrants
(Leaving Their State of Birth), 1975–80

New York to Florida   229,879
New York to New Jersey   109,105
New York to California   100,382
California to Oregon   76,016
California to Washington   71,261

108

FIGURE 4.1 *(continued)*

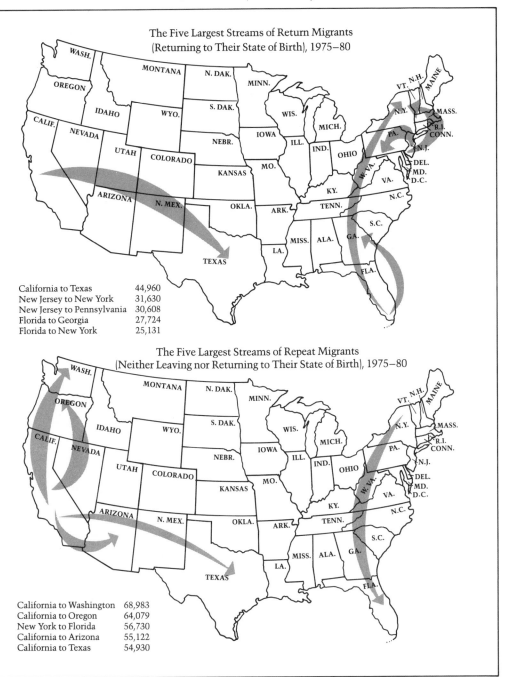

The Five Largest Streams of Return Migrants
(Returning to Their State of Birth), 1975–80

California to Texas	44,960
New Jersey to New York	31,630
New Jersey to Pennsylvania	30,608
Florida to Georgia	27,724
Florida to New York	25,131

The Five Largest Streams of Repeat Migrants
(Neither Leaving nor Returning to Their State of Birth), 1975–80

California to Washington	68,983
California to Oregon	64,079
New York to Florida	56,730
California to Arizona	55,122
California to Texas	54,930

ients of two of the largest streams of migrants leaving their state of birth (see the second map in Figure 4.1). On this basis, Oregon and Washington can claim that their inmigration of native Californians represents two very large streams of persons leaving (if not fleeing, abandoning, or deserting) their birthplace. In general, the five largest streams of persons leaving their state of birth follow the same paths as the five streams with the largest total number of migrants.

Return and repeat migrants do not follow these well-beaten paths. The largest stream of return migrants in 1975–80 was made up of persons leaving California to go back to Texas. To some extent this stream is simply the retracing of a well-worn path because from the 1930s through the 1960s one of the nation's five largest migration streams was from Texas to California (as shown by the maps in Figure 3.1). The large flow of return migrants along this path in 1975–80 probably represents some persons going home to retire and others returning because of the very rapid expansion of the Texas economy in the late 1970s.

Two other large streams of return migrants originated in New Jersey, with one terminating in New York and the other in Pennsylvania. A convenient rationale for these two streams is not immediately evident. They may partly reflect reporting birthplace on an occurrence basis rather than mother's usual residence at time of birth; if so, then persons born in hospitals just across the New Jersey border in Philadelphia or New York would be recorded as return migrants (rather than primary migrants) if they moved to Pennsylvania or New York. Other large streams of returnees went from Florida to Georgia and from Florida to New York State; the latter has been attributed in part to a flow of persons who initially leave New York to retire in Florida but at advanced ages return to New York to enter retirement homes, move in with relatives, or be near geriatric hospitals.[7]

Four of the five major streams of repeat migrants originate in California. California is often pictured as attracting highly mobile persons for whom the state is said to be the end of the line, the point from which further westward migration is impossible. California probably does fit this description to some extent, but according to the last of the maps in Figure 4.1, it also sends many such persons to other states, particularly Washington, Oregon, Arizona, and Texas.

Another large stream of repeat migrants was from New York state to Florida. New York state also serves as a conduit through which flows another group of repeat migrants—persons born abroad. Such persons were about 23 percent of migrants from New York to New Jersey, 19

[7]Jeanne C. Biggar, *The Graying of the Sunbelt: A Look at the Impact of U.S. Elderly Migration* (Washington, DC: Population Reference Bureau, 1984), pp. 5–7.

percent of migrants from New York to Florida, and 17 percent of migrants from New York to California. Nationwide, persons born abroad were only 6 percent of interstate migrants in 1975–80. New York state not only receives large numbers of migrants from outside the United States (42 percent of all persons moving to New York state in 1975–80 were from outside the United States—higher than any other state), but it also sends many elsewhere.

Decomposing interstate migration streams in these ways shows that many actually consist of persons with dissimilar prior migration experience. Further insight can be obtained by looking at a wider spectrum of states than simply those at either end of the largest streams. And the size of various streams of primary, return, and repeat migrants needs to be interpreted in terms of the numbers of persons eligible to move and the propensity to move among those eligible. For example, knowing simply that some states have a high proportion of returnees among their inmigrants does not reveal whether the explanation is a high rate of return movement or a paucity of others who want to move to the state in question.

Disaggregating migration rates according to migrants' prior mobility can also help answer a question raised in the previous chapter about why several Rustbowl states which had severe job losses in the late 1970s had low outmigration rates. Did they have low outmigration rates because their populations were made up of comparatively few earlier inmigrants who may be outmigrants in later intervals? Or, alternatively, do these states have low outmigration rates simply because few of their natives move elsewhere?

Return and Repeat Movers: The View from Individual States

Table 4.2 highlights the states where return and repeat migrants are greatly overrepresented or underrepresented. It shows the 10 states with the highest and lowest percentages of inmigrants and outmigrants who were (1) leaving their state of birth, (2) returning to it, or (3) making a repeat (nonreturn) move in 1975–80.

Persons leaving their state of birth represented a high proportion of migrants to several states of net inmigration in 1975–80, including New Hampshire, Wyoming, Arizona, Vermont, Florida, and Nevada. For these states migrants leaving their state of birth were at least 41 percent of total inmigrants. Some like Wyoming, Arizona, Florida, and Nevada have had substantial inmigration for a long time and probably attract

TABLE 4.2

States with a Very High or Very Low Proportion of Inmigrants or Outmigrants Aged 5 and Over Who Were Leaving Their State of Birth, Returning to Their State of Birth, or Making Repeat (Nonreturn) Interstate Moves: 1975–80

Migrants Leaving Their State of Birth				Migrants Returning to Their State of Birth			
Migrants to		Migrants from		Migrants to		Migrants from	
New Hampshire	48.8%	Pennsylvania	58.3%	West Virginia	33.9%	Alaska	28.0%
Wyoming	43.6	New York	57.5	Pennsylvania	27.9	Nevada	28.0
Arizona	42.9	Ohio	51.5	Alabama	26.4	Florida	27.0
Vermont	42.9	Iowa	51.5	Iowa	26.2	Wyoming	25.8
Florida	42.6	West Virginia	50.7	Mississippi	25.4	Arizona	24.0
Nevada	41.1	Wisconsin	49.8	Kentucky	25.3	South Carolina	23.9
Delaware	39.6	Michigan	49.3	Ohio	25.1	North Carolina	23.5
Colorado	39.6	Minnesota	49.3	South Dakota	23.9	Hawaii	23.4
Wisconsin	38.2	Illinois	48.3	Minnesota	23.5	Colorado	23.2
Alaska	37.9	Massachusetts	48.2	Michigan	23.4	Oklahoma	23.0
⋮		⋮		⋮		⋮	
U.S. average	33.0	U.S. average	39.4	U.S. average	15.1	U.S. average	18.1
⋮		⋮		⋮		⋮	
Maryland	31.3	Maryland	27.1	New Hampshire	9.7	Iowa	15.1
Alabama	31.2	New Mexico	26.0	Maryland	9.7	Minnesota	14.6
Texas	30.8	Virginia	24.0	California	8.6	Michigan	14.6
Pennsylvania	30.2	Colorado	22.5	Wyoming	8.4	Illinois	14.6
Massachusetts	30.0	Wyoming	22.3	Colorado	8.1	Ohio	14.6
District of Columbia	29.5	Florida	21.1	Hawaii	5.5	New Jersey	14.4
Hawaii	28.0	Arizona	18.6	Florida	5.3	Wisconsin	14.4
Illinois	27.4	Hawaii	16.1	Arizona	4.7	Massachusetts	12.7
California	25.2	Nevada	13.9	Alaska	3.8	Pennsylvania	10.9
New York	17.6	Alaska	11.4	Nevada	3.2	New York	8.8

TABLE 4.2 (continued)

Migrants Born in the U.S. but Moved Neither to Nor from
Their State of Birth in 1975–80

Migrants to		Migrants from	
Alaska	45.7%	Alaska	55.5%
Nevada	42.1	Nevada	52.9
Wyoming	41.9	Arizona	51.8
Idaho	40.2	Colorado	49.5
Arizona	39.6	Wyoming	48.7
Oregon	39.3	Hawaii	48.4
Colorado	39.2	Virginia	48.4
New Mexico	38.9	Maryland	48.2
District of Columbia	38.8	District of Columbia	45.8
Virginia	38.6	Florida	45.3
.		.	
.		.	
.		.	
U.S. average	30.5	U.S. average	36.4
.			
.			
.			
Rhode Island	27.5	Kentucky	32.7
Wisconsin	26.8	Massachusetts	31.7
Michigan	25.9	Wisconsin	31.7
Massachusetts	25.8	Iowa	31.2
Illinois	25.8	Michigan	30.9
West Virginia	25.0	Illinois	30.3
California	24.6	Ohio	30.3
Pennsylvania	23.8	West Virginia	29.4
New Jersey	21.1	Pennsylvania	26.1
New York	16.0	New York	19.9

NOTE: The U.S. averages are different in the columns labeled "Migrants to" and "Migrants from" because the former includes movers from abroad. Movers from abroad are in the base of all immigrants but are not included as any of the three types of immigrants specified.

the natives of a wide variety of states. Others like New Hampshire and Vermont may appeal to the natives of nearby states; for example, New Hampshire's lower taxes may have attracted capital and new residents from neighboring Massachusetts in the late 1970s.

Natives were a high proportion of outmigrants from a few states with chronic outmigration. More than one half of the persons leaving Pennsylvania, New York, Ohio, Iowa, and West Virginia were leaving their state of birth. States with net outmigration over long periods tend to have relatively few inmigrants in their populations and their potential migrants therefore consist mostly of natives. Hence, it should not be too surprising to find that most persons leaving such states are native sons and daughters. In sharp contrast, states that have had substantial inmigration in recent decades have populations with many newcomers, and most persons leaving such states are the inmigrants of the past. More than three out of every four persons leaving Arizona, Hawaii, Nevada, and Alaska in 1975–80 were inmigrants from earlier periods (see columns 4 and 6 of Table 4.2).

These statistics, which were not tabulated in earlier censuses, illustrate Goldstein's point that high mobility rates in some areas may simply reflect the frequent movement of a few people and that some areas with many outmigrants are simply passing on to other areas the persons they earlier received through migration.[8] For other states, however, outmigrants are mostly natives in whom the state may have made a substantial investment in schooling, and for this reason a state may be losing more through migration than is immediately evident. A traditional approach in migration research has been to evaluate areas' gains and losses of human capital by comparing the educational and skill levels of inmigrants and outmigrants; but if the outmigrants are mostly natives whose schooling (at least primary or secondary education) was paid for by the area of outmigration, then the losses through migration may be greater than suggested by conventional approaches. A more thorough and exact approach to calculating gains and losses of human capital might take a longer accounting period in consideration and include the background of migrants beyond the most recent move.

Return migrants were a high proportion of inmigrants to several

[8]Sidney Goldstein, "Repeated Migration as a Factor in High Mobility Rates," *American Sociological Review* 19 (October 1954): 536–541; "Migration and Occupational Mobility in Norristown, Pennsylvania," *American Sociological Review* 20 (August 1955): 72–76; *Patterns of Mobility, 1910–1950: A Method for Measuring Migration and Occupational Mobility in the Community* (Philadelphia: University of Pennsylvania Press, 1958); and "The Extent of Repeated Migration: An Analysis Based on the Danish Population Register," *Journal of the American Statistical Association* 59 (December 1964): 1121–1132.

states with substantial past outmigration. One third of all persons moving to West Virginia in 1975–80 were born in West Virginia, and returnees were at least one fourth of migrants to Pennsylvania, Alabama, Iowa, Mississippi, Kentucky, and Ohio. Obviously, many persons moving to areas losing population through migration are natives going home. Analogously, many persons leaving states with high population turnover are going home. Over one fourth of migrants from Alaska, Nevada, Florida, and Wyoming were going back to their state of birth.

More often, however, migrants leaving high-turnover states are the highly mobile persons who are neither leaving nor moving back to their state of birth. A majority of persons leaving Alaska, Nevada, and Arizona were persons who were "just passing through"—persons who had moved in from somewhere else and were leaving in 1975–80 but not to go back to their state of birth. These persons had lived in at least three states and would probably live in others. Colorado, Wyoming, Hawaii, Virginia, Maryland, the District of Columbia, and Florida also had a high representation of repeat movers among their outmigrants. Large military installations in Hawaii, Virginia, Maryland, and Florida may contribute to these states serving as temporary stopping points in a pattern of frequent moving by a few highly mobile persons.

These data demonstrate that a few states receive and then seem to send elsewhere—or trade among themselves—frequent movers who may be highly responsive to alternative opportunities or work for the military or large national or multinational organizations that frequently relocate employees. Alaska, Nevada, Wyoming, Arizona, and Colorado stand out in Table 4.2 as having high proportions of frequent movers among both their inmigrants and their outmigrants. Some states—New York and California in particular—might have ranked higher if they did not rely so heavily on migration from overseas. Nearly 42 percent of persons moving to New York in 1975–80 were living outside the United States in 1975; for California the figure was 35 percent.

Rates of Return and Repeat Migration for States

The rate at which states receive migrants from other states and then send them on to still other states cannot be inferred from Table 4.2, which simply shows the states with very high or very low proportions of primary, return, and repeat movers among their inmigrants or outmigrants. The fact that many persons moving to West Virginia and Pennsylvania are return migrants does not necessarily mean that there is a high rate of return movement to these two states; it may mean that few persons other than natives who earlier left have reason to move to West Virginia or Pennsylvania.

Calculating rates of inmigration and outmigration for each of the three types of inmigrants and outmigrants needs to be done with careful attention to the proper bases and is more complex than the national rates shown in Table 4.1. The rates should be computed on an at-risk basis so as to represent migrants as a percentage of persons eligible to make each of the three types of moves to and from each state. The first step is to limit the universe to persons who were born in the United States and were living in the United States in 1975. The bases for calculating at-risk rates of outmigration for each state are as follows:

- The base for the rate of primary outmigration from state X is the number of persons born in state X and living in state X in 1975.

- The base for the rate of return outmigration and the rate of repeat outmigration from a given state X is the number of persons living in state X in 1975 and born in the United States but outside state X. This base consists of persons who moved to state X before 1975 and in 1975–80 are "at risk" of either going back to their state of birth or moving along to another state.

At-risk rates of inmigration are not as straightforward. They were calculated as follows:

- The base for the primary inmigration rate to state X is all persons born in the United States but outside state X and living in their state of birth in 1975. Such a base is quite large and so rates appear small compared with the others.

- The base for the return inmigration rate to state X is the number of persons born in state X and living outside state X in 1975 but in the United States.

- The base for the repeat inmigration rate to state X is all persons born in the United States but outside state X and living in the United States in 1975 but not in their state of birth.

Here, then, are five bases for calculating the six rates of in- and outmigration for each state. Both the numerator and denominator of the rates are limited to persons aged 5 and over in 1980. States that rank very high or very low on the three rates of outmigration are shown in Table 4.3 and are discussed first. States with very high or very low inmigration rates are shown in Table 4.4 and will be discussed more fully in a later section. Data for all states are given in Appendix C.

A few states rank high on all three rates of outmigration as they send many natives to other states and send many former inmigrants either back to their states of birth or onward to still other states. Alaska,

TABLE 4.3

States That Rank High or Low on Three Rates of Outmigration
for Persons Aged 5 and Over: 1975–80

Primary Outmigration Rate		Return Outmigration Rate		Repeat Outmigration Rate	
District of Columbia	19.4%	Hawaii	18.0%	Hawaii	37.2%
Alaska	12.4	Alaska	13.8	Alaska	27.3
Nevada	12.4	North Dakota	12.3	North Dakota	22.4
Wyoming	10.3	Mississippi	9.8	District of Columbia	21.5
Idaho	9.8	North Carolina	9.7	Maine	18.7
Montana	9.2	South Carolina	9.4	South Dakota	18.5
Colorado	8.9	Kentucky	9.2	Virginia	18.0
Delaware	8.7	Wyoming	9.2	Nebraska	17.9
Arizona	8.6	South Dakota	9.2	Vermont	17.8
South Dakota	8.6	Louisiana	8.8	Wyoming	17.4
.		.		.	
.		.		.	
.		.		.	
Mississippi	5.1	Wisconsin	5.6	New Jersey	11.7
Wisconsin	4.8	Connecticut	5.6	Oklahoma	11.7
Kentucky	4.5	Minnesota	5.6	Indiana	11.2
Tennessee	4.3	Maryland	5.4	Texas	11.1
Georgia	4.3	Ohio	5.2	Ohio	10.9
Alabama	4.2	New Jersey	5.0	Michigan	10.2
South Carolina	3.9	Oregon	4.8	Washington	9.9
Louisiana	3.8	Michigan	4.8	Oregon	9.7
North Carolina	3.6	Washington	4.8	Florida	9.6
Texas	3.4	California	4.1	California	8.3

NOTE: Rates are on an "at risk" basis and show outmigrants from each state as a percentage of the population eligible to make each of the three types of moves.

Wyoming, and South Dakota are among the top ten states on each of these rates of outmigration. In the case of Alaska, 12.4 percent of persons born in Alaska and living there in 1975 moved to a different state by 1980. Among persons who had moved to Alaska from elsewhere in the United States, 13.8 percent went back to their state of birth and 27.3 percent left but did not go back to their state of birth.

Other states, however, display highly discrepant rankings according to the three rates of outmigration. A number of southern states—Mississippi, South Carolina, Louisiana, and North Carolina—had distinctly low rates of outmigration among their natives (column 1) but very high rates of outmigration on the part of previous inmigrants who were leaving to go back to their state of birth (column 2). In the case of North Carolina, for example, only 3.6 percent of its natives left the state be-

TABLE 4.4

States That Rank High or Low on Three Rates of Inmigration
for Persons Aged 5 and Over: 1975–80

Primary Inmigration Rate		Return Inmigration Rate		Repeat Inmigration Rate	
Florida	0.66%	California	11.7%	Texas	3.2%
California	0.58	Florida	10.9	Virginia	1.8
Texas	0.43	Utah	10.9	Washington	1.5
Arizona	0.21	Texas	10.9	New York	1.3
Virginia	0.19	Oregon	10.4	North Carolina	1.1
New Jersey	0.18	Washington	10.1	Ohio	1.1
Colorado	0.18	Louisiana	7.5	California	1.1
Illinois	0.18	Tennessee	7.3	Pennsylvania	1.0
Georgia	0.17	Michigan	7.3	Florida	1.0
Washington	0.17	North Carolina	7.2	Oregon	1.0
.		.		.	
.		.		.	
.		.		.	
Wyoming	0.04	Rhode Island	4.5	Idaho	0.1
Maine	0.03	Vermont	4.5	Hawaii	0.1
Alaska	0.03	Iowa	4.4	Iowa	0.1
Montana	0.03	Kansas	4.4	Nebraska	0.1
District of Columbia	0.03	Alaska	4.1	New Hampshire	0.1
Rhode Island	0.02	Mississippi	3.9	Alaska	0.1
Delaware	0.02	Nebraska	3.9	District of Columbia	0.1
North Dakota	0.02	South Dakota	3.6	Montana	0.1
Vermont	0.02	North Dakota	3.2	Maine	0.1
South Dakota	0.02	District of Columbia	2.1	Delaware	0.04

NOTE: Rates are on an "at risk" basis and show inmigrants to each state as a percentage of the population eligible to make each of the three types of moves.

tween 1975 and 1980 and only one state (Texas) had a lower rate of exodus among natives. Among persons who had moved to North Carolina from elsewhere, 9.7 percent went home between 1975 and 1980—a rate of return exceeded by only four other states. These southern states with low rates of outmigration among their natives and high rates of return migration tended to have moderate rates of repeat outmigration.

Table 4.3 can also be used to interpret more fully the flows of primary, return, and repeat migrants mapped in Figure 4.1. In particular, Table 4.3 shows that the large flows of repeat migrants from California (the last map in Figure 4.1) do not represent a high rate of exodus among persons who move to California, for among all the states California has the lowest rates of return and repeat outmigration. Thus, California sends large numbers of return and repeat migrants to other states only because it receives large numbers of inmigrants. Persons who move to California from other states have a comparatively low rate of moving on to still other states. More so than for other states with high population turnover, California really does seem to be the "end of the line."

Outmigration from the Great Lakes States

Another use of the three outmigration rates shown in Table 4.3 is to interpret more fully the conclusion of Chapter 3 that although several Rustbelt states lost many jobs in the 1970s, their rates of outmigration were below average. In light of substantial deterioration of economic conditions in the 1970s, the low rate of exodus in 1975–80 seemed puzzling. It could not be explained by differences in underlying age composition, even though some Rustbelt states—which include Michigan, Ohio, Pennsylvania, and perhaps other Great Lakes states—had comparatively old populations partly because net outmigration over several decades removed many younger, more mobile persons. Another possible interpretation is that since these states have had net outmigration for quite some time, their low outmigration rates may derive from their having in their populations a low proportion of frequent movers who are very sensitive to alternative opportunities and quickly move in response to the shifting fortunes of different areas of the country.

A simple test of this hypothesis is to compare rates of outmigration among natives of the states, as was illustrated in column 1 of Table 4.3 for the top 10 and bottom 10 states. The complete listing, presented in Appendix A, does give a somewhat different picture than that suggested by the preceding chapter, which did not distinguish migrants by prior mobility status. Ohio's ranking is raised by limiting the outmigration rate to natives; Ohio's overall outmigration rate in 1975–80 was 39th among the states but 25th when limited to natives. The rankings of Michigan and Pennsylvania are also raised, but not by much. Michigan's overall outmigration rate was 45th among the states, and the outmigration rate of its natives was ranked 38th. Pennsylvania's overall outmigration rate was 49th, and the outmigration rate of its natives was 40th among the states.

The conclusion seems to be that for the most part the Great Lakes states had below-average rates of outmigration in 1975–80 simply because their natives were less likely to engage in interstate migration than were natives of most other states. The considerable publicity given to migration from this part of the country hid the fact that the rate of departure was comparatively low. One can only speculate as to why, in spite of serious economic dislocations in the 1970s, natives of America's traditional core manufacturing region remained more strongly tied to their home state than natives of most other states. Perhaps high manufacturing wages in the region have tended to raise rates of homeownership or in other ways increased locational ties to the area or produced strong union ties. Perhaps because of past low rates of outmigration, many of the natives have relatives who live near them and whom they do not want to leave. Whatever the explanation, the simple rates of movement of natives and nonnatives illustrate that the effects of economic conditions on migration may be mediated by a host of prior conditions.

Inmigration Rates

The inmigration rates of Table 4.4 offer a complementary perspective to the outmigration rates of Table 4.3. A few states have consistently high rates of attraction for (1) the natives of other states still living in their state of birth, (2) their own natives who have moved to other states, and (3) persons who have left their state of birth. Florida, California, Texas, and Washington are in the top ten states on each of these three rates of inmigration. These states generally had substantial net inmigration in 1975–80, and so it may not be too surprising to find that they appeal to persons with varying prior exposure to migration.

In fact, the three rates of inmigration tend to be more highly correlated than the three rates of outmigration. The zero-order correlation between columns 1 and 2 of Table 4.4 (but for all 50 states and the District of Columbia) is .69, indicating a fairly strong association between the degree to which states appeal to the natives of other states and the degree to which they draw back their own natives who have left. The zero-order correlation between the inmigration rate of natives of other states and the inmigration rate of persons living in other states (but not in their state of birth) is also high—.62, indicating that states that draw in many natives of other states also draw back many persons who have left their state of birth. Correlations among the outmigration rates are lower. The correlation between the outmigration rate of natives (column 1 of Table 4.3 but for all states and the District of Columbia) and the rate at which states send previous inmigrants back to their state of birth (column 2) is only .06, and the correlation between the outmigration rate of natives and that of repeat, nonreturn migrants is .28. At a minimum, these simple correlations show that the outmigration rates of persons of varying prior migration experience are less highly correlated across states than inmigration of persons with different migration experiences.[9] These correlations suggest that growing areas rather uniformly attract—and declining areas repel—migrants with a variety of migratory backgrounds; but areas seem less consistently to send their natives and previous inmigrants to other locations.

The middle column of Table 4.4 is probably what most people have in mind when they think of the rate of return migration. This column shows, for example, that among native Californians who were living in other states in 1975, 11.7 percent moved back to California by 1980. No state had a higher rate of return, although between 1975 and 1980 Florida, Utah, Texas, Oregon, and Washington "recaptured" at least 10 percent of their natives who had moved away by 1975.

The data compiled for the middle column of Table 4.4 also show that the high percentage of return migrants among all movers to West Virginia and Pennsylvania, as reported in Table 4.2, was *not* due to a high rate of return. As discussed earlier, returnees were about 34 percent of all migrants to West Virginia and 28 percent of migrants to Pennsylvania in 1975–80. Though more reliant than other states on former natives as a source of inmigrants, these two states are not among the top 10 in rates of return movement. Among the 50 states and the District of Columbia, Pennsylvania ranks 35th and West Virginia ranks 39th in rates of return inmigration; natives who had left Pennsylvania or West Virginia were less than one half as likely to go home in 1975–80 as natives of states with the highest rates of return migration. Pennsylvania and West Virginia have many returnees among their inmigrants largely because they attract comparatively few natives of other states.

This perspective on return inmigration illustrates a perennial difficulty in interpreting local migration surveys. An observer recording who moves to West Virginia or Pennsylvania—and probably localities in these and some other states—would find that many newcomers were not newcomers at all but "locals" returning home. The temptation is to conclude that many who leave later return, but only national data test such a hypothesis by showing the proportion of outmigrants who return.

Since metropolitan areas or other localities vary greatly in the proportion of inmigrants who are returnees, this variation can strongly influence attempts to compare areas according to inmigrants' characteristics, motivations, and reasons for choosing their destination. Almost

---

[9]When primary, return, and repeat migration are measured in the manner allowed by census data, some of the resulting rates of movement are not independent. For example, inmigrants tend to be in the childbearing years and may be prone to move again, and the children born to migrants to state X are natives of state X. If the inmigrant parents move on to another state, they raise the repeat outmigration rate from state X and their children born in state X raise the outmigration rate of natives of state X.

certainly returnees will have different motivations and reasons for choosing their destination than other migrants, and studies that compare areas according to why migrants select them may produce spurious conclusions without taking into account the composition of migrants according to prior residential background.

Back to the 1950s

With extant data, it is not possible to extend back in time the precise kinds of comparisons just featured. The 1940 census publications contained no cross-tabulations of state of birth and residence five years earlier, and the 1960 and 1970 publications did not show inmigrants and outmigrants differentiated by birthplace for geographical areas smaller than the nine divisions, which are formed by grouping states.[10] The divisions, however, have featured prominently in migration analyses, as is shown in the next chapter. And it is useful to demonstrate how different regions of the country changed between the 1950s and the 1970s as to sources and types of inmigrants and outmigrants.[11]

To do this, inmigrants and outmigrants for each of the nine divisions for the three intervals were disaggregated to show migrants who were (1) leaving their division of birth, (2) returning to their division of birth, and (3) moving between divisions but not leaving or returning to their division of birth. Figure 4.2 shows a map of states and divisions, and Table 4.5 shows the percentage of each division's inmigrants and outmigrants who were first-time, return, and repeat migrants in 1955–60, 1965–70, and 1975–80.

These data are useful in demonstrating that areas of rapid growth initially derive their inmigrants largely from persons leaving their area

---

[10]Increasing the size of areal units ordinarily decreases the observed volume and rate of migration. Going from states to divisions as the migration-defining areas decreases the amount of primary, return, and repeat migration. However, as size of areal units increases, the amount of return migration tends to be reduced less than the amount of primary or repeat migration. The reason is that increasing the size of areas increases one's chances of returning to "area" of birth. For example, a person born in Mississippi but living in New York in 1975 and Alabama in 1980 would be classified as a repeat migrant over the 1975–80 period when states are used as migration-defining areas but as a return migrant when divisions are used because Mississippi and Alabama belong to the same division. The rates of primary and repeat migration decrease as size of areal units increases, but the rate of return migration increases as size of areal units increases.

[11]These materials draw heavily upon work previously reported in Larry Long and Kristin A. Hansen, "Trends in Return Migration to the South," *Demography* 12 (November 1975): 601–614; and "Interdivisional Primary, Return, and Repeat Migration," *Review of Public Data Use* 5 (March 1977): 3–10.

FIGURE 4.2

Regions and Geographic Divisions of the United States

of birth and persons who are repeat movers. Over time there develops somewhat greater balance as return migrants come to constitute a larger proportion of inmigrants. For example, consider the Pacific division whose overall migration is strongly influenced by California. The Pacific division's population grew very rapidly after World War II and has continued to grow at a comparatively rapid pace. Over time the Pacific division has come to rely less on persons leaving their area of birth and more on returnees and repeat movers as a source of immigration. Persons leaving their divison of birth were 65.8 percent of all inmigrants in 1955–60, 58.7 percent of inmigrants in 1965–70, and 58.3 percent in 1975–80. Concomitantly, the Pacific division has come to rely increasingly on returnees, who were 8.1 percent of inmigrants in 1955–60, 12.8 percent in 1965–70, and 16.9 percent in 1975–80. Repeat migrants have increased from 26.1 percent of inmigrants in 1955–60 to 28.4 percent in 1965–70 and 29.4 percent in 1975–80.

TABLE 4.5

Percentage of Inmigrants and Outmigrants Aged 5 and Over Who Were Primary, Return, or Repeat Migrants, by Division: 1955–60, 1965–70, and 1975–80

	Inmigrants			Outmigrants		
	Leaving Division of Birth	Returning to Division of Birth	Making Other Inter-divisional Moves	Leaving Division of Birth	Returning to Division of Birth	Making Other Inter-divisional Moves
New England						
1955–60	55.3%	23.0%	21.8%	63.6%	17.1%	19.3%
1965–70	53.3	24.0	22.7	52.6	22.6	24.8
1975–80	50.7	24.4	24.9	52.9	20.1	27.1
Middle Atlantic						
1955–60	51.5	31.7	16.9	72.6	13.6	13.9
1965–70	43.1	38.6	18.3	69.5	15.7	14.9
1975–80	42.8	36.3	20.9	62.4	18.2	19.4
East North Central						
1955–60	59.7	24.3	16.0	60.8	20.1	19.1
1965–70	51.4	29.8	18.8	60.0	21.2	18.8
1975–80	37.9	42.8	19.2	71.9	13.6	14.5
West North Central						
1955–60	47.9	33.5	18.6	67.0	15.9	17.2
1965–70	46.6	32.7	20.7	60.1	19.9	20.0
1975–80	44.1	32.8	23.1	55.8	20.9	23.2
South Atlantic						
1955–60	63.1	17.0	19.9	50.2	26.6	23.2
1965–70	59.2	18.6	22.2	43.3	31.6	25.1
1975–80	59.9	17.5	22.6	37.7	32.6	29.6
East South Central						
1955–60	43.1	40.9	15.9	70.4	16.0	13.6
1965–70	44.5	37.6	17.9	61.1	21.8	17.1
1975–80	46.2	31.7	22.1	49.5	26.7	23.8
West South Central						
1955–60	47.1	31.4	21.4	59.3	19.9	20.9
1965–70	45.4	30.8	23.8	53.4	23.2	23.4
1975–80	48.3	25.2	26.6	44.9	27.4	27.7
Mountain						
1955–60	61.1	12.2	26.7	36.6	29.4	34.1
1965–70	56.7	14.3	29.0	36.1	30.3	33.6
1975–80	57.5	13.2	29.2	30.3	34.9	34.8
Pacific						
1955–60	65.8	8.1	26.1	26.9	38.6	34.5
1965–70	58.7	12.8	28.4	31.0	36.4	32.5
1975–80	53.8	16.9	29.4	35.4	32.0	32.5

NOTE: Excluded are persons born outside the United States or living outside the United States five years before the census.

These findings are hardly surprising. They simply mean that even if rates of outmigration from areas of rapid growth remain constant, the number of outmigrants should rise slightly and increase the pool of potential returnees, and more returnees will more nearly balance the composition of inmigrants among primary, repeat, and return migrants. Explaining who moves to the Pacific division and why has increasingly come to entail accounting for the return of natives to the division and the behavior of repeat (nonreturn) migrants.

Return migrants also come to be an increasing source of inmigrants to regions experiencing increasing net outmigration. Consider the East North Central division (Michigan, Ohio, Indiana, Illinois, and Wisconsin). As shown in the next chapter (Figure 5.1), this division had a modest amount of net inmigration in the early 1950s but has had accelerating net outmigration since then. From the 1950s to the 1970s it tended to lose industrial jobs and was less able to attract natives of other states. Persons leaving their division of birth to move to the East North Central division declined from 59.7 percent of the division's inmigrants in 1955–60 to 51.4 percent in 1965–70 and 37.9 percent in 1975–80. Return migrants grew from 24.3 percent of inmigrants in 1955–60 to 29.8 percent in 1965–70 and 42.8 percent in 1975–80. Increasingly, then, inmigrants to the East North Central division are people who have lived there before. Returnees have grown as a percentage of inmigrants because of the very rapid decline in the number of natives of other areas who are attracted to the East North Central division.

Return migrants become less important as a region experiences an initial upsurge in inmigration—for example, the West South Central division in the 1970s. This division (consisting of Texas, Oklahoma, Louisiana, and Arkansas) attracted many new residents during the 1970s as a result of an oil boom and associated rapid growth in other sectors of the economy. Return migrants declined from 31.4 percent of the region's inmigrants in 1955–60 to 25.2 percent in 1975–80. The proportion of inmigrants who were repeat movers increased from 21.4 percent in 1955–60 to 26.6 in 1975–80.

By 1975–80 persons leaving their division of birth were most highly represented among persons moving to the South Atlantic states (59.9 percent of all inmigrants) and least important among persons going to the East North Central division (37.9 percent of inmigrants). Returnees were most important among migrants to the East North Central division (42.8 percent of inmigrants) and least important among migrants to the Mountain states. Repeat migrants were most highly represented among migrants to the Pacific division (29.4 percent of the total) and least represented among migrants to the East North Central division.

This view of the changing composition of inmigrants over a 20-year period gives a new perspective of the origins of migrants to growing and declining regions. A surge of growth changes not only the number but the composition of inmigrants: The proportion of first-time and repeat migrants increases and the proportion of returnees decreases. With maturity, however, the proportions tend to balance out somewhat. As regions shift to overall net outmigration or experience growing outmigration, the proportion of inmigrants who are returnees increases.

The Changing Backgrounds of Outmigrants

As regional migration balances change, the backgrounds of outmigrants change in ways that parallel those of inmigrants. For example, the Pacific division had net inmigration steadily over the 1950–80 period, but its outmigrants increasingly came to consist of natives of the Pacific division and decreasingly consisted of persons going back to their division of birth. As shown in Table 4.5, persons born in the Pacific division were 26.9 percent of the division's outmigrants in 1955–60 but 35.4 percent in 1975–80. Persons leaving the Pacific division to go home were 38.6 percent of outmigrants in 1955–60 but only 32.0 percent in 1975–80. The proportion of outmigrants who were repeat movers slipped from 34.5 percent in 1955–60 to 32.5 percent in 1975–80.

Concomitantly, persons leaving an area of growing outmigration increasingly consist of natives of the area. As the East North Central division changed from modest net inmigration in the 1950s to substantial outmigration in the 1970s, the proportion of outmigrants who were natives rose from 60.8 percent in 1955–60 to 71.9 percent in 1975–80. As discussed in Chapter 3, the overall propensity to migrate from the states of the East North Central division increased only moderately during this period, but because these states were attracting few migrants from other states their populations increasingly came to consist of natives; and as economic hard times hit with a suddenness in the 1970s, these states had comparatively few residents other than natives to send to other regions of the country.

Improving economic conditions in a region also change the composition of outmigrants. The oil boom and an expanding economy in the West South Central division accelerated net inmigration and kept more natives at home. Natives declined from 59.3 percent of outmigrants from the West South Central division in 1955–60 to 44.9 percent in 1975–80. Persons going home and repeat migrants made up a growing proportion of outmigrants from the West South Central division between the late 1950s and the late 1970s.

Overall, the data in Table 4.5 on the changing origins of inmigrants and outmigrants from the nine divisions give a new perspective to who moves to or from areas of growth or decline. The figures mean that an initial surge of net inmigration is associated with changes in the composition of inmigrants (proportionately more first-time and repeat migrants and fewer returnees) and outmigrants (fewer natives and more returnees and repeat migrants). A sharp increase in net outmigration probably changes the composition of inmigrants to proportionately fewer first-time migrants and more returnees, and the composition of outmigrants is likely to change to include proportionately more natives and fewer returnees. These changes mean that shifts in net migration balances are associated with changes in the make-up of both inmigrants and outmigrants according to exposure to previous migration and knowledge of areas of destination. As net outmigration grows, one expects an increasing number of inmigrants to have knowledge of the area because they consist increasingly of returnees. As net inmigration increases, the changing mix may bring in relatively more people with little prior exposure to the area but more people with prior exposure to migration through repeat movement in the past.

Three Types of Net Migration

If a region's inmigrants and outmigrants can be classified into these three types, then its net migration can be separated into components attributable to (1) persons leaving their area of birth, (2) persons moving to their area of birth, and (3) others who are neither moving from nor to their area of birth. Table 4.6 presents these figures for the nine divisions for the 1955–60, 1965–70, and 1975–80 migration intervals.

Table 4.6 shows that regions seldom have net inmigration or net outmigration for all three types of migrants. The net inmigration to areas with substantial net inmigration is typically attributable to the movements of persons leaving their areas of birth and to repeat migrants. For example, the Pacific division had a very large volume of net inmigration during the period of study, and Table 4.6 shows that this net inmigration was attributable to the movements of persons leaving their state of birth and repeat, nonreturn migrants. Table 4.6 shows that from domestic sources (excluding persons born outside the United States or living outside the United States in 1975) the Pacific division had a net inmigration of 429,495 persons aged 5 and over in 1975–80. When one considers only the movements of persons leaving their division of birth, the Pacific division's net gain was 562,848. Of return mi-

TABLE 4.6

Decomposition of Each Division's Net Migration into Persons Aged 5 and Over Leaving Their Division of Birth, Returning to Their Division of Birth, or Making Other Moves Between Divisions: 1955–60, 1965–70, and 1975–80

	Net Migration from Domestic Sources	Persons Leaving Division of Birth	Persons Returning to Division of Birth	Other Interdivision Migrants
New England				
1955–60	−56,633	−72,773	16,357	−217
1965–70	−905	4,069	8,442	−13,416
1975–80	−181,331	−109,797	−8,007	−63,527
Middle Atlantic				
1955–60	−490,797	−536,167	87,754	−42,384
1965–70	−610,357	−703,962	148,761	−55,156
1975–80	−1,136,246	−1,016,305	77,389	−197,330
East North Central				
1955–60	−392,774	−254,710	−20,571	−117,493
1965–70	−304,329	−327,818	81,014	−57,525
1975–80	−1,412,272	−1,361,170	105,539	−156,641
West North Central				
1955–60	−391,035	−397,166	63,046	−56,915
1965–70	−255,915	−274,851	63,615	−44,679
1975–80	−185,720	−227,918	86,268	−44,070
South Atlantic				
1955–60	467,399	465,817	−47,891	49,473
1965–70	621,668	629,453	−98,787	91,002
1975–80	906,684	1,017,186	−164,925	54,423
East South Central				
1955–60	−303,157	−382,792	106,282	−26,647
1965–70	−160,746	−228,160	88,788	−21,374
1975–80	168,927	48,383	98,348	22,196
West South Central				
1955–60	−160,588	−201,144	68,883	−28,327
1965–70	96,979	−41,400	111,569	26,810
1975–80	754,047	401,994	164,913	187,140
Mountain				
1955–60	247,626	313,346	−83,354	17,634
1965–70	69,505	229,998	138,351	−22,142
1975–80	656,416	684,779	−157,270	128,907
Pacific				
1955–60	1,079,959	1,065,589	−190,506	204,876
1965–70	544,100	712,671	−265,051	96,480
1975–80	429,495	562,848	−202,255	68,902

NOTE: Excluded are persons born outside the United States or living outside the United States five year before the census.

grants, the Pacific division sent 202,255 more than it received; and of repeat migrants, it received 68,902 more than it sent.

In general, areas with overall net inmigration typically have net inmigration from first-time migrants and repeat migrants. Areas with overall net outmigration similarly tend to have net outmigration of first-time and repeat migrants. Streams of return migrants typically produce negative balances for regions with (overall) net inmigration and positive balances for areas of net outmigration.

Although regions rarely have a net gain or loss from all three sources, it is possible to suggest the circumstances under which regions might do so. The East North Central division in 1955–60 is shown to have net outmigration from all three sources, although comparatively high nonresponse to both the place-of-birth and residence-five-years-ago questions means that small numbers should be interpreted very cautiously. This division in 1955–60 was just beginning to experience the first shocks of economic restructuring and loss of jobs and a shift from positive to negative overall migration balances. As it did so, it began to send more of its natives to other regions and in return received fewer natives leaving their division of birth, producing net outmigration of persons leaving their division of birth. It also began to send more previous inmigrants back home, producing net outmigration of return migrants. But as it sent more former inmigrants back to places of birth or onward to other areas, its stock of previous inmigrants was diminished so that it had fewer to send. By 1965–70 the return outmigration stream no longer offset the return inmigration stream, and the division had a positive balance between the streams of return inmigrants and return outmigrants.

Another exception to the rule that regions rarely have net gain or loss from all three sources is the West South Central division in 1975–80. There the circumstances were almost opposite those characterizing the East North Central division in the late 1950s. The West South Central division in the late 1970s was experiencing an oil boom and very rapid growth in jobs. It was beginning to keep more of its own natives and was attracting more natives from other states. In earlier decades, however, the West South Central division had sent many of its natives to other states, as was shown in the preceding chapter (see Figure 3.1). The division, therefore, had a large pool of potential returnees from which to draw, and it seemed to draw them back in large numbers in 1975–80 (see Figure 4.1). These circumstances gave the West South Central states positive balances of migrants leaving their division of birth, return migrants, and repeat migrants. But as the West South Central division draws down the pool of potential return migrants, it, too, will shift to net outmigration of return migrants.

These migration dynamics are completely invisible in estimates of net intercensal migration or the postcensal estimates of net migration. Nor can they be seen in the usual census figures on gross migration not disaggregated by place of birth. Taking into account prior mobility of current migrants clearly improves understanding not only of gross flows but also of net flows and gives a clearer picture of who accounts for changes in migration balances. Rarely are censuses fully utilized in these ways to describe or model the interactions of primary, return, and repeat migration in changing an area's population.

Age of Primary, Return, and Repeat Migrants

Up to now, attention has been devoted entirely to the numbers of persons leaving their area (state or division) of birth, returning to it, or making a repeat, nonreturn move. Perhaps a good way of identifying who is likely to be making each of these three types of moves is to look at rates of movement by age and level of education. Chapter 2 argued that of the characteristics commonly identified in censuses, these two were among the most consistent in identifying who is likely to move long distances. In order to gain a perspective on who are the first-time, return, and repeat migrants and to see if the migration differentials noted in Chapter 2 apply to each of these three types of moves, rates of moving were calculated by age and by years of school completed. Single-year-of-age probabilities of leaving one's state of birth, returning to it, or making a repeat, nonreturn interstate move are shown in Figure 4.3. The rates are on an "at risk" basis, and the bases are the same as discussed earlier in the chapter for national rates of leaving one's state of birth, returning to it, or making a repeat, nonreturn interstate move.

Chapter 2 presented the "classic" age profile of migration that has been observed in the United States and in many other countries. Rates are typically high among young children (because they have young parents), low among persons of high school age, and at a peak among persons in their early 20s. Rates then decline fairly rapidly and are often observed to rise slightly at retirement ages. Figure 4.3 shows that this age profile of migration is actually a composite of three distinct age curves associated with movement from state of birth, back to it, or onward to another state.

The "typical" curve most clearly characterizes persons leaving their state of birth. The age curve of return migration is at its peak among children aged 5–9, suggesting a high rate of return to state of birth on

FIGURE 4.3

Rates of Leaving State of Birth, Returning to State of Birth, or Making Repeat (Nonreturn) Interstate Moves, by Single Years of Age: 1975–80

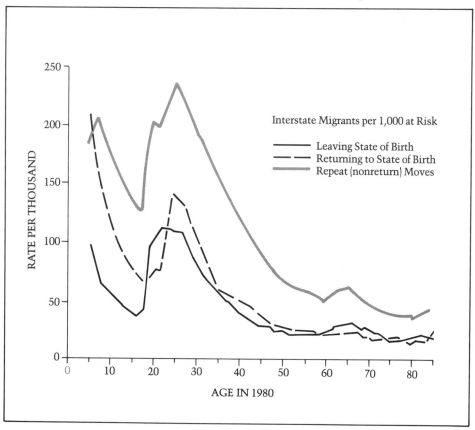

the part of young parents. Return migration reaches a secondary peak among persons aged 25–29 and sharply declines with age, showing no perceptible upturn at age 65. At every age except the very youngest, rates of repeat migration are far higher than rates of leaving or returning to state of birth. Rates of repeat migration are comparatively low among persons in their late teens and peak at ages 25–29 (all ages refer to 1980, after migration occurred). Rates of repeat migration then decline with age with a slight turning up around age 65.

The age profile of return migration clearly shows that it cannot be described as primarily a phenomenon of retirees "going home" to re-

FIGURE 4.4

Rates of Leaving State of Birth, Returning to State of Birth, or Making Repeat (Nonreturn) Interstate Moves, by Years of School Completed and Five-Year Age Groups (25–69): 1975–80

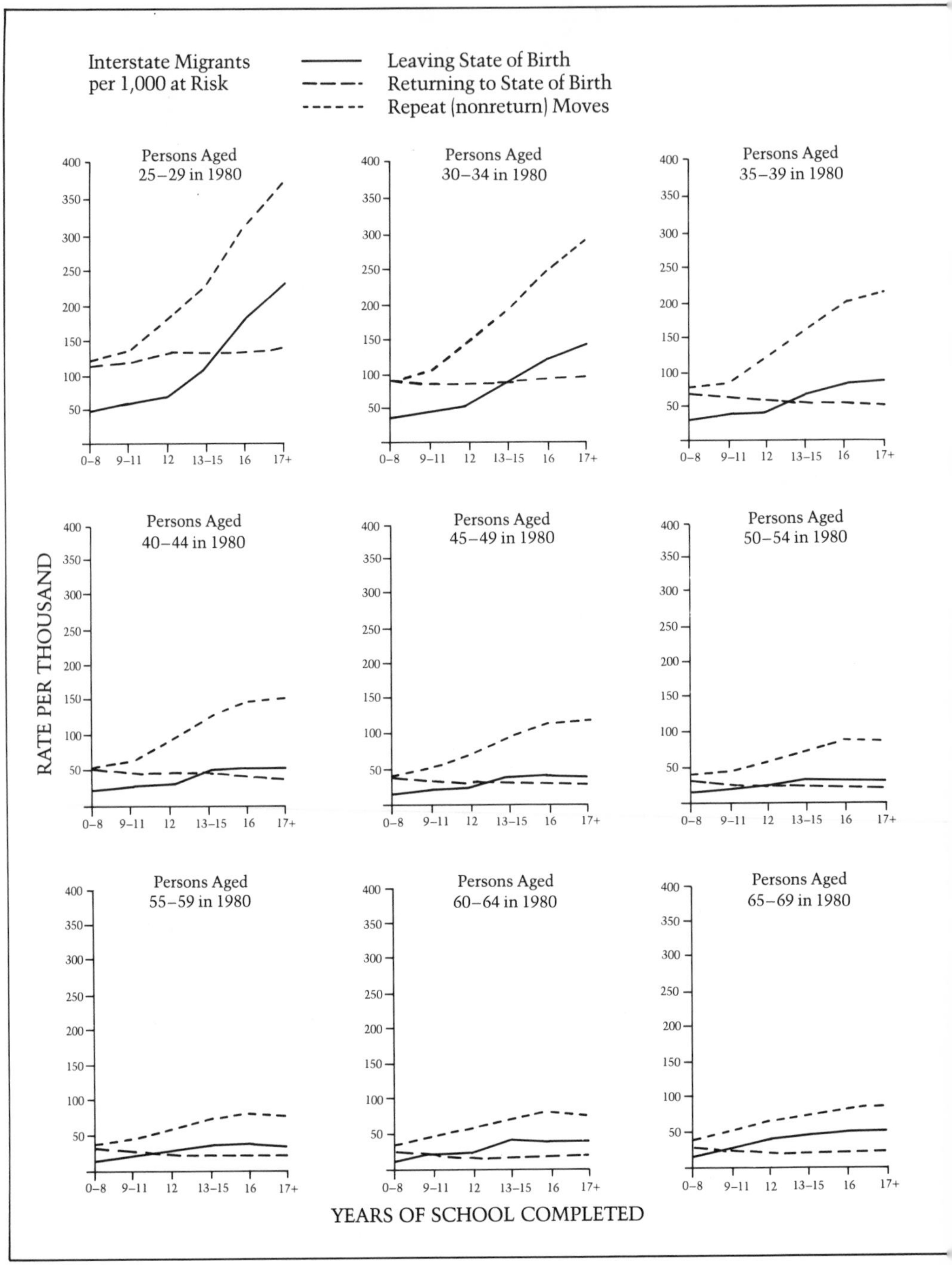

Interstate Migrants per 1,000 at Risk
Leaving State of Birth
Returning to State of Birth
Repeat (nonreturn) Moves
Persons Aged 25–29 in 1980
Persons Aged 30–34 in 1980
Persons Aged 35–39 in 1980
Persons Aged 40–44 in 1980
Persons Aged 45–49 in 1980
Persons Aged 50–54 in 1980
Persons Aged 55–59 in 1980
Persons Aged 60–64 in 1980
Persons Aged 65–69 in 1980
RATE PER THOUSAND
400
350
300
250
200
150
100
50
0–8
9–11
12
13–15
16
17+
YEARS OF SCHOOL COMPLETED

verse the migration of their youth. The median age of persons returning to their state of birth in 1975–80 was 26.9 years—greater than the median of 23.2 for migrants leaving their state of birth but less than the median of 28.9 for repeat, nonreturn interstate migrants. Since these ages relate to the end of the migration interval, one may assume that the migrants were somewhat younger at the time they moved (or the time of their last move) during the 1975–80 period.

In Figure 4.3 the slight upturn that is sometimes noted in national migration rates around age 65 is almost entirely attributable to persons leaving their state of birth or making repeat, nonreturn moves. The absence of a visible increase in the propensity to return to one's state of birth at retirement suggests that the longer one stays away from "home," the less likely is one to return to it. The increased propensity to leave one's state of birth around age 65 could be a regional phenomenon, for Chapter 3 showed (see Figure 3.4) a marked increase in the propensity of residents of several northeastern states to engage in interstate migration around age 65. These states have a high proportion of natives in their population and large migration streams to Florida. The increase in the rate of repeat, nonreturn migration around age 65 might be a phenomenon of persons who have lived in many areas in their lifetime, have strong attachments to none, and may be exercising choice among many possible places to retire to.

Education of Primary, Return, and Repeat Migrants

Looking at the age-specific probabilities of leaving state of birth, returning to it, or making repeat, nonreturn moves offers a somewhat different view of who moves than the national rates not differentiated by prior mobility status of the population. Does differentiating the population by prior mobility status also offer insights not available from the presentation in Chapter 2 of migration differentials by level of education? Specifically, does the positive association between level of education and propensity to move between states characterize migration from state of birth, back to it, and migration onward to other states? For each of these three types of migration, Figure 4.4 shows migration probabilities by age and years of school completed.

The positive association between years of school completed and likelihood of migrating is entirely the product of persons leaving their state of birth or making repeat, nonreturn moves. At no age is level of education strongly associated with whether or not one goes back to one's state of birth. At ages 35–50 there appears to be a modest inverse association between level of education and probability of returning to state of birth.[12]

Persons who have less than eight years of school and are living outside their state of birth are about as likely to go back to their state of birth as they are to move onward to another state. At higher levels of education, however, persons who have left their state of birth are far more likely to move onward than they are to go back to their state of birth, and the higher the level of education, the greater the likelihood of choosing to move on but not back to state of birth. Higher levels of education for the once-migrated group seem to offer more knowledge of other places, more employment options, or other reasons to engage in repeat migration.

At every age group and educational level, persons who have left their state of birth are more likely to move than persons living in their state of birth. This consistent differential may mean that migrants learn by doing, for at every educational level persons who have moved once find it comparatively easy to do so again. The results seem to suggest that at least insofar as interstate migration is concerned, those who move the most are those with the highest levels of education.

These results challenge the notion that chronic movers are drifters who move from place to place without setting down roots or finding steady employment. The data for Figure 4.4 suggest that throughout life repeat interstate migrants are most likely to be highly qualified persons with the most choices among employment opportunities. Of course, missing is information on intrastate moves and the actual number of moves, and it is quite possible that excessive mobility among persons with weak job attachment occurs over the shorter, intrastate distances. Also missing is knowledge of how soon persons move again after an initial move; the census data measure movement only over a five-year interval and may miss many moves. Beyond some point hypermobility surely interferes with the accumulation of location- or firm-specific capital and flattens an individual's earnings curve; hypermobility likely entails different types, levels, and frequencies of moving for persons of different educational attainment and occupational position.

---

[12]One should not conclude that under all circumstances there is no association between level of education and probability of return migration. One study reported that among southern-born blacks living in the North in 1965, the probability of going back to the South by 1970 was positively associated with level of education. Larry Long and Kristin A. Hansen, "Selectivity of Black Return Migration to the South," *Rural Sociology* 42 (Fall 1977): 317–331.

Summary and Conclusion

For some persons, migration can beget further migration. If migration is a cumulative experience, the barriers to the first move or first few moves may be the hardest to overcome, and subsequent moves may build upon knowledge or contacts acquired from earlier moves. For particular areas, the presence of large numbers of migrants may increase the mobility potential of nonmigrants, for many migrants in an area may increase awareness of other areas and encourage outmigration. As shown in Chapter 6, inmigration to metropolitan areas seems to correlate positively with mobility within them.

Whether such processes work in reverse is not clear. The migration-begets-migration theme seems to suggest that migration will increase over time, but it is not increasing, and its composition seems to consist increasingly of persons who have moved before. High and rising levels of nonresponse and changes in census questions and processing procedures make difficult the precise measurement of how the composition of interstate migrants has been altered by changes in the propensity of the general population to leave their state of birth, to go back to it, or to move onward to another state. The data suggest that the propensity to leave one's state of birth was lower in the late 1970s than the late 1950s, but of those who had already left their state of birth, the propensity to move again was moderately higher in the late 1970s than the late 1950s. Over this period, persons leaving their state of birth made up a declining proportion of interstate migrants, and repeat (nonreturn) migrants were a growing proportion.

Such results imply some reorientation from the traditional concern with who moves. Perhaps more attention should be directed at identifying persons whose mobility is blocked and who are not able to move. A long-standing approach has been to look upon the problems of migration as associated with the adjustment, accommodation, and assimilation of persons who move and are often assumed to do so involuntarily. This aspect of migration is highly visible and fairly easily measured by surveys that identify who migrates and compare the socioeconomic status of migrants and nonmigrants at places of destination. More difficult, however, is measuring the effects of selective—and at times involuntary—nonmigration. Selective nonmigration can mean more young persons looking for employment close to home because their parents can subsidize living costs. It can mean more persons choosing to go to a local college or university rather than one in another state that offers a course of study that would be more beneficial after graduation. It can mean that workers facing unemployment in areas of economic decline opt for early retirement or accept downward mobility because of "sunk" capital in a house that would be lost by moving to a more expensive area. The costs of nonmigration are very hard to study.

Return migration to state of birth tends to occur within a short time after leaving. Rates of leaving state of birth are highest among persons in their early 20s, and rates of return are highest among persons in their mid to late 20s. There appears to be no measurable upturn in rates of return to state of birth at retirement, suggesting that the longer a person stays away from state of birth, the lower the likelihood of returning. The upturn in interstate migration rates around age 65 is the product of an increased propensity to leave state of birth (probably some northern states) and an increased propensity to move onward (but not back to state of birth) among persons living outside their state of birth.

Return migrants figure prominently among migrants to areas of long-term outmigration. The reason is not a high rate of return among people who leave areas of chronic outmigration; the reason is that such areas attract few natives of other areas. Return migrants to an area are more likely than other migrants to have knowledge of where they are moving to and to have relatives in the area; for this reason alone, migrants to areas of outmigration will exhibit different decision-making processes and invoke different criteria for choosing their destinations than migrants to growing areas. Studies of migration decision making need to institute careful controls for migrants' prior moves and residential background.

Growth cycles alter the composition of migrants to an area. Sudden economic growth in an area previously characterized by outmigration may increase the rate of return to the area but not the proportion of inmigrants who are returnees. Very rapid growth is likely to increase the proportion of inmigrants who are repeat movers or first-time migrants. When areas shift toward accelerated outmigration, they rapidly lose their previous inmigrants, and the proportion of outmigrants who are natives tends to rise.

5

INTERREGIONAL MIGRATION, RACE, AND PUBLIC POLICY

THIS CHAPTER concentrates on the effects of internal migration, at least some that are currently measurable and operate on a fairly large geographical scale. As applied to geographical areas, the with-what-effect questions associated with migration are often approached through the how much and who questions, for quite obviously migration has greater effects when the volume is great or the degree of selectivity is high. Even if volume and selectivity are only moderate, migration may affect areas of destination if the migrants differ appreciably from the destination population in terms of culture, religion, race, language, or other socioeconomic variables.

The effects of internal migration are often raised in the context of interregional movements, and the chapter reviews the magnitude of net migration gains and losses for the major regions of the country from 1880 to 1984. One of the effects of large migration flows is simply to change the age composition of areas of substantial gain or loss so that a certain momentum to total population change is established. When migration removes many young persons it diminishes the reproductive potential of areas of outmigration, and by adding persons of reproductive age to areas of destination, migration can generate a demographic shock wave that persists long after the initial inmigration.

Some of the most intensely debated consequences of migration have involved the effects—or presumed effects—of the very substantial redistribution of the black population of the South to large cities in the

North and West in the three decades after World War II. Many policy debates arose as to the degree to which various social problems—particularly unemployment, poverty, and welfare dependence—were interregionally transferred through this and other South-to-North flows. The chapter assesses research which led to a revision of traditional theories of the presumed disadvantages of rural birth and the adjustment of rural-origin migrants to northern cities after World War II. Under some circumstances black migrants were found to be doing better economically than nonmigrants of similar age and educational level.

A changing debate is illustrated by the shift of concern over the effects of migration of the poor on welfare burdens in areas of destination to more recent concern over the effects that welfare payments may have in inhibiting migration of the poor. Policies intended to influence migration have often been raised with particular reference to the poor, either to decrease or, more recently, to increase their mobility. Less common are migration policies or programs proposed as a means of affecting the movement of the nonpoor or well-to-do, except indirectly. Economic development of lagging areas is sometimes advocated as a way of keeping talented youth in their areas of origin and relying on their nonmigration to foster growth and development. In cases like these, subsidies to develop infrastructure may be proposed as policies to foster selective nonmigration, and their success might be judged with a view to the degree to which they reduce outmigration of persons with specific skills or talents. In contrast, more direct types of policy intervention have at various times called for programs to reduce, increase, or redirect migration of low-income or unemployed persons. The chapter reviews the debate on these questions and the degree to which regions of the country have imported or exported poverty through migration.

The chapter also takes advantage of data from the 1940, 1960, 1970, and 1980 censuses to identify interregional migration streams of highly educated persons and those with little formal education. The data allow some approximations as to which regions over this period of time have gained and which have lost human capital through interregional migration.

The topics covered are those that have been the subject of considerable public debate and for which fairly firm empirical evidence is available. The chapter concludes by noting that the effects of migration exist for individuals and areas. Neither is particularly well measured.

Regional Dimensions of U.S. Internal Migration

Most interregional migration streams are highly selective by age, with persons at young-adult ages being greatly overrepresented. About the only exceptions to this generalization are streams of retirees moving to Florida, Arizona, and a few other locations. Age selectivity by itself is often great enough to have significant impact simply by altering the age composition of origin or destination areas.

For example, over many decades outmigration from farming areas of the Midwest and South removed such a large proportion of persons of childbearing age that many counties in the 1950s registered more deaths than births, and population decline threatened the viability of many villages and small communities. The irony of this effect is that at the peak of the baby boom in the 1950s nearly one half of the nation's 3,100 counties were decreasing in population, with a large proportion being in the Great Plains region of the Midwest.[1] Natural decrease (more deaths than births) was the product of current as well as past outmigration that had removed young people and brought about rapid aging of population and decreased reproductive potential.

Gaining areas usually expand in the proportion of population of childbearing age, and an additional momentum to growth tends to be established in net inmigration areas. The extensive migration to Sunbelt states in the 1970s brought in many young persons whose childbearing will continue to add to population growth in the 1980s even if net inmigration abates. The irony to this momentum is that a wave of inmigration can obviate some of the features of areas that initially attracted migrants. Job opportunities certainly played a role in the migration to Sunbelt states in the 1970s, but these states will now have to add jobs especially rapidly in order to avoid incurring higher unemployment in the 1980s simply because many of the inmigrants of the 1970s have children who will be entering the labor force in the 1980s.

The migration to Sunbelt states in the 1970s also illustrates that the effects of migration can be a function of not only numbers and characteristics of migrants but also the rapidity of change. In some ways the redistribution of population out of the Northeast and Midwest and to the South and West in the 1970s represented a continuation of patterns evident in the 1960s. The total magnitude of change was unprecedented, however, and is illustrated in Figure 5.1, which shows average annual net intercensal migration from 1890 to 1984 for each of the four major regions and the nine divisions that form the regions. The reason for showing data for both regions and divisions is that some data are avail-

---

[1]Calvin L. Beale, "Rural Depopulation in the United States: Some Demographic Consequences of Agricultural Adjustments," *Demography* 1, no. 1 (1964): 264–272. The tendency of outmigration to bring about population aging was also noted for metropolitan areas that later came to lose population; see Edgar Rust, *No Growth: Impacts on Metropolitan Areas* (Lexington, MA: Lexington Books, 1975). For a more complete and up-to-date treatment of the effects of metropolitan growth or decline see Chapters 5 and 6 of the 1980 census monograph *Regional and Metropolitan Growth and Decline*, by William H. Frey and Alden Speare, Jr.

FIGURE 5.1

*Average Annual Net Migration for the Four Major U.S. Regions
and the Nine Divisions They Comprise: 1880–1984 (in thousands)*

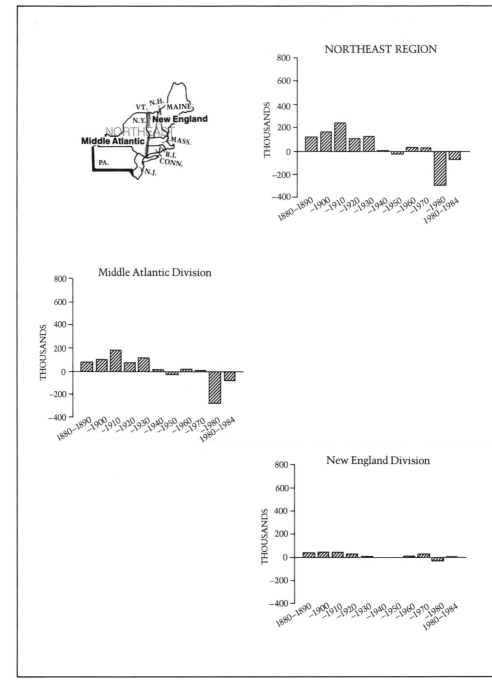

FIGURE 5.1 *(continued)*

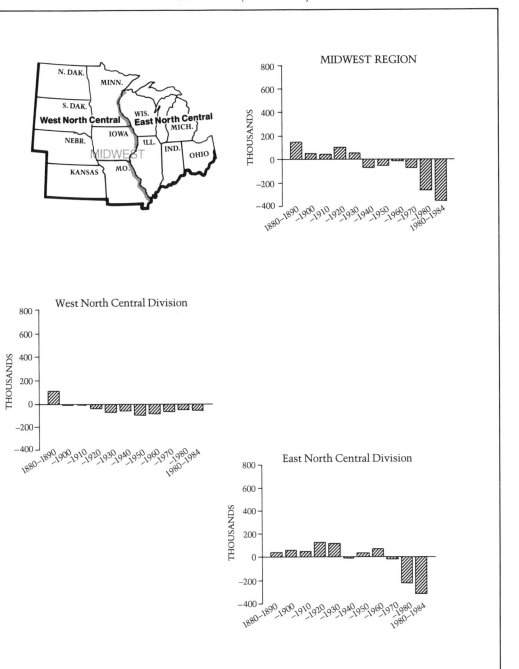

FIGURE 5.1 *(continued)*

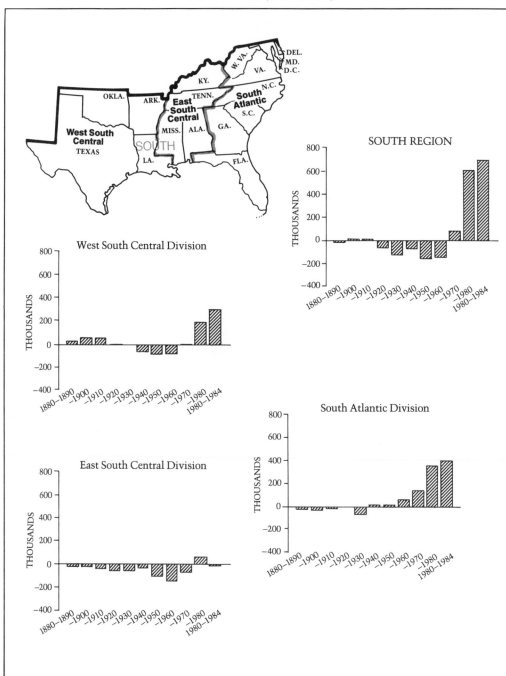

FIGURE 5.1 *(continued)*

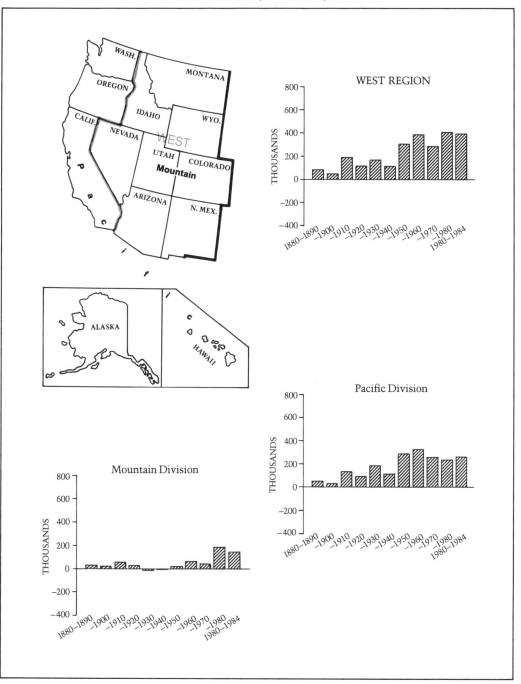

able only for the regions and other data are available for the divisions (see Appendix A for sources of data).

The Northeast region as a whole had substantial net inmigration in the late nineteenth century and through the 1920s, when new legislation sharply curtailed immigration. The region had very small migration balances in the 1930s and 1940s but had net inmigration in the 1950s and 1960s. The region's overall net inmigration in these two decades was due entirely to the migration of blacks from the South; as noted in the next section, the Northeast as a whole has had net outmigration of whites rather steadily since World War II. The net outmigration in the 1970–80 decade was unprecedented and was not maintained in the early 1980s. Most of the net outmigration of the 1970s was accounted for by the Middle Atlantic division (New York, Pennsylvania, and New Jersey).

Like the Northeast, the Midwest as a whole had net inmigration from the late nineteenth century through the 1920s. Unlike the Northeast, however, the Midwest has had net outmigration almost continuously since then. The substantial net outmigration from the Midwest in the 1970–80 decade was an acceleration of a pattern evident since the Great Depression, and outmigration from the region remained high in the early 1980s. The more industrialized states of the Midwest (Ohio, Michigan, Indiana, Illinois, and Wisconsin, which make up the East North Central division) collectively had net inmigration in the 1950s and 1960s but have been the biggest losers of population through migration since then.

The South as a whole had modest migration balances until World War I. The region had substantial outmigration in the 1920s as conditions in agriculture deteriorated and as immigration, which had been going mostly to the North, was curtailed and led northern employers to look elsewhere to fill jobs. Despite a high rate of exodus from some southern states during the Great Depression, outmigration from the region slowed as economic opportunities diminished in the North in the 1930s. With World War II net outmigration from the South increased and the region's net migration remained highly negative in the 1950s (due largely to net outmovement of blacks). The South shifted to net inmigration in the 1960–70 decade, and the volume of inmigration increased markedly in the 1970–80 decade and remained high in the early 1980s. The net inmigration was accounted for in large part by the South Atlantic division (particularly Florida) and the West South Central division (particularly Texas). Even the East South Central division (Mississippi, Alabama, Kentucky, and Tennessee) collectively had net inmigration in the 1970s, reversing net outmigration in all previous decades of the twentieth century. In the early 1980s, however, the East South Central division reverted to having net outmigration.

144

The West region has had net inmigration for each decade for the period covered, although many states have had fluctuating net migration balances that reflect the boom-and-bust cycles of economies based on mining, logging, and industrial activities like aircraft manufacturing. The Pacific division, which since the 1950s has included Alaska and Hawaii, has had net inmigration for each decade of the twentieth century, and the Mountain division had net inmigration in the 1970s and early 1980s at a level far above previous decades.

This backdrop to regional migration gains and losses over long periods of time underscores the development of the regional shifts of population that have received so much recent attention. Some of the regional changes in net migration balances since World War II are explainable only when the figures are disaggregated by race. Concern with composition of migration flows clearly came to rival concern with sheer volume of migration after World War II.

Migration of Blacks

The divergent migration flows of blacks and whites is illustrated in Figure 5.2, which shows net migration for the two racial groups for the four regions from 1920 to 1984. The series begins with 1920 because migration of blacks from the South was small before that date.[2] The slow development of outmigration of blacks from the South may seem surprising or puzzling in light of legally sanctioned discrimination and limited economic opportunities for blacks in the South after the Civil War and continuing into the twentieth century, but the relatively small migration of blacks to the North before 1920 is probably attributable in part to the large volume of immigration to the North. As long as immigrants were available for blue collar jobs, there probably were diminished incentives for blacks to leave to compete for employment in expanding industries of the North. It seems plausible to assume that in many contexts immigration may substitute for and reduce the volume of internal migration, but this hypothesis has not been extensively researched.

An alternative interpretation of the limited migration of blacks from the South in the late nineteenth century stresses the obvious advantage to white landowners in maintaining a large supply of black la-

---

[2]A historical account of specific black migration streams is provided in Daniel M. Johnson and Rex R. Campbell, *Black Migration in America: A Social Demographic History* (Durham, NC: Duke University Press, 1981).

FIGURE 5.2

Average Annual Net Migration of Blacks and Whites, for the Four Major Regions:
1920–84 (in thousands)

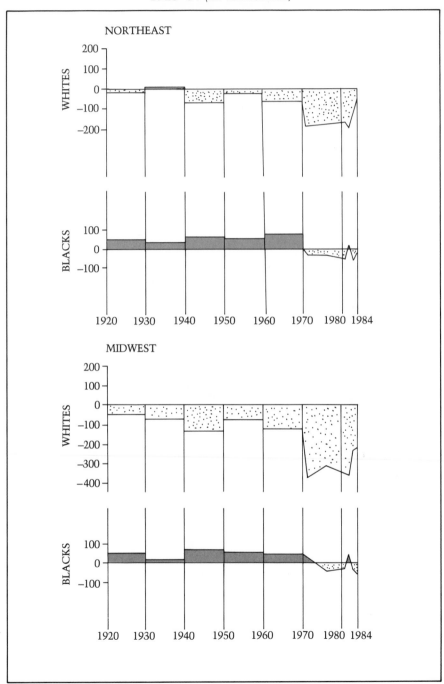

FIGURE 5.2 *(continued)*

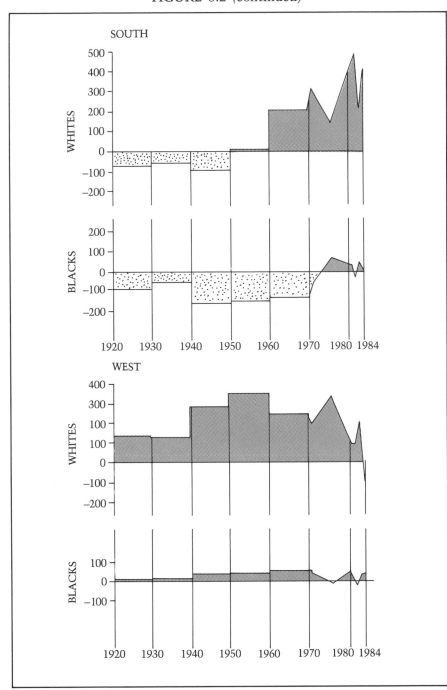

NOTE: Data for 1920–70 are annual averages of estimates of net intercensal migration. Data after 1970 are from Current Population Survey questions on residence one year earlier; linear interpolations were made for missing CPS data in 1972–75 and 1977–80.

borers and preventing an exodus that might create labor scarcities and drive up wages. There is considerable anecdotal evidence of harassment of blacks who had to use public transportation to leave the South.[3] And there is reason to believe that various labor laws were specifically enacted to reduce migration of blacks.[4] For example, one-year labor contracts were supported by legislation that made abandoning a job a criminal offense rather than merely a civil offense. Also, vagrancy laws sometimes meant that a black person without a job or tangible property as means of support could be arrested as a vagrant. Other laws severely restricted recruitment of labor by northern employers by imposing outrageously high licensing fees and stringent restrictions on activities that might be interpreted as "enticing" black laborers. Whatever the motivation or intent, such legislative and enforcement practices would certainly seem to restrict migration of blacks from the South in the Jim Crow era.

With World War I and the curtailment of immigration, blacks began to migrate in larger numbers. In the late nineteenth century and the early years of the twentieth century, censuses found only about 15 percent of blacks living outside their state of birth compared with about 22 percent of whites. By 1920 about 20 percent of blacks were living outside their state of birth, as were 24 percent in 1930—about the same as for whites. Since then, blacks have tended to be somewhat more likely than whites to leave their state of birth.[5]

The Northeast and Midwest were the main recipients of the increased migration of blacks from the South after World War I. Both regions had net inmigration of blacks and net outmigration of whites from the 1920s through the 1960s (except for a small volume of net inmigration of whites to the Northeast in the 1930s).

The South had net outmigration of blacks and whites from 1920 to 1950. After 1950 the South began to have net inmigration of whites but continued to have net outmigration of blacks until the 1970s. In a sense, therefore, the South had similar patterns of black and white migration for a long period of time before 1950 (net outmigration of both racial

---

[3]Emmett J. Scott, *Negro Migration During the War* (New York: Arno Press, 1969 [1919]). Chapter 7, "Efforts to Check the Movement," gives examples of efforts to keep blacks from leaving the South.

[4]The examples are taken from Jennifer Roback, "Exploitation in the Jim Crow South: The Market or the Law?" *Regulation* 8 (September–December 1984): 37–43.

[5]As mentioned in Appendix B, blacks tend to have somewhat lower period (as opposed to lifetime) rates of long-distance movement. That is, although the black population is as likely as, or more likely than, the white population to be living outside their state of birth at the time of a census, blacks are somewhat less likely to move between states over a one- or five-year period. Only part of the lower period rates of interstate migration of blacks can be attributed to lower levels of education among blacks and less representation in high-mobility occupations.

groups) and after the early to mid-1970s (net inmigration of both racial groups). The South's divergence of net flows of blacks and whites between these two dates may have served to focus attention on whether different motives governed migration of blacks and whites.[6]

The West has had net inmigration of both blacks and whites

[6]When early results of the 1970 census showed that the South had changed to net inmigration, the Census Bureau held a press conference to mark this demographic milestone. Asked why the region continued to have net outmigration of blacks, the Secretary of Commerce replied, "I have no doubt that higher welfare benefits in the North are a factor." When questioned further he added that ". . . greater job opportunities [in the North] would be the chief motivating factor." "Negro Migration to North Found Steady Since '40's," *New York Times*, March 3, 1971, p. 1.

Models of migration of blacks and whites in the 1960s and 1970s seemed to routinely include welfare benefits as a variable. In general, they produced inconclusive—at least always debatable—results and no firm evidence that migration of blacks was strongly influenced by level or availability of welfare benefits. The extensive debate on the degree to which migration of blacks and whites was influenced by welfare benefits included David E. Kaun, "Negro Migration and Unemployment," *Journal of Human Resources*, 5 (Spring 1970): 191–207; Bernard M. Bass and Ralph A. Alexander, "Climate, Economy, and the Differential Migration of White and Nonwhite Workers," *Journal of Applied Psychology* 56, no. 6 (1972): 518–521; Janet Rothenberg Pack, "Determinants of Migration to Central Cities," *Journal of Regional Science* 13, no. 2 (1973): 249–260; Gordon F. DeJong and William L. Donnelly, "Public Welfare and Migration," *Social Science Quarterly* 54 (September 1973): 329–344; Richard J. Cebula, Robert M. Kohn, and Richard C. Vedder, "Some Determinants of Interstate Migration of Blacks, 1965–1970," *Western Economic Journal* 11 (December 1973): 500–505; Richard J. Cebula, "Local Government Policies and Migration," *Public Choice* 19 (Fall 1974): 85–93; Richard J. Cebula, "Interstate Migration and the Tiebout Hypothesis: An Analysis According to Race, Sex and Age," *Journal of the American Statistical Association* 69 (December 1974): 876–879; Richard J. Cebula, "Migration, Economic Opportunity, and the Quality of Life: An Analysis for the United States According to Race, Sex, and Age," *Annals of Regional Science* 9 (March 1975): 127–133; Richard J. Cebula and Robert M. Kohn, "Public Policies and Migration Patterns in the United States," *Public Finance* 30, no. 2 (1975): 186–196; Richard J. Cebula, "On the Impact of State and Local Government Policies on Human Migration: A Log-Linear Analysis," *Review of Regional Studies* 5 (Winter 1975): 61–67; Joseph A. Ziegler, "Interstate Black Migration: Comment and Further Evidence," *Economic Inquiry* 14 (September 1976): 449–453; Morris M. Kleiner and William T. McWilliams, Jr., "Analysis of Alternative Labor-Force Population Migration Forecasting Models," *Annals of Regional Science* 11 (July 1977): 74–85; Robert Premus and Robert Weinstein, "Non-White Migration, Welfare Levels, and the Political Process: Some Additional Results," *Review of Regional Studies* 7 (Spring 1977): 11–19; Rishi Kumar, "More on Nonwhite Migration, Welfare Levels, and the Political Process," *Public Choice* 32 (Winter 1977): 151–154; S. B Jones-Hendrickson, "A Note on Nonwhite Migration, Welfare Levels and the Political Process: A Comment," *Public Choice* 33 (1978): 131–134; and Paul G. Athus and Joseph Schachter, "Interstate Migration and the New Federation," *Social Science Quarterly* 64 (March 1983): 35–45.

Much of this literature resulted from the failure of the early ecological models to control for socioeconomic differences between black and white populations and a concomitant failure to disentangle the covariation of (1) level of earnings, (2) size or availability of welfare, (3) size of black population, and (4) northern location. Because of these design inadequacies which arise partly from data unavailability, different studies might conclude that whites were more likely—and blacks less likely—to move to areas with (1) moderate but growing earnings levels, (2) stingy welfare benefits, (3) small black populations, and (4) warm climates.

throughout the twentieth century, although the volume of black net inmigration to the West was quite small before the 1940s. For each of the four regions the reliance on survey statistics for the period since 1970 may suggest fluctuations that actually are sampling variability.[7]

In ways that are impossible to measure precisely, the current socio-economic position of blacks relative to whites reflects migration patterns over more than a century. Blacks were slow to leave the South, which after the Civil War remained a region highly dependent on agriculture and offered limited economic advancement. At a relatively early date whites began to leave in substantial numbers for the West as well as the industrializing North. The black exodus began later and reached its peak in the two and a half decades after World War II—a time when the South's economy was rapidly restructuring itself in ways that would eventually add new jobs at a faster rate than in the North.[8] Today, a large proportion of the black population lives in central cities of northern metropolitan areas which have lost many jobs and experienced deteriorating living conditions for several decades. The present status of blacks would be quite different if blacks instead of white immigrants had moved to these same cities when their industrial bases were expanding. Some consequences of migration are measurable, but the consequences of nonmigration—though no less real—are almost never measurable.[9]

[7]As discussed in Appendix A, there are at the present time no "official" estimates of net migration by race by state (or other subnational areas) for 1970–80. The post-1970 data in Figure 5.2 come from available Current Population Surveys that asked for migration information on a one-year basis—specifically, 1970–71, 1975–76, 1980–81, 1981–82, 1982–83, and 1983–84. Gross and net flows for 1970–80 at the regional level have also been studied using other Current Population Surveys which showed net migration for 1970–71, 1970–73, 1970–74, 1970–75 and similar intervals for the latter half of the decade. During the first half of the decade the South shifted from net outmigration to essentially a zero net migration balance of blacks, with the balance subsequently being significantly greater than zero (a long migration interval that records more migration is more likely to detect statistically significant flows). The 1980 census showed that the South had a net inmigration of blacks over the 1975–80 interval.

[8]Part of the restructuring of the South's economy in the late 1940s and 1950s was the mechanization of agriculture and the displacement of large numbers of black farm workers. For counties of the South, Fligstein correlated various measures of farm mechanization with other variables and net migration of blacks and whites over several decades. See Neil Fligstein, *Going North: Migration of Blacks and Whites from the South, 1900–1950* (New York: Academic Press, 1981); and "The Transformation of Southern Agriculture and the Migration of Blacks and Whites, 1930–1950," *International Migration Review* 17, no. 2 (1983): 268–290. As southern agriculture was being transformed, an oft-debated chicken-and-egg question was the degree to which mechanization of agriculture reduced the demand for unskilled labor and thereby encouraged outmigration or, alternatively, outmigration of unskilled labor tended to push agricultural wages upward and encourage mechanization.

[9]Some of the reasons for studying nonmigration are identified in Peter Uhlenberg, "Noneconomic Determinants of Nonmigration: Sociological Considerations for Migration Theory," *Rural Sociology* 38 (Fall 1973): 296–311.

The Largest Streams of Black Migrants

The gradual development of net outmigration of blacks from the South may have resulted from a stepwise pattern characterized by streams that became longer and began to take blacks directly to northern destinations. Figure 5.3 pictures the five largest streams of black interstate migrants in the late 1930s, 1950s, 1960s, and 1970s.

Since Ravenstein's work in the nineteenth century (see Chapter 2) many demographers, geographers, and sociologists have been concerned with the degree to which migration streams develop as a result of successive short-distance movements, which are sometimes referred to as "step-migration" or migration by stages. In the nineteenth century and in many Third World countries today, migration streams often appear to develop as a sequence of moves—from, say, a rural area to the nearest village, then to a regional city, and perhaps finally to a major city of national importance. This type of migration reflects migrants' limited economic resources and limited knowledge of alternatives, and under such circumstances the friction of distance is great. Whether black migration from the South developed in this fashion cannot be answered unequivocally, but between the 1930s and the 1950s major black migration streams appear to have increased in length so as to remove more blacks from the South.

In 1935–40 the five largest black interstate migration streams were all within the South and between contiguous states. The largest was from Georgia to neighboring Florida. Another took migrants from South Carolina to North Carolina, and still another from North Carolina northward to Virginia. Other large streams went from Mississippi northward to Tennessee and from Louisiana to Texas.

By the 1950s many of these streams had lengthened and terminated in northern states. In 1955–60 the stream from Georgia to Florida was still the largest, but black migration from South Carolina terminated in New York instead of North Carolina, and the stream from North Carolina terminated in New York rather than Virginia. In a similar fashion, the stream from Mississippi terminated in Illinois rather than Tennessee. By 1955–60 a stream from Texas to California had become one of the five largest streams of black interstate migrants.

In 1965–70 the largest interstate migration stream of blacks was the suburban movement from the District of Columbia to Maryland; a large proportion of these moves covered the short distance from the District of Columbia to adjacent Prince Georges County in Maryland. The second largest stream was the previously established flow from Mississippi to Illinois. Perhaps the most visible change in the major streams of black interstate migrants was a westward redirection of movement. The

FIGURE 5.3

The Five Largest Streams of Black Interstate Migrants:
1935–40, 1955–60, 1965–70, and 1975–80

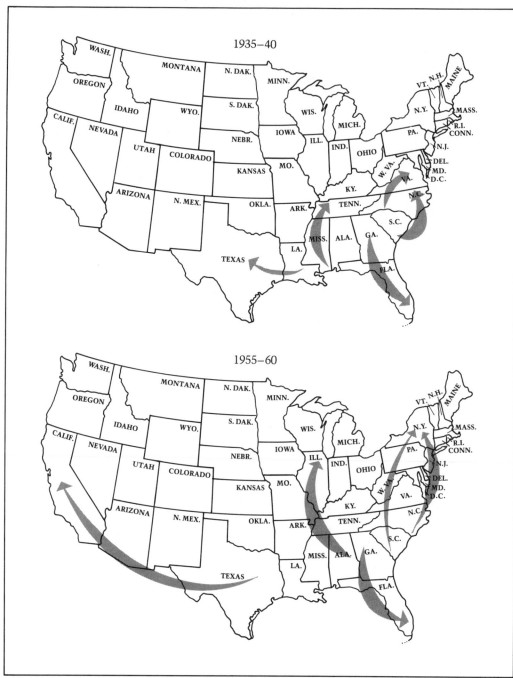

FIGURE 5.3 *(continued)*

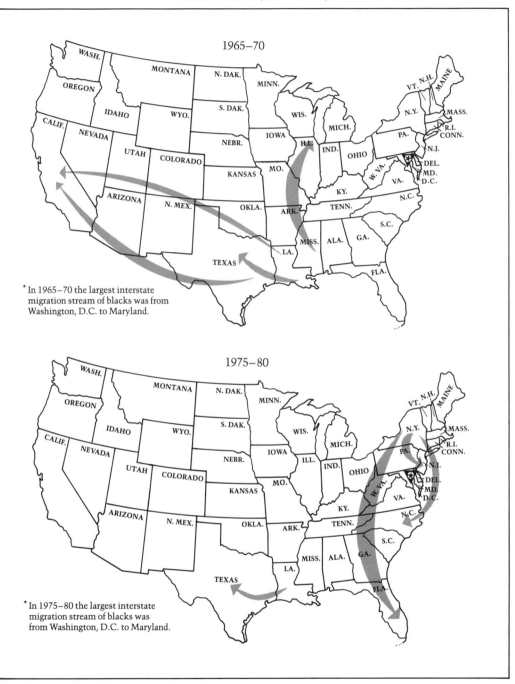

1965–70

* In 1965–70 the largest interstate migration stream of blacks was from Washington, D.C. to Maryland.

1975–80

* In 1975–80 the largest interstate migration stream of blacks was from Washington, D.C. to Maryland.

other three of the five largest streams went from Louisiana to California, from Louisiana to Texas, and from Texas to California.

By 1975–80 North-to-South flows dominated the map of black interstate migration. The largest stream was still the suburban movement from Washington, D.C., to Maryland, and it was joined by one from New York to New Jersey that probably also included many city-to-suburb moves. The second largest stream was from New York to Florida (among whites this was the largest interstate stream in 1975–80). Another of the five largest was from New York to North Carolina—reversing what had been one of the largest in 1955–60. The Louisiana-to-Texas stream remained among the five largest, but in 1975–80 none of the five largest streams of black migrants was to California.

One cannot help being struck by the reversed direction of many of the arrows in the 1975–80 map compared with the 1955–60 map. In 1955–60 three of the five arrows pointed north, but in 1975–80 three of the five pointed south. Many of the black migrants from New York to North Carolina in 1975–80 were returnees—43 percent were born in North Carolina. Black migrants from Washington, D.C., to Maryland were divided among persons born in D.C. (48 percent) and persons making repeat moves (neither moving from nor to their state of birth); 41 percent of blacks moving from D.C. to Maryland were born in neither area, and many probably were earlier migrants from southern states who were suburbanizing just as whites were. The Louisiana-to-Texas stream was dominated by blacks leaving their state of birth (77 percent were born in Louisiana). In the New York-to-Florida stream a rather small proportion were born in New York State (25 percent) and a surprisingly high proportion reported a birthplace outside the United States (37 percent).

Consequences of the Migration of Blacks

At its peak, from 1940 to 1970, the black exodus from the South cumulated to a net outmigration of over 4 million persons—somewhat larger than Italian immigration to the United States between 1890 and World War I, the peak period of Italian immigration. The black exodus removed a very large number of persons from a rural life in the South to some of the largest urban areas in the North and changed the demographic composition in places of destination.

Ironically, however, some of the impacts of black migration have probably been overstated. For example, black migration after World War II clearly altered the racial composition of major cities of destination, in some of which blacks came to be a majority of the population. Washington, D.C., became a majority-black city by 1960. Detroit went from 16 percent black in 1950 to 44 percent black in 1970 and 63 percent black in 1980. Cleveland's population was 16 percent black in 1950, 39 percent black in 1970, and 44 percent black in 1980. Baltimore became a predominantly black city after 1970. Detroit, Chicago, Newark, Gary, and many other cities came to have black mayors.

What is sometimes overlooked in such figures is that changes in racial composition reflect not simply black inmigration but also a concurrent white outmigration. In fact, the increase in the percentage black in northern cities after World War II usually was due more to white suburbanization than to black cityward movement. The outmigration of whites tended to be demographically more important than black inmigration or higher rates of natural increase in increasing the percentage black in 11 of the 12 cities with the largest black populations in 1970.[10] For these 11 cities white outmigration tended to account for more than half of the increase in the percentage black between 1950 and 1970.

Of course, migration of the two groups may not be independent, for, as discussed in the next chapter, high rates of inmigration to cities seem to be associated with high rates of outmigration. A high rate of inmigration of blacks might encourage white outmovement to new homes and suburban schools, and a high rate of outmigration of whites from northern cities could encourage black inmigration by creating housing vacancies. Such processes can feed upon themselves. By 1980 enough blacks had joined the migration to suburbs that the proportion of the nation's blacks living in central cities of metropolitan areas declined for the first time.[11]

Studies of the migrant and nonmigrant black populations in large cities of the North led to a reassessment of some aspects of conventional theories of adjustment and accommodation of migrants to cities. Until the 1970s, assessments of migrant-native differences were predicated on the theory that rural-to-urban migrants arrived with less education, fewer skills, and less experience and familiarity with job-hunting and job-holding, and as a result of these disadvantages of rural birth migrants' earnings throughout life were presumed to remain below those of urban natives.

These expectations led to interpretations that had important implications regarding the origin of urban conditions and the nature and du-

---

[10]Larry Long, "How the Racial Composition of Cities Changes," *Land Economics* 51 (August 1975): 258–267.

[11]Larry Long and Diana DeAre, "The Suburbanization of Blacks," *American Demographics* 3 (September 1981): 16–21 and 44.

ration of black-white inequality. The temptation was to interpret many measures of deteriorating economic conditions and quality of life in a number of large northern cities in the 1950s and 1960s as a consequence, partly, of the volume of black migration from the rural South. At various times, increasing unemployment, crime, welfare dependence, and changes in family composition in large cities of the North in the 1950s and 1960s were attributed in substantial part to the post–World War II influx of southern blacks.[12] According to this view, such urban problems to a large degree originated outside the cities themselves, and reducing or alleviating urban problems would depend on reducing or redirecting migration streams from the South. Such a perspective suggested that time would heal urban problems with the gradual reduction of rural-to-urban migration streams (birth rates in the rural South were seen to be falling and outmigration was changing the age distribution in a way that was unfavorable to continued high fertility).

Another implication of applying past theories of rural-to-urban migration to northern cities in the 1950s and 1960s was that black-white income differences would be diminished as the proportion of the black population born and raised in the urban North increased. Large differences in economic status between blacks and whites in the North were seen as a reflection of the disadvantages of rural birth on the part of blacks, with differences being diminished as more blacks were exposed to the economy and lifestyle of the North.[13]

Both expectations were challenged, however, by research published in the early 1970s. Data from many sources, including the 1960 and 1970 censuses and several large surveys, produced similar and complementary evidence showing that black South-to-North migrants had lower levels of education than otherwise similar northern nonmigrant blacks, but the migrants from the South after a few years of residence were more likely to be employed and less likely to be poor or on welfare than the urban nonmigrants in places of destination. The explanation

---

[12]For references, see Larry Long, "Poverty Status and Receipt of Welfare among Migrants and Nonmigrants in Large Cities," *American Sociological Review* 39 (February 1973): 46–56; and Larry Long and Lynne R. Heltman, "Migration and Income Differences between Black and White Men in the North," *American Journal of Sociology* 80 (May 1975): 1391–1409.

[13]The classic statement of this point of view was by Banfield: "The income of the Census Negro is low as compared to that of the white. However, when one controls for region of origin, rural or urban origin, and education, the difference is greatly reduced. Much of what looks like 'racial' poverty is really 'rural Southern poverty.' " Edward C. Banfield, *The Unheavenly City* (Boston: Little, Brown, 1970), p. 71. Controlling for the variables mentioned in the quotation was found to increase black-white income differences as of 1970, as reported in Long and Heltman, "Migration and Income Differences."

for the greater economic success of the migrants was their stronger attachment to the labor force; in particular, they were more likely to avoid unemployment even if it meant taking lower status jobs than nonmigrant blacks in northern cities. The result was that northern-born blacks were more likely, when employed, to have a white collar occupation, but the southern-born, after a few years of residence in the North, were more likely to be employed and proportionately fewer were on welfare or had incomes below the poverty level. Most studies at this time focused on black migrants to the North because the net migration of whites had already begun to shift to the South.

Quite clearly, traditional theories of migrant-nonmigrant differences in large urban settings were not fully applicable to the black population of northern cities in the late 1950s and 1960s. The evidence for this conclusion was produced by many authors from independent data sources and seemed quite consistent, but an explanatory scheme was never fully developed. One approach was to look at circumstances and conditions at migrants' origins that might contribute to explaining why they were willing to take low-status—perhaps "dead end"—jobs so as to avoid unemployment and welfare dependence more successfully than black urban nonmigrants. The migrants were leaving an environment where expectations from work were modest, leading them to look forward to little from work except a paycheck which, though small by northern standards, was likely to seem satisfactory by what they might have expected in the South.[14] Because the migrants were not well integrated into local communities and were not "street wise," they might be less well informed as to alternatives to working, like how to avail themselves of welfare or unemployment benefits for which they were eligible or how to profit from the underground economy. In other words, not being "assimilated" into the host community seemed to be associated with taking and keeping jobs that might not otherwise have been filled and provided enough income to keep proportionately more of the migrants than the natives off welfare.

Another possibility was that the migrants may have been positively selected on unmeasured variables like motivation, initiative, self-reli-

---

[14]One study used the National Longitudinal Surveys to compare attitudes toward jobs and work among southern-born and northern-born blacks in the North. The conclusion was that in evaluating jobs the migrants gave heavier emphasis to wages than the nonmigrants, who mentioned numerous nonpecuniary aspects of employment, like whether the work is enjoyable, personally rewarding, or allows one to work with congenial co-workers. Arvil V. Adams, and Gilbert Nestel, "Interregional Migration, Education, and Poverty in the Urban Ghetto: Another Look at Black-White Earnings Differentials," *Review of Economics and Statistics* 58 (May 1976): 156–166.

ance, or other attributes that distinguished them from nonmigrants at places of origin or destination. Such attributes are almost never measured, and so their relative importance cannot be accurately assessed. Interpretations of the above-mentioned research findings of this period emphasized an important role of unmeasured variables, suggesting that under some circumstances their influence could overcome the ostensible disadvantages of rural birth. Selective return migration was also a plausible hypothesis, so that perhaps the southern-born who stayed in the North were "doubly selected" by a return of the least qualified. Empirical evidence did not support this hypothesis, however.[15]

Still another approach to explaining observed migrant-nonmigrant differences among northern blacks was that conditions at destination may have handicapped nonmigrants compared with black migrants from the South. The departure of jobs from cities and the infiltration of crime, drugs, and discipline problems in the schools of many inner city neighborhoods may have given nonmigrant children a bad start on life— a situation compounded by city-to-suburb movement of economically successful families and the removal of positive role models from inner city neighborhoods. This view shifted attention to the debilitating effects of cities on nonmigrants in them.

The case of black migrants from the South to the urban North in the late 1950s and 1960s came to illustrate modifications to long-standing generalizations about migrant-nonmigrant differences arising out of the adjustment, accommodation, and assimilation of migrants. Some of the expected disadvantages of migrants were found not to persist beyond a relatively short period of residence in destination cities, and migrant-nonmigrant differences came to be seen as much more complex than previously thought, arising not only out of differences in the characteristics of migrants and nonmigrants but also out of the relative circumstances at origin and destination. Research suggested a need to focus not only on the disadvantages that can be experienced by migrants but also on the disadvantages that can accrue to nonmigrants.

---

[15]One approach was to use census data to compare persons born in the South and living in the North in both 1965 and 1970 with return migrants defined as persons born in the South and living in the North in 1965 but back in the South in 1970. This approach showed positive selectivity of return migration among southern-born blacks even when age was controlled for. The black return migrants to the South were slightly better educated, in fact, than nonreturn black migrants of comparable age. See Larry Long and Kristin A. Hansen, "Selectivity of Black Return Migration to the South," *Rural Sociology* 42 (Fall 1977): 317–331. The obvious limitation to this approach is that the data fail to capture those who returned after a very short stay in the North; for example, a person who left the South in 1966 but returned in 1968 should be considered a return migrant but would not be counted as ever having left the South by the migration question used in the 1970 census.

Poverty Status of Interregional Migrants

Even though some groups of South-to-North migrants fared better economically than comparable groups of nonmigrants in northern cities in the late 1950s and 1960s, did the South still export poverty via migration? There were many reasons for supposing this to be the case, for the South was traditionally the nation's lagging economic region; and even as the region shifted to net inmigration by 1970, it might continue to have net outmigration of low-income persons. Low-income persons might have fewer sources of information than others and might continue along well-beaten migration paths even after relative economic conditions in the North and South had changed. Also, a significant share of the South's poverty population consisted of blacks who might feel that regardless of rates of economic growth in the South, few opportunities were open to them, and they might continue to move North even as some economic indicators came to favor the South.

A suggested policy intervention in the 1960s was that an attack on urban problems in the North might begin in the South. The U.S. government was advised during this period that "the roots of much of the poverty in the metropolitan North are traceable to the rural South" (p. 288) and that "the migration streams originating in the rural South form the crucial link in a system of poverty" (p. 291).[16] The evidence for this point of view consisted of little more than noting low levels of educational attainment and high levels of poverty in the rural South and substantial migration from the region in the 1940s, 1950s, and early 1960s.

The southern region as a whole probably continued to have net outmigration of low-income persons for a few years after its overall net balance shifted from negative to positive. But the South seems to have changed rather quickly in the early 1970s from an exporter to an importer of poverty, according to Table 5.1, which uses the measure of poverty developed for statistical purposes by the federal government in the mid-1960s.

The measure of poverty developed in the 1960s was based on Department of Agriculture data on minimum food needs, and the poverty line was set at three times the dollar cost of a minimum food basket, adjusted for family size and updated annually for inflation.[17] This mea-

---

[16]John F. Kain and Joseph J. Persky, "The North's Stake in Southern Rural Poverty," in President's National Advisory Commission on Rural Poverty, *Rural Poverty in the United States* (Washington, DC: U.S. Government Printing Office, 1968).

[17]For a fuller discussion of the measure of poverty, see, among other publications, U.S. Bureau of the Census, "Characteristics of the Population Below the Poverty Level: 1983" *Current Population Reports*, series P-60, no. 147 (Washington, DC: U.S. Government Printing Office, 1985). For data from the March 1984 CPS (income in 1983), the poverty line for a family of four was $10,178.

TABLE 5.1

*Poverty Status of Migrants to and from the Four Major Regions
of the United States: Selected Periods to 1984 (in thousands)*

	Immigrants[a]		Outmigrants		Net Migration	
	Above Poverty	Below Poverty	Above Poverty	Below Poverty	Above Poverty	Below Poverty
South						
Birth to 1967[b]	4,103	467	6,544	941	−2,441	−474
1968–71 (annual average)	1,076	187	1,025	231	51	−44
March 1975–March 1976	1,014	178	889	100	125	78
March 1980–March 1981	1,076	301	739	151	337	150
March 1981–March 1982	1,237	245	798	214	439	31
March 1982–March 1983	933	277	749	225	184	52
March 1983–March 1984	1,144	254	778	196	366	58
West						
1968–71 (annual average)	818	196	640	88	178	108
March 1975–March 1976	826	141	522	78	304	63
March 1980–March 1981	720	152	580	130	140	22
March 1981–March 1982	784	147	686	133	98	14
March 1982–March 1983	673	208	517	128	156	80
March 1983–March 1984	704	130	703	184	1	−54
Northeast						
1968–71 (annual average)	495	64	655	80	−160	−16
March 1975–March 1976	416	38	589	78	−173	−40
March 1980–March 1981	411	53	583	122	−172	−69
March 1981–March 1982	351	122	585	100	−234	22
March 1982–March 1983	364	75	505	120	−141	−45
March 1983–March 1984	383	104	480	99	−97	5
Midwest						
1968–71 (annual average)	796	115	864	163	−68	−48
March 1975–March 1976	589	81	843	181	−256	−100
March 1980–March 1981	560	90	864	192	−304	−102
March 1981–March 1982	651	142	953	209	−302	−67
March 1982–March 1983	562	99	760	187	−198	−88
March 1983–March 1984	628	193	899	203	−271	−10

[a]Excludes movers from abroad.

[b]Refers to inmigrants, aged 14 and over living in the South at the time of the 1967 Survey of Economic Opportunity but born elsewhere in the United States; and to outmigrants, aged 14 and over born in the South but living elsewhere in the United States in 1967. Parallel tabulations were not prepared for the other three regions; data are from Bowles et al. (1973), pp. 112–117. Other data refer to persons aged 1 and over and come from the Current Population Survey. CPS data are not available for 1972–75 or 1977–80. See text for definition of poverty and its limitations.

sure has been regularly reported in the Census Bureau's Current Population Surveys, which are about as close as one can come to developing a time series to measure poverty status of interregional migrants at the time they move.[18] The well-known limitation of the initial poverty measure is that it failed to include noncash benefits, which for the poor can include food stamps, subsidized housing, and other services provided at no cost to the recipient or at below-market prices. Noncash benefits have increased much faster than cash benefits, and in recent years attempts have been made to adjust the measure to take noncash benefits into account, although the data in Table 5.1 have not been adjusted.

The data suggest that the southern region as a whole did indeed export poverty until sometime in the early to mid-1970s. As of 1967, there were an estimated 467,000 non–southern-born persons in the South with incomes below the poverty level; other regions had 941,000 southern-born persons below the poverty level, suggesting a cumulative net outmigration of 474,000 southern-born persons below the poverty level. Of course, the South at this time was an even larger exporter of nonpoor persons—2,441,000 according to Table 5.1. For 1968–71 the South probably continued to have net outmigration of persons below the poverty level and net inmigration of persons above it at the time they moved. Since the mid-1970s the South appears to have been an annual net importer of persons below the poverty level. Hence, after changing to overall net inmigration in the 1960s, the southern region continued to export poverty via migration for up to ten years.

The Midwest seems to have had net outmigration of poor and nonpoor persons rather steadily from the late 1960s to the early 1980s. The Northeast has steadily had net outmigration of the nonpoor during this period and seems also to have had net outmigration of the poor, although the Northeast's estimated net outmigration of the poor is low and the numbers are subject to considerable sampling variability. The West has tended to have net inmigration of both poor and nonpoor, although the more recent data show a fluctuating pattern due partly to sampling variability.

Knowing whether a region is exporting or importing poverty on a "current" basis is useful for purposes of policy planning and evaluation, but it is equally important to know how many of the low-income migrants from a region remain poor and become a burden on their areas of destination. The nation's poverty population is a fluid population that undergoes considerable turnover. Some of the interregional migrants

---

[18]The Current Population Survey measures migration and income over nearly overlapping 12-month intervals. Taken in March, the survey typically asks about migration in the 12 months preceding the survey and income during the preceding calendar year.

who are poor when they move are college students or persons leaving college to take their first job and after a few paychecks will become nonpoor. Others are persons who may have been unemployed for quite a while and are moving to take a job which will make them nonpoor. Retirees with low incomes could be motivated to move to the South where living costs are low and they might inflate the number of poor inmigrants, but other evidence suggests that their influence on these figures is quite small.[19]

The real test of whether a region imports or exports poverty is not only how many low-income persons annually move in or out, but how long they remain poor and whether they return or move on to other regions.[20] One might expect areas with growing numbers of jobs and net inmigration of nonpoor persons to have net inmigration of the poor also, and the data in Table 5.1 generally seem to support this idea for the recent past, at least for the four large regions.

Do Welfare Benefits Stimulate Migration?

An important countervailing theory to the idea that the poor and nonpoor move in similar directions is that migration of the poor (at least a significant portion of the poor) is governed to an important degree by differential availability of public assistance and various forms of welfare benefits administered by local areas. This idea is a variation of the Tiebout hypothesis, which asserts that people do indeed "vote with their feet" and move to areas that, within the budgetary constraints of their household, conform to the household's needs, values, and interests.[21] According to this view, parents with children who attend or will attend public schools are likely to move to neighborhoods with good schools, subject to budgetary and other constraints (like location of work). Similarly, it was thought that the poor would be attracted to areas that of-

[19]Larry Long, "Interregional Migration of the Poor: Some Recent Changes," *Current Population Reports*, series P-23, no. 73 (Washington, DC: U.S. Government Printing Office, 1978).

[20]Data on duration of residence, as collected in the 1976 Survey of Income and Education, allow some insights into short-term versus long-term interregional transmissions of poverty. Data from the SIE showed that for each of the four regions migrants with a duration of residence of two or three years were less likely to be poor than those with a duration of less than one year; this information suggests that the annual figures exaggerate the amount of long-term poverty that is interregionally transferred by migration. In none of the four regions, however, did the likelihood of being poor seem to vary inversely with duration of residence. See Long, "Interregional Migration of the Poor."

[21]Charles M. Tiebout, "A Pure Theory of Local Expenditures," *Journal of Political Economy* 64 (October 1956): 416–424. How the Tiebout model came to be expanded to migration research in general, and the presumed welfare-migration connection in particular, is discussed in Richard J. Cebula, *The Determinants of Human Migration* (Lexington, MA: Lexington Books, 1979), pp. 91–103.

fered generous welfare payments, either in the form of high monthly benefits or the ease of getting on or staying on welfare.

By the late 1960s there was considerable belief that the high level of welfare benefits in some northern states was inducing some migration that otherwise would not have occurred. A common practice was to compare the meager average monthly AFDC (Aid to Families with Dependent Children) payments in some southern states (particularly Mississippi and South Carolina) with the much higher amounts—often three to four times higher—in some northern states like New York. In the early 1960s the South was having net outmigration and welfare rolls were rising much faster in New York and many other states than in Mississippi and its southern neighbors; many people believed that the two trends were related via migration.[22]

From a behavioral point of view, one might argue that low-income persons in the South were aware of higher benefit levels in the North but were unable to discount them for the higher costs of living and thus were "lured" to the North. Alternatively, one might argue that potential migrants may have been aware of higher benefits in the North but migrated for employment reasons, only to lack needed skills and eventually fall back on welfare.

Both conservatives and liberals seemed to agree that some kind of connection existed. A positive view was that welfare benefits in the North assisted some migrants (or many migrants, depending on one's point of view) during a period of adjustment while searching for employment and housing. A negative view was that the high cost of such assistance represented a tax that the South was imposing upon the North. Either view might be interpreted as support for some kind of nationalization of welfare or at least some reduction of differences among states in the size of benefits offered or the administration of programs.[23]

---

[22]References to expert opinion as well as endorsements of this hypothesis in popular magazines are given in Larry Long, "Poverty Status and Receipt of Welfare among Migrants and Nonmigrants in Large Cities."

[23]Michael C. Barth, "Migration and Income Maintenance," in President's Commission on Income Maintenance, *Technical Studies*, (Washington, DC: U.S. Government Printing Office, 1970). One study specifically concluded that the provisions in President Nixon's proposal for a Family Assistance Plan would "reduce somewhat the black migration from the South to northern metropolitan areas" (p. 225). John F. Kain and Robert Schafer, "Income Maintenance, Migration, and Regional Growth," *Public Policy* 20 (Spring 1972): 199–225. A later proposal for a negative income tax allegedly would "(1) increase the rate of migration, (2) induce people to move to locations with better environments, and (3) induce people to reduce their hours of work." Michael C. Keeley, "The Effect of a Negative Income Tax on Migration," *Journal of Human Resources* 15 (Fall 1980): 695–706. Another study, using a different data source, concluded that "programs such as the negative income tax effectively relax the cost and risk constraints facing poor households." Richard L. Kaluzny, "Determinants of Household Migration: A Comparative Study by Race and Poverty Level," *Review of Economics and Statistics* 57 (August 1975): 269–274.

The belief that generous welfare payments in some jurisdictions might attract inmigration that otherwise might not occur or restrict outmigration—and perpetuate poverty—among current recipients was strong enough that some northern jurisdictions introduced duration-of-residence requirements (usually one year) as a condition for being eligible for welfare. Such requirements were in a few states written into legislation and constitute one of the few instances of recent legislative attempts to restrict migration. The constitutionality of such legislation was challenged in several cases which were ultimately decided in 1969 by the Supreme Court, which found the duration-of-residence requirements to be unconstitutional as a violation of the Equal Protection Clause of the Fourteenth Amendment or the Due Process Clause of the Fifth Amendment.[24]

Research never fully or clearly identified how much, if any, migration was welfare-induced or what effect it had on localities. The reason was that at the time the issue was so intense (say, from the mid-1960s to the mid-1970s) there were no data allowing researchers to observe poverty status, use of public assistance, and migration of a representative (and sufficiently large) sample of the entire population over reasonably long periods of time. Censuses provided large, representative data sets and were tabulated by income, but the obvious problems were that family status was measured at the time of the census (April), income was measured over the preceding calendar year, and migration could have occurred at any time (or more than once) during the preceding five years. Nevertheless, the supply of such tabulations led to regression models attempting to describe how the migration of low-income families differed from that of middle- or high-income families.[25] The results of such macro models were ambiguous.

Virtually every study, however, suggested that the chronically poor probably tended to drift toward (or settle in) high-welfare states. Whether such apparent effects were large enough or occurred with sufficient regularity and consistency to have important effects on public programs was the major unanswered question. More recent research, using a variety of data sources and statistical methods, tends to reinforce the view that inmigration of the poor accounted for very little of the increase in the welfare population in high-benefit areas, but the chroni-

---

[24]Margaret K. Rosenheim, "The Constitutionality of Durational Residence Requirements," *Social Service Review* 44 (March 1970): 82–93.

[25]For example, Frederick B. Glantz, "Migration and Economic Opportunity: The Case of the Poor," *New England Economic Review* (March–April 1973): 14–19; and Frederick B. Glantz, "The Determinants of Intermetropolitan Migration of the Poor," *Annals of Regional Science* 9 (July 1975): 25–39.

cally poor, when they do move, may exhibit a modest tendency to gravitate toward high-benefit areas.[26]

Do Welfare Benefits Inhibit Migration?

By the late 1970s the debate had changed from whether geographical variability in public welfare programs stimulated migration to whether welfare benefits inhibited it. As reduction in the nation's poverty population began to slow, the concern shifted to whether the poor were sufficiently responsive to job opportunities in different areas and whether they were tied to cities that had declining industries and declining opportunities for welfare recipients to escape the benevolent bonds of public assistance. A review in the early 1980s by the Committee on National Urban Policy of the National Research Council said little about the effects of geographical variability in inducing or redirecting migration of the poor. Instead, it wondered if the U.S. population—poor and nonpoor alike—was becoming immobile and insufficiently responsive to employment opportunities which had expanded greatly in the 1970s in the South and in many rural locations. The review concluded that ". . . differences among areas in worker support systems, ranging from unemployment insurance, union contracts containing callback provisions for senior workers, *and differences in state welfare benefits . . .* tend to reduce the propensity of workers to strike out for a new community and an uncertain future."[27] [Emphasis added.] Several strategies for increasing worker mobility were suggested, including a national job information system and national assumption of welfare costs. Part of the appeal of the latter proposal was that "the benefits to the nation in income gains from increased mobility could conceivably offset some of the cost."[28]

The report of the National Research Council's Committee on National Urban Policy appeared after a presidential commission's report on urban policy, *Urban America in the Eighties.* This controversial report focused on the then-prevailing rapid rates of economic growth in the South and West and in a number of rural locations as signs of an economic realignment and restructuring, and it looked upon migration as a necessary corollary of growth. Trying to revitalize declining cities

---

[26]Edward M. Gramlich and Deborah S. Laren, "Migration and Income Redistribution Responsibilities," *Journal of Human Resources* 19, no. 4 (1984): 489–511.

[27]Committee on National Urban Policy, National Research Council, *Rethinking Urban Policy* (Washington, DC: National Acacemy Press, 1983), p. 111.

[28]Committee on National Urban Policy, *Rethinking Urban Policy,* p. 118.

through massive federal subsidies was looked upon as wasteful relative to other strategies. It recommended that "the numerous poor and un-skilled urban residents" be assisted

> . . . by removing barriers to mobility that prevent people from migrat-ing to locations of economic opportunity, and by providing migration assistance to those who wish and need it. People-to-jobs strategies, whether by retraining or relocation or both, should receive the same degree of emphasis that is now reserved for jobs-to-people strategies.[29]

The two reports illustrate the changed emphasis from the migra-tion-promoting to the migration-inhibiting effects of areal differences in public assistance programs. The reasons for the shift in focus included the changes in observed migration patterns (net inmigration of both the poor and the nonpoor to the South by the mid-1970s, as discussed ear-lier) and highly publicized changes in the composition of the poverty-level population (more single-parent families and fewer married-couple families). Because of the changes in composition, more poverty-level families qualify and have been accepted on the welfare rolls; this fact alone should increase the migration-reducing effects relative to the mi-gration-increasing effects of public assistance programs.

Throughout the period from, say, the early 1960s to the early 1980s welfare payments probably never did have the migration-inducing ef-fects they were popularly believed to have for the nonwelfare poor. But for the poor on welfare, some migration-inhibiting effects probably ex-isted throughout the period. Figure 5.4 shows age-specific rates of mov-ing within counties, between counties within a state, and between states for three groups of female, single-parent families for 1968–71: those who were nonpoor and not receiving public assistance, those who were below the poverty level and received public assistance, and those who were below the poverty level and did not receive public assistance. The data come from tabulations of the microdata files of Current Pop-ulation Surveys in 1968, 1969, 1970, and 1971; they were cumulated in order to increase the sample size and adjusted to reflect constant dollars. These data represent family status as of March, mobility status mea-sured over the preceding 12 months, and income, poverty status, and receipt of cash payments from public assistance programs measured over the preceding calendar year. Poverty status was computed in the same manner as discussed previously. Figure 5.4 is limited to female single-parent families because most states at that time banned husband-

---

[29]President's Commission for a National Agenda for the Eighties, Urban America in the Eighties (Washington, DC: U.S. Government Printing Office, 1980), p. 5.

FIGURE 5.4

Annual Rates of Moving Within Counties, Between Counties Within a State, and
Between States, for Families Maintained by a Woman (No Husband Present),
According to Age, Poverty Status, and Receipt of Cash Payments
from Public Assistance: 1968–71

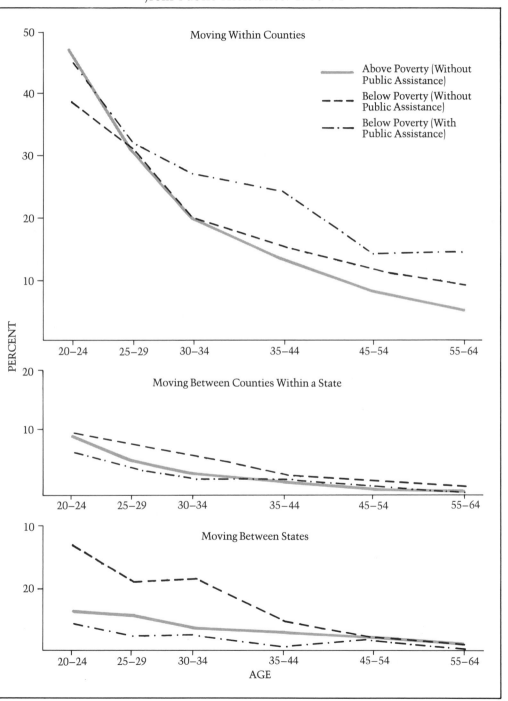

wife couples from welfare programs. The time period probably represents the peak of interest in the hypothesis that welfare payments in high-benefit states were encouraging some migration.

On the one hand, these data might be cited as evidence that the welfare poor lead residentially unstable lives. The three groups have about equally high rates of intracounty moving at ages 20–30, but at later ages the welfare poor seem less able than others to settle down. Of course, for many of the welfare poor the proximate cause of their getting on welfare may have been an eviction, a family breakup, or some other event connected with residential mobility. The point is that the welfare poor seem to make more short-distance moves between ages 30 and 65 than the nonpoor or the nonwelfare poor. Still, all three groups exhibit some declines in intracounty rates of moving after the peak in the early 20s, testifying to the near universality of the generalization that rates of residential mobility reach a peak at this age group and then decline, perhaps increasing somewhat at very advanced ages as institutionalization or health problems force the very old to change their living arrangements.

On the other hand, these data can be cited as evidence that the welfare poor may to some degree be immobilized insofar as interstate migration is concerned. The bottom panel of Figure 5.4 suggests that the welfare poor are somewhat less likely than the nonpoor or the nonwelfare poor to move between states, at least for female single parents between the ages of 20 and 54. Hence, receipt of welfare does seem to tie a family to the state where benefits are received, but the effects appear to be quite small. The most important message communicated by the bottom panel of Figure 5.4 is that the nonwelfare poor (female-headed families, in this case) seem to have higher rates of interstate migration than either the welfare poor or the nonpoor, at least up to around age 50.

For female-headed families, there do not appear to be any meaningful differences among the three groups in rates of moving between counties within a state (the middle panel of Figure 5.4). All three groups appear to be similarly likely to make moves of this type, and the rates appear to decline with age.

These data are useful partly to illustrate the difficulties of disentangling temporal priority (if not causality) among changes in residence, marital status, and use of public assistance. Some of the low-income women supporting families at any given time will later remarry and become nonpoor or at least get off welfare and thereby acquire different patterns of residential mobility and migration. For others, welfare is still only a transitional state, arising out of a family breakup or emergency. The cross-sectional views featured in Figure 5.4 give only a glimpse of a complex sequence of events that can be fully captured only with longitudinal data.

Should Migration of the Poor Be Subsidized?

Welfare can tie the poor down not only by giving them a "stake" in their area of current residence, but in other ways, too. Almost all public assistance programs prohibit the cumulation of savings or assets, and possession of a car or only a few hundred dollars in savings can be justification for removing a family from the rolls. The effect of such administrative regulations is to keep the welfare poor from acquiring the resources to finance a job search or migration. There seems to be consensus among policy analysts that an effect along these lines exists (even if it cannot be quantified) and because of the long-term movement of entry-level jobs from central cities some type of assisted migration would benefit cities and the chronically poor in them.[30]

Subsidized job-search or relocation assistance has often been discussed with respect to two groups: (1) experienced workers who become unemployed as a result of plant closures, technological change, or international competition, and (2) persons who live in areas of persistent economic hardship, like Appalachia or the rural South, and are unlikely to secure employment where they live. A number of experimental programs aimed at the latter group have been tried from time to time as a means of reducing poverty and increasing national output by matching workers and jobs.

Evaluating these programs has been difficult, however.[31] Although

[30]Franklin J. James and John P. Blair, "The Role of Labor Mobility in a National Urban Policy," *American Planning Association Journal* 49 (Summer 1983): 307–315; John D. Kasarda, "Urban Change and Minority Opportunities," in Paul E. Peterson, ed., *The New Urban Reality* (Washington, DC: Brookings Institution, 1985); Gordon L. Clark, *Interregional Migration, National Policy, and Social Justice* (Totowa, NJ: Rowman & Allanheld, 1983), chap. 3.

[31]Problems in evaluating programs of the 1960s are illustrated in H. Tyrone Black, Loren C. Scott, Lewis H. Smith, and William A. Sirmon, "On Moving the Poor: Subsidizing Relocation," *Industrial Relations* 14 (February 1975): 63–77; P. B. Beaumont, "On Moving the Poor: Subsidizing Relocation" [comment], *Industrial Relations* 16 (February 1977): 107–110; and H. Tyrone Black, Loren C. Scott, Lewis H. Smith, and William Sirmon, "Reply to Mr. Beaumont," *Industrial Relations* 16 (February 1977): 111–113. A strong case for relocation assistance for unemployed workers, based on the Employment and Training Administration's Job Search and Relocation Assistance program begun in 1976, is presented by Charles F. Mueller, "Migration of the Unemployed: A Relocation Assistance Program," *Monthly Labor Review* 104 (April 1981): 62–64. All relocation offices were located in southern states, and Mueller reports (p. 62) that the program seemed to enhance mobility "for the young, black persons, men, and persons with lower levels of education."

the costs are known, measuring the benefits tends to be elusive. Almost any return migration may be interpreted as program failure, and a perennial question is whether the programs simply pay for migration that would have occurred anyway. With regard to the latter criticism, many of the relocatees do tend to be young, single persons who, following national patterns, are likely to move, but focusing efforts specifically at hard-to-move groups (for example, families with children) will likely increase costs of the program and may adversely affect other measures of program success. A difference between the more recent calls for relocation assistance and past programs is that the more recent ones would likely face even more obstacles in that they directly address the welfare poor, and to be successful programs may have to provide many other services—for example, remedial education, training in specific job skills, and instruction in basic work habits. Also, the slower rate of economic growth and changed economic structure and circumstances (like competition from immigrants—legal or illegal—for low-wage jobs) would probably make it more difficult now than in the past to demonstrate program successes.

Moreover, such programs may not enjoy widespread public support according to Gallup polls. In 1974, 1975, 1977, and 1981 the Gallup Poll asked this question of its sample of adults (1,500 to 1,600 persons aged 18 and over):

> A plan has been proposed to invite *welfare families now living in ghetto areas of large cities* to move to areas of the nation where living conditions and job opportunities are better. The government would pay the costs of moving as well as living costs until these families found jobs. Would you favor or oppose such a plan?[32] [Emphasis added.]

Those favoring the unnamed plan were 48 percent of the sample in 1974, 47 percent in 1975, 49 percent in 1977, and 44 percent in 1981. Those opposng the plan varied between 42 and 48 percent of the sample, with 7 to 9 percent having no opinion. No clear trend is evident, except that less than a majority of the adult population seemed to favor subsidizing the migration of welfare families.

In 1985 the question was changed in potentially significant ways. The target population was changed from "welfare families now living in ghetto areas" to "unemployed people now living in large cities." And instead of saying that the government would "pay the costs of moving as well as living costs until these families found jobs," the question

---

[32]Gallup Poll, *Gallup Report*, no. 188, May 1981, pp. 32–33.

simply stated that "the Federal government would provide housing vouchers *to help pay* the family rent anywhere in the U.S." (emphasis added).[33] The changed wording would seem to broaden the appeal of the question by not limiting the target population simply to the welfare poor and by suggesting lower costs for the relocation assistance. Fifty-one percent said they would favor this plan—possibly a slight increase over the earlier version. Forty percent opposed the 1985 version, and 9 percent had no opinion.

Young persons, blacks, and low-income households seem most likely to favor relocation assistance. Especially noteworthy is the inverse association between household income and support for programs providing relocation assistance. The most recent version of the Gallup question asked about relocation assistance for "unemployed people" and was favored by 60 percent of persons in households with under $10,000 annual income but was favored by only 41 percent of those in households with annual incomes of $50,000 or more. A similar relationship characterized response to the earlier version of the question about relocation assistance for "welfare families living in ghetto areas." When the "welfare families" version was asked in 1981, it was favored by 55 percent of persons in households with an annual income under $5,000 but only 36 percent of those in households with an income of $25,000 or more. And when the same "welfare families" question was asked in 1974, it was favored by 66 percent of persons in households with an income under $3,000 but only 41 percent of those with an income of $20,000 or more.[34] These successive surveys suggest that support for assisted migration is strongest among those who probably view themselves or friends and relatives as likely beneficiaries, and support seems weakest among persons who view themselves as having to pay for such a program.

Proposals for the federal government to increase the mobility of the unemployed or the poor go back a long way in time and have been tried on a limited basis. The more recent proposals may be an idea whose time has come again as a way of aiding both places (large cities) and people, but the drawbacks are still the difficulty of measuring benefits and what seems like a lack of broad support in the population at large.

---

[33]The full question in 1985 was: "A plan has been proposed to help unemployed people now living in large cities to move to areas where job opportunities are better. Under the plan, the Federal government would provide housing vouchers to help pay the family rent anywhere in the U.S. Would you favor or oppose such a plan?" The cross-tabulations discussed in the text are presented in the *Gallup Report*, no. 239, August 1985, pp. 29–30.

[34]Gallup Poll, *Gallup Opinion Index*, no. 116, February 1975.

Selectivity of Migration: Regional Views

Much of this chapter has focused on migration of the low-income and welfare populations, but an assessment of the effects of migration obviously requires looking at a much broader spectrum of migrants and the populations they leave and join. Concern with whether an area's stock of human capital is being eroded or augmented typically tends to focus on the migration of persons with high levels of education, valuable skills, or entrepreneurial or other sought-after talents. Gain or loss of such persons can effect gradual but profound changes over long periods of time.

This recognition of the heterogeneity of migrants and the possibility that regions of outmigration might be losing their "best" people is part of what is sometimes called the cumulative-disequilibrium model of migration and regional development. The neoclassical model implied convergence as labor and capital flowed to regions offering higher marginal returns, until returns were equalized. But if economically depressed regions lose human capital to other regions, they can in effect subsidize growth elsewhere and convergence of factor returns may not occur.[35]

In asking who leaves and the effect on an area's population, one possibility is that areas of outmigration may tend to lose persons at the educational extremes. That is, some areas may have a higher-than-average exodus of persons with little education and few reasons to stay and also a higher-than-average exodus of those with high educational potential who depart for greater opportunities elsewhere. Those left behind may be persons in the middle with strong ties to the area, like location-specific capital or other assets. The evidence in Chapter 2 on migration differentials seems to provide little support for this hypothesis because for the nation as a whole the association between years of school completed and the probability of moving between states was strong and positive (Table 2.4). But this national pattern could be misleading if it obscures widely varying regional patterns. Another reason for thinking that the relationship between educational level and outmigration may not always be linear is the belief that some states may have in effect encouraged the least-well-educated to leave by offering few services (like public assistance or subsidized housing) to retain them. Their outmigration from areas of origin could be induced, in a Tiebout-like

---

[35]The neoclassical and cumulative-disequilibrium models are reviewed in Clark (*Interregional Migration, National Policy, and Social Justice*), who demonstrates many exceptions to expectations derived from a strictly neoclassical approach to migration and argues for some interventionist policies rather than rely entirely on market forces and migration to equalize factor returns.

fashion, by other areas that offer services appealing to persons with little education and limited ability to compete in labor markets.

As in Chapter 2, the census measure of years of school completed provides the only test for the occurrence of a U-shaped outmigration rate. The nine divisions are the smallest geographical areas for which tabulations on educational levels of inmigrants, outmigrants, and migration streams were prepared from the four censuses that have collected comparable migration data over five-year intervals, and only the 25–34 age group is common to these tabulations. For this age group, outmigration rates specific for years of school completed at the census date (that is, the end of the migration interval) were computed on an "at risk" basis and are displayed in Figure 5.5 for each division for 1935–40, 1955–60, 1965–70, and 1975–80. These materials are a prelude to identifying the "best-educated" and "worst-educated" migration streams and their effects on educational levels in each division.

The change in the enumeration of college students after the 1940 census probably does not seriously bias comparison with later data. In 1940 college students were counted as resident at their parents' address but at their school address thereafter. At each census some 25-to-34-year-olds reported their school address as their previous residence regardless of where the census might have counted them when they were in school.

For each of the four migration intervals and for each division except the Pacific there appears to be a strong, positive association between educational level and probability of moving to another division. Persons with four or more years of college are sometimes three to four times as likely to leave their division of residence than persons who finished grade school but went no further. For the Pacific states (California, Oregon, Washington and, beginning in 1960, Alaska and Hawaii) the association between educational level and outmigration is weaker but still positive. Why persons with college degrees are only modestly more likely to leave the Pacific division than persons with less than a high school education is not clear. The Pacific division since the 1930s seems to have had below-average rates of outmigration of persons with college degrees, whereas residents of the Pacific states with less than a high school education seem to have outmigration rates not too different from similarly educated persons in other divisions.

There is no evidence of a U-shaped relationship between years of school completed and rate of outmigration. For the East North Central division (Ohio, Michigan, Indiana, Illinois, and Wisconsin) there seem to be few differences in outmigration rates for persons with 0–8, 9–11, or 12 years of school, but thereafter more years of schooling seem to be associated with higher rates of exodus. The positive association between

FIGURE 5.5

*Rates of Outmigration from Each Division, for Persons Aged 25–34,
by Level of Education: 1935–40, 1955–60, 1965–70, and 1975–80*

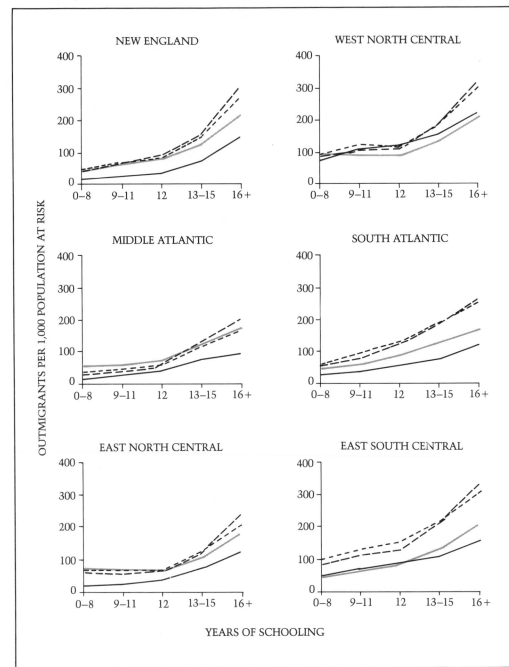

FIGURE 5.5 *(continued)*

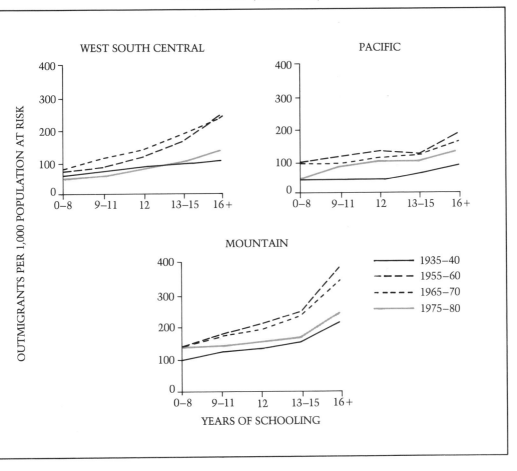

educational level and likelihood of migrating over long distances appears to be geographically widespread since at least the 1930s and has characterized regions of net inmigration as well as net outmigration.

Two qualifications need to be noted. One is the fact that the geographical divisions featured in Figure 5.5 are large and if data were available for smaller areas like towns or counties one might find evidence of a U-shaped curve of outmigration. Also, the data are limited to persons aged 25–34 at the time of the census and who could have been 20 to 29 when they moved. Areas that simultaneously lose their "best and worst" through migration possibly do so as some drop out of school and other leave at age 18, immediately after high school graduation. If this happens, it would not be reflected in the data used for Figure 5.5.

Rates of inmigration were also calculated on an "at risk" basis but are not presented here. They showed a strong and positive association with years of school completed for each of the nine divisions except the East South Central (Mississippi, Alabama, Kentucky, and Tennessee). The probability of migrating to the East South Central division showed only a modest, but still positive, association with migrants' educational level.

As might be expected, the nine divisions are more alike in terms of inmigration and outmigration of the highly educated than the poorly educated. The greater mobility of college graduates over long distances generates greater similarity among areas, but it also generates more criss-crossing moves that are often canceling. Interdivisional migration of persons with less than a high school education is more nearly uni-directional and tends more clearly to follow established channels with comparatively small countercurrents.

Streams of the Best-Educated (and Other) Migrants

The educational level of migrants from a region should be expected to reflect the educational level of the region's population, after control-ling for age. This expectation is generally borne out in Figure 5.6, which maps the five (out of 72) interdivisional migration streams with the low-est educational levels, and Figure 5.7, which maps the five migration streams with the highest educational levels (again restricted to persons aged 25–34).

Historically, the East South Central division (Mississippi, Alabama, Tennessee, and Kentucky) and the West South Central division (Texas, Oklahoma, Louisiana, and Arkansas) have contained areas of low edu-cational attainment. Not surprisingly, in the late 1930s these two divi-sions accounted for migration streams with extensive representation of persons of very limited educations. In the late 1930s more than half of all 25-to-34-year-olds moving from the East South Central states to the more industrialized East North Central states had completed fewer than eight years of schooling and probably were only marginally literate. Other streams of poorly educated migrants from the East South Central states during this period went to the West North Central division (nearly 50 percent had under eight years of school) and to the South Atlantic division (43.5 percent had under eight years of school). The West South Central states sent streams of poorly educated migrants to the Mountain and Pacific states. However, for each of these areas of origin, the outmigration rate was positively associated with migrants' educational level, and the poorly educated migrants leaving the East South Central and West South Central states were less likely to depart than persons with higher educational levels.

The map for 1955–60 shows considerable similarity to the one for 1935–40. Three of the five streams with high concentrations of persons with limited education still originated in the East South Central division and still terminated in the East North Central, West North Central, and South Atlantic divisions. Another stream of poorly educated migrants still went from the West South Central states to the Pacific states. The major change is the appearance of a stream of poorly educated migrants going from the more industrialized and better educated East North Central states to the East South Central states. This stream at first seems puzzling since the East South Central states at that time were more highly rural and offered very few services, benefits, or other attractions for persons with very little formal education. The explanation for the arrow from the East North Central to the East South Central states in 1955–60 is return migration. More than half of these migrants were born in the East South Central states and, in a sense, were "going home." This migration stream is an "echo" of past migration streams.

The data for 1955–60 illustrate rising levels of educational attainment. In 1935–40, 53.8 percent of migrants from the East South Central division to the East North Central division had only a grade-school education, but by 1955–60 only 34.8 percent of migrants in this stream had this level of education. The other streams also showed considerable reduction in the proportion of migrants possessing this minimum amount of education.

By 1975–80 the stream weighted by return migrants from the East North Central states to the East South Central states took first place in the ranking of interdivisional streams of migrants with the lowest educational credentials. Also by 1975–80 the long-standing stream of poorly educated migrants from the West South Central to the Pacific division was replaced by one in the opposite direction—again reflecting a strong influence of return migration.

The 1975–80 data demonstrate continued rises in educational levels. By then, persons with no more than an eighth-grade education represented at most only about 5 or 6 percent of the 25-to-34-year-old migrants moving between divisions. Persons at this age and with this low level of education had at times represented 50 percent of migrants in some streams in the 1930s.

The well-educated, as shown in Figure 5.7, have traveled different paths, as might be expected. In 1935–40 the five migration streams with the best-educated persons aged 25–34 all originated or terminated in New England. In 1935–40 the best-educated migration streams con-

FIGURE 5.6

*The Five Interdivisional Migration Streams Showing the Percentage of Migrants
Aged 25–34 with 0–8 Years of School Completed:
1935–40, 1955–60, 1965–70, and 1975–80*

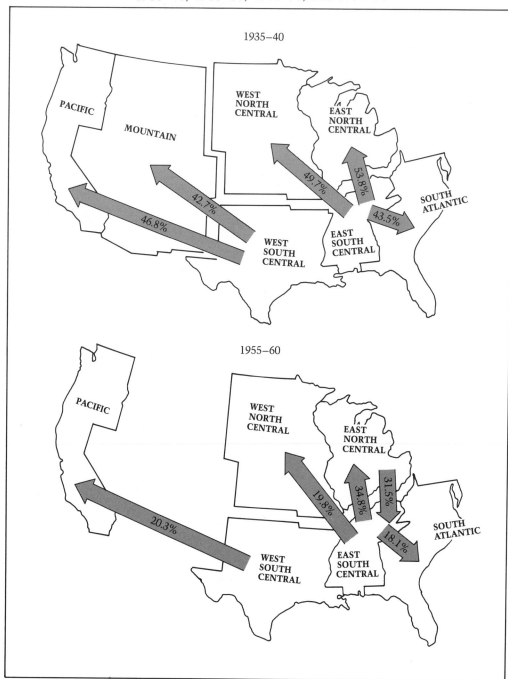

FIGURE 5.6 *(continued)*

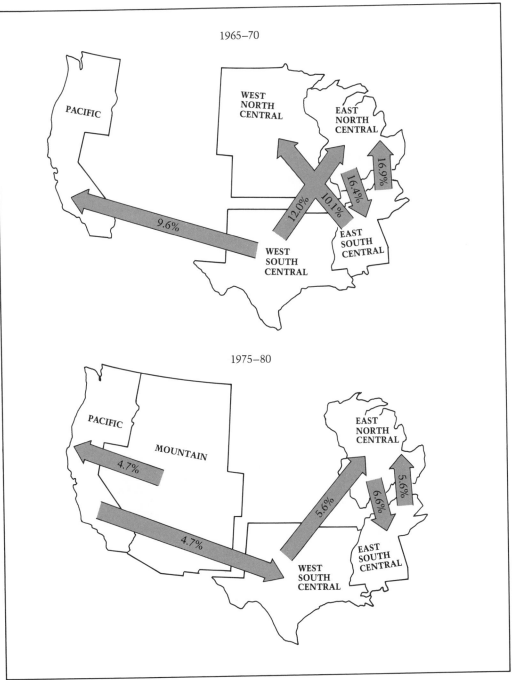

FIGURE 5.7

The Five Interdivisional Migration Streams Showing the Percentage of Migrants Aged 25–34 with Four or More Years of College: 1935–40, 1955–60, 1965–70, and 1975–80

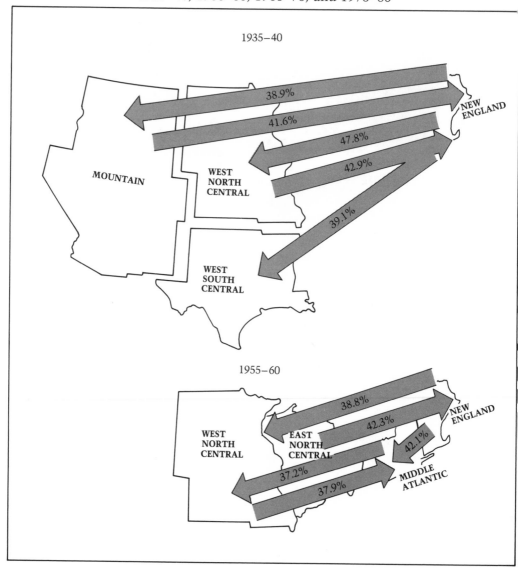

FIGURE 5.7 *(continued)*

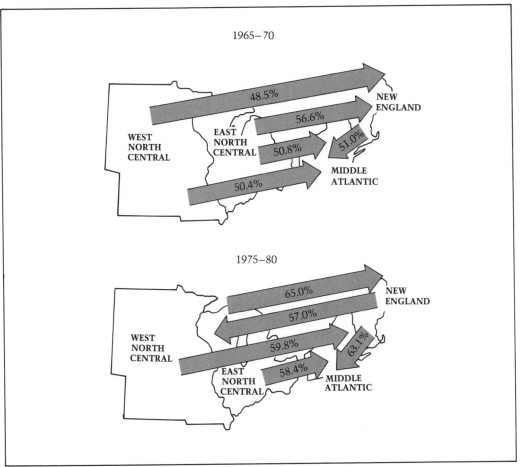

1965–70

1975–80

sisted of population exchanges between New England and the Mountain states, the West North Central states, and the West South Central states. The prominent role of New England as the origin or terminus of the best-educated migrants results from the export-industry role played by New England's institutions of higher education.

College graduates represented close to 40 percent of all 25-to-34-year-old migrants in some migration streams to and from New England in the late 1930s. For that time, these were extraordinarily well-educated persons. There were proportionately as many college graduates in some migration streams from New England as there were persons with only an eighth-grade education leaving the East South Central states in the late 1930s, at least for this age group.

By 1955–60 New England was playing a somewhat less prominent role and the Middle Atlantic states had become more prominent in migration streams with many college graduates. Then and later, the interdivisional streams of the best-educated migrants were entirely within the North, representing movement to or from New England, the Middle Atlantic division, the East North Central division, and the West North Central division. Interestingly, the best-educated migration streams in 1955–60 tended to have proportionately somewhat fewer college graduates than the best-educated streams in 1935–40.

Since the 1960s the best-educated migration streams have continued to be movements within the North. In 1965–70 and 1975–80 the best-educated interdivisional migration stream among persons aged 25–34 was from the East North Central division to New England. Nearly 57 percent of the migrants in this stream in 1965–70 had a college degree, as did 65 percent in 1975–80. In general, for the last 20 years the streams of the mostly highly educated migrants have followed a few well-worn paths among northern states, whereas the poorly educated migrants travel along more paths, some of which represent return flows of poorly educated migrants in previous periods of time.

Effects of Migration on Educational Levels

Granted that college graduates and persons with an eighth-grade education have traveled different migration paths, an unanswered question is how their movements affect educational levels of different areas of the country. Has migration tended to raise the educational level of some areas and lower it in others? Census data offer a way of answering this question. For each of the five-year migration intervals, one can estimate the educational level at the beginning of the interval by taking the end-of-period population at each educational level and adding to it outmigrants at that educational level and then subtracting inmigrants. In Table 5.2 the results of these data manipulations are shown. Movers from abroad have been excluded from both the end-of-period and beginning-of-period populations, and persons not reporting residence five years earlier were also excluded from the 1940, 1960, and 1970 census data. For each of the four migration intervals, the columns of the table show net migration, the percentage distribution of the beginning-of-period population according to years of school completed, and the end-of-period population distributed according to years of school completed.

Comparisons of the beginning-of-period and end-of-period populations seem to suggest small changes attributable to migration, but even small changes can cumulate over time to have significant effects. A fairly consistent effect since the 1950s is for the East South Central states to lose college graduates through migration and to have the proportion of college graduates in their population lowered as a result of migration. Of course, the proportion of college graduates in the population of the East South Central division has risen over the decades simply because a rising proportion of population has enrolled in and completed college. But since the 1950s the increase in the proportion of college graduates in the East South Central division has been offset to some degree by net outmigration of college graduates. The irony, of course, is that even though the worst-educated migration streams have tended to originate in the East South Central states, migration seems to have done more to erode the number of college graduates in the region than the number of persons with only an eighth-grade education.

Consider the effect of migration in 1955–60 on the proportion of the East South Central division's 25-to-34-year-old population with only a grade school education and the proportion with college degrees. At that time the low educational levels in the East South Central states were highly publicized and, as mentioned earlier, were sometimes cited as the "source" of poverty, unemployment, or other urban problems in the North. As can be seen in Table 5.2, the East South Central states had net outmigration of persons with 0–8 years of school completed, but there was also net outmigration of persons with 16 or more years of school completed. The net outmigration of persons at the bottom of the educational distribution had negligible effect on the proportion of the division's population with 0–8 years of schooling. About 34 percent of the 1955 population had this level of education, as did 34 percent of the 1960 population. Though smaller in absolute terms, the net outmigration of persons with 16 or more years of schooling lowered the proportion of the population at this educational level from 7.9 percent to 7.5 percent. The same type of change characterized the East South Central division in 1965–70 and 1975–80. A case can be made that the stock of human capital in the East South Central division was eroded through migration during this period.

A caveat in interpreting such statistics is that it is impossible from the data to ascertain where college graduates obtained their college educations. Many of the 20-to-29-year-olds (age at beginning of the migration intervals) who left the East South Central or other divisions obtained their college degrees in their place of destination. For this reason, it is impossible to say precisely to what extent the apparent outmigration of college graduates from an area represents that area's contribution to another region's stock of human capital.

TABLE 5.2

The Effect of Internal Migration on Educational Levels, for Persons Aged 25–34, by Division: 1935–40, 1955–60, 1965–70, and 1975–80

Years of School	1935–40			1955–60			1965–70			1975–80		
	Net Migration	1935 Population	1940 Population	Net Migration	1955 Population	1960 Population	Net Migration	1965 Population	1970 Population	Net Migration	1975 Population	1980 Population
New England												
0–8	980	36.9%	37.2%	46	15.7%	15.9%	249	9.0%	9.0%	−47	4.1%	4.2%
9–11	−383	21.6	21.7	−2,406	21.8	21.9	−1,415	15.8	15.8	−1,854	7.5	7.6
12	−2,574	27.3	27.3	−3,687	37.8	38.0	−2,636	41.7	41.7	−14,080	35.6	35.7
13–15	−1,057	6.9	6.8	−2,673	11.7	11.6	1,566	15.0	15.2	−11,703	22.7	22.7
16 or More	−3,012	7.2	7.0	−6,794	12.9	12.5	−2,581	18.5	18.4	−20,986	30.2	29.8
Middle Atlantic												
0–8	2,482	43.9	44.2	3,431	14.8	15.1	−1,790	9.0	9.1	−7,024	4.2	4.3
9–11	−7,068	22.4	22.4	−9,289	24.1	24.2	−4,093	17.8	17.9	−16,563	9.6	9.8
12	−11,475	20.9	20.8	−27,214	39.1	38.9	−10,236	43.8	44.0	−82,875	39.2	39.7
13–15	−4,760	5.7	5.7	−11,479	10.0	9.8	−13,025	12.8	12.6	−75,550	20.4	20.1
16 or More	−3,486	7.1	7.0	−5,654	11.9	11.9	−7,982	16.6	16.5	−104,689	26.6	26.1
East North Central												
0–8	27,409	35.5	35.9	12,472	16.2	16.5	10,185	7.9	8.1	−4,112	3.5	3.6
9–11	5,084	24.8	24.8	−6,588	23.4	23.3	13,618	18.4	18.6	−12,148	10.5	10.7
12	−1,453	26.2	26.0	−4,345	40.1	40.0	31,025	45.7	46.1	−51,034	41.8	42.4
13–15	−2,095	7.6	7.5	−2,078	10.2	10.2	167	13.2	13.2	−49,492	21.4	21.3
16 or More	−4,467	6.0	5.8	−4,585	10.0	9.9	−28,135	14.7	14.0	−98,060	22.8	22.0
West North Central												
0–8	−33,055	38.6	39.8	−7,965	16.5	16.7	−813	7.1	7.3	−1,060	2.5	2.5
9–11	−27,810	18.5	18.4	−13,354	18.1	18.1	−2,648	13.3	13.6	238	7.2	7.3
12	−47,491	27.1	26.6	−24,718	42.0	42.3	−12,358	47.1	47.8	−8,626	40.8	41.2
13–15	−20,545	9.8	9.5	−11,844	12.6	12.5	−11,393	15.7	15.5	−12,969	24.1	24.1
16 or More	−15,020	6.0	5.7	−15,972	10.8	10.4	−28,642	16.9	15.8	−30,288	25.5	24.8
South Atlantic												
0–8	−1,007	56.1	55.2	−6,514	27.9	27.7	−895	13.8	13.7	2,416	6.1	6.1
9–11	8,683	18.2	18.2	−707	23.1	23.1	−2,570	21.5	21.3	3,286	12.7	12.6
12	15,610	14.9	15.2	7,016	29.9	30.1	−10,268	39.2	38.6	7,431	38.2	37.9
13–15	8,337	5.8	6.0	188	9.3	9.3	3,261	12.3	12.3	6,762	20.9	20.8
16 or More	11,132	4.9	5.3	1,072	9.8	9.8	31,881	13.1	14.0	50,152	22.0	22.6

TABLE 5.2 (continued)

Years of School	1935–40 Net Migration	1935 Population	1940 Population	1955–60 Net Migration	1955 Population	1960 Population	1965–70 Net Migration	1965 Population	1970 Population	1975–80 Net Migration	1975 Population	1980 Population
East South Central												
0–8	−29,926	61.3	61.4	−21,495	34.0	34.1	−5,952	18.0	18.2	1,814	8.6	8.6
9–11	−10,660	16.6	16.5	−13,107	22.3	22.4	−8,048	21.2	21.4	3,009	14.8	14.9
12	−7,382	13.1	13.1	−15,576	27.4	27.7	−11,508	37.9	38.4	7,601	39.2	39.5
13–15	−2,826	5.3	5.3	−5,983	8.3	8.3	−6,851	11.1	11.0	2,694	18.4	18.5
16 or More	−1,149	3.6	3.7	−11,020	7.9	7.5	−19,382	11.9	10.9	−10,441	19.1	18.6
West South Central												
0–8	−41,724	49.1	48.7	−13,305	25.4	25.5	−3,935	14.0	13.9	4,138	7.6	7.4
9–11	−17,236	21.6	21.5	−9,813	21.5	21.7	1,262	19.5	19.7	14,149	12.3	12.0
12	−10,250	17.2	17.2	−14,725	30.6	30.8	2,389	37.7	37.9	61,150	36.6	36.4
13–15	−2,186	7.3	7.4	−9,380	11.5	11.4	−1,458	14.4	14.4	48,518	21.9	22.1
16 or More	2,473	4.9	5.1	−14,057	10.9	10.5	−6,145	14.4	14.1	59,349	21.7	22.1
Mountain												
0–8	8,878	33.4	33.6	3,365	16.0	15.5	−1,831	8.2	8.0	1,430	3.0	2.9
9–11	3,192	22.4	22.2	9,409	21.2	21.2	−1,485	15.8	15.7	7,816	7.7	7.5
12	4,730	26.3	26.2	18,294	36.2	36.4	494	40.3	40.3	50,630	35.0	34.9
13–15	2,608	11.1	11.2	9,869	14.4	14.7	3,295	18.3	18.7	44,747	29.2	29.3
16 or More	1,637	6.8	6.8	5,723	12.2	12.2	−1,022	17.4	17.3	43,019	25.1	25.4
Pacific												
0–8	65,963	23.6	24.7	29,965	11.8	12.0	4,782	6.4	6.4	2,445	5.3	5.2
9–11	46,198	24.1	23.8	45,855	22.6	22.4	5,379	15.7	15.3	2,067	8.7	8.5
12	60,285	32.7	32.2	64,955	37.1	36.4	13,098	40.2	39.3	29,803	33.3	32.6
13–15	22,524	11.5	11.5	33,380	16.3	16.1	24,438	21.4	21.5	46,993	29.6	29.4
16 or More	11,892	8.1	7.8	51,287	12.2	13.2	62,008	16.2	17.6	111,944	23.1	24.3

NOTES: The net migration figure excludes moves from abroad. The beginning-of-period population is estimated by taking the end-of-period population, adding outmigrants, adding inmigrants, movers from abroad, and subtracting inmigrants, movers from abroad, and persons not reporting residence five years earlier. The end-of-period population excludes movers from abroad and persons not reporting residence five years earlier.

Since the 1930s migration has tended to lower the percentage of New England's population with four or more years of college, but to some extent this effect simply reflects the many colleges and universities in the region. Migration has also tended to lower the proportion of the East North Central division's population with four or more years of college. Since the 1950s migration has tended to raise the proportion of college graduates in the Pacific division's population. The other divisions exhibit variable effects of migration on educational levels.

For 1975–80 migration acted to lower the proportion of college graduates in the North (New England, Middle Atlantic, East North Central, and West North Central) and to raise the proportion of college graduates in the South and West (except for the East South Central division). On this basis, the redistribution of population in the 1970s from Frostbelt to Sunbelt did seem, within the limitations of available data, to constitute a transferral of human capital.

Summary and Conclusion

The consequences and effects of internal migration may exist at both the individual and areal levels. This chapter has concentrated exclusively on the areal effects, but considerable attention has been directed at the potentially harmful effects of migration on families in general and children in particular. Migration is sometimes seen as leading to geographical separation of the generations that make up extended families, with children becoming increasingly separated from their grandparents and other relatives. Even if the average distance separating members of extended families were greater now than it was in a more idyllic and stable past, the cause probably has less to do with increased migration than affluence that allows considerable housing choices and forces fewer adult children to live with their parents or care for dependent relatives in their home. There is a tendency for popular writers to note that more persons live alone now than did a generation or two ago and look to migration as a cause of isolation of family members and anomie and loneliness,[36] even though such social patterns may well be the product of increased personal incomes and more income support programs (for example, Social Security) that allow individuals greater freedom of choice in their living arrangements.

[36]For example, Ralph Keyes, *We, the Lonely People* (New York: Harper & Row, 1973); and Suzanne Gordon, *Lonely in America* (New York: Simon & Schuster, 1975). Some of the same themes appear in Vance Packard's *A Nation of Strangers* (New York: McKay, 1972).

Recent research has suggested that much previous research on the effects of frequent moving on individuals was methodologically unsound. A study of frequently relocated employees of large corporations found that "[mental] health consequences of residential change are not uniformly negative or positive."[37] What may appear to be effects of frequent moving or what may be expressed by respondents as the effects of moving may actually represent antecedent conditions and personality factors. For this population there appear to be few direct links between mobility and psychological well-being.

Frequent migration may, however, keep some children from making expected progress from one grade to the next. One study used census data on age and modal grade of enrollment for children aged 8–17 and found that when family income and composition were controlled for, children who had made several interstate moves were less likely than other children to be enrolled at or above the modal grade for their age.[38] In general (that is, without controls for parents' socioeconomic status), children who have moved frequently are more likely than other children to be at or above the modal grade for their age because they have parents with above-average educational levels. Long-term outmigration of the well-educated from an area may remove children who do well on tests of achievement and performance and in this way lower measures of children's IQ and school achievement in areas of chronic outmigration. A study in the early 1960s administered IQ and achievement tests to a nationally representative sample of school children and reported that children in areas of heavy population loss tended to score nearly one standard deviation below those of similar age in areas growing faster than average for their region.[39] Many factors may contribute to explaining this result, including the possibility of selective outmigration.

When the concern is the effects of migration on individuals, the most common public policy response seems to be to increase mobility of needy populations through direct subsidies to migration and through decreasing the psychic costs and the uncertainty of moving by providing information about job opportunities in different areas. Proposals for increasing mobility of the unemployed or low-income persons or families by these means periodically arise, but programs for achieving these ends

---

[37]Daniel Stokols, Sally A. Shumaker, and John Martinez, "Residential Mobility and Personal Well-Being," *Journal of Environmental Psychology* 3 (1983): 5–19.

[38]Larry Long, "Does Migration Interfere with Children's Progress in School?" *Sociology of Education* 48 (Summer 1975): 369–381.

[39]U.S. National Center for Health Statistics, *School Achievement of Children by Demographic and Socioeconomic Factors;* and *Intellectual Development of Children by Demographic and Socioeconomic Factors* (Washington, DC: U.S. Government Printing Office, 1971).

are difficult to evaluate and may not enjoy widespread public support. Although the focus is on the effect of migration on individuals, such programs would most likely have their greatest effect on outmigration areas with large numbers of persons dependent on public support.

When the effect of migration on areas is at issue, the most common policy response seems to come from areas of destination that desire to prevent inmigration of unwanted new residents.[40] The opposite approach—preventing outmigration of talented, skilled, or otherwise desirable current residents—is seldom approached directly although area redevelopment schemes or programs to foster economic growth are often justified as preserving human capital in regions of chronic outmigration. Efforts to inhibit inmigration have typically been intended to prevent the inmovement of low-income persons who might increase welfare burdens. Mobility-inhibiting effects may also exist at the local level, for zoning plans and growth-limiting policies may serve to keep out new residents.[41]

---

[40]Occasionally one finds policies intended to increase the outmigration of unwanted residents, particularly those not native to the area. For example, in 1985 welfare officials of Hennepin County, Minnesota, proposed to use public funds to give one-way bus tickets to welfare applicants who were not native to Minnesota. "Courts Balk Minnesota on Slashing Welfare Rolls," *New York Times*, September 22, 1985, p. 35.

[41]Peter A. Morrison, "Migration and Rights of Access: New Public Concerns of the 1970's," in Mark Baldassare, ed., *Cities and Urban Living* (New York: Columbia University Press, 1983).

6

METROPOLITAN AND
NONMETROPOLITAN MOBILITY

T HIS CHAPTER addresses a number of questions that are usually considered separately in the various research literatures dealing with geographical mobility within and between metropolitan and nonmetropolitan settings. Previous chapters have focused on geographical mobility at the national, regional, and state levels. Regions and states have long served as spatial aggregates for migration research, and even rural-to-urban migration has often been analyzed as an interregional phenomenon. In the late 1960s and early 1970s, however, several developments gave renewed attention to movements between metropolitan and nonmetropolitan locations, among metropolitan areas, and within metropolitan areas.

Perhaps the most highly publicized new development was the discovery in the early 1970s that about 1970 nonmetropolitan territory changed from being a net exporter to a net importer of population through migration. This discovery set in motion a very active search for new theories and explanations of movement between these generic classifications of residential location, and the search may be intensified by a shift of net migration balances back toward metropolitan territory in the early 1980s. This chapter reviews how this migration change was identified, the methods used to communicate it to disbelievers, and new data that were developed to explain it. This chapter extends this line of research by analyzing changes in the propensity of the U.S. population to move between metropolitan and nonmetropolitan locations between the mid-1970s and the early 1980s. During this period migration balances from all sources (including abroad) reverted once again to favor metropolitan territory.

The chapter also shows how much of the nation's migration can be characterized as intermetropolitan, between metropolitan and nonmetropolitan territory, and between nonmetropolitan locations. The purpose is to evaluate the common assertion that as the United States became a predominantly urban nation, most migration became essentially interurban. The most common approach to explaining intermetropolitan migration is with econometric models which infer determinants of migration from characteristics of metropolitan areas of origin or destination. The chapter identifies recent modifications that incorporate new variables to account for increased migration to many smaller metropolitan areas, particularly those in the Sunbelt.

The chapter then shifts to an intrametropolitan perspective for the purpose of assessing the incidence of residential mobility in different metropolitan areas. Large central cities have traditionally been viewed as having transient populations, but little hard evidence has been produced to evaluate the degree to which contemporary cities conform to this view. The chapter compares the level of residential mobility for individual cities and their suburban rings, proposes ways of accounting for interurban differences in residential mobility, and compares recent and historical evidence on the level of urban residential mobility.

The Nonmetropolitan Turnaround of the 1970s

The shift of nonmetropolitan territory to net inmigration about 1970 was to migration researchers what the baby boom—at least the sustained baby boom—was to fertility researchers. Both demographic developments were unforeseen, both required new techniques and approaches for purposes of description and explanation, and both fundamentally challenged existing theories.

As is the case with all scientific discoveries, the exact timing of the discovery that nonmetropolitan territory had shifted to net inmigration is subject to dispute. But identifying how the new pattern was detected, verified, and communicated to wide, often disbelieving, audiences provides a textbook illustration of some of the methods and materials of migration research.

Some analysts set the turnaround discovery date at 1973 with the release of data from the Census Bureau's Current Population Survey

(CPS) on migration between 1970 and 1973.[1] This survey was the first to publish data from a revision of the traditional CPS migration question, which since 1948 had measured internal migration simply in terms of movement within and between counties and states. The redesigned question not only measured migration in this way but also measured flows between cities and suburban territory and metropolitan and nonmetropolitan locations. The Current Population Survey taken in March 1973 asked respondents where they lived in March 1970, and the results showed that for this three-year period more people moved to nonmetropolitan territory than from it.[2] This snippet of news about migration received considerable public attention.[3] The results of this single survey were soon confirmed by aggregating into metropolitan and nonmetropolitan categories the Census Bureau's estimates of net migration for counties for 1970–73. These 1970–73 estimates were the first annual estimates of net migration prepared by the Census Bureau at the level of individual counties.

Others date communication of an incipient nonmetropolitan turnaround to congressional testimony by Calvin Beale in 1969.[4] Beale said that estimates of population change at the county level prepared by the Census Bureau on an experimental basis in the late 1960s showed renewed growth in the nonmetropolitan sector. Not until the 1970s did the Census Bureau prepare such estimates annually. Had the county estimates been prepared earlier or the CPS question changed earlier, the discovery might have occurred earlier and served to document a gradual transition of nonmetropolitan territory from a net exporter to a net importer of people through migration.

Beale's 1969 congressional testimony did not set new directions in migration research, but he later analyzed net migration for counties for 1970–74 in a short publication that became a model for subse-

[1]Larry Long, "Back to the Countryside and Back to the City in the Same Decade," in Shirley Bradway Laska and Daphne Spain, eds., *Back to the City: Issues in Neighborhood Renovation* (New York: Pergamon Press, 1980), pp. 61–76.

[2]U.S. Bureau of the Census, "Census Bureau Reports Migration Loss in Nation's Metropolitan Areas During Last Three Years." *U.S. Department of Commerce News* (press release CB73-338), 1973.

[3]*New York Times*, "Urban Areas Show Drop in Population," November 24, 1973, p. 36. This headline did not quite fit the short article which simply reported that the March 1973 CPS showed that metropolitan areas collectively had a net outmigration since 1970. Neither urban areas nor metropolitan territory experienced a drop in total population in the 1970s.

[4]John M. Wardwell and David L. Brown, "Population Redistribution in the United States During the 1970s," in David L. Brown and John M. Wardwell, eds., *New Directions in Urban-Rural Migration: The Population Turnaround in Rural America* (New York: Academic Press, 1980), p. 17. Beale's testimony was before the Ad Hoc Subcommittee on Urban Growth of the Subcommittee on Banking and Currency, U.S. House of Representatives.

quent studies of the nonmetropolitan migration turnaround.[5] He classified counties not simply as metropolitan or nonmetropolitan, but he divided the latter according to whether they were adjacent to a metropolitan area. Even the nonmetropolitan counties not adjacent to a metropolitan area were found to have experienced a turnaround from net outmigration in the 1960s to net inmigration in the early 1970s. Hence, the turnaround was not simply a spillover of population growth from metropolitan areas into exurban or suburbanizing counties that were still technically classified as nonmetropolitan. The CPS data were not tabulated to allow for this test and so were not accepted as incontrovertible proof that a new migration pattern existed. Beale's study offered a convincing proof of the hypothesis that a new migration pattern had come into existence as nonmetropolitan counties clearly removed from a metropolitan area were collectively experiencing net inmigration.

New Research Directions

As subsequent data confirmed the pattern noted by Beale's proof, most researchers accepted the evidence as demonstration that a new migration pattern existed and warranted explanation.[6] Subsequent analyses generally sought to fill in the picture by (1) examining who was moving to the distinctly less urban settings that were having the unexpected net inmigration, (2) charting what had changed (more migration to rural locations or less migration from them), (3) achieving greater geographical specificity by concentrating on particular locations rather than simply the national or broad regional levels, and (4) searching for new theoretical paradigms to account for the new trend.

Data from the Current Population Survey helped supply answers to the who-is-moving question. Tucker compared data from the March

[5]Calvin L. Beale, *The Revival of Population Growth in Nonmetropolitan America*, Economic Research Service ERS-605 (Washington, DC: U.S. Department of Agriculture, 1975).

[6]For another proof emphasizing the Hoover index as a measure of population concentration and deconcentration in the United States, see Daniel R. Vining, Jr., and A. Strauss, "A Demonstration that the Current Deconcentration of Population in the United States is a Clean Break with the Past," *Environment and Planning A* 9 (July 1977): 751–758. Similar evidence of dispersal of population beyond core regions was produced for a number of other countries, notably parts of Western Europe and Japan, and served to convince researchers of the significance of new migration patterns in the 1970s. Evidence for other countries is presented in Daniel R. Vining, Jr., and Thomas Kontuly, "Population Dispersal from Major Metropolitan Regions: An International Comparison," *International Regional Science Review* 3 (Fall 1978): 49–73; and Daniel R. Vining, Jr., and Robert Pallone, "Migration between Core and Peripheral Regions: A Description and Tentative Explanation of the Patterns in 22 Countries," *Geoforum* 13, no. 4 (1982): 339–410.

1975 Current Population Survey and the 1970 census, each of which asked respondents about place of residence five years earlier and each tabulated the results according to the same geographical boundaries for metropolitan territory.[7] Tucker showed that the shift of nonmetropolitan territory from net outmigration in 1965–70 to 1970–75 resulted from a 12 percent decrease in the number of nonmetropolitan-to-metropolitan migrants and a 23 percent increase in the number of metropolitan-to-nonmetropolitan migrants. At most age groups the rate of exodus from nonmetropolitan territory was found to have declined and the departure rate from metropolitan areas was found to have increased between 1965–70 and 1970–75. Nonmetropolitan territory continued in the latter period to have a net loss of persons aged 20–24.

Other studies used the same data but examined race and socioeconomic composition of metropolitan and nonmetropolitan migration flows. The net migration gain of nonmetropolitan territory in 1970–75 included whites (but not blacks), persons at every educational level, and persons with clerical and sales occupations, craftsmen and operatives, and laborers and service workers.[8] These studies demonstrated that the nonmetropolitan migration gains were broad based and included many demographic groups.

A different approach to research on nonmetropolitan inmigration was to identify the characteristics of counties that were associated with net inmigration. Beale developed cross-tabulations of nonmetropolitan counties at the time of the 1960 and 1970 censuses according to postcensal net migration.[9] He found that for nonmetropolitan counties

---

[7]C. Jack Tucker, "Changing Patterns of Migration between Metropolitan and Nonmetropolitan Areas in the United States: Recent Evidence," *Demography* 13 (November 1976): 435–443.

[8]James J. Zuiches and David L. Brown, "The Changing Character of the Nonmetropolitan Population, 1950–75," in Thomas R. Ford, ed., *Rural U.S.A.: Persistence and Change* (Ames: Iowa State University Press, 1978), pp. 55–72. Their comparisons of 1965–70 and 1970–75 migration were also included in Peter Morrison's *Rural Renaissance in America?* (Washington, DC: Population Reference Bureau, 1976). A more detailed analysis showing greater retention of population in nonmetropolitan areas and greater rates of migration to nonmetropolitan territory when controlling for both age and educational level was presented in C. Jack Tucker, "Age and Educational Dimensions of Recent U.S. Migration Reversal," *Growth and Change* 12 (April 1981): 31–36. Even after 1970, however, the net exchange of population between the metropolitan and nonmetropolitan sectors tended to depress somewhat several measures of overall socioeconomic status in nonmetropolitan territory; see Daniel T. Lichter, Tim B. Heaton, and Glenn V. Fuguitt, "Trends in the Selectivity of Migration between Metropolitan and Nonmetropolitan Areas: 1955–1975," *Rural Sociology* 44 (Winter 1979): 645–666.

[9]Calvin L. Beale, "The Recent Shift of United States Population to Nonmetropolitan Areas, 1970–75," *International Regional Science Review* 2 (Winter 1977): 113–122. Comparable analyses for earlier periods were presented in Calvin L. Beale and Glenn V. Fuguitt, "The New Pattern of Nonmetropolitan Population Change," in Karl E. Taeuber, Larry L. Bumpass, and James A. Sweet, eds., *Social Demography* (New York: Academic Press, 1978), pp. 157–177.

median family income was strongly associated with net migration gains in the 1960s but not in the 1970s; thus, net migration was less clearly going to the relatively high-income nonmetropolitan counties. He also found that population density in nonmetropolitan counties and level of urbanization (measured by size of largest city) were positively associated with growth (or minimization of migration losses) in the 1960s but not in the 1970s, suggesting movement to less dense, less urban settings in the nonmetropolitan sector. From these types of results, he inferred changed motives for migration: "On the average, people are simply not moving to or between nonmetropolitan counties in a manner associated with the income levels of areas, suggesting that many of them are not moving for monetary motivations."[10]

A similar approach was used by McCarthy and Morrison, who developed an ordinary-least-squares model of characteristics of counties associated with net inmigration or outmigration. They concluded that "previous growth advantages associated with manufacturing and government related activity appear to have diminished in the 1970s, and retirement and recreation have emerged as important growth-inducing activities in the nonmetropolitan sector."[11] This was further evidence that new patterns of migration were being observed and that areal characteristics previously associated with attracting migrants were less clearly doing so in the 1970s.

New Information, New Theories

These two sources of data—survey statistics from the CPS and estimates of net migration for counties—were soon supplemented by other sources of information on the "new migration." The Continuous Work History Sample (CWHS) was derived from forms filed by employers of workers covered by Social Security and represented a longitudinal, annual sample of workers. The forms were supposed to reflect job location, and year-to-year changes in job location were taken to be migration. The CWHS had the distinct advantage of being able to show earnings (at least those covered by Social Security) both before and after moving. Its limitations included errors and inconsistencies in the filing of reports (mostly a tendency for employers to report employment at a

---

[10]Beale, "The Recent Shift of United States Population," p. 116.
[11]Kevin F. McCarthy and Peter A. Morrison, "The Changing Demographic and Economic Structure of Nonmetropolitan Areas in the United States," *International Regional Science Review* 2 (Winter 1977): 123–142.

company's headquarters rather than branch plants) and the inability to control for variables that influence earnings of individuals (weeks worked, hours worked, and so on).

The CWHS demonstrated that (1) metropolitan territory had net in-migration of workers for successive periods in the 1960s but net out-migration in the early 1970s, (2) the net movement of jobs to nonmet-ropolitan locations accelerated between 1970 and 1976, and (3) earnings were growing faster for the nonmetropolitan sector than the metropoli-tan average in the early 1970s.[12] Such results supplemented the strictly demographic analyses by showing the economic base of nonmetropoli-tan population growth. Public release of the CWHS was halted by the late 1970s because of concerns over privacy and confidentiality.

Analyses of the CWHS stressed the economic foundations of the new migration toward nonmetropolitan territory, whereas noneconomic interpretations were generally offered by researchers who collected or analyzed data on self-reported reasons for moving. One of these under-takings was the survey of migrants to 75 midwestern counties with high net inmigration in 1970–75.[13] These data were collected from inter-views with households who were in the 1976 or 1977 telephone direc-tories but not the 1970 directories of the counties surveyed. The survey asked about reasons for leaving previous county of residence and reasons for choice of destination. The tabulations controlled for type of origin (metropolitan or nonmetropolitan) and demographic characteristics of respondents. The study concluded that ". . . the major stated motiva-tions for leaving places of origin, especially among those from metro-

[12]Regional Economic Analysis Division, "Work Force Migration Patterns, 1960–73," *Survey of Current Business* 56 (October 1976): 23–28. This work was later updated to 1976 in Vernon Renshaw, Howard Friedenberg, and Bruce Levine, "Work-Force Migration Pat-terns, 1970–76," *Survey of Current Business* 58 (February 1978): 17–20. Other researchers extended these analyses of the CWHS by developing a more complex set of origins and destinations, based on size of metropolitan areas and adjacency or nonadjacency of non-metropolitan counties. See John M. Wardwell and C. Jack Gilchrist, "Employment Decon-centration in the Nonmetropolitan Migration Turnaround," *Demography* 17 (May 1980): 145–158; David L. Brown, "Spatial Aspects of Post-1970 Work Force Migration in the United States," *Growth and Change* 12 (January 1981): 9–20; and Dan L. Tweed, James W. Longest, Eugene H. Owen, and Patricia A. Dabbs, "Labor Force Deconcentration in the United States: An Examination of the Relative Impacts of Intrasystemic and Intersystemic Movement," *Review of Public Data Use* 9 (July 1981): 133–142.

[13]James D. Williams and Andrew J. Sofranko, "Motivations for the Inmigration Com-ponent of Population Turnaround in Nonmetropolitan Areas," *Demography* 16 (May 1979): 239–255. James D. Williams and David Byron McMillen, "Migration Decision Mak-ing among Nonmetropolitan-Bound Migrants," in Brown and Wardwell, *New Directions in Urban-Rural Migration*, pp. 189–211. James D. Williams and David Byron McMillen, "Location-Specific Capital and Destination Selection among Migrants to Nonmetropolitan Areas," *Rural Sociology* 48 (Fall 1983): 447–457. Andrew J. Sofranko and Frederick C. Fliegel, "The Neglected Component of Rural Population Growth," *Growth and Change* 14 (April 1983): 42–49.

politan areas, are 'quality of life' considerations."[14] This conclusion seemed to apply even to migrants of labor force age.

This type of conclusion was also offered by researchers who developed regression models that used net migration as the dependent variable and sets of independent variables to measure economic activity or opportunity as well as amenities or quality-of-life attributes of counties. Such models found that over time economic variables explained a declining proportion of variation and the amenity variables explained a growing proportion of variation, even when net migration was restricted to persons of labor force age.[15] Perhaps it is to be expected that over time economic characteristics of counties would come to be less closely associated with net migration because of the increasing ability of people to live in adjoining counties where living costs are lower and residents can easily commute across county boundaries. As discussed in Chapter 2, commuting can come to be an alternative to migration as technology, values, or other forces cause the various forms of spatial mobility to become substitutable. Only a few studies correlated economic features of counties on the basis of the location of employment (rather than workers' residence), but in most cases the results were interpreted as suggesting changing rankings of attributes of areas as potential places of residence and hence changing reasons for moving or selection among alternative destinations by migrants.

This hypothesis helped make sense of the unexpected net inmigration to nonmetropolitan territory in the 1970s, but it rested on somewhat shaky ground. First, surveys of reasons for moving seldom ask comparable questions or code or process the data in the same ways, and there is simply no time series to document for the general population a changing set of reasons for moving or choosing destinations. Second, the regression models of net migration for counties typically employed fairly simple statistical designs and usually used net migration rather than more detailed data on specific origins and destinations of migrants.

More complex designs seem to yield somewhat different conclusions. A study of gross migration for 1955–60 and 1965–70 for metropolitan and nonmetropolitan State Economic Areas[16] used a three-stage

[14]Williams and Sofranko, "Motivations for the Inmigration Component of Population Turnaround in Nonmetropolitan Areas."

[15]Tim B. Heaton, William B. Clifford, and Glenn V. Fuguitt, "Temporal Shifts in the Determinants of Young and Elderly Migration in Nonmetropolitan Areas," *Social Forces* 60 (September 1981): 41–60; Steve H. Murdock, Banoo Parpia, Sean-Shong Hwang, and Rita R. Hamm, "The Relative Effects of Economic and Noneconomic Factors on Age-Specific Migration, 1960–1980," *Rural Sociology* 49, no. 2 (1984): 309–318.

[16]State Economic Areas, basically, are metropolitan areas as of 1950 and groups of nonmetropolitan counties. They were extensively used as tabulation categories for migration data in the censuses of 1950, 1960, and 1970.

least-squares model to conclude that "the most notable changes between the 1950s and 1960s are not in the realm of determinants of migration, but rather the determinants of employment growth which in turn affects migration."[17] According to this view, the faster growth of jobs in nonmetropolitan locations in the 1970s facilitates the increased movement to (and retention of migrants in) such locations by persons who value the various amenities characteristic of less urban settings. Hence, employment growth in nonmetropolitan counties is the ecological explanation of more migration to nonmetropolitan territory, and migrants to them are self-selected individuals who value nonmetropolitan lifestyles and express amenities or quality-of-life considerations when asked why they have chosen to move to such areas.

This distinction between ecological and individual explanations helps to put in perspective another line of reasoning based on surveys of migration preferences. Surveys going as far back as the late 1940s asked respondents where they would prefer to live, and respondents were usually given a flashcard listing different types of residential environments—for example, on a farm, in the open countryside but not on a farm, in a small town, in a small city, in the suburbs of a large metropolitan area, or in a large city. The results showed that more people were living in large metropolitan areas than preferred to, and if people could achieve their residential preferences, more would migrate to nonmetropolitan territory. These data were sometimes used to argue in favor of population policies that would allow or encourage population redistribution toward smaller cities and towns.[18]

As net migration balances were observed to tilt toward the nonmet-

---

[17]James D. Williams, "The Nonchanging Determinants of Nonmetropolitan Migration," *Rural Sociology* 46 (Summer 1981): 183–202. Perhaps the only other dissenting view that increased migration to nonmetropolitan territory reflects an increased role of noneconomic motivations is Stephen A. Hoenack, Jose Antonio Peris, and William C. Weiler, "Can Economic Incentives Explain the Recent Population Movements to Nonmetropolitan Areas?" *Annals of Regional Science* 18 (November 1984): 81–93. This study used time-series analyses of annual net migration of elementary school children in Minnesota's nonmetropolitan counties from 1951 through 1978.

[18]James L. Sundquist, *Dispersing Population: What America Can Learn from Europe* (Washington, DC: Brookings Institution, 1975), chaps. 1 and 7. Some of the early (pre-1970) interpretations are reviewed in James J. Zuiches and Glenn V. Fuguitt, "Residential Preferences: Implications for Population Redistribution in Nonmetropolitan Areas"; and Sara Mills Mazie and Steve Rawlings, "Public Attitude Towards Population Distribution Issues," in U.S. Commission on Population Growth and the American Future, *Population, Distribution, and Policy*, edited by Sara Mills Mazie, (Washington, DC: U.S. Government Printing Office, 1972). The Commission-sponsored survey showed that a majority of the U.S. population felt the federal government should discourage the growth of large metropolitan areas and should encourage more people and industry to move to "smaller cities and towns." See Mazie and Rawlings, "Public Attitude Towards Population Distribution Issues, pp. 612–614.

ropolitan sector in the early 1970s, the results of such surveys were interpreted to mean that more persons were achieving their residential preferences through migration. Size-of-place preferences were polled in national samples of the United States, the state of Wisconsin, and the state of Pennsylvania.[19] Most research on where respondents lived and where they would like to live introduced some controls for individual characteristics like race, age, sex, income, and previous residential experiences (for example, residence at age 16). The results showed whites expressing more fondness than blacks toward the idea of migrating to a rural area, and younger persons showed stronger preference than older persons for nonmetropolitan residence even though the younger were much less likely to have been born or raised in a rural area or small town. In general, achievement of residential preferences would result in migration of many demographic subpopulations toward less urban settings, although many of the potential metropolitan-to-nonmetropolitan migrants would stay in a metropolitan area if their preferred move would entail significant income sacrifice or would leave them too far from a metropolitan area.[20]

Migration trends were hard to discern in the surveys of residential preferences. Because the various surveys used different ways of classifying current residence and asked slightly different questions, they showed little clear evidence of increasing preference for migration to rural or less urban locations. They probably are best interpreted as meaning that faster job growth in many nonmetropolitan settings in the 1970s allowed more metropolitan residents to move to nonmetropolitan settings in achievement of long-standing preferences.

Patterns of the 1980s

The post-1980 estimates of net migration for counties have shown a shift in the balance of net migration again in favor of the metropolitan

[19]The Wisconsin survey was reported in Zuiches and Fuguitt, "Residential Preferences." The Pennsylvania survey was reported in Gordon F. DeJong, "Residential Preferences and Migration," *Demography* 14 (May 1977): 169–178; and Gordon F. DeJong and Ralph R. Sell, "Population Redistribution, Migration, and Residential Preferences," *Annals of the American Academy of Political and Social Sciences* 429 (January 1977): 130–144.
[20]Glenn V. Fuguitt and James J. Zuiches, "Residential Preferences and Population Distribution," *Demography* 12 (August 1975): 491–504; and James J. Zuiches, "Residential Preferences in Migration Theory," in Brown and Wardwell, *New Directions in Urban-Rural Migration*, pp. 163–188.

TABLE 6.1

Net Migration for Central Cities, the Suburban Balance of Metropolitan Areas, and Nonmetropolitan Territory: 1975–76 to 1983–84 (in thousands)

	1975–76	1980–81	1981–82	1982–83	1983–84
Central Cities	− 1,955	− 2,236	− 2,569	− 2,231	− 1,749
Suburban Territory	+ 1,560	+ 1,927	+ 2,360	+ 2,254	+ 2,100
Nonmetropolitan Territory	+ 395	+ 194	+ 149	− 22	− 351

NOTES: Data are from March Current Population Surveys, which asked where persons aged 1 and over lived on March 1 of the preceding year. Movers from abroad are excluded. Boundaries of metropolitan areas and central cities are as of 1970. Comparable data are not available for 1977–80.

sector,[21] although the nonmetropolitan sector does not have the volume or rate of outmigration characteristic of the 1960s or earlier decades of large rural-to-urban migration. Since a variety of theoretical perspectives were invoked to explain the shift of the balance toward the nonmetropolitan sector in the early 1970s and since there evolved no unified theory with predictive power, there is no clear guide to finding an explanation of the drift back to net inmigration to metropolitan territory in the 1980s. One approach is simply to retrace the developments of the early 1970s and find out which demographic groups participated in the changes and which flows changed to alter the net migration balances.

Table 6.1 documents the nonmetropolitan territory's shift of net migration from positive to negative between the mid-1970s and the early 1980s. The data are from the Current Population Survey and reflect constant boundaries of central cities and metropolitan areas as of 1970. Hence, the data do not reflect the extensive restructuring of metropolitan-area boundaries as new metropolitan areas were carved out of nonmetropolitan territory and as other nonmetropolitan counties were incorporated into the fringes of metropolitan areas. For these purposes,

[21]Estimates of 1980–84 net migration for counties aggregated into metropolitan and nonmetropolitan territory are presented in U.S. Bureau of the Census, "Patterns of Metropolitan Area and County Population Growth: 1980 to 1984," *Current Population Reports*, series P-25, no. 976 (Washington, DC: U.S. Government Printing Office, 1985). Personal income between metropolitan and nonmetropolitan territory converged between 1969 and 1979 but diverged again in favor of metropolitan areas after the 1979 recession. See Daniel H. Garnick, "Patterns of Growth in Metropolitan and Nonmetropolitan Areas: An Update," *Survey of Current Business* 65 (May 1985): 33–38. The ability of the neoclassical economic model to explain metro-nonmetro differences in population and income from 1959 to 1981 is reviewed in Daniel H. Garnick, "Shifting Balances in U.S. Metropolitan and Nonmetropolitan Area Growth," *International Regional Science Review* 9, no. 3 (1984): 257–273.

"suburban" includes all residents of a metropolitan area outside the central city or cities.

The data suggest gradual change. The net inmigration to nonmetropolitan territory observed in the early 1970s persisted through the decade, began to decline in 1980–82, and changed to net outmigration by 1983–84. Nonmetropolitan territory went from net inmigration of about 395,000 in 1975–76 to net *out*migration of 351,000 in 1983–84. Concomitantly, net outmigration from central cities declined from 1,955,000 in 1975–76 to 1,749,000 in 1983–84, and net inmigration to suburbs grew from 1,560,000 in 1975–76 to 2,100,000 in 1983–84. The figures exclude movers from abroad; including them would affect the city figures somewhat more than the suburb or nonmetropolitan figures. Sampling variability for net migration is large, and precise comparisons should not be inferred; the general conclusion is simply that the survey data suggest gradual rather than abrupt change in net migration.

No single age group clearly accounted for these changes. As shown in Table 6.2, central cities had net inmigration for no age groups, whereas suburbs seem to have had net inmigration in almost every age group for each of the two one-year intervals. For both periods, central cities may have had their greatest losses among persons in their late 20s, and suburbs may have had their greatest gains in this age group.[22]

Nonmetropolitan territory seems to have had net inmigration at all ages except 15–24 in 1975–76, although the apparent net inmigration at other ages does not represent statistically significant results. This information, in conjunction with Tucker's analysis of 1965–70 and 1970–75 data,[23] suggests that nonmetropolitan territory never developed net inmigration among persons aged 15–24 in the 1970s. By 1983–84 nonmetropolitan territory may have had net inmigration only for persons over age 45.

Another approach to describing the changes is to look at specific flows that underlie the net movements featured in Tables 6.1 and 6.2. Table 6.3 shows the change in the number of movers and the change in

---

[22]Because of sampling variability, one should not draw this inference solely from the data in Table 6.2. Other migration data suggest this pattern, however. For example, see the estimates of net intercensal migration by age for several central cities and suburban counties in Larry H. Long and Paul C. Glick, "Family Patterns in Suburban Areas: Recent Trends," in Barry Schwartz, ed., *The Changing Face of the Suburbs* (Chicago: University of Chicago Press, 1976): 39–67. Such a pattern is consistent with documentation that family size was much smaller for nonmetro-to-metro movers than metro-to-nonmetro movers, with the latter family size resembling that found for city-to-suburb movers. See Ralph B. White, "Family Size Composition Differentials between Central City-Suburb and Metropolitan-Nonmetropolitan Migration Streams," *Demography* 19 (February 1982): 29–36.

[23]Tucker, "Changing Patterns of Migration."

TABLE 6.2

Net Migration by Age, for Central City, Suburban, and Nonmetropolitan Residential Categories: 1975–76 and 1983–84 (in thousands)

Age	Central Cities		Suburbs		Nonmetropolitan	
	1975–76	1983–84	1975–76	1983–84	1975–76	1983–84
1–4 Years	− 124	− 199	99	242	25	− 43
5–9 Years	− 152	− 88	100	71	52	17
10–14 Years	− 120	− 141	78	141	42	0
15–19 Years	− 167	− 145	188	183	− 21	− 38
20–24 Years	− 306	− 165	381	359	− 75	− 194
25–29 Years	− 367	− 341	257	411	110	− 70
30–34 Years	− 182	− 240	143	274	39	− 34
35–44 Years	− 192	− 194	150	252	42	− 58
45–54 Years	− 155	− 75	100	60	55	15
55–64 Years	− 121	− 64	46	18	75	46
65–74 Years	− 48	− 49	18	45	30	4
75 or more years	− 21	− 48	− 3	44	24	4
All ages 1+	− 1,955	− 1,749	1,560	2,100	395	− 351

NOTES: Sampling errors associated with these estimates of net migration are very large. See U.S. Bureau of the Census, *Current Population Reports,* series P-20, no. 305. Movers from abroad are excluded.

TABLE 6.3

Changing Gross Flows and Rates of Migration for Central Cities, Suburban Territory, and Nonmetropolitan Territory, for Persons Aged 1 and Over: 1975–76 and 1983–84 (in thousands)

	Movers			Rates of Moving		
	1975–76	1983–84	Percentage Change	1975–76	1983–84	Percentage Change
From Cities to Suburbs	3,499	4,045	+ 15.6	.061602	.067335	+ 9.3
From Cities to Nonmetro	1,106	1,041	− 5.9	.019472	.017329	− 11.0
From Suburbs to Cities	1,822	2,300	+ 26.2	.024078	.026942	+ 11.9
From Suburbs to Nonmetro	1,371	1,217	− 11.2	.018118	.014256	− 21.3
From Nonmetro to Cities	828	1,037	+ 25.2	.012823	.014710	+ 14.7
From Nonmetro to Suburbs	1,254	1,572	+ 25.4	.019421	.022299	+ 14.8

NOTES: Rates of moving in the specified streams are expressed on an "at risk" basis. The base is obtained by taking the end-of-period population, adding outmigrants from the category, and subtracting inmigrants. The rate is the number of outmigrants from the category divided by the base. Computing rates to six decimals is done only for illustrative purposes; large sampling errors are associated with the rates of moving and estimates of percentage change. Data are from Current Population Surveys of 1976 and 1984.

the rates of movement among the three residential categories. The city-to-suburb and suburb-to-city flows include movers within as well as between metropolitan areas.

The various migration streams seem to have changed in the expected ways. That is, the nonmetropolitan territory's change from net inmigration in 1975–76 to net outmigration in 1983–84 resulted from fewer movers from cities and suburbs to nonmetropolitan territory and more movers from nonmetropolitan territory to cities and suburbs.

More specifically, the rate of city-to-nonmetropolitan moving declined by 11.0 percent, resulting in a 5.9 percent decline in the number of movers in this stream between 1975–76 and 1983–84. The suburb-to-nonmetropolitan rate of moving fell 21.3 percent, decreasing by 11.2 percent the number of movers in this stream. The counterflows increased. The rate of moving from nonmetropolitan locations to cities increased by 14.7 percent, raising by 25.2 percent the number of movers in this stream. And the rate of moving from nonmetropolitan locations to suburbs rose by 14.8 percent, raising the number of movers in this flow by 25.4 percent. Hence, the two flows out of metropolitan areas (one originating in cities and the other in suburbs) and the two flows out of nonmetropolitan territory (one terminating in cities and the other in suburbs) changed in a consistent fashion.

The four flows were not, however, of equal importance in changing the net migration balance. It is possible to quantify the contribution of changes in each of the four gross flows in changing net migration by comparing the observed flows with what would be expected if age-specific rates of moving at the earlier period were maintained. To do this, one computes the base population exposed to the "risk" of migrating at the earlier and more recent migration intervals, controlling for age since the age composition can change. The base population is simply the end-of-period population minus inmigrants during the migration interval, plus the outmigrants from the area (or residential category, in this case). The rate of movement in a specified stream is obtained by dividing the outmoving stream by the base for the residential category of origin. The results of these data manipulations are illustrated in Figure 6.1.

The observed nonmetropolitan net migration for 1983–84 was −351,000. One would have expected net *in*migration of 482,000 if there were no change in the 1975–76 age-specific rates of moving (1) from cities to nonmetropolitan territory, (2) from suburbs to nonmetropolitan territory, (3) from nonmetropolitan territory to cities, and (4) from nonmetropolitan territory to suburbs. The difference between the observed and expected net migration can be attributed to 171,000 fewer city-to-nonmetropolitan movers, 355,000 fewer suburban-to-nonmetropolitan movers, 119,000 more movers from nonmetropolitan territory to cities,

FIGURE 6.1

Components of the Difference Between Observed and Expected Net Migration for Nonmetropolitan Territory in 1983–84

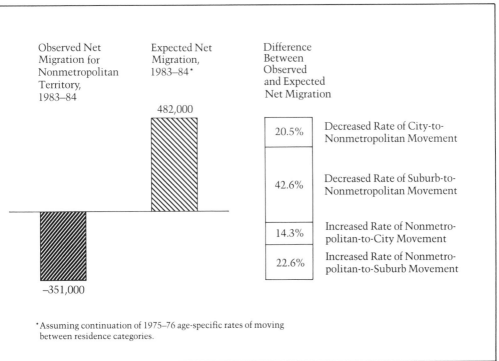

Observed Net Migration for Nonmetropolitan Territory, 1983–84	Expected Net Migration, 1983–84*	Difference Between Observed and Expected Net Migration

482,000

20.5%	Decreased Rate of City-to-Nonmetropolitan Movement
42.6%	Decreased Rate of Suburb-to-Nonmetropolitan Movement
14.3%	Increased Rate of Nonmetropolitan-to-City Movement
22.6%	Increased Rate of Nonmetropolitan-to-Suburb Movement

−351,000

*Assuming continuation of 1975–76 age-specific rates of moving between residence categories.

and 188,000 more movers from nonmetropolitan territory to suburbs than expected if age-specific rates of moving in 1975–76 continued into 1983–84. As illustrated in Figure 6.1, these data mean that 20.5 percent of the change in net migration can be attributed to a decreased rate of movement from cities to nonmetropolitan territory, 42.6 percent to a decreased rate of movement from suburbs to nonmetropolitan territory, 14.3 percent to an increased rate of movement from nonmetropolitan territory to cities, and 22.6 percent to an increased rate of movement from nonmetropolitan territory to suburbs.

This information shows that nonmetropolitan net migration changed from positive to negative between 1975–76 and 1983–84 more as a result of fewer metropolitan-to-nonmetropolitan movers than as a result of more nonmetropolitan-to-metropolitan movers. The rate of moving out of metropolitan areas changed less than the rate of moving into them (as shown in Table 6.3), but because the metropolitan base is much larger than the nonmetropolitan base the decline in the rate of exodus from metropolitan areas affected the net flow more than the increased rate of movement to metropolitan territory.

These rather mechanical manipulations of migration data suggest that the net balance of movement between metropolitan and nonmetropolitan territory changes as a result of consistent alterations in propensities to move. The specific flows among cities, suburbs, and nonmetropolitan territory do not all change at the same rate, but they do seem to change together, as a system of population flows linking these residential categories. At least this was the case for the flip-flop of the metropolitan-nonmetropolitan migration balance between the mid-1970s and the early 1980s.

The fundamental reality that underlies the rather modest net migration balances between metropolitan and nonmetropolitan aggregates may be relative stability rather than volatility, for the net balances seem small when viewed against the gross flows. The net migration of 395,000 in favor of nonmetropolitan territory in 1975–76 was the result of nearly 4,600,000 moves between the two residential categories. The net migration of 351,000 in favor of metropolitan territory in 1983–84 was the result of nearly 4,900,000 moves between the two categories.

Over long periods of time, the two broad aggregates have probably converged in many ways. Urbanization in the United States has been diffuse and has spread urban facilities and amenities to the countryside to such a degree as to have curbed the massive rural-to-urban movements that dominated the nation's internal migration for much of the twentieth century. In the 1970s metropolitan territory became more rural, and nonmetropolitan territory became more urban.[24] These developments facilitate moves between what is technically metropolitan (or urban) and nonmetropolitan (or rural) and support the idea that at advanced stages of development internal migration ceases to be characterized by massive, largely unidirectional flows between highly dissimilar (for example, urban and rural) environments and instead consists mostly of circular movements among essentially similar residential environ-

[24]Metropolitan areas are predominantly, but not entirely, urban since they are composed of whole counties which may be partly rural. The Census Bureau definition of urban has changed over the years and by 1980 included residents of incorporated places of 2,500 or more inhabitants and also residents of fairly densely settled territory (1,000 persons per square mile) around urban agglomerations of 50,000 or more population. In 1960 and 1970 about 88 percent of the population of metropolitan territory was urban by Census Bureau definitions. By 1980 the proportion of metropolitan residents who were urban fell to about 85 percent. Nonmetropolitan territory rose from 59 percent urban in 1970 to 62 percent urban in 1980. The reason for the "ruralization" of metropolitan territory in the 1970s was that many nonmetropolitan counties reclassified as metropolitan during the decade were so highly rural that they brought down the urban percentage for the metropolitan average. These data are from Larry Long and Diana DeAre, "Repopulating the Countryside: A 1980 Census Trend," *Science*, 217 (September 17, 1982): 1111–1116.

ments.[25] Areas become similar through diffusion of economic growth and reduction of differences in level of living, but economic differentiation continues to occur as areas find themselves at different stages of the product life cycle (innovative productive processes arise in some areas, are diffused to others, and the cycle repeats itself although possibly in different areas). When large socioeconomic differences separate urban and rural locations, there is great concern with adjustment, accommodation, and assimilation of migrants into their new (urban) environments. With the reduction of such differences, concerns shift to whether the migration causes individuals to become less attached to places and the effects on community life and structure.

Future metropolitan-nonmetropolitan or urban-rural migration balances depend on many things. One is economic developments that in unexpected and indirect ways may favor either more urban or less urban locations. A study of nonmetropolitan job growth suggested that increased international competition in the 1970s forced many U.S. firms to search hard for ways to cut costs by relocating all or part of their operations to lower-cost, often nonmetropolitan areas of the country.[26] In this view, rural areas did not steal jobs from metropolitan areas but kept jobs at home rather than lose them to other countries. By the 1980s, however, the cost-cutting benefits of relocation may have been used up, and the competitiveness of U.S. firms in an international context may have shifted from strategies that emphasize cost-cutting by relocating to strategies that focus on *in situ* developments based on new technologies like robotics or more extensive computerization. Such technologies typically originate in and are first applied in metropolitan areas, and their successful implementation would likely shore up metropolitan-area populations.

Another consideration impinging on future metropolitan (urban) and nonmetropolitan (rural) migration balances is simply the way these and other broad categories of residential locations are defined, especially the aggressiveness with which nonmetropolitan territory is reclassified as metropolitan. Virtually every city or town of moderate size and am-

---

[25]A classic formulation was Wilbur Zelinsky, "The Hypothesis of the Mobility Transition," *Geographical Review* 61 (April 1971): 219–249. This work and other theories of trends in the volume and form of spatial mobility are reviewed in Chapter 2. The application to contemporary urban-rural migration exchanges is developed in John M. Wardwell, "Equilibrium and Change in Nonmetropolitan Growth," *Rural Sociology* 42 (Summer 1977): 156–179.

[26]Larry Long and Diana DeAre, "Repopulating the Countryside: A 1980 Census Trend"; "The Slowing of Urbanization in the United States," *Scientific American* 249 (July 1983): 33–41; and "Metropolitan-Nonmetropolitan Industrial Changes and Population Redistribution," paper presented at the annual meeting of the American Association for the Advancement of Science, Detroit, May 30, 1983.

bition would prefer to be a metropolitan area because there is a great deal to be gained and very little to lose in becoming metropolitan. Government grants tend to reward metropolitan status, and since measures of market size and advertising rates charged by the media are often based on official (governmental) sets of boundaries, most existing metropolitan areas are desirous of adding more counties to their territory and thereby adding more people to their "market."[27] In a society where most migration is between generally similar but slightly different environments, the orientation of migration research may shift from the dichotomous metropolitan-nonmetropolitan or urban-rural focus of the past to more complex, but more analytically useful, categorizations of origin and destination.

Intermetropolitan Migration

One often reads that most migration in the United States and other economically advanced nations is interurban, whereas at some earlier time rural-to-urban flows were dominant and still are the most common form of migration in many less developed countries. Documenting just when the interurban movements came to be the characteristic form of migration within the United States is not possible with extant information, for there is not a consistent series of migration data classified by urban and rural origin and destination. By 1950 the country as a whole had become predominantly metropolitan, with 56 percent of the population living in one of the 168 areas then recognized as Standard Metropolitan Areas.[28] At that time metropolitan areas were built around cities of 50,000 or more population, and however one were to define what is migration or what is urban, it is unlikely that interurban flows could have constituted a majority of internal migration before 1950.

Table 6.4 offers perhaps the closest approximation to measuring how much internal migration is interurban by showing how many moves between counties within a state and between states originated or

[27]Why areas desire to be metropolitan and some rewards of that status are illustrated in Sam Allis, "Localities Aim for Lucrative Rank of Standard Metropolitan Areas," *Wall Street Journal*, December 16, 1980, p. 31; "Make Mine Metropolitan," editorial, *Washington Post*, January 2, 1984, p. A20; and Calvin L. Beale, "Poughkeepsie's Complaint, or Defining Metropolitan Areas," *American Demographics* 6 (January 1984): 29–31 and 46–48.

[28]By 1984 there were 257 metropolitan areas, called Metropolitan Statistical Areas, encompassing 76 percent of the nation's 1980 population. Figures on the number and population of metropolitan areas are given in U.S. Bureau of the Census, 1980 Census of Population and Housing, *Metropolitan Statistical Areas*, Supplementary Report, PC-S1-18, (Washington, DC: U.S. Government Printing Office, 1984).

TABLE 6.4

Distribution of the U.S. Population Aged 1 and Over According to Metropolitan-Nonmetropolitan Status and Amount of Intercounty (within a state) and Interstate Movement To, From, Within, or Between Metropolitan Areas: 1975–76 to 1983–84

	1975–76	1980–81	1981–82	1982–83	1983–84
Distribution of Population					
Percentage of U.S. Population in					
Metropolitan areas	67.7%	67.6%	67.6%	67.8%	68.0%
Nonmetropolitan territory	32.3	32.4	32.3	32.2	32.0
Distribution of Movers Between					
Counties Within a State					
Percentage Who Moved					
Within a metropolitan area	24.7	22.0	21.5	22.4	21.2
Between metropolitan areas	22.1	28.3	28.9	27.9	28.9
Metropolitan to nonmetropolitan	17.6	15.1	14.2	12.9	12.4
Nonmetropolitan to metropolitan	12.6	11.5	12.7	12.5	14.2
Nonmetropolitan to nonmetropolitan	23.0	23.1	22.7	24.3	23.2
Distribution of Interstate Movers					
Percentage Who Moved					
Within a metropolitan area	2.9	2.4	2.5	2.9	2.9
Between metropolitan areas	43.7	45.1	44.1	46.4	42.4
Metropolitan to nonmetropolitan	19.7	19.2	19.5	17.9	18.6
Nonmetropolitan to metropolitan	18.7	20.3	19.1	18.3	22.0
Nonmetropolitan to nonmetropolitan	15.0	13.0	14.8	14.5	14.1

NOTES: Metropolitan-area boundaries are as of 1970. Data are from March Current Population Surveys.

terminated in metropolitan areas. The metropolitan boundaries in Table 6.4 are as of 1970; by 1984 this set of boundaries encompassed 68 percent of the U.S. population, but moves from one metropolitan area to another constituted less than a majority of interstate moves.

Moves from one metropolitan area to another made up 42.4 percent of interstate moves in 1983–84. Moves from metropolitan areas to non-metropolitan territory made up 18.6 percent of interstate moves, and moves from nonmetropolitan territory to metropolitan areas made up another 22.0 percent of interstate moves. Hence, 83 percent of interstate migration begins or ends in a metropolitan area (excluding intrametropolitan moves).

One can express the same results differently by saying that just over 40 percent of interstate migration in 1983–84 was between metropolitan and nonmetropolitan locations. In a sense, therefore, 4 in 10 interstate moves were between environments (metropolitan and nonmetropolitan) that historically have been distinct. Other interstate moves include those that begin and end in nonmetropolitan locations (14.1 percent of all interstate moves in 1983–84), and a few that begin and end in the same metropolitan area (2.9 percent).

The picture is understandably a little different when restricted to moves between counties within a state. For these moves, intermetropolitan migration is less important and moves within a metropolitan area or between nonmetropolitan locations are more important than is the case for interstate migration.

What this information seems to demonstrate is considerable heterogeneity of interstate migration in terms of metropolitan and nonmetropolitan origins and destinations. It is true that according to these categories, the modal interstate move is from one metropolitan area to another, but such moves represented less than one half of interstate migration in the early 1980s according to 1970 metropolitan-area boundaries. As these boundaries are updated, intermetropolitan moves will rise as a proportion of interstate migration. The general conclusion, in some ways a little surprising, is that even though the United States became a predominantly metropolitan nation around 1950, by the early 1980s intermetropolitan migration was still not a majority of interstate moves.

Intermetropolitan migration is most often analyzed and explained not in terms of its volume relative to other types of moves but in terms of econometric models of migration flows among metropolitan areas. The appeal of using metropolitan areas rather than states as the origin and destination of migration streams is that metropolitan areas may represent labor markets and thus for labor force migration are preferable to states whose heterogeneity includes urban as well as rural moves which may represent entirely different decision-making processes. Research on intermetropolitan migration streams derives in large part from Lowry's 1966 study, which in some ways represents an important turning point in research on U.S. internal migration.[29]

Prior to Lowry's work the number of migrants from one city to another was often looked upon simply as a function of the population of the city of origin, the population of the city of destination, and the distance between them. Data for testing such models were often from privately collected surveys of recent migrants, as detected in places of destination. A famous elaboration upon this approach was by Samuel Stouffer, who proposed adding two variables: the number of intervening opportunities and the number of competing migrants.[30] Stouffer's work guided a great many research undertakings, but the major shortcomings were operationalizing the notions of intervening opportunities and com-

---

[29]Ira S. Lowry, *Migration and Metropolitan Growth: Two Analytical Models* (San Francisco: Chandler, 1966).

[30]Stouffer's work is summarized and updated to 1955-60 in Omer R. Galle and Karl E. Taeuber, "Metropolitan Migration and Intervening Opportunities," *American Sociological Review* 31 (February 1966): 5–13.

peting migrants and the inability of the model to forecast or account for changing migration flows.

Stouffer's final formulation was based on data from the 1940 census on 1935–40 migration flows among all U.S. cities of over 100,000 population. As metropolitan areas came to replace cities as the preferred ecological unit, the Census Bureau came to tabulate migration data for metropolitan areas. Lowry's model was for 1955–60 migration flows among metropolitan areas of 250,000 or greater population. It posited the number of migrants from metropolitan area i to metropolitan area j (M_{ij}) to be:

$$M_{ij} = k[U_i/U_j \cdot W_j/W_i \cdot L_iL_j/D_{ij}].$$

U_i and U_j represent unemployment as a percentage of the civilian non-agricultural labor force at i and j; W_i and W_j represent the average hourly manufacturing wage at i and j; L_i and L_j represent the nonagricultural labor force at i and j; and D_{ij} equals the airline distance from i to j. Converted to logarithms, the equation becomes:

$$\log M_{ij} = \log k + \log U_i - \log U_j - \log W_i$$
$$+ \log W_j + \log L_i + \log L_j - \log D_{ij}$$

and it is easy to see that migration from metropolitan area i to metropolitan area j is expected to be positively associated with the unemployment rate at i, the wage rate at j, and the size of the labor forces at i and j, and negatively associated with the unemployment rate at j, the wage rate at i, and the distance between i and j.

A voluminous research literature evolved from elaborations of this basic formulation of intermetropolitan migration streams and the more traditional approaches which take net migration (1950–60 or 1960–70) or gross inmigration and outmigration (1955–60 or 1965–70) for metropolitan areas as the dependent variable. The persistence of the more traditional approaches which use inmigration or outmigration streams (not specific as to origin or destination) or simply net migration is accounted for by data availability, for such data were disaggregated by age, race, and other characteristics, whereas the stream flows among metropolitan areas were not disaggregated by characteristics of migrants.

Subsequent models—whether elaborations of the Lowry model or the other approaches which focus simply on inmigrants, outmigrants, or net migration—may be characterized as emphasizing three major themes. One consists of adjustments and refinements to the Lowry-type variables. These have included efforts to measure all predictor variables at the beginning of the migration interval so as to eliminate simultaneity bias and to develop alternatives to a simple unemployment rate, which often was found not to have the expected positive effect on outmigration and the negative effect on inmigration.[31] Another adjustment is to the income-opportunity variable (sometimes measured by mean earnings, per capita income, or median family income) to take into account differences in cost of living. Adjustments for cost of living generally improve the fit of regression models, suggesting that migrants and potential migrants do make some allowances for differences among metropolitan areas in cost of living.[32] Cost of living data, however, are often available only for a few large metropolitan areas which may not be representative of metropolitan areas in general.

Besides adjusting and refining the Lowry-type variables, another extension of metropolitan migration models in the 1970s was the addition of variables to the right-hand side of the regression equation. Most commonly, variables were added to reflect climate or overall quality of life in order to account for the shift of migration toward Sunbelt metropolitan areas. Measures of the climate of metropolitan areas have been numerous and have included number of days per year when the temperature falls below freezing; micrograms of suspended particulate matter per cubic meter of air; the absolute deviation of an area's mean January and July temperatures from 65 degrees Farenheit (intended to measure moderate climates with modest seasonal variation); the average relative humidity during June, July, and August; the average wind speed during December, January, and February; and average January snowfall.[33] Some

---

[31]Gary S. Fields, "Place-to-Place Migration: Some New Evidence," *Review of Economics and Statistics* 61 (February 1979): 21–32. Fields used labor turnover instead of rates of unemployment.

[32]Gary Fields, "Labor Force Migration, Unemployment, and Job Turnover," *Review of Economics and Statistics* 57 (November 1976): 407–415; and Richard J. Cebula, *The Determinants of Human Migration* (Lexington, MA: Lexington Books, 1979): 53–59. The general issue is made more complex through considerations that some age groups may be more sensitive than others to cost-of-living differences or to some components (for example, housing) than others among the list of goods priced for family units; besides, family budgets need not reflect persons who migrate alone or in nonfamily households. Some recent experiments with alternative formulations for cost-of-living adjustments include Stephen M. Renas and Rishi Kumar, "The Cost of Living, Labor Market Opportunities, and the Migration Decision: Some Additional Evidence," *Annals of Regional Science* 15 (November 1981): 74–79; Gershon Alperovich, "The Cost of Living, Labor Market Opportunities and the Migration Decision: A Case of Misspecification," Comment," *Annals of Regional Science* 17 (March 1983): 94–97; Jung Duk Lim, "The Cost of Living, Labor Market Opportunities and the Migration Decision: A Case of Misspecificaton? a Comment" *Annals of Regional Science* 17 (November 1983): 83–88.

[33]Philip E. Graves, "A Reexamination of Migration, Economic Opportunity, and the Quality of Life," *Journal of Regional Science* 16 (April 1976): 107–115; Gershon Alperovich, Joel Bergsman, and Christian Ehemann, "An Econometric Model of Migration between U.S. Metropolitan Areas," *Urban Studies* 14 (June 1977): 135–145; Stephen M. Renas and Rishi Kumar, "Desirability of Climate and the Spatial Allocation of Migrants: A Statistical Inquiry," *Review of Regional Studies* 8 (Winter 1978): 52–59; Philip E. Graves, "A Life-Cycle Empirical Analysis of Migration and Climate, by Race," *Journal of Urban Economics* 6 (April 1979): 135–147; and Philip E. Graves, "Income and Migration Revisited," *Journal of Human Resources* 14 (Winter 1979): 112–121.

researchers have experimented with combining the aforementioned measures with measures of other noneconomic amenities (such as availability of health care and presence of good schools) into a single overall index of "quality of life."[34] In almost every formulation the climate variables or overall quality-of-life indexes add to explained variation but not always in consistent ways, partly because climate may have different effects for migrants of different age or economic status, and the available data often have not allowed appropriate disaggregation of the migration variable.

Other sets of variables have also been added to the right-hand side of the equation in an attempt to identify the effect of public policies and programs on metropolitan migration. The underlying theory is that people act as consumers and "vote with their feet" in choosing among metropolitan areas. Among the variables most often included are tax rates, size or availability of unemployment payments, and size or availability of public assistance.[35] The effects of such variables are not always as might be expected, partly because of the inability to disaggregate the migration variables into population groups that are most likely to be sensitive to each of the policy-relevant variables.

All of the models of metropolitan migration reviewed here have at least one feature in common: They are *macro* models in which the dependent variable is gross inmigration or outmigration for individual metropolitan areas, net migration, or migration flows between each pair of metropolitan areas. Most have employed single-equation estimation techniques, although simultaneous-equation methods have also been employed to estimate mutually determined variables.[36] Micro models based on data for individual migrants have also been introduced to account for puzzling findings from the macro models. For example, the latter have found inconsistent effects of a metropolitan area's unemployment rate on its rates of inmigration, outmigration, or net migration, seeming to suggest that an area's unemployment rate does not have much effect on migration. Use of individual-level survey data,

---

[34]Ben-chieh Liu, "Differential Net Migration Rates and the Quality of Life," *Review of Economics and Statistics* 57 (August 1975): 329–337; David A. Larson and Walton T. Wilford, "A Note on Differential Net Migration and the Quality of Life," *Review of Economics and Statistics* 62 (February 1980): 157–162; Chang-Tseh Hsieh and Ben Chieh Liu, "The Pursuance of Better Quality of Life: In the Long Run, Better Quality of Social Life Is the Most Important Factor in Migration," *Review of Economics and Sociology* 42 (October 1983): 431–440; Stephen M. Renas and Rishi Kumar, "Climatic Conditions and Migration: An Econometric Inquiry," *Annals of Regional Science* 17 (March 1983): 69–78.

[35]See Fields, "Place-to-Place Migration Flows: Some New Evidence"; and Cebula, *The Determinants of Human Migration*, pp. 91–145.

[36]Michael J. Greenwood, "A Simultaneous-Equations Model of Urban Growth and Migration," *Journal of the American Statistical Association* 70 (December 1975): 797–810; and Michael J. Greenwood, *Migration and Economic Growth in the United States* (New York: Academic Press, 1981), 169–182.

however, along with ecological measures of metropolitan areas shows that the migration of unemployed persons is strongly influenced by the area's unemployment rate.[37]

Another feature common to the attempts to model metropolitan migration is the lack of explicit attention to the nonmetropolitan migration turnaround. None was designed to predict and none was evaluated in terms of ability to predict (even on an *ex post* basis) the increased migration from metropolitan areas or the decreased migration to them. This shortcoming is likely to be remedied only with better information on migrants' origins and destinations and explicit attention to the determinants of migration between more urban (metropolitan) and less urban (nonmetropolitan) locations.

The Incidence of Geographical Mobility

Up to now, the focus has been on the changing migration flows between the generic categories of metropolitan and nonmetropolitan locations and attempts to model migration for individual metropolitan areas. Unanswered is whether the incidence of geographical mobility varies according to city, suburban, and nonmetropolitan locations. Granted that migration flows between metropolitan and nonmetropolitan residential categories have changed in unexpected ways over the last 15 years, has the incidence of short- or long-distance moving been altered for metropolitan or nonmetropolitan territory? Do cities really conform to descriptions of them as having restless populations characterized by high turnover and extensive geographical mobility? Or, alternatively, in predominantly metropolitan societies, can rural populations accurately be described as sessile and sedentary? Table 6.5 presents an attempt to answer these questions, at least for the period from 1970 to 1984.

This period represents a time when metropolitan and nonmetropolitan migration flows were more nearly in balance than historically was the case, and it was also a time when the nation's residential mobility rate was generally declining, as discussed in Chapter 2. The comparisons between 1970–71 and the later periods in Table 6.5 can be mislead-

---

[37]Julie DaVanzo, "Does Unemployment Affect Migration?—Evidence from Micro Data," *Review of Economics and Statistics* 60 (November 1978): 504–514. DaVanzo used data from the University of Michigan Panel Study of Income Dynamics; for a similar study using microdata from the 1970 census, see Frank J. Navratil and James J. Doyle, "The Socioeconomic Determinants of Migration and the Level of Aggregation," *Southern Economic Journal* 43 (April 1977): 1547–1559.

TABLE 6.5

Percentage of Population Aged 1 and Over Changing Residence in One Year, by Type of Move and Area of Residence After Moving: 1970–71 to 1983–84

	1970–71	1975–76	1980–81	1981–82	1982–83	1983–84
Percentage of Population Who Changed Residence in Preceding 12 Months						
Metropolitan	18.7%	17.5%	17.7%	17.3%	16.7%	17.8%
Central Cities	19.9	18.7	19.8	19.6	19.0	20.2
Suburbs	17.9	16.7	16.2	15.7	15.1	16.1
Nonmetropolitan	18.7	18.0	16.4	16.5	16.3	16.1
Nonfarm	19.9	NA	NA	NA	NA	NA
Farm	9.6	NA	NA	NA	NA	NA
Percentage of Population Who Moved Within a County						
Metropolitan	12.0	11.1	10.9	10.7	10.4	11.0
Central cities	14.1	12.9	13.3	13.2	13.0	13.3
Suburbs	10.3	9.7	9.3	9.1	8.7	9.5
Nonmetropolitan	10.4	10.1	9.4	9.4	9.5	8.9
Nonfarm	11.0	NA	NA	NA	NA	NA
Farm	5.3	NA	NA	NA	NA	NA
Percentage of Population Who Moved Between Counties Within a State						
Metropolitan	2.4	3.0	3.1	3.1	3.0	3.4
Central cities	1.9	2.5	2.8	2.9	2.8	3.4
Suburbs	2.9	3.4	3.4	3.1	3.2	3.4
Nonmetropolitan	4.2	4.3	4.0	3.7	3.8	4.0
Nonfarm	4.4	NA	NA	NA	NA	NA
Farm	2.5	NA	NA	NA	NA	NA
Percentage of Population Who Moved Between States						
Metropolitan	3.4	2.8	2.8	2.9	2.7	2.8
Central cities	3.0	2.6	2.7	2.7	2.6	2.8
Suburbs	3.7	3.1	2.9	3.0	2.8	2.8
Nonmetropolitan	3.5	3.2	2.8	3.1	2.8	2.9
Nonfarm	3.8	NA	NA	NA	NA	NA
Farm	1.6	NA	NA	NA	NA	NA

NOTES: NA means "not available." Data are from Current Population Surveys. Data for 1970–71 reflect metropolitan boundaries in 1960; other data reflect metropolitan boundaries in 1970. Top panel includes movers from abroad.

ing because the 1970–71 data represent 1960 metropolitan-area boundaries, whereas the later periods reflect 1970 boundaries. As new metropolitan areas were created from what had been nonmetropolitan territory in 1960 and as other nonmetropolitan counties were added to the fringe of older metropolitan areas, growth and mobility were transferred out of the nonmetropolitan sector.

To some extent, the data do suggest somewhat higher rates of residential mobility among city residents than among suburbanites or nonmetropolitan residents. A central city resident picked at random in 1984 had a .202 chance of having changed residence in the preceding 12 months; for suburbanites and nonmetropolitan residents the probability was .161. The central city residential mobility rate may have increased modestly between 1975–76 and 1983–84, the suburban rate did not consistently change, and the nonmetropolitan rate seems to have decreased.

The higher central-city rate of residential mobility reflects more short-distance moving. About 13.3 percent of 1984 residents of central cities had moved within the same county in the preceding 12 months compared with 9.5 percent of suburbanites and 8.9 percent of nonmetropolitan residents.

Central cities, however, do not appear to have higher rates of intermediate- or long-distance moving. About 3.4 percent of 1984 central city residents had moved between counties within a state during the preceding 12 months, as had 3.4 percent of suburbanites and 4.0 percent of nonmetropolitan residents. About 2.8 percent of central city residents had moved between states, as had 2.8 percent of suburbanites and 2.9 percent of nonmetropolitan residents. There is no clear evidence of trend in these rates of moving between 1975–76 and 1983–84, and no evidence of systematic differences among the three residential categories.

These broad residential categories mask enormous variation among individual localities. Some of this variation can be illustrated by focusing on individual cities and the suburban balance of their metropolitan areas, as is done in Table 6.6, which presents rates of moving for the central city and suburban portions of 21 large metropolitan areas. These 21 were included in earlier research and represent simply the largest areas that were separately identified on the computer tapes that were then available. Metropolitan areas of the Northeast and Midwest are overrepresented, but the 21 areas include both growing and declining locations and each of the major regions of the country is represented by at least one metropolitan area. To increase the effective sample size, data from Current Population Surveys of March 1982, 1983, and 1984 were combined, but sampling variability is still great and small differences should be interpreted very cautiously.

The percentage of the population who had changed residence in the preceding 12 months ranged from a low of 11.1 in Philadelphia to a high of 33.1 in Dallas. Other cities with very low rates of residential mobility were New York City (11.9 percent), Buffalo (14.1 percent), and Baltimore (14.2 percent). All of the low-mobility cities lost population in the 1970s and might be expected to have populations characterized by people "left behind" as more mobile residents departed for the nearby suburbs or other parts of the country. Still, the differences are great. The proportion of Philadelphia's population in 1982–84 that moved to or within the city

TABLE 6.6

Percentage of Population Aged 1 and Over Changing Residence in the Preceding 12 Months, by Type of Move, for 21 Large Cities and Their Suburbs: Averages for 1982, 1983, and 1984

	Percentage Changing Residence		Percentage Moving Within a County		Percentage Moving Between Counties Within a State		Percentage Moving Between States	
	Central City	Suburbs	Central City	Suburbs	Central City	Suburbs	Central City	Suburbs
New York City	11.9%	11.5%	6.3%	6.6%	3.5%	2.6%	1.0%	1.6%
Chicago	16.3	11.9	13.1	7.0	1.4	2.5	0.9	1.9
Los Angeles–Long Beach	21.0	17.3	14.9	12.4	3.3	2.5	1.7	1.6
Philadelphia	11.1	12.7	7.9	6.8	1.9	3.5	1.1	1.8
Detroit	21.1	9.9	17.9	6.4	1.5	2.4	1.3	1.0
San Francisco–Oakland	21.2	18.4	11.2	9.8	7.6	5.4	1.9	2.3
Boston	23.0	11.3	14.5	6.0	4.5	3.1	3.2	1.7
Pittsburgh	16.6	8.7	11.1	6.2	3.3	1.2	2.1	1.2
St. Louis	16.7	13.3	11.7	7.1	3.5	2.3	1.6	3.7
Washington, D.C.	18.1	18.5	10.1	7.0	0.9	4.9	6.2	5.7
Cleveland	18.7	13.2	13.9	9.0	3.3	1.9	1.0	2.0
Baltimore	14.2	12.6	11.1	6.3	2.2	4.5	0.6	1.5
Newark	16.3	12.3	11.2	6.9	1.4	2.8	3.7	2.2
Minneapolis–St. Paul	23.3	16.5	15.3	7.4	4.1	5.1	3.4	3.7
Buffalo	14.1	6.7	9.3	4.9	2.3	0.7	2.5	0.5
Houston	30.3	20.7	19.2	9.4	5.3	7.4	4.9	3.7
Milwaukee	20.8	8.5	13.6	4.7	4.6	2.1	1.7	1.7
Paterson–Clifton–Passaic	20.1	11.5	12.1	5.3	3.8	3.6	2.1	1.7
Cincinnati	23.6	17.2	19.6	10.6	2.3	3.0	1.4	3.6
Dallas	33.1	24.7	21.6	13.1	6.1	6.0	4.5	5.1
Atlanta	23.3	18.3	12.2	8.3	7.7	4.7	2.6	4.6

NOTES: Boundaries of cities and metropolitan areas are as of 1970. "Suburbs" means the entire balance of metropolitan areas outside the central city. "Percentage changing residence" includes movers from abroad. Data are from Current Population Surveys of March 1982, 1983, and 1984.

215

was less than the proportion of Dallas's population that had moved *within* the city; the incidence of intercounty migrants in Dallas's population was nearly as great as the percentage of Philadelphia's population that had moved to or within the city.

The high-mobility cities do not necessarily represent areas of rapid growth. Besides Dallas, other cities with high rates of residential mobility include Houston (30.3 percent), Cincinnati (23.6 percent), Atlanta (23.3 percent), Minneapolis–St. Paul (23.3 percent), and Boston (23.0). Of these cities, Dallas and Houston grew rapidly and the others lost population in the 1970s. Among other cities with annual residential mobility rates of 20 percent or greater, Los Angeles–Long Beach grew, but San Francisco–Oakland, Detroit, Milwaukee, and Paterson–Clifton–Passaic did not. Clearly, the proportion of a city's population that has moved is a function of more than just growth—a point that will be returned to shortly.

For almost all of the 21 metropolitan areas, the proportion of population that had moved in the preceding 12 months was higher in the central city than the suburban territory, primarily reflecting higher rates of intracounty moving on the part of central city residents. Comparing cities and suburbs in rates of intercounty movement is difficult because some cities may spread over several counties. For example, the rates of moving between counties within a state are quite high for Atlanta in part because the city spreads across three counties, and rates of interstate migration are very high for Washington, D.C., because it is, for statistical purposes, treated like a state and a city-to-suburb or a suburb-to-city move counts as interstate migration.

Many of the cities and suburban areas shown in Table 6.6 had residential mobility rates below the 16.1 percent for the entire nonmetropolitan population in 1984. Although the cities tend to have higher rates of intracounty moving than nonmetropolitan territory, many of the suburbs have lower intracounty rates than for nonmetropolitan territory as a whole. These comparisons suggest that there is little evidence for the notion of a general "urban" versus "rural" level of geographical mobility. What one finds instead is extensive place-to-place variability, partly reflecting the diffusion of growth toward fringe locations and toward many newer metropolitan areas in the South and West over the last 15 or 20 years.

Urban Residential Mobility of Owners and Renters

One approach to accounting for mobility differences between cities and suburbs and among metropolitan areas might be through differences in population composition. For example, locations whose populations are overrepresented with persons who are known to be highly mobile would be expected to display high geographical mobility. One of the most consistently reported differences in the mobility of urban populations is between owners and renters. Renters are regularly reported to be more likely to change residence than owners, and since cities almost always have a higher proportion of renters than owners, perhaps the higher residential mobility of cities can be at least partly accounted for in this way. To test this proposition, residential mobility rates of the 21 cities and suburban areas shown in Table 6.6 are shown for owners and renters in Table 6.7.

With some apparent exceptions, central city homeowners seem to have higher rates of residential mobility than suburban homeowners. Residential mobility differences between central city and suburban

TABLE 6.7

*Annual Residential Mobility Rates of Owners and Renters
and the Percentage of Persons Aged 1 and Over Living in Rental Housing,
for 21 Large Cities and Suburbs: Averages for 1982, 1983, and 1984*

| | Percentage Changing Residence | | | | Percentage Who Live in Rental Housing | |
| | Owners | | Renters | | | |
	Central City	Suburbs	Central City	Suburbs	Central City	Suburbs
New York City	6.0%	6.9%	13.0%	19.4%	67.5%	31.0%
Chicago	7.7	5.3	22.4	35.2	52.2	20.4
Los Angeles–Long Beach	9.3	8.6	28.8	28.3	54.5	39.9
Philadelphia	7.0	6.5	20.5	32.0	29.0	21.7
Detroit	11.1	4.7	38.4	35.4	35.4	16.5
San Francisco–Oakland	9.7	9.5	28.5	32.5	58.7	34.7
Boston	7.6	5.6	30.3	24.4	64.1	27.5
Pittsburgh	6.7	5.1	28.5	23.3	44.6	19.6
St. Louis	5.1	8.5	28.7	31.9	49.3	20.2
Washington, D.C.	10.1	9.4	22.8	40.9	55.9	25.9
Cleveland	7.1	5.9	32.0	33.6	44.0	25.4
Baltimore	6.7	6.4	21.6	37.3	48.7	19.2
Newark	1.5	5.9	20.0	27.0	80.2	28.8
Minneapolis–St. Paul	8.1	9.0	44.7	46.9	40.2	19.3
Buffalo	8.7	3.2	20.5	28.6	46.1	11.3
Houston	11.6	15.1	51.8	44.7	44.2	18.5
Milwaukee	7.4	4.8	36.3	23.8	43.3	19.7
Paterson–Clifton–Passaic	8.3	4.6	23.6	24.7	63.0	29.9
Cincinnati	10.1	8.6	35.8	49.8	51.6	20.8
Dallas	17.9	12.3	46.3	51.8	50.4	30.1
Atlanta	7.6	7.8	39.0	39.6	47.5	30.6

NOTES: Boundaries of cities and metropolitan areas are as of 1970. "Suburbs" means the entire balance of metropolitan areas outside the central city. "Percentage changing residence" includes movers from abroad. Data are from Current Population Surveys of March 1982, 1983, and 1984.

owners are typically small, and the rates are subject to very large sampling variability. Still, for 15 of the 21 metropolitan areas central city homeowners appear to have been more likely than suburban homeowners to have moved in the last year. Hence, homeowners conform to the image of greater residential mobility in cities than in suburbs.

For renters, the picture is different. Central city renters seem less mobile than suburban renters. Although the sampling errors are very large for such small bases, still in 15 of the 21 metropolitan areas central city renters seem less likely to have moved in the last year than suburban renters. Thus, renters do not conform to the image of higher residential mobility in cities than suburbs.

Why central city renters might have lower residential mobility than suburban renters is not immediately evident. One possibility is that the renter category includes public housing, which is more common in central cities than in suburbs. In some cities families may have to wait years before being accepted in public housing, suggesting that, once accepted, occupants of public housing may have comparatively long durations of residence. Another possibility is rent control, which is also more common in cities than suburbs. Where rent control is stringent and landlords can raise rents only modestly in occupied units, the probable outcome is for renters to stay in their units for relatively long periods of time. Both of these explanations suggest factors that reduce turnover in central city rental units. The surveys from which Tables 6.6 and 6.7 were derived did not allow tests for these explanations.

Residential mobility differences among metropolitan areas cannot be attributed to differences in level of homeownership. In general, metropolitan areas that have high rates of overall mobility tend to have high rates for both owners and renters. The comparatively low rates of residential mobility in older metropolitan areas of the Northeast and Midwest tend to characterize both owners and renters, and the high rates in growing metropolitan areas of the Southwest still stand out. For example, on average only 6.0 percent of New York City homeowners changed residence annually in the 1982–84 period compared with 17.9 percent of homeowners in Dallas. Homeowners in Dallas, in fact, appear more residentially mobile than renters in New York City. For these two cities, differences in rates of residential mobility reflect growth and population turnover that cannot be attributed to differences in the incidence of homeownership.

These data confirm that renters typically do have higher rates of residential mobility than owners, although the differences would be somewhat less if owner-renter status were measured before moving rather than after moving, as is done in Table 6.7. The data did not permit such measurement or further cross-tabulation. The table does show, however, considerable variation among areas in residential mobility rates of owners and renters, reflecting areal differences in overall population growth and, possibly, local policies that may reduce the average mobility of the renter population by affecting its composition.

Relating Intermetropolitan and Intrametropolitan Mobility

Most research on intrametropolitan mobility has not attempted to explain differences among metropolitan areas—in sharp contrast to research on intermetropolitan migration. Analyses of intrametropolitan movement have been characterized by micro models, often using data collected by individual researchers, to explain how households decide to move or stay and to account for the likelihood of an individual household's moving. Models of intermetropolitan migration have consisted largely of macro models that use publicly available data (usually from censuses) to account for areal differences in inmigration, outmigration, net migration, or place-to-place flows. In essence, the former focus on variability among individuals or households, and the latter focus on variability among areas.

Other differences also distinguish the two research traditions. Research on movement among metropolitan areas has stressed the importance of distinguishing between the factors that enter into the decision to move and the factors that influence the choice of destination by movers. In many models of intrametropolitan mobility, however, the outcome is dichotomous—either the household moves or it does not. It has been suggested, however, that the allocation of intrametropolitan movers among neighborhoods can be modeled in much the same way as models of intermetropolitan migration that focus on the allocation of migrants among metropolitan areas;[38] this approach has not been widely used because censuses or large public surveys almost never collect or tabulate data on neighborhood-to-neighborhood movement.

Models of intrametropolitan mobility have drawn heavily on an older research tradition concerned with mobility differentials observed in cross-sectional surveys. The likelihood of moving locally (and local mobility is more commonly analyzed on an intraurban basis than within rural environments) has been most often related to the notion of stage in the life cycle, which has usually included age, marital status,

---

[38]Gershon Alperovich, "Economic Analysis of Intraurban Migration in Tel-Aviv," *Journal of Urban Economics* 14 (1983): 280–292.

and number and ages of children. In light of rising divorce rates and a growing variety of living arrangements, the notion of intraurban moves being linked to such common life-cycle events as getting married or the birth of the first child loses some of its theoretical or predictive significance. Other household characteristics often incorporated in models of intraurban mobility include whether the dwelling is owned or rented, the adequacy of the dwelling unit (for example, bedrooms relative to the number of children), and overall satisfaction with the dwelling unit or the neighborhood.[39]

Much of the research on intrametropolitan mobility derives from work done in the late 1960s and 1970s that related household mobility to the notion of "residential stress," which occurs as new needs arise and cause a household to reassess the adequacy of its current dwelling; and after investigating the choices available within budgetary and other constraints, the household decides to move or stay. Residential stress is often measured by such changes in household composition as the birth of a child, the impending enrollment of a child in school, or a relative's joining the household. Sometimes "contextual" factors are included—for example, a change in the nature of the neighborhood. This line of research has focused almost exclusively on explaining mobility differences among households as a function of characteristics of the household or neighborhoods.[40]

One approach to explaining intermetropolitan differences in the amount of intrametropolitan mobility is by recognizing that locational "stress" can come not only from household changes but also from circumstances external to the household and representative of changes in metropolitan areas. Insight into these processes was provided by urban sociologists and human ecologists in the 1920s who described how migrants to cities at that time tended to settle in inner areas near the central business district and displaced the residents of those areas. Households that left these inner neighborhoods tended to move slightly

[39]A review of the literature and an analysis that presents the case for the independent effects of housing and neighborhood satisfaction is presented in Alden Speare, Jr., Sidney Goldstein, and William Frey, *Residential Mobility, Migration and Metropolitan Change* (Cambridge, MA: Ballinger, 1975). More recent works are reviewed, with some emphasis on geographical perspectives, in W. A. V. Clark, "Recent Research on Migration and Mobility: A Review and Interpretation," *Progress in Planning* 18 (1982): 5–56, especially chap. 3 on intraurban migration. An economic perspective is given in John M. Quigley and Daniel H. Weinberg, "Intra-Urban Residential Mobility: A Review and Synthesis," *International Regional Science Review* 2 (Fall 1977): 41–66.

[40]Perhaps the only exception is John L. Goodman, "Linking Local Mobility Rates to Migration Rates: Repeat Movers and Place Effects," in W. A. V. Clark, ed., *Modelling Housing Market Search* (New York: St. Martin's Press, 1982). Goodman used the Panel Survey of Income Dynamics to show that the probability of a household's moving within a metropolitan area was, other things being equal, positively affected by the overall population growth rate.

farther from the central business district, thereby setting in motion more residential mobility and waves of invasion and succession. The implication seems to be that a high volume of inmigration would cause a larger shock to the system and generate more local residential mobility ("invasion and succession") than a small volume of inmigration. Over a cross-section of cities one might expect a positive correlation between the inmigration rate and the local mobility rate.

Another perspective which suggests a positive correlation between inmigration and local mobility is furnished by geographers who have found that long-distance migration (sometimes called "total displacement migration") is often followed by subsequent moves within the area (called "partial displacement migration").[41] The theory is that migration to a metropolitan area is always made with varying degrees of uncertainty, and after moving to an area a household acquires greater knowledge of the area and can achieve through moving a better fit between its needs and aspirations and the available housing and neighborhoods—hence, one might expect that the greater the inmigration, the greater the local moving.

An adequate test of these ideas might involve time-series analyses with appropriate lags between inmigration rates and local mobility rates, or it might be done with longitudinal data for individual households. Neither is possible for the 21 cities and suburban areas included in Table 6.6. Nevertheless, assuming that (1) intercounty movement approximates migration and intracounty movement approximates local mobility and (2) lags between inmigration and local mobility are not very great, one can draw some inferences about the association between inmigration rates and local mobility rates.

First, one might expect the association to be higher for cities than for suburban counties, which are on average less extensively developed and have more room for new construction, so that heavy inmigration would generate less "locational stress." Second, one might expect the association for cities to decline over time, especially older cities that have attracted fewer and fewer inmigrants and have had substantial population loss (for example, St. Louis city, included in Table 6.6, lost one half of its population between 1950 and 1984). Third, one might expect the correlation for suburban areas to increase over time, reflecting a "filling up" of many suburban areas.

Figure 6.2 depicts the regression of the intracounty rate of moving (plotted on the y axis) and the intercounty rate of moving (plotted on the x axis) for 20 of the cities and suburban areas listed in Table 6.6

[41]Curtis C. Roseman, "Migration as a Spatial and Temporal Process," *Annals of the Association of American Geographers* 61 (September 1971): 589–598; John S. Adams, D. J. Caruso, E. A. Nordstrand, and R. I. Palm, "Intraurban Migration," *Annals of the Association of American Geographers* 63 (March 1973): 152–55.

FIGURE 6.2

Regression of Intracounty Rates of Moving on Intercounty Rates,
for 20 Large Cities (1949–50, 1968–71, and 1982–84)
and Their Suburbs (1968–71 and 1982–84)

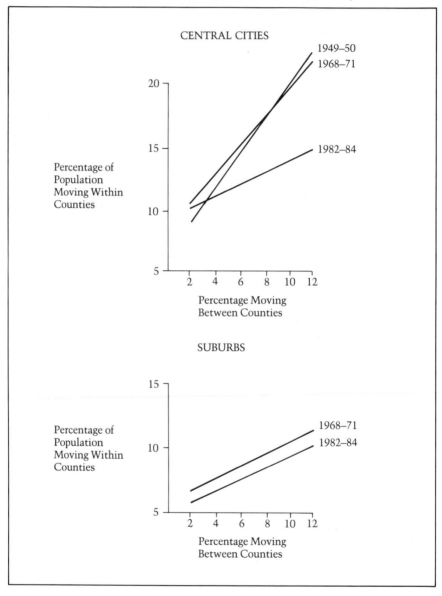

(Atlanta was excluded because data were not available in 1968–71). The 1949–50 data are from the 1950 census, the only U.S. census to include a question on residence one year earlier. The 1968–71 data were tabulated from microdata files of Current Population Surveys of 1968, 1969, 1970, and 1971; and the 1982–84 data from microdata files of Current Population Surveys of 1982, 1983, and 1984. Each of the Current Population Surveys asked about residence one year earlier. Intercounty movers include movers from abroad. The data did not permit further disaggregating for owners and renters or other population categories.

The aforementioned expectations are generally borne out. First, the association between intercounty and intracounty movement is greater for cities than suburbs. Second, for cities the association betweeen intercounty and intracounty moving dropped between 1950 and the early 1980s, as indicated by successive declines in the slope of the regression line. For the 20 cities the correlation (r^2) between annual intercounty and intracounty moving dropped from .57 in 1949–50, to .34 in 1968–71, and to .13 in 1982–84. For suburbs, the correlation between intercounty and intracounty rates rose from .06 in 1968–71 to .26 in 1982–84.

Such results do not constitute a definitive test of a theory. Perhaps the best that can be claimed is that they provide some support for the notion that high inmigration rates to cities have served to generate short-distance moving; but as older cities (and the 20 cities are overrepresented by older urban areas) have lost population and as migration to them declined, less local moving can be accounted for by inmigration rates.

One could, of course, continue to add variables to the regression equation to take into account other characteristics of cities and metropolitan areas—including, for example, rent control, rate of new housing construction in suburban areas, and changes in mortgage rates and housing affordability. The limitation is the small number of metropolitan areas for which one-year rates of moving were available.[42] Figure 6.2 is

---

[42]One-year mobility rates are available for a larger number of areas from the metropolitan area samples of the American Housing Surveys. Mobility is measured somewhat differently in the AHS (the mobility question is asked only of the householder or household head) than in the CPS (where the question is asked of each person), and attention was restricted to the CPS because the series could be extended farther back in time. AHS data for 42 metropolitan areas sampled in the 1970s exhibit a positive association between inmigration and movement within them; see Goodman, "Linking Local Mobility Rates to Migration Rates," p. 210. The five-year data from censuses do not show an association between inmigration and local mobility. For the 20 cities included in Figure 6.2, the correlation between intercounty moving and intracounty moving in 1965–70 was .004. The five-year interval is apparently too long and combines too many multiple moves of the same persons to show any association between inmigration and local moving.

intended to illustrate a positive but declining association between in-migration rates and local mobility in large cities.

Some evidence of urban residential mobility for earlier periods comes from work by sociologists and historians who have sought to study population turnover from year-to-year comparisons of city directories, utility disconnects, and other sources of data. This literature does not reflect a systematic methodology, is often vague about the area being studied (whether the entire city or only part), and may overstate mobility as a result of errors and inconsistencies in the city directories. Nevertheless, almost all imply a downward trend in residential mobility.

For example, one study reported annual residential mobility rates for Omaha, Nebraska, of about 21 percent in the late 1920s, 13 percent in the mid-1930s, and 20 percent from 1942 to 1945.[43] St. Louis was reported to have had annual mobility rates of 36 percent in the 1920s and Cleveland was said to have had a rate of 25 percent in the mid-1930s.[44] The proportion of population who had moved in several small but growing cities of Illinois in 1930 was reported to have exceeded 40 percent annually.[45] Boston is reported to have had annual rates of intracity moving of 30 percent in the 1890s.[46] And in Norristown, Pennsylvania, Goldstein reported consistent declines in intracity moving from 1910 to 1950.[47] For the areas studied, the reported rates of moving imply marked declines in urban residential mobility during the twentieth century.

Many studies of urban residential mobility were undertaken during periods of rapid growth or extensive invasion and succession. The work by sociologists was often undertaken for the purpose of associating urban residential mobility with various social problems—juvenile delinquency, family breakups, mental disorders—and they may have contributed to a belief that American cities in general are characterized by permanently high and disruptive amounts of population turnover.

---

[43]T. Earl Sullenger, "The Social Significance of Mobility: An Omaha Study," *American Journal of Sociology* 55 (May 1950): 559–563.

[44]Theodore Caplow, "Incidence and Direction of Residential Mobility in a Minneapolis Sample," *Social Forces* 27 (May 1949): 413–417.

[45]William Albig, "The Mobility of Urban Population: A Study of Four Cities of 30,000 to 40,000 Population," *Social Forces* 11 (March 1933): 351–367.

[46]Stephen Thernstrom and Peter R. Knights, "Men in Motion: Some Data and Speculations about Urban Population Mobility in Nineteenth Century America," in Tamara K. Hareven, ed., *Anonymous Americans: Explorations in Nineteenth Century Social History* (Englewood Cliffs, NJ: Prentice-Hall, 1971).

[47]Sidney Goldstein, *Patterns of Mobility, 1910–1950: The Norristown Study* (Philadelphia: University of Pennsylvania Press, 1958): 211–214.

Summary and Conclusion

Varying sources of data that lend themselves to differing research methods have strongly influenced the nature of research in three areas of metropolitan and nonmetropolitan mobility: the unexpected nonmetropolitan migration turnaround of the 1970s, movement between metropolitan areas, and movement within metropolitan areas. Analysis of the first has come from census and survey statistics on gross migration flows, intercensal estimates of net migration for counties, and privately collected surveys of reasons for moving and residential preferences. A variety of explanations for the nonmetropolitan turnaround were offered: a shift of many kinds of jobs to less urban settings in the 1970s; a greater willingness on the part of a sizable segment of the population to trade some degree of income maximization in order to realize longstanding preferences for less urban residential environments; growing leisure time and a tendency to spend it around rural recreational centers made accessible by better transportation and three-day weekends; and a growing number of retirees whose choice of rural retirement locations can be employment-generating for other persons.

After 1980 the net migration balance again shifted to favor the metropolitan sector. To date, no explanatory scheme has satisfactorily accounted for the unprecedented fluctuations of metropolitan-nonmetropolitan migration balances over the last 15 years. During this time, however, the net exchanges have been comparatively small, and the shift of net migration back toward the metropolitan sector in the early 1980s does not represent the massive net redistribution to metropolitan areas characteristic of the 1950s and 1960s. The more recent shift of net migration back toward the metropolitan sector suggests the need for a dynamic approach that relates the urban-rural implications of national economic restructuring and the changing ability of different demographic subgroups to act on the basis of residential preferences.

Research on migration among metropolitan areas has often been undertaken on the theory that individual metropolitan areas come closer than other spatial aggregates to representing the space over which migration decisions are made. Migration to, from, or between metropolitan areas has been characterized by macro models based on publicly available data on net migration, gross inmigration and outmigration, or migration flows among metropolitan areas. Research in the last decade and a half has emphasized extensions of classical economic models by adding new variables to represent the effects of climate, amenities, or quality of life in individual metropolitan areas or their policies, like taxes and welfare spending. What has not been possible is a time-series approach that can demonstrate the changed effect of climate (a constant) or how changes in public policies and programs affect migration flows.

Studies of intrametropolitan mobility have emphasized micro models of household decision making, often using privately collected data for a single metropolitan area. These approaches emphasize how households decide to move or stay and sometimes how they evaluate neighborhoods. They are intended to explain who engages in local moving, and they do not very well account for differences among metropolitan areas in rates of local moving. Differences among metropolitan areas in the amount of intrametropolitan mobility appear to be considerable and not explainable in terms of differences in such compositional factors as how many households own or rent. The amount of intrametropolitan mobility appears to be positively related to inmigration.

On average, central cities of metropolitan areas have somewhat more short-distance moving than is found in suburbs or nonmetropolitan territory, but large, older cities of the Northeast and Midwest have rather low rates of residential mobility. Chapter 8 compares their residential mobility with that found in large metropolitan areas of Great Britain and Japan.

7

REASONS FOR MOVING

A LMOST never do censuses ask movers why they moved, but censuses have been a major source for inferring the motivational bases underlying geographical mobility, especially long-distance movement. In the last two decades the dominant approach to identifying causes of migration has been with econometric models that account for migration to, from, or between areas or simply the net migration of areas. Variability among areas in any of these measures of migration is typically accounted for by models that include sets of variables to measure economic conditions and climatic, environmental, or quality-of-life factors that may strengthen or weaken economic pushes and pulls. With a Sunbelt shift of population in the 1970s and a movement away from large metropolitan areas to rural and smaller urban locations, noneconomic variables received increased attention. The universal conclusion, discussed in Chapter 6, was that noneconomic variables increased the ability of models to account for variability of migration among areas or at least were more important in the 1970s than in preceding decades in explaining migration flows.

The alternative to inferring the motives and causes of migration from observed flows is to ask migrants why they move, perhaps inquiring as to why migrants left the area of previous residence and why they chose their place of destination. This approach received renewed attention in the 1970s as many researchers sought to identify more precisely the characteristics of less urban locations that attracted new residents from metropolitan areas. The goal often seemed to be to identify attributes of areas that might not be measured in common statistical sources. A common research design was to identify samples of migrants to nonmetropolitan locations through use of new listings in phone books, utility hookups, or other sources and to conduct personal interviews with the inmigrants, asking about reasons for moving. Almost all studies concluded that noneconomic, quality-of-life amenities played a very important role in the movement to less urban locations in the 1970s.

This chapter briefly reviews the case for and against analyzing geographical mobility by means of survey questions on reasons for moving, and it evaluates the evidence from attempts to assess reasons for moving on national surveys. It illustrates the use of large surveys of the nation as a whole to evaluate reasons for interstate migration, focusing on retirement and desire for change of climate as "causes" of such migration.

The Pros and Cons of Asking Reasons for Moving

The limitations of asking movers why they moved are well known and often cited:

- Respondents may not know or may not be able to verbalize the reasons for their behavior. Or they may not be able to separate among many considerations those that influenced their decisions. Respondents may not be able to distinguish among competing reasons for moving or staying held by different household members, and since most mobility in developed countries consists of household moves rather than individuals migrating alone, respondents may not be able to identify the ways that individuals' reasons for wanting to move or stay get compromised when household mobility decisions are made.

- Some respondents may have reasons for lying, intentionally misrepresenting, or rationalizing why they move. Some may be leaving unpleasant family circumstances or business failures, or for other reasons may want to withhold from interviewers the circumstances surrounding their leaving one location for another.

- By focusing on the proximate determinants of mobility, reasons-for-moving surveys may fail to detect long-range planning that underlies a decision to move from one location to another. For individuals who have distant planning horizons, a particular move may be part of an anticipated chain or sequence of moves, and the reasons for a particular move may not be representative of the motivations underlying the intended sequence of moving.

- Reasons-for-moving surveys may oversimplify reality because of the constraints imposed by the limited space on survey questionnaires or the limited time available for interviews. Because of constraints of sample size or budget, many surveys use a small number of predetermined reasons or collapse reported reasons into a very limited number of categories which are too broad and too vague to provide insight into motivation. Also, the lack of convention on which aspects of migration motivations to probe for sometimes results in questions that guide respondents toward giving answers that the researcher is looking for.

For some purposes, however, a reasons-for-moving approach is desirable or even preferable to inferring motivation from observed flows:

- Some bases for moving may be identifiable only through self-reporting. For example, considerable theorizing has been devoted to the voluntary and involuntary aspects of moving. To identify how much local moving is forced upon persons by housing conversions and demolitions, rent increases, and other circumstances thought to force a move, there may not be a practical alternative to asking movers about these or related circumstances.

- Some groups of movers—and their characteristics—can hardly be identified and compared except through personal interviews. For example, over the last decade or so a large literature has arisen concerning the migration of retirees, but many studies simply examine movers around age 60 or 65 or even all movers over age 60 or 65. Surveys may be a desirable way of identifying persons moving in connection with retiring from full-time participation in the labor force, and surveys may be the only basis for identifying the social and economic characteristics of these persons and comparing them with other groups of movers or retirees who do not move. Self-reporting becomes particularly important when persons at "retirement" ages leave a job or career and "retire" to a new area but continue working, perhaps part time.

- Surveys offer an advantage of assessing a variety of influences on the decision to move or the choice of destination. For example, considerations of retirement may begin to influence migration decisions much earlier than age 65 or common ages of withdrawal from the labor force. Some middle-aged persons may accept opportunities to relocate to locations where they may later want to retire.

These advantages of assessing reasons for moving have not been fully exploited in major surveys of internal migration. The rest of this chapter assesses the evolution of some major national surveys of reasons for moving and exploits some of the strengths of the American Housing Survey, which at present has the most extensive set of questions on reasons for moving.

Early Attempts to Identify Reasons for Moving

National surveys of reasons for moving date back at least to the Current Population Survey taken in October 1946 and its attempt to identify the "causes" of migration related to World War II demobilization.[1] The survey asked for the respondent's last county of residence as a civilian and then asked, "Why did . . . leave his last county of residence?" Interviewers were given six categories for classifying responses: to look for work, to take a job, housing problems, change in marital status, head of family moved, or simply "other" (specify). When the data were tabulated, two additional categories were shown—moved to join head of family and health—apparently in response to analyses of the "other" category. Multiple reasons were accepted and no attempt was made to establish a "main" or "primary" reason. This survey did not identify retirement as a reason for moving.

The 1946 survey reported that about one half of all persons moving from one county to another "did so because the head of their family moved."[2] When the "head's" reason for moving was assigned to family members, about 56 percent of intercounty moves could be attributed to moving to take a job or to look for work. Intracounty moves were not counted.

The next use of the CPS to measure reasons for moving was in 1963.[3] This time, moves within counties were recorded as well as moves between counties, and the question was reworded to ask, "Why did . . . move here?" Thus, the emphasis was shifted from reason for leaving the earlier residence to reason for choosing the new one.

In the 1963 survey the reasons-for-moving-here question was asked only of men 18 to 64. The list of reasons was expanded from the 1946 survey to record "job transfer," "easier commuting" and "to enter or

---

[1]U.S. Bureau of the Census, "Postwar Migration and Its Causes in the United States: August, 1945, to October, 1946," *Current Population Reports*, series P-20, no. 4 (Washington, DC: U.S. Government Printing Office, 1947).

[2]U.S. Bureau of the Census, "Postwar Migration and Its Causes," pp. 2–3.

[3]U.S. Bureau of the Census, "Reasons for Moving: March 1962 to March 1963," *Current Population Reports*, series P-20, no. 154 (Washington, DC: U.S. Government Printing Office, 1966).

leave armed forces" and the focus of the earlier "housing problems" reason was changed to "better housing" and "forced moves" [because of housing]. "Health" was again tabulated as a reason for moving, but there was no provision for identifying retirement as a reason for moving, probably because the survey was limited to men aged 18–64. No attempt was made for the respondent to establish priority among multiple reasons for moving, but tabulation procedures imposed a ranking, giving top priority to "take a job" followed by "to look for work" and "job transfer."

This survey was the first to establish the dominance of what appeared to be housing-related reasons for moving within counties. About 60 percent of all reported reasons (included multiple reasons) for moving within counties were in the two housing categories ("better housing" and "forced move"). Nearly as high a percentage of intercounty moves were attributed to job-related considerations (to take a job, to look for work, a job transfer, easier commuting, or to enter or leave the armed forces).

The Census Bureau report on the survey found that intercounty movers appeared to be somewhat more likely than intracounty movers to give more than one reason for moving. The report concluded that this difference "suggest[s] that migration tends to be perceived with somewhat greater frequency as a more complicated operation than movement within counties."[4] Unlike the report for the 1946 survey, which was said to show the causes of migration, the report for the 1963 survey carefully noted that "brief inquiries on reasons for moving do not necessarily produce a definitive catalog of the causes of mobility, although they do provide some useful insights."[5]

Recent Attempts to Identify Reasons for Moving

The next attempt of the Census Bureau to assess reasons for moving on a national basis was the inauguration of the Annual Housing Survey in 1973, renamed the American Housing Survey after 1981 when the survey became biennial. From 1973 to 1978 the AHS asked, "What is the main reason [household head, later 'householder'] moved from his previous residence?" Like the CPS of 1946, the AHS during this period seemed to focus on reasons for leaving the previous residence rather than reasons for choosing the current residence. Unlike the earlier sur-

---

[4]U.S. Bureau of the Census, "Reasons for Moving," p. 3.
[5]U.S. Bureau of the Census, "Reasons for Moving," p. 4.

veys, however, the AHS focused on householders rather than individual members of households.

The AHS questionnaires from 1973 to 1978 listed far more reasons than the earlier surveys. The approximately 30 reasons listed in the AHS included job-related reasons that were similar to those in the Current Population Survey of 1963. The AHS featured an expanded set of "family" reasons to reflect setting up and dissolution of households, changes in marital status and family size, and moves "to be closer to relatives." Other reasons included moves in response to neighborhood conditions, moves undertaken in order to purchase a new home, moves undertaken for "schools," and various reasons for involuntarily moving (displaced by urban renewal or similar action, eviction, desire for lower rent or less expensive home, and natural disasters). Retirement was added as a reason for moving along with a desire for a change of climate. Unlike the Current Population Surveys of 1946 and 1963, health was not included as a reason for moving. Also unlike the earlier surveys, the Annual Housing Surveys from 1973 through 1978 made no provision for recording multiple reasons for moving.

In 1979 the AHS questionnaire was modified in order to record multiple reasons for moving by the householder and to identify reasons for picking the neighborhood moved to. No published figures from the expanded set of questions are available.

Probably the only other federal survey to ask reasons for moving is the Health Interview Survey. It has used migration questions similar to the Current Population Surveys prior to the 1970s; that is, it identified moves within counties, between counties within a state, and between states. It has also asked about frequency of moving and distance moved. Like the Current Population Surveys of 1946 and 1963, it has focused on reasons for moving for each person, but rather than emphasize reasons for leaving the earlier residence, as was done in the Current Population Surveys, the HIS emphasizes reasons for choosing the current location by asking: "What is the reason . . . moved here? Was it because . . . changed jobs, because . . . retired, because of . . . health, or was it for some other reason?" Each person is asked if there is more than one reason and asked to identify the main reason. Answers were recorded in seven categories: job—self, retired—self, health—self, job—other person, retired—other person, health—other person, and "other." These data have not been systematically analyzed.

Perhaps the clearest conclusion from this review of Federal surveys of reasons for moving is that they have had a checkered past.[6] They

---

[6]A well-known nonfederal national survey of reasons for migrating was carried out in 1962 and 1963 and reported in John B. Lansing and Eva Mueller, *The Geographic Mobility of Labor* (Ann Arbor: Survey Research Center, University of Michigan, 1967).

have, however, shown increasing sophistication in the framing of questions and a recognition of "new" reasons (i.e., retirement) and noneconomic considerations (i.e., change of climate) as bases for long-distance moving. The recent American Housing Surveys have also drawn upon research findings and have distinguished, at least for local moves, between reasons for leaving one residence or neighborhood and reasons for choosing a new residence or neighborhood. But inconsistent processing of data and inadequate or noncomparable tabulations have hampered cumulation of findings. At a minimum, surveys of reasons for moving have demonstrated "heterogeneity of migrant types and migration reasons."[7] The significance of such a conclusion is that attempts to model or explain large migration flows face the challenge of incorporating a great variety of explanatory frameworks and variables.

Main Reasons for Interstate Migration

Recent American Housing Surveys are probably the richest publicly available source for analyzing reasons for moving. Part of the expanded set of questions on reasons for moving is illustrated in Figure 7.1; additional questions, not shown, asked about moves that implied housing displacement and reasons for choosing the new residence or new neighborhood. These expansions of the questionnaire were introduced in 1979 and have been continued; earlier versions had a more restricted list of reasons for moving and did not allow for recording multiple reasons for moving. What follows draws upon responses to the questions shown in Figure 7.1.

Mobility status in the AHS was obtained by asking for duration of residence in current dwelling unit for the "reference person," usually the person in whose name the unit is owned or rented. When the housing unit is jointly owned or rented, any of the persons who jointly own or rent the unit may be listed as the reference person. Reference persons with a duration of residence of less than one year were asked to report the locality of previous residence, but the microdata tapes identified state of previous residence and whether previous residence was metropolitan (central city or balance of a metropolitan area) or in a nonmetropolitan location. The survey tapes did not identify movement in terms of the traditional county-based classification (i.e., moves within counties and those between counties). In view of these limitations, the great-

---

[7]Curtis C. Roseman, "Labor-Force Migration, Non-Labor Force Migration, and Non-Employment Reasons for Migration," *Socio-Economic Planning Sciences* 17, nos. 5–6 (1983): 311.

FIGURE 7.1

Reasons for Moving Identified in the Annual Housing Surveys of 1979, 1980, and 1981

Section VI – RECENT MOVERS SUPPLEMENT – Continued

48. Please look at this card.

SHOW FLASHCARD F

What are the reasons . . . (Reference person) **moved FROM that residence?**

(Mark all answers given)

EMPLOYMENT

(410)
*
- 1 ☐ Job transfer
- 2 ☐ To look for work
- 3 ☐ To take a new job
- 4 ☐ Entered or left U.S. Armed Forces
- 5 ☐ Retirement
- 6 ☐ Commuting reasons

(411)
*
- 7 ☐ To attend school
- 8 ☐ Other employment reasons – *Specify*

FAMILY

(412)
*
- 09 ☐ Needed larger house or apartment
- 10 ☐ Divorced or separated
- 11 ☐ Widowed

(413)
*
- 12 ☐ To be closer to relatives
- 13 ☐ Newly married
- 14 ☐ Family increased

(414)
*
- 15 ☐ Family decreased
- 16 ☐ To establish own household
- 17 ☐ Other family reasons – *Specify*

OTHER

(415)
*
- 18 ☐ Neighborhood overcrowded
- 19 ☐ Change in racial or ethnic composition of neighborhood
- 20 ☐ Crime

(416)
*
- 21 ☐ Wanted neighborhood with children
- 22 ☐ Wanted neighborhood without children
- 23 ☐ Wanted better neighborhood

(417)
*
- 24 ☐ Wanted more expensive place or better investment
- 25 ☐ Wanted to own residence
- 26 ☐ Wanted better house

(418)
*
- 27 ☐ Wanted to rent residence
- 28 ☐ Wanted residence with more conveniences
- 29 ☐ Lower rent or less expensive house

(419)
*
- 30 ☐ Wanted change of climate
- 31 ☐ Displaced by urban renewal, highway construction, or other public activity
- 32 ☐ Displaced by private action

(420)
*
- 33 ☐ Schools
- 34 ☐ Natural disaster
- 35 ☐ Other – *Specify*

INTERVIEWER INSTRUCTION ➡

Two or more boxes marked in item 48 – *Ask 49*

If only ONE box is marked in item 48 – *Transcribe code to item 49 and fill Check item M, page 25*

49. Of the reasons you just mentioned, what was the MAIN reason . . . (Reference person) **moved from that residence?**

(421) ☐☐ Box number of MAIN reason

est comparability with past chapters appeared to lie in focusing on interstate and interregional moves.

A basic issue concerns how much long-distance migration (interstate moves in this case) can be attributed to economically oriented migrants changing jobs or looking for work and to other migrants whose movement is attributable to noneconomic considerations like family-oriented moves, retirement moves, or amenity-seeking moves. These are essentially empirical questions, but their answers greatly affect attempts to derive theoretically based models of long-distance migration.

Table 7.1 shows the reasons for interstate migration of households (specifically household "reference persons") in 1979, 1980, and 1981; the three surveys, each taken in the fall of the year, were combined. Only reasons accounting for at least 2 percent of interstate moves are shown in Table 7.1, and only the "main" reasons are shown.

In terms of these "main" reasons for moving, about 22.2 percent of

TABLE 7.1

Selected Main Reasons[a] for Household "Reference Persons" Moving Between States in the 12 Months Preceding the 1979, 1980, and 1981 Annual Housing Surveys (in thousands)

	Reference Persons Moving Between States	Percentage Distribution
Job transfer	1,388	22.2%
To look for work	392	6.3
To take a new job	1,167	18.7
Entered or left U.S. armed forces	215	3.4
Retirement	151	2.4
To attend school	352	5.6
Other employment reasons[b]	201	3.2
Divorced or separated	165	2.6
To be closer to relatives	537	8.6
Other family reasons[c]	190	3.0
Wanted change of climate	373	6.0
Other reasons specified on form [d]	358	5.7
Other reasons[e]	633	10.1
Reasons not reported	128	2.0
Total	6,250	100.0

[a]All categories (shown in Figure 7.1) accounting for at least 2 percent of interstate moves made by household reference persons.

[b]Reason no. 8, Figure 7.1.

[c]Reason no. 17, Figure 7.1.

[d]All reasons shown in Figure 7.1 and not included above.

[e]Reason no. 35, Figure 7.1.

household interstate relocations between 1979 and 1981 were due to job transfers. Another 18.7 percent were due to the household reference persons taking a new job; 6.3 percent were to look for work; and 3.2 percent were due to unspecified employment-related reasons. In a sense, therefore, about one half of household moves between states during this period of time were primarily attributable to well-known economic motivations.

The other one half of interstate household moves reflected a great variety of reasons. Moves to be closer to relatives accounted for 8.6 percent; another 2.6 percent were due to becoming divorced or separated and in some cases probably represented moves to be near relatives. Six percent of interstate moves were undertaken because of a desire for a change of climate; 5.6 percent were to attend school; and 3.4 percent were to enter or leave the armed forces. Retirement moves were 2.4 percent of interstate movement of households. Nearly 16 percent of interstate movers reported a reason that was not one of the categories listed on the form. Only 2.0 percent failed to give a reason for their move.

These data suggest that a substantial fraction of migration is constrained in terms of choice of destination and is not accounted for by models or concepts of migration decision making that postulate a two-stage process, the first consisting of the decision to move and the second consisting of a choice of destination.[8] For example, a job transfer normally means that the destination is determined when the decision to move is made. Moves to be near relatives usually mean that the destination is determined, and some of the other family-related reasons probably mean that the destination of a move is determined by the location of family members that the mover is joining or moving near. Together, these two types of circumstances—job transfers and moves for various family reasons—suggest that perhaps one third or more of interstate migration consists of movers with highly constrained choice as to destination.

A case can be made that a great many moves are not accounted for by classic economic approaches linking long-distance migration to employment opportunities. Interstate moves to attend school (5.6 percent of interstate moves) or to retire (2.4 percent) do not appear to conform to traditional models. Many of the 10.1 percent of moves that could not be classified in one of the 34 preset categories may have represented

---

[8]This conclusion was reached by Sell in earlier analyses of AHS data for 1973–77 on movement between metropolitan and nonmetropolitan locations. See Ralph Sell, "A Research Note on the Demography of Occupational Relocations," *Social Forces* 60 (March 1982): 859–865; and "Analyzing Migration Decisions: The First Step—Whose Decision?" *Demography* 20 (August 1983): 299–311.

persons seeking lifestyles and values that do not appear to be governed strictly by economic considerations. But it is easy to overemphasize the role of such influences, even for groups with great locational freedom—like retirees. An earlier study of AHS data for the mid-1970s found that nearly 12 percent of household heads for whom retirement was the main reason for moving were employed in the week preceding the survey.[9] Since some retirement moves may be part of career changes and not full-time withdrawal from the labor force, even the migration of retirees may be governed by employment considerations that are not immediately evident from reports of main reasons for moving.

Age and Reasons for Moving

To some extent the major reasons for long-distance moving—whether reported by migrants themselves or inferred from migration flows—reflect the age composition of the population at large. If the young and the old move for different reasons, then at a given point in time the dominant reasons for moving depend partly on the representation of different age groups in the population from which migrants are drawn. It seems not unreasonable to suppose that new entrants in the labor force are likely to be moving to take jobs and to look for work. Persons who have been in the work force for several years may find themselves transferred or may wish to move to new jobs. Moves connected with retirement come much later in life, but since retirement has been occurring at younger and younger ages, the effect of retirement on migration decisions is likely to exist much earlier than the "traditional" retirement age of 65.

But what stages in a person's life cycle are likely to characterize some of the other reasons identified in Table 7.1? For example, interstate moves whose "main" motivation was the search for a better climate were 6 percent of all interstate moves by households in the study period. Are these the moves of young, ecology-minded persons? Or are they the moves of middle-aged persons who have secured a financial standing that allows them the "luxury" of emphasizing certain quality-of-life considerations as to where to live? Do moves to be closer to relatives represent young persons going back home to rejoin their parents after completing college or military service? Or is the situation just the

[9]Larry H. Long and Kristin A. Hansen, "Reasons for Interstate Migration: Jobs, Climate, and Other Influences," *Current Population Reports*, series P-23, no. 81 (Washington, DC: U.S. Government Printing Office, 1979) p. 20.

opposite: are such movers very old persons who need to live near their children on whom they depend for help with chores?

Part of the answer to these questions is simply to look at reported reasons by age of the household "reference person," as is done in Table 7.2. These data show the distribution of main reasons for interstate migration at successive ages and is best used to determine to what extent the distribution of reasons for moving is influenced by the age distribution of movers.

As expected, the importance of job transfers rises with age and then falls off. Job transfers account for about 15 percent of the interstate migration of household reference persons under age 25, rising to about 30 percent at ages 35–44. By ages 55–59, it is back down to about 15 percent.

Moves to take a new job account for nearly 22 percent of interstate migration at ages under 30 and then gradually become less often mentioned. The third major economic reason—to search for work—was cited by 9.7 percent of interstate migrants under age 25 but at later ages no pattern is evident; from ages 25 to 60 interstate moves to look for work account for 4.4 to 6.7 percent of all interstate moves.

Moves to retire begin to appear well before age 65. Such moves may represent 3 percent of the interstate migration of households in their forties, and by ages 60–64 retirement accounts for about 23 percent of interstate migration. Persons aged 65–69 appear to be somewhat less likely than persons aged 60–64 to report retirement as the main reason for moving between states.

Among households moving between states, the percent who cite climate as the main reason for moving appears to be much greater for those over age 50 than those under age 50. Among households under age 50 only about 3 to 5 percent of those moving between states cite a desire for a climate change as the main reason for moving. Between ages 50 and 64, however, about 13 to 15 percent of households moving between states said that climate was the main reason for their move. At ages 65–69 climate was cited as the main reason by 30 percent of interstate migrants, exceeding the percentage reporting retirement.

Moves to be near relatives are more common among old than among young interstate migrants. Movers citing this as the main reason for moving were about 4.2 percent of all interstate movers under age 25 and only a moderately higher percentage among movers from age 25 to age 45. After age 45 or so moves to be near relatives begin to rise as a proportion of all interstate movers, reaching 21.5 percent of migrants aged 65–69 and nearly 45 percent among migrants over age 70.

At every age heterogeneity of motives is suggested by the fairly large proportion of moves in the "all other" category, which represents

TABLE 7.2

Percentage Distribution of Main Reasons for Moving Between States in the 12 Months Preceding the Annual Housing Surveys of 1979, 1980, and 1981, by Age of Household Reference Person

	All Ages	Age of Reference Person										
		Under 25	25–29	30–34	35–39	40–44	45–49	50–54	55–59	60–64	65–69	70 and Over
Job transfer	22.2%	14.8%	25.0%	28.4%	32.6%	30.2%	24.7%	23.7%	15.4%	9.7%	0.0%	0.0%
Look for work	6.3	9.7	5.9	5.6	6.7	4.4	5.0	6.2	6.6	1.5	0.0	2.9
Take new job	18.7	21.8	21.7	21.6	19.3	18.7	19.1	16.0	9.0	6.5	0.5	0.8
Armed forces	3.4	6.9	5.2	2.5	0.8	3.5	1.1	0.0	0.0	0.0	0.0	0.0
Retirement	2.4	0.0	0.0	0.1	1.4	2.9	3.8	2.8	10.7	23.3	14.9	6.2
Attend school	5.6	15.4	6.9	2.9	2.4	0.0	0.6	0.0	0.7	0.0	0.0	0.0
Be closer to relative	8.6	4.2	6.9	7.2	6.0	5.7	8.6	12.8	13.7	14.9	21.5	44.7
Change climate	6.0	2.9	4.7	3.2	5.3	4.6	3.6	13.2	15.0	14.1	30.2	13.4
All other	26.8	24.4	23.8	28.5	25.5	30.0	33.5	25.3	29.0	30.0	32.8	32.0
Total (000s)	6,250	1,362	1,352	988	694	471	338	252	235	203	143	211

between 25 and 33 percent of interstate migrants at the various age groups. This category probably attests to a genuine variety of motivations, preferences, and values underlying movement between states.

These data illustrate how future changes in the age distribution of interstate migrants might affect the distribution of reported reasons for moving. The oldest members of the baby boom are now in their forties, and as they grow older the proportion of interstate moves due to desires to live in an area with a preferred climate or to retire will likely increase, assuming no massive economic or social dislocations. Accordingly, moves due to classical economic reasons like job transfers or moves to take new jobs could decline if an aging work force follows patterns of the past. Of course, these are not predictions. If increased foreign competition causes more Americans to lose their jobs, more moves in search for work or to take new jobs could characterize the later work force ages.

Business cycles almost certainly affect the likelihood that some reasons for moving will be cited. The number of job transfers may rise with economic expansion or may depend on the level of corporate profits. Moves to take new jobs almost surely fall when the economy is generating new jobs at a slow rate and rise as hiring accompanies a recovery. The three surveys combined for analysis here include 1979, 1980 (a recessionary year), and 1981 (a year of economic expansion). Business cycle effects on reasons for moving are blurred when these three years are combined, but the data represent similar kinds of "average" experiences that are analyzed in census questions on migration over a five-year period. The major reason for combining three surveys was to increase the effective sample size. The years chosen were the first with the new questions on reasons for moving.

Age-Reason-Specific Rates of Interstate Migration

The data presented in Table 7.2 simply show why movers in different age groups moved. Such data can show the relative importance of different reasons at different ages, but Table 7.2 should not be interpreted as showing the likelihood of interstate migration being "caused" by the various reasons shown. For example, among interstate migrants a desire to live close to relatives is more likely to be cited as the main reason for having moved among old than among young migrants; this does not necessarily mean that a desire to be near relatives is more likely to induce migration among the young than among the old. A higher proportion of young persons than old will move in a given period of time, and there are in the aggregate more young than old interstate

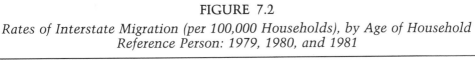

FIGURE 7.2

Rates of Interstate Migration (per 100,000 Households), by Age of Household Reference Person: 1979, 1980, and 1981

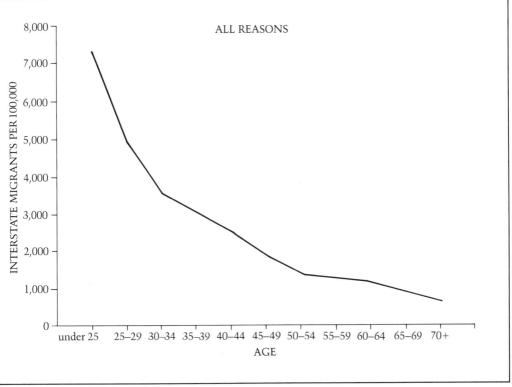

NOTE: Mobility interval is the 12 months preceding the three national surveys.

migrants. If in the population at large 1 percent of young persons and 1 percent of old persons are motivated to move for a given reason (e.g., to move where the climate is better), that reason will probably constitute a larger proportion of old than young movers simply because there are fewer old than young movers.

These distinctions are often invoked to explain why migration probabilities are highest among young adults and decline with age, as discussed at length in Chapter 2 and illustrated in Figures 2.1 and 2.2. Many explanations of why migration peaks early in life simply state that reasons that induce or impel migration are concentrated at young-adult ages. Retirement is often cited as the only life-cycle event whose migration-inducing properties increase with age, at least up to a point.

FIGURE 7.3

*Rates of Interstate Migration (per 100,000 Households), by Age of
Household Reference Person and Main Reason for Moving:
1979, 1980, and 1981*

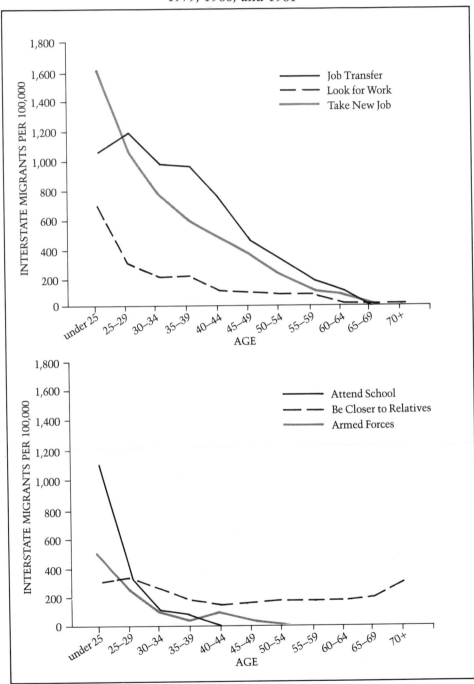

NOTE: Mobility interval is the 12 months preceding the three national surveys.

FIGURE 7.3 *(continued)*

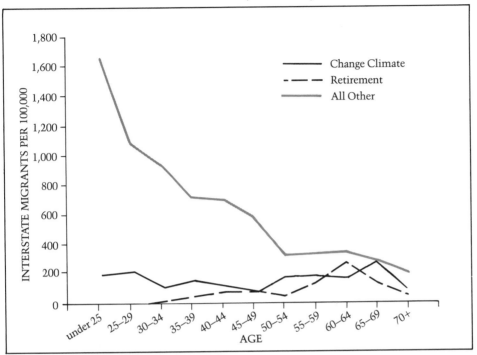

Whether desires to be near relatives or to live where the climate is better are more likely to "cause" migration at some ages than others has never been demonstrated.

To test for such effects, it is necessary to decompose the age-specific rates of interstate migration into cause-specific rates. To do this, one takes interstate migrants at each age group moving for each reason for moving and divides by the total population at each age group. The result can be interpreted as the rate of interstate migration attributable to each of several "causes"—in this case, main reasons for moving. Figure 7.2 illustrates the age pattern of "total" rates of moving (the sum of all the reasons), based on each household reference person's age. Figure 7.3 then presents age- and reason-specific rates. Summing the rates in the nine charts in Figure 7.3 produces the curve shown in Figure 7.2.

Most of the nine "cause-specific" rates of moving decline with age, but not all do and not all decline at the same rate. For example, the rate of interstate migration produced by job transfers appears to decline with age somewhat less rapidly than do moves to take a new job. Moves to attend school obviously fall off very quickly with age, as do moves to look for work.

Moves to enter or leave the armed forces predominantly reflect leaving the armed forces since personnel living in barracks are not included in household surveys like the American Housing Survey. The degree to which entering or leaving the Armed Forces induces interstate migration understandably declines quickly after age 25 but may increase at ages 40–45, an age when persons who entered the armed forces right after high school or college have completed 20 years of service and become eligible to retire.

Particularly interesting are the relatively flat lines in the charts for moves to be closer to relatives and moves to achieve a change of climate. Interstate movers over 50 were earlier shown to be more likely to cite these reasons than movers under 50. But Figure 7.3 shows that these two reasons are no more likely to generate interstate migration among the old than among the young. Stated differently, the data mean that a 25-year-old person picked randomly in the population is not measurably more likely than a 65-year-old person to move to another state in order to be near relatives or to live where the climate is better. Older persons who have moved are more likely to report these reasons because fewer old persons move.

The only reason whose migration-inducing effects seem to increase with age is retirement. The likelihood of moving between states for the purpose of retiring appears to peak at ages 60–64 and then declines at ages 65–69 and declines further at the 70-and-over age category.

In general, Figure 7.3 supports the idea that the familiar age curve of migration is a composite of many cause- or reason-specific probabilities of moving. Most have their greatest effect before age 25 and very quickly decline with age. Others, like job transfers, may peak somewhat later and decline less rapidly with age. A few, like desires to be near relatives or to live in an area with a better climate, do not vary much with age. Of measured migration-inducing reasons, only retirement seems to increase with age, although at advanced ages health problems and a decreased ability to care for oneself may induce movement into homes of relatives or to institutionalized settings; these moves are not represented in the AHS data since the questions on reasons for moving were asked only of household reference persons.

Secondary Reasons for Moving

Most interstate migrants (household reference persons) reported only one reason for their interstate move. The percentage distribution of all other reasons cited for moving from one state to another are given in Table 7.3. Note that the base is total reasons cited and not the num-

TABLE 7.3

Percentage Distribution of Reasons Other Than Main Reason for Moving Between States in the 12 Months Preceding the Annual Housing Surveys of 1979, 1980, and 1981, by Age of Household Reference Person

	All Ages	Age of Reference Person										
		Under 25	25–29	30–34	35–39	40–44	45–49	50–54	55–59	60–64	65–69	70 and Over
Job transfer	2.3%	1.3%	2.7%	3.2%	3.5%	1.5%	3.5%	3.1%	3.1%	0.0%	0.0%	0.0%
Look for work	6.1	9.7	8.5	4.5	6.8	2.2	6.1	5.0	2.0	0.0	0.0	0.0
Take new job	8.5	8.3	11.5	10.1	7.8	13.0	7.9	9.7	3.8	0.0	0.0	2.6
Armed forces	1.5	1.9	2.0	1.3	1.8	2.1	3.1	0.0	0.0	0.0	0.0	0.0
Retirement	3.3	0.0	0.6	0.0	0.4	7.3	0.0	6.0	7.4	19.8	27.7	10.8
Attend school	2.8	10.3	1.8	1.1	0.4	0.0	0.0	0.0	0.0	0.0	0.0	0.0
Be closer to relatives	13.2	9.5	12.1	14.0	14.9	13.0	13.9	11.5	16.3	21.8	13.0	20.1
Change climate	9.8	9.1	8.9	8.9	9.4	8.1	16.1	13.0	5.8	11.2	14.5	14.3
All other	52.5	49.9	51.8	57.0	55.2	52.8	49.4	51.7	61.7	47.2	44.9	52.2
Total (000s)	1,907	405	426	301	211	106	88	79	81	81	63	67

NOTE: The "total" is the number of secondary reasons cited and not the number of movers citing secondary reasons for moving.

ber who cited more than one reason. Although these reasons are here termed "secondary," several reasons could have been offered by a respondent, but except for designating one reason as the main reason, no ranking was asked for.

Secondary reasons were more likely than main reasons to fall into the "all other" category, which at most age groups accounted for a majority of secondary reasons. This finding means that secondary reasons are even more varied and heterogeneous than primary reasons for moving, further supporting the notion that migration decisions are complex and influenced by many considerations.

Of the specific secondary reasons mentioned, the one most often cited was to be closer to relatives. This reason was 13.2 percent of all the secondary reasons given. Since it represented only about 8.6 percent of main reasons, it is more important as a secondary than a primary reason for interstate migration. It accounts for nearly 22 percent of all secondary reasons mentioned among interstate migrants at ages 60–64, the age when retirement is most likely to be cited as the main reason for interstate migration. These figures suggest that although persons of retirement age may in principle have considerable locational freedom, many take into account the location of relatives in choosing where to retire.

Also mentioned fairly frequently as a secondary reason for moving is the desire for a change of climate. This reason represented 6 percent of main reasons for interstate moving but almost 10 percent of secondary reasons. Like the desire to be closer to relatives, the desire for a change of climate appears to be more important as a secondary than as a primary motivation for interstate migration.

Moves to look for work are about as important as a secondary reason as they are as a main reason. Just over 6 percent of main reasons and just over 6 percent of secondary reasons for interstate migration of household reference persons were to look for work. As a main reason for moving, moves to look for work are far overshadowed by job shifts where the new location is determined (either as job transfers or taking new jobs), and the data on secondary reasons suggest that among persons who move between states to look for work, perhaps one half give top priority to something other than the search for work. Those who said that a search for work was a secondary consideration may be saying that a desire to be near relatives, a desire for a good climate, or something else determined where they moved and thus where they searched for work.

The reason most often cited as a main reason for interstate migration was mentioned relatively infrequently as a secondary reason. Job transfers were 22.2 percent of main reasons but only 2.3 percent of secondary reasons. Obviously job transfers, when they occur, dominate over other considerations. Perhaps those few for whom job transfers were only a secondary consideration had turned down other opportunities in order to transfer to a preferred location.

At most ages most persons gave only one reason for moving from one state to another. Since young persons are more likely to move than older persons, one might think that the young would give more reasons for their moving. But Tables 7.2 and 7.3 do not support this interpretation. The mean number of reasons cited by interstate migrants was 1.3, a figure which did not strongly vary by age of migrant.

Interregional Streams

Up to now the emphasis has been on interstate migration in general, but reasons for moving may be particularly useful in identifying the bases for the substantial migration of population to the South and West. On the one hand, the South and West experienced rapid growth in total employment during the period of study, and one would expect movement to these two regions to be heavily influenced by traditional economic considerations. On the other hand, noneconomic factors like climate are often cited as inducements to leave the Northeast and Midwest for the South or West. To examine these competing explanations of interregional migration, Table 7.4 was constructed to show inmigrants and outmigrants for each of the four major census regions and the main and secondary reasons for moving. A map showing the four regions and the states in each region was presented in Chapter 5 (Figure 5.1).

In order to obtain a count of persons moving to each region, the household reference person's mobility status and reason or reasons for moving were assigned to each person in the household. In Table 7.4 the top panel simply counts the number of each region's inmigrants and outmigrants by main reason for moving. The second panel is a percentage distribution of main reasons for moving, and the third panel is a percentage of main and all other reasons, and so exceeds 100.0 percent.

For each of the main reasons the implied net migration is often very small and should be interpreted cautiously. It comes as no surprise that from 1979 to 1981, the period covered by the table, the Northeast and Midwest had net outmigration of persons in households where the reference person was being transferred, looking for work, or taking a new job. For example, these three reasons took an estimated 896,000 persons to the Midwest and took 1,587,000 persons from the Midwest to other

TABLE 7.4

*Main and All Other Reasons for Persons Moving to and from
Each of the Four Census Regions in the 12 Months
Preceding the Annual Housing Surveys of 1979, 1980, and 1981 (in thousands)*

	To Northeast	From Northeast	To Midwest	From Midwest	To South	From South	To West	From West
Migrants by Main Reason for Moving								
Job transfer	290	473	447	674	848	714	599	324
Look for work	81	65	98	275	277	173	137	79
Take new job	234	287	351	638	744	448	374	330
Armed forces	45	50	97	90	133	152	104	87
Retirement	3	57	23	87	149	29	32	34
Attend school	52	72	69	101	119	89	112	89
Be closer to relatives	107	85	195	201	299	238	166	244
Change climate	13	267	38	324	381	109	325	58
All other	287	371	366	551	855	648	563	500
Total	1,112	1,727	1,684	2,941	3,805	2,600	2,412	1,745
Percentage Distribution of Migrants by Main Reason for Moving								
Job transfer	26.1%	27.4%	26.5%	22.9%	22.3%	27.5%	24.8%	18.6%
Look for work	7.3	3.8	5.8	9.4	7.3	6.7	5.7	4.5
Take new job	21.0	16.6	20.8	21.7	19.6	17.2	15.5	18.9
Armed forces	4.0	2.9	5.8	3.1	3.5	5.8	4.3	5.0
Retirement	0.3	3.3	1.4	3.0	3.9	1.1	1.3	1.9
Attend school	4.7	4.2	4.1	3.4	3.1	3.4	4.6	5.1
Be closer to relatives	9.6	4.9	11.6	6.8	7.9	9.2	6.9	14.0
Change climate	1.2	15.5	2.3	11.0	10.0	4.2	13.5	3.3
All other	25.8	21.5	21.7	18.7	22.5	24.9	23.3	28.7
Total	100.0	100.0	100.0	100.0	100.0	100.0	100.0	100.0
Percentage Distribution of All Reasons for Moving								
Job transfer	26.3%	28.0%	27.7%	23.5%	22.9%	28.4%	26.0%	19.7%
Look for work	9.1	5.7	6.7	12.3	9.2	8.4	8.8	5.6
Take new job	22.7	19.5	23.9	24.4	22.2	19.7	18.5	21.5
Armed forces	4.6	3.5	6.4	3.6	4.1	6.8	5.3	5.6
Retirement	1.1	5.2	2.2	3.7	5.3	2.8	2.9	2.6
Attend school	4.7	4.9	4.6	4.5	3.6	4.3	6.3	5.1
Be closer to relatives	15.2	10.1	15.1	10.4	12.6	12.4	10.9	20.9
Change climate	4.4	21.2	3.2	17.6	15.5	6.0	18.5	5.6
All other	40.2	35.1	34.4	34.2	36.5	38.6	41.1	29.2
Total	128.1	133.2	124.2	134.2	131.8	127.4	138.1	115.8

NOTE: The estimate of persons was obtained by assigning to each household member the reference person's mobility status and reason or reasons for moving.

regions. Like the Midwest, the Northeast had net outmigration due to these reasons, and the South and West gained these economically motivated migrants.

The South and West also appear to gain from persons moving for ostensibly noneconomic reasons. Ten percent of migrants to the South and 13.5 percent of migrants to the West during this period said that the desire for a change of climate was the main reason for moving. The desire for a change of climate was the main reason reported by 15.5 percent of persons leaving the Northeast and 11.0 percent of persons leaving the Midwest during the study period.

Moving to be near relatives was mentioned fairly frequently, but such moves appear to bring about little net redistribution of population. Insofar as main reasons for moving are concerned, these moves sometimes represented 10 percent or more of regional inmigrants or outmigrants, but in most cases they were nearly canceled by persons moving in the opposite direction to be near relatives. On a regional basis, moves for this reason essentially represent circulation rather than net redistribution of population.

Only a small amount of the South's net inmigration was directly attributable to retirees. About 149,000 moves to the South during the study period were in households where the main reason for moving was retirement, and they represented about 3.9 percent of the South's inmigrants. Perhaps surprisingly, the West appears to have no measurable net migration gain from persons for whom retirement was the main reason for moving. Retirees were only 1.3 percent of migrants to the West, and as many moved from as moved to the West for this reason.

Some reasons for moving, like a desire for a climate change, take on increased importance as secondary factors in migration decision making. For example, the desire for a change of climate was the main reason given by 15.5 percent of migrants from the Northeast, but an additional 5.7 percent of migrants from the Northeast mentioned this reason as a secondary consideration. In total, therefore, 21.2 percent of migrants from the Northeast mentioned the desire for a change of climate as a consideration in their decision to leave the region. Similarly, for 11.0 percent of migrants from the Midwest a desire for a better climate was the main reason for moving, and another 6.6 percent mentioned climate as a secondary consideration; in all, 17.6 percent of migrants from the Midwest were moving at least in part to achieve a preferred climate.

Moves to be near relatives also figure prominently as secondary reasons for moving, particularly among migrants to the Northeast and from the West. For about 9.6 percent of migrants to the Northeast a desire to be near relatives was the main reason for moving, but when secondary reasons are considered, about 15.2 percent of migrants to the Northeast were moving at least partly in order to be near relatives. For nearly 21 percent of migrants from the West a desire to be near relatives was the main or a secondary consideration in their moving. The temptation is to conclude that many of these moves from the West and to the Northeast are return migration—persons who are "going home." But there is really no direct evidence for this interpretation. Neither why persons were moving to be near relatives nor exactly what relatives (parents, siblings, cousins, and so on) they were moving to be near can be inferred from the coded response. Perhaps the most unequivocal interpretation is that without such locational preferences, there would be fewer migrants from the West and fewer to the Northeast.

As before, the strongly economic reasons for moving are usually cited as the main rather than a secondary reason for moving. Relatively few people cite job transfers or moves to take a new job as secondary reasons for moving.

Perhaps the most surprising result of this regional view of reasons for moving is the role of desires to achieve a change of climate or to be near relatives as secondary considerations in migration decisions. Probably no one would have predicted that one in five migrants leaving the Northeast between 1979 and 1981 was moving with climatic preferences as the primary or secondary consideration. Also surprising (at least not previously demonstated) was that another one in five migrants from the West was exercising a preference to live near relatives, either as a main or secondary consideration. Although most persons move for only one reason, secondary reasons provide a fuller and more complete understanding of migration decision making than is obtained by focusing on "main" reasons.

Summary and Conclusion

The desire to know why movers move is widespread and has many practical applications and uses. Researchers have been suspicious about the quality of such data, doubting that movers can or are willing to explain why they left their last residence or how they chose their destination. Studies of reasons for moving have not produced comparable time-series data, for some have been based on nonrepresentative samples and others have asked questions that seem biased toward producing anticipated conclusions. From surveys of reasons for moving there is no firm evidence for or against the widespread notion that reasons for moving have changed over the last several decades in favor of noneconomic motives like a desire to live where the weather is nice, where recreational opportunities are present (whether mountains for skiing or beaches for surfing), or where other quality-of-life amenities exist. Places possessing such attributes—warm weather, ski resorts, and the like—have tended to grow in population in recent years, but their growth may reflect an increasing ability of employers to relocate near such areas. Simply stated, changing migration patterns that favor places with comfortable climates or other amenities do not necessarily mean that reasons for moving have changed.

The data analyzed in this chapter were for interstate migrants and were taken from Annual Housing Surveys that seem designed more for the analysis of local moves than long-distance migration. Nevertheless, the results suggest that a rather parsimonious set of categories (job transfer, look for work, take new job, enter or leave armed forces, retirement, attend schools, be closer to relatives, or to seek a change of climate) usually account for 70 or 80 percent of the "main" reasons for interstate or interregional moves, varying somewhat by age of migrants and region of origin or destination. These are encouraging results and suggest the possibility of developing consistent time-series data on reasons for long-distance migration.

An important use of such data is to identify the things that people consider when they move long distances. This chapter presented the first data for the United States as a whole on the number of reasons for moving reported by interstate migrants. The average number of reasons for moving was 1.3, and the secondary reasons were more heterogeneous and less easily classified than main reasons. The secondary reasons most often cited appeared to represent personal values, like a desire to live near relatives or to achieve a climatic preference.

INTERNATIONAL COMPARISONS
OF GEOGRAPHICAL MOBILITY

H OW LONG people stay in one house or in one location is an important consideration in characterizing the lifestyles of individuals and understanding the degree to which organizations and institutions in different countries adapt to turnover associated with geographical mobility. As noted in Chapter 2, many nineteenth-century commentaries on internal migration were concerned with how nations might differ and how differences might be related to other national traits. The reasons that there has been comparatively little contemporary research on differences among countries in internal spatial mobility are not hard to identify.

First, few international conventions guide the collection of statistics on internal migration. Extensive guidelines have come to govern the collection and presentation of statistics on fertility and mortality—the other two basic demographic variables—but nothing comparable exists for statistics on internal spatial mobility. Most countries that collect data on internal migration do so for whatever local administrative areas are important to them—gemeinden in Germany, parishes in France, municipios in Latin America, and a great variety of local governments in other countries. Like counties and other political jurisdictions in the United States, these areas vary greatly in size, shape, and social and political significance within and among nations. There is no completely unambiguous way of comparing movement among, say, counties in the

United States and the aforementioned administrative areas of other countries. Collectively calling the various areas "communities" does not make them communities, for as observed in Chapter 1 some U.S. counties or county equivalents cover 20,000 square miles (an area larger than the Netherlands) and are 10,000 times as large as the smallest U.S. county equivalent.

Second, because of the heavy reliance on censuses and surveys in the United States, the unit of observation is movers, whereas the continuous population registration systems in Europe and elsewhere record moves. Population registration systems typically require a person moving from area A to area B to register both the departure in area A and the arrival in area B, and the accounts of arrivals and departures are usually balanced annually in the central statistical office. But within a year's time if the migrant from A to B moves back to A another move will have occurred and will be counted by a system of continuous population registration; the latter move may not be counted by survey questions like those in the United States which ask, "Where did you live one year ago?"

Another difference arises because the survey and census questions are limited to persons aged 1 and over for the residence-one-year question, whereas persons under age 1 are included in the count of moves recorded by population registration systems. That is, if a couple living in area A have a baby in A and during the same calendar year move to area B, the baby's move will be counted as a departure from A and an arrival in B. Survey questions of the where-did-you-live-one-year-ago type would not count the baby's move if the baby had not passed its first birthday by the time of the interview. Still another element of noncomparability may arise if a person moves from A to B, registers both the departure and arrival, but dies very shortly after moving to B; surveys are obviously limited to persons alive at the survey date.

For these reasons, the number of moves is almost always greater than the number of movers, but no formula has been derived for translating the moves counted by continuous population registration into movers. A problem in devising a universal conversion factor is that population registration systems vary according to which moves from A to B must be reported. Sometimes a move that is intended to be for only a month or two is defined as "temporary" and either need not be reported or is counted in a special category different from permanent moves. But in other cases a move of this duration is deemed a "relocation" and is to be entered into the regular accounts of departures and arrivals. Rarely do statistical offices make special tabulations to convert the number of moves into the numbers of movers.

Among censuses there are also many sources of noncomparability in statistics on internal migration.[1] One concerns the length of the interval over which mobility is measured. One-year and five-year intervals are often used, but the five-year rates are not five times the one-year rates because of return and repeat moves and the greater mortality over the five-year interval. Some work has been done on methods of converting one- and five-year mobility rates, but to date they have been applied in only a few instances and it is not clear how stable the conversion factors are over time.[2] Some countries use mobility intervals other than one or five years; the 1975 census of France asked about residence seven years earlier so as to identify residence at the preceding national census taken in 1968.[3] Still other countries rely on different types of questions or measures, like duration of residence in the current locality of residence. There has been very little systematic research on converting duration-of-residence data to period rates of migration.[4]

Because of these sources of noncomparability, national or international statistical organizations rarely compile compendia of internal migration statistics of different countries. Fertility and mortality data, in contrast, are regularly assembled by statistical offices for comparison and analysis for virtually all nations of the world. Migration researchers

[1]A survey by the United Nations in the 1970s found that of 121 countries responding, the most commonly collected information on migration was place of birth, obtained for 107 countries. Place of residence for a fixed prior date (usually one or five years earlier) was collected by 75 of the 121 countries, and 70 obtained data on duration of residence. United Nations, *Statistics of Internal Migration: A Technical Report*, series F, no. 23 (New York: United Nations, 1978).

[2]P. H. Rees, "The Measurement of Migration, from Census Data and Other Sources," *Environment and Planning A* 9, no. 3 (1977): 247–272; P. H. Rees, "Multiregional Mathematical Demography: Themes and Issues," *Environment and Planning A* 15 (December 1983): 1571–1583; and Pavel Kitsul and Dimiter Philipov, "The One-Year/Five-Year Migration Problem," in Andrei Rogers, ed., *Advances in Multiregional Demography* (Laxenburg, Austria: International Institute for Applied Systems Analysis, 1981).

[3]Based on U.S. data for one-, two-, three-, four-, and five-year migration intervals, Courgeau estimated one-year rates from the seven-year mobility interval used in the 1975 census of France. Daniel Courgeau, "Comparaison des migrations internes en France et aux États-Unis," *Population* 37 (November–December 1982): 1184–1188.

[4]Duration-of-residence questions typically ask how long a person has lived continuously in the locality of current residence or, alternatively, the date the person moved into the current locality for persons who have not lived their whole life in the locality of current residence. Such questions also typically ask for the name of the locality or country of previous residence. A person who reports a duration of residence of exactly two years and names a different locality of residence two years earlier is clearly a nonmover among localities over the preceding 12 months, but residence five years ago obviously cannot be inferred. Similarly, a person who moves from A to B and lives in B for four years before moving back to A will be recorded as having moved by a duration-of-residence question but not in a where-did-you-live-five-years ago question. And without controls for age, comparability is made even more difficult because the questions on residence one or five years earlier are limited to persons at least 1 year old or 5 years old, whereas duration-of-residence tabulations often are not disaggregated in sufficient age detail to identify children under specified ages.

typically must go to original sources—reports from censuses or population registers, microdata tapes, or special tabulations—in order to obtain data. For individual researchers, these activities tend to be costly and time consuming, especially when many countries are involved.

The chapter reports on such an undertaking. It focuses on residential mobility—meaning all persons changing usual residence without regard to administrative boundaries crossed or distance moved. From extant theories that attempt to account for residential mobility of households, hypotheses are derived about how countries differ. The chapter investigates how individual metropolitan areas in several countries compare as to rates of residential mobility. The chapter presents two other approaches to comparing the amount of spatial mobility within different countries: (1) identifying distance moved from the distance between the population centers of localities of origin and destination and (2) inferring migration distances from movements among administrative areas of successively larger average size. There is no perfect answer to the question, "To what degree are the inhabitants of country X more (or less) geographically mobile than the inhabitants of country Y?" Only approximations are possible and are illustrated in what follows.

Hypotheses About Residential Mobility

One approach that has been used before is to focus on the total amount of residential mobility that takes place within countries without regard to whether boundaries of local administrative areas are crossed.[5] Surveys or censuses in several countries have asked respondents, "Did you live in this residence on this date one year ago (five years ago)?" Persons answering no are then asked to name the locality or area of residence one or five years earlier. When the number of persons answering no is divided by the total population aged 1 or 5 and over, the result is often called the residential mobility rate and provides a measure of the probability of changing usual residence and is applicable in different countries.

As mentioned briefly in Chapter 6, virtually all theories of residen-

---

[5]These materials draw heavily from previous work done in collaboration with Celia Boertlein of the Census Bureau. Some early results of this collaboration were published in Larry Long and Celia Boertlein, *The Geographical Mobility of Americans: An International Comparison* (Washington, DC: U.S. Government Printing Office, 1976). This publication reprints questions from the 1970 or 1971 censuses of Australia, Canada, Great Britain, Japan, and the United States on residence one or five years previously.

tial mobility are built around micro models that attempt to describe or explain the behavior of individuals or households. Most residential mobility covers only short distances, so most theories of residential mobility are really theories of local mobility. Typically the decision to stay in or move from a dwelling is seen to be the first of two stages of decision making. The second stage is the choice of new dwelling or new neighborhood after the decision to move has been made.

The decision to stay or move is commonly thought to be strongly related to life-cycle events—leaving one's parental home to go to school or work, leaving school or a first job for other employment, and then getting married. Other moves may also occur as a couple move from a rented apartment to an owned dwelling or as a couple move to a neighborhood with good schools in time for their first child to enroll in school. Later in life, additional moves may occur as the last child leaves home and the couple find they have less need for a large house and may move to a smaller house or apartment or to retire. All of these—and some other moves—are associated with commonly occurring transitions in life. A weakness of this general approach is the growth of divorce, nonfamily living arrangements, and extramarital childbearing over the last two decades; such developments mean that residential changes are less clearly tied to traditional life-cycle transitions.

Besides moves related to life-cycle events, other residential changes occur as a result of conditions that change the satisfaction with the house or the neighborhood. As additional children are born, a house may be re-evaluated as not having enough bedrooms or bathrooms, and the decision may be to renovate or move. If a relative joins the household, special new needs may be created that cause a household to consider remodeling or moving. If the socioeconomic character of the neighborhood changes or if there is commercial invasion of the neighborhood, a household may decide to look for another residence in a different neighborhood. These changes in equilibrium conditions are said to create "locational stress."

Some moves are less clearly tied to life-cycle transitions or to events that create "locational stress." Some occur simply because occupationally successful households find that they can afford to "move up" to a bigger or better house in a more desirable neighborhood. All decisions involving mobility are constrained by the household's budget and anticipated future earnings, including those from household members who may enter the labor force partly for the purpose of enabling the household to move in order to achieve housing desires. Decisions are also constrained by the household's awareness space—the area over which the household possesses or acquires knowledge of neighborhoods or housing opportunities.

These theories have been supported by extensive empirical research, and all have increased understanding of why persons or households change residence.[6] In models of residential change, the dependent variable is often dichotomous—either the person or household moves or it does not—and the various life-cycle transitions, the conditions that create "locational stress," and the degree of personal satisfaction with the housing unit or neighborhood have been found to contribute to explaining why persons or households move or stay. Although they were devised to account for mobility differences among persons or households rather than areas, this line of theory development may hold some implications for explaining how countries differ in rates of residential mobility.

Some researchers have suggested that at least in industrialized nations life-cycle events dictate a certain minimum number of residence changes. If this is the case and there is general similarity in the number of life-cycle stages in different countries, then the difference between a minimal level and the observed level of mobility might be attributed to conditions not directly related to life-cycle transitions. A large supply of cheap housing, a high level of prosperity or affluence, or other circumstances might allow more moves for each life-cycle stage in some countries than in others.

What is the minimum number of moves in a lifetime? Describing urban North America, one study suggested five: "Life-cycle stages account for at least five of the eight or nine moves that might be expected in a lifetime as an individual grows up, leaves home, marries, has children, and ages" (p. 630).[7] In other words, a person might expect to move at least once as a child, again when moving away from his or her par-

---

[6]The premier study of residential mobility was Peter Rossi's *Why Families Move* (Glencoe, IL: Free Press, 1955). The idea that in addition to life-cycle events, residential change may come from the development of locational stress from family or neighborhood conditions was developed by Julian Wolpert, "Migration as an Adjustment to Environmental Stress," *Journal of Social Issues* 22 (October 1966): 92–102. The idea that places and neighborhoods have special utility that varies by life-cycle stage and other household factors derives largely from the work of Lawrence Brown and colleagues, as cited in the references. Related to the notion of place utility is the simple matter of how households evaluate their neighborhood in deciding whether to stay (and perhaps remodel) or move; the theme is developed by Alden Speare and colleagues, as cited in the bibliography. Another approach that supplements a strict life-cycle explanation of why residential mobility occurs is the notion that broad cultural norms affect evaluation of the adequacy of housing (for example, the belief, and in some cases regulations, that require teen-age children of the opposite sex to have separate bedrooms); this line of work was used by Butler et al. and by Earl Morris in numerous works cited in the bibliography. Work by W. A. V. Clark and others cited in the bibliography has drawn from all of the perspectives in developing models of spatial patterns of residential movement. Many writers have commented on the lack of consensus as to precisely the life-cycle stages relevant to explaining residential mobility, and there is little work on how recent changes in marriage and divorce have affected the utility of the life-cycle approach in explaining residential mobility.

[7]James W. Simmons, "Changing Residence in the City: A Review of Intraurban Mobility," *Geographical Review* 58 (October 1968): 622–651.

ents, again at marriage, again when building a family with children, and a fifth time later in life to move to a smaller dwelling after the children have left home, to make a retirement move, or to adjust housing in response to health or other considerations late in the life cycle. A later study, also with an urban orientation, suggested three or four moves in a lifetime:

> Even if no other factors entered the picture, most people would move three or four times during their lives when they leave home, marry and experience the changing needs of a growing family. However, superimposed on these demographic events are many other situations which give rise to residential moves.[8]

It is these "other situations" which are likely to be variable among countries and contribute to different frequencies of lifetime moving. These two statements were derived from observations of North America, but both suggest that a national residential mobility rate that implies three to five changes of residence per person over a lifetime is close to a minimum level for industrial nations.

This line of theoretical development suggests at least two hypotheses that are amenable to testing.

> *Hypothesis 1:* Industrial countries vary in their rates of residential mobility primarily as a result of the average number of moves per life-cycle stage and the relative representation of frequent movers in their populations.

"Residential mobility" refers to all changes of usual residence. The relative incidence of frequent movers might be detected by comparing residential mobility rates over short and long intervals. In high-mobility countries the ratio of the one-year residential mobility rate to the five-year rate should be high, indicating that much of the moving over the five-year period is accounted for by a few people who move repeatedly. Existence of either or both of the two effects implies that differences among countries in rates of residential mobility will be less over a long interval than over a short interval.

> *Hypothesis 2:* Since the life-cycle stages most clearly associated with residential changes are concentrated at the "young adult" age range, relative differences among nations in residential mobility rates should be least at this age range.

---

[8]Eric G. Moore, *Residential Mobility in the City* (Washington, DC: Association of American Geographers, 1972), p. 1.

Hypothesis 2 is straightforward and can be tested with age-specific rates of residential mobility.

Testing Hypotheses About Residential Mobility

Table 8.1 shows residential mobility rates over one- and five-year periods ending in 1970 or 1971 for 10 countries and Hong Kong and Puerto Rico.[9] The 1970–71 round of censuses provides a benchmark period for which the most detailed data (by age, for example) for the largest number of countries are available. The last column of the table shows the approximate number of moves per person in a lifetime implied by the rates of residential mobility shown in columns 1 and 3. Moves in a lifetime were estimated by the life table methods discussed in Appendix B. Technically speaking, the last column refers to "years with moves" for the data do not count more than one residence change in a year (nor do they count as movers persons who left and returned to their address within the year over which mobility was measured). When available, age-specific data for one-year mobility intervals and a 1967 life table were used to estimate lifetime moves; in other cases inferences were made from the five-year rates of moving.

The table shows that rates of residential mobility are high in the United States and about as high in Australia, Canada, and Hong Kong. Over a 12-month period 19.2 percent of the U.S. population changed residence compared with 17.1 percent in Australia. Over a five-year period, the proportion changing residence was 47.0 percent in the United States, 43.4 percent in Australia, 46.6 percent in Canada, and 51.3 percent in Hong Kong. Puerto Rico also had a comparatively high five-year residential mobility rate of 44.3 percent. These figures include movers from abroad; excluding movers from abroad lowers the rates somewhat, as can be seen from the table.

---

[9]Data for Hungary and Taiwan are from population registers of residential moves recorded over a year; these data were adjusted to represent movers per 100 persons aged 1 and over from information provided by Shigemi Kono, "Evaluation of the Japanese Population Register Data on Internal Migration," *International Population Conference, London, 1969*, vol. 4 (Liège, Belgium: International Union for the Scientific Study of Population, 1972), pp. 2766–2775. Data for France are from Daniel Courgeau, "Baisse de la mobilité residentielle." *Population et Sociétés* 179 (April 1984). Data for the other countries come from censuses or from government-sponsored national surveys which included questions on usual residence one or five years earlier. The estimate of migration expectancy for Australia is for 1975–76 and is taken from D. T. Rowland, *Population and Educational Planning* (Canberra: Australian Government Publishing Service, 1983), p. 93. Other data were obtained from official publications or from personal correspondence with statistical offices.

TABLE 8.1

Percentage of Population Residentially Mobile in 10 Countries and Hong Kong and Puerto Rico: 1970 or 1971

	Percentage Changing Residence in One Year[a]		Percentage Changing Residence in Five Years[b]		Approximate Number of Residence Changes per Person in a Lifetime[c]
	Including Movers from Abroad	Excluding Movers from Abroad	Including Movers from Abroad	Excluding Movers from Abroad	
Australia	17.1%	15.6%	43.4%	39.4%	10 or 11
Canada	NA	NA	46.6	44.3	12 or 13
France	10.4	NA	NA	NA	6 or 7
Great Britain	11.8	11.1	37.2	35.9	7 or 8
Hong Kong	NA	NA	51.3	49.7	12 or 13
Hungary[d]	11.2	11.2	NA	NA	7 or 8
Ireland	5.1	4.3	NA	NA	3 or 4
Japan	12.0	12.0	35.9	35.8	7 or 8
New Zealand	15.4	14.1	37.5	35.0	9 or 10
Puerto Rico	NA	NA	44.3	37.9	10 or 11
Taiwan[d]	10.0	NA	NA	NA	6 or 7
United States	19.2	18.6	47.0	43.2	12 or 13

NOTE: NA means "not available."

[a]Persons aged 1 and over.

[b]Persons aged 5 and over.

[c]Estimated by life table methods using age-specific data for one-year intervals, when available. Estimate refer to years with moves. See Appendix B for statement of methods.

[d]Estimated from population registration and may overstate movers per 100 persons aged 1 and over.

The rate for New Zealand is slightly less—15.4 percent over a one-year period and 37.5 percent over a five-year period. Somewhat lower annual rates of 10 to 12 percent per year characterized France, Great Britain, Hungary, Japan, and Taiwan in 1970 or 1971. An annual residential mobility rate of 10 percent has also been reported for West Germany.[10] The lowest rate shown in Table 8.1 is for Ireland, where only 5.1 percent of the population moved in the 12 months preceding the 1971 census.

As the last column of the table shows, Ireland's annual rate of residential mobility translates into the minimum three or four moves per person in a lifetime as postulated in the quotations presented above. A slightly higher level of movement, implying six to eight lifetime changes of residence, seems to characterize France, Great Britain, Hun-

[10]John O'Loughlin and Gunter Glebe, "Intraurban Migration in West German Cities," *Geographical Review* 74 (January 1984): 4.

gary, Japan, and Taiwan. The rates for New Zealand and Puerto Rico probably mean 9 to 11 residence changes, and the rates for the United States, Canada, and Australia, and Hong Kong imply 11 to 13 residence changes per person over a lifetime. These figures suggest considerable differences in lifestyles derived simply from differences in lifetime "quotas" of moves. The detailed calculations of mobility expectancy presented in Appendix B suggest that by age 20 or 21 a typical American will have moved as often as the typical resident of Ireland does in a lifetime. At least this was the case in 1970–71.

In order to test the first hypothesis, Table 8.2 shows the ratio of the one-year rates to the five-year rates for the five countries for which such data were available. Also shown is the ratio of the one- and five-year rates of the other countries to the one- or five-year rates of the United States.

As hypothesized, the one-year/five-year ratio appears to be somewhat higher in the high-mobility countries. The ratio is .41 in the United States and New Zealand and .39 in Australia compared with .32 in Great Britain and .33 in Japan. These figures mean that in the United States the annual rate of moving in 1970–71 was 41 percent of the five-year rate. If there were no return and repeat moving, the one-year rate would be one fifth the five-year rate; if all moves in a five-year period were persons moving again and again, the one-year rate would equal the five-year rate. The higher the one-year/five-year ratio, the greater the implied incidence of repeat moving over the five-year period. The ratio seems high in the high-mobility countries, suggesting that repeat moves disproportionately account for at least some of the "excess" mobility found in the United States, Australia, and New Zealand. But data were available for only five countries, and the results should not be inter-

TABLE 8.2

Ratio of One-Year Rate to Five-Year Rate of Residential Mobility and Ratio to U.S. Rate for Australia, Great Britain, Japan, and New Zealand: 1970 or 1971

	Ratio of One-Year Rate to Five-Year Rate	Ratio to U.S. Rate[a]	
		One-Year Interval	Five-Year Interval
Australia	.39	.89	.92
Great Britain	.32	.61	.79
Japan	.33	.63	.76
New Zealand	.41	.80	.80
United States	.41	1.00	1.00

[a]Rates include movers from abroad.

preted as a definitive test of the hypothesis that a greater incidence of repeat movers in their populations helps account for why some countries have high annual rates of residential mobility.

Such results suggest that countries may differ not only in the mean number of moves to be expected in a lifetime but also in the distribution of population according to the actual number of moves. That is, the mean number of moves in a lifetime, as estimated by life table techniques, may be more highly skewed by a relatively few frequent movers in countries with high annual rates of residential mobility.

The other part of the first hypothesis was that the high-mobility countries generate more mobility per life cycle stage. With available data, there seems no way to effectively test for this possibility. The various countries tend to tabulate residential mobility data by age (to be discussed next) but not age *and* the timing of marriage, the birth of children, or other common indicators of life-cycle stage. Such data might be created from microdata files but do not now exist.

In Table 8.2 differences among countries are less when measured over a five-year interval than a one-year interval. Over a one-year period, for example, the residential mobility rate in Britain is 61 percent of the U.S. rate, but over a five-year period the British rate is 79 percent of the U.S. rate. For each of the other countries except New Zealand, the ratio of the residential mobility to the U.S. rate is higher for the five-year interval than the one-year interval; for New Zealand the ratio is the same for the one- and five-year intervals. The longer interval increases the possibility that a person will move at least once and reduces the apparent differences among nations.

Residential Mobility by Age

The relationship between age and residential mobility, as described in Chapter 2 (see especially Figure 2.2) seems generally applicable to other countries.[11] Figure 8.1 shows one-year rates of residential mobility

[11]The basic shape of the curves displayed in Figure 8.1 applies to an even greater variety of countries which provide data on movers between localities. In almost all, rates of movement between localities are high among young children and low among teen-agers, rising to a peak among persons in their 20s and then declining with age. An upturn in rates with the onset of retirement from the labor force is not universal. Mathematical expressions of these regularities (the relatively sharp decline up to the age of leaving school, the rapid rise with separation from the nuclear family, and the more gradual decline with increasing age at least up to the time of exit from the labor force) are presented in Luis J. Castro and Andrei Rogers, "What the Age Composition of Migrants Can Tell Us," *Population Bulletin of the United Nations*, no. 15 (1983): 63–79; and "Patterns of Family Migration," *Environment and Planning A* 15 (February 1983): 237–254.

FIGURE 8.1

Percentage of Population Changing Residence in One Year, by Age, for the United States, Great Britain, Japan, Ireland, and New Zealand: 1970 or 1971

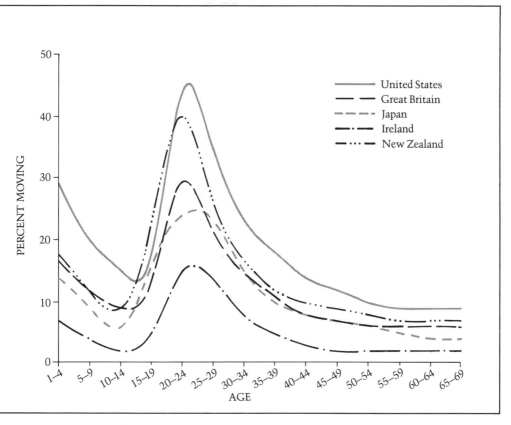

by age for the United States, Great Britain, Japan, New Zealand, and Ireland for 1970 or 1971. These five countries provided tabulations by five-year age groups.

In each country rates of moving are relatively high among children under age 5, reflecting the high mobility of their young parents. Rates of residential mobility reach a low point among persons around their mid-teens and then rise very rapidly to a peak among persons in their early 20s. After the peak is reached, rates decline fairly rapidly and then begin to decline more gradually with age. The low rate of residential mobility that characterizes persons in their mid-teens also characterizes persons in their 40s.

The visual image conveyed by Figure 8.1 is one of rough similarity

263

among the five countries in the association between age and the probability of changing residence. To some extent, this similarity supports the life-cycle approach to explaining residential mobility. In each country mobility is high among persons in their late teens or in their 20s as they leave their parental home to complete their education, find jobs, get married, and so forth. High mobility in the early family-building years is shown by the high rates of moving among children under age 5 or 10. Mobility seems to decline as the children become teen-agers and as their parents settle into careers and neighborhoods.

The second hypothesis stated that countries would be most alike in rates of moving at the ages where mobility is greatest. To facilitate testing this hypothesis, Table 8.3 shows, age by age, the ratio of the residential mobility rate for each of the countries to the U.S. rate.

The hypothesis is at least partially supported. The boxes in the table highlight the age group where the ratio to the U.S. rate is highest, and the ratios reach their peak somewhere between the late teens and the late 20s. Relative to the U.S. rate, the British and Japanese rates of residential mobility are greatest at ages 15–19. The New Zealand rate exceeds the U.S. rate at age 15–19 and is very close to the U.S. rate at ages 20–24. The residential mobility rate for Ireland comes closer to the U.S. rate at ages 25–29 than at any other age.

TABLE 8.3

Ratio of One-Year Residential Mobility Rates in Great Britain, Japan, New Zealand, and Ireland to the U.S. Rate, by Age: 1970 or 1971

| Age | Ratio to U.S. Rate | | | |
	Great Britain	Japan	New Zealand	Ireland
1–4 Years	.60	.47	.63	.23
5–9 Years	.59	.45	.59	.18
10–14 Years	.58	.41	.60	.15
15–19 Years	.72	.90	1.24	.30
20–24 Years	.66	.53	.89	.33
25–29 Years	.64	.66	.77	.41
30–34 Years	.65	.63	.74	.35
35–39 Years	.63	.57	.70	.29
40–44 Years	.62	.57	.73	.24
45–49 Years	.61	.57	.74	.20
50–54 Years	.63	.58	.80	.19
55–59 Years	.59	.55	80	.18
60–64 Years	.64	.52	.83	.21
65–69 Years	.66	.48	.78	.24

Differences among countries in the exact shape of the overall age curve associated with residential mobility are doubtlessly influenced by differences in school-leaving ages, median age at first marriage, median age of women when they have their first baby, and how soon young couples are able to acquire housing that cultural and social norms say is suitable for raising a family. In other words, the exact timing of life-cycle events varies somewhat, but because these events are typically concentrated between the late teens and late 20s, countries seem to be more similar somewhere within this age range than at younger or older ages, at least as concerns the probability of changing usual residence over the course of one year.

Precise comparisons are also affected by differences in coverage of the various data sources. The one-year U.S. data are from a household sample that excludes most institutional population—for example, military personnel living in barracks, persons detained in jails or prisons, persons in long-term hospitals, and others in group quarters. In the U.S. survey, however, college students living in dormitories are supposed to be counted in their parents' household. Data for the other countries are from censuses which presumably include institutional population, some of whom have high residential mobility rates. These differences in coverage between a household sample and a census might be particularly great at ages 18–22 when many young persons are in the military or in other group quarters. But the relatively high U.S. rates persist through ages 25–29, supporting the hypothesis that differences will be least somewhere at the young-adult ages.

In Table 8.3 residential mobility differences among the five countries tend to be greatest at ages 5–9 or 10–14; that is, the ratios are lowest at this age range. This pattern may mean that in the United States residential changing tends to extend over a longer span of the family-raising stage of the life cycle. Maybe it reflects differences among countries in marital stability of parents with children at these ages. Whatever the explanation, the U.S. rate seems to be high, relative to the rate for the four other countries, for school-age children and their parents.

In each of the five countries there was a sex differential associated with the probability of moving during the one-year interval. The data are not shown, but the rise in the late teens in rates of moving tended to begin earlier for women than for men, to attain a higher peak for women than for men, and to decline earlier for women than for men. A major reason for the differences in the timing of residential mobility of men and women is the younger age at marriage for women than for men and a tendency for women to marry men who are slightly older. Part of the difference may also derive from an understatement of mobility of

TABLE 8.4

One-Year Rates of Residential Mobility in Selected Large Metropolitan Areas of the United States, Great Britain, Japan, New Zealand, and Ireland, for Persons Aged 1 and Over: 1970 or 1971

Metropolitan Areas	Population of Metropolitan Area (in thousands)	Percentage Changing Residence in One Year		
		Entire Metropolitan Area	Central City or Cities	Remainder of Metropolitan Area
United States				
New York	14,706	13.3%	13.7%	12.8%
Chicago	7,613	17.5	17.6	17.3
Los Angeles–Long Beach	8,235	22.4	22.5	22.4
Philadelphia	4,628	13.6	13.2	13.9
Detroit	4,247	17.3	19.5	15.8
San Francisco–Oakland	3,121	23.3	23.3	23.3
Boston	2,619	15.0	15.4	14.9
Pittsburgh	2,608	11.6	12.3	11.4
St. Louis	2,273	18.4	22.4	17.1
Washington, D.C.	2,773	21.4	24.8	20.1
Cleveland	1,871	14.3	20.2	11.4
Baltimore	1,908	18.9	18.7	19.0
Newark	1,828	14.9	17.8	14.2
Minneapolis–St. Paul	1,713	19.6	22.5	17.7
Buffalo	1,215	14.4	16.3	13.5
Houston	1,646	25.1	23.9	28.5
Milwaukee	1,246	14.5	17.4	11.2
Paterson–Clifton–Passaic	1,305	13.4	13.7	13.3
Cincinnati	1,090	18.7	22.3	15.8
Dallas	1,478	29.3	34.2	23.5
Great Britain				
Greater London Conurbation	7,345	12.6	14.4	11.4
South East Lancashire Conurbation (Manchester)	2,353	11.1	NA	NA
West Midlands Conurbation (Birmingham)	2,332	10.6	NA	NA
West Yorkshire Conurbation (Leeds)	1,699	11.0	NA	NA

men who in their late teens or early 20s join the military or work or study abroad. Men who are highly mobile may also be less likely to be enumerated in censuses or surveys.

Data for only five countries do not constitute a definitive test of the hypothesis that rates of moving among industrialized countries are most similar at the young-adult ages when rates are highest. The data tend to support the hypotheses but should not be interpreted as proving it. These five countries were selected for the simple reason that they provided the most comparable data on rates of residential mobility by age.

TABLE 8.4 *(continued)*

Metropolitan Areas	Population of Metropolitan Area (in thousands)	Percentage Changing Residence in One Year		
		Entire Metropolitan Area	Central City or Cities	Remainder of Metropolitan Area
Central Clydeside Conurbation (Glasgow)	1,698	10.7	NA	NA
Merseyside Conurbation (Liverpool)	1,246	9.8	NA	NA
Tyneside Conurbation (Newcastle)	794	11.0	NA	NA
Japan				
Keihin Metropolitan Area	22,941	15.8	16.5	15.2
Tokyo city	—	—	16.1	—
Yokohama city	—	—	17.2	—
Kawasaki city	—	—	18.3	—
Keihanshin Metropolitan Area	15,056	14.0	13.6	14.3
Kyoto city	—	—	12.0	—
Osaka city	—	—	13.1	—
Sakai city	—	—	15.4	—
Higashiosaka city	—	—	14.3	—
Kobe city	—	—	14.7	—
Amagasaki city	—	—	15.5	—
Chukyo (Nagoya) Metropolitan Area	6,488	12.2	13.7	11.5
Kitakyushu Metropolitan Area	4,013	13.9	17.7	10.6
Sapporo Metropolitan Area	1,462	22.1	24.6	16.7
Sendai Metropolitan Area	1,255	12.6	18.8	8.0
Hiroshima Metropolitan Area	1,368	15.6	19.0	13.5
New Zealand				
Auckland Urban Area	634	17.7	19.4	16.2
Wellington Urban Area	300	18.4	22.4	14.9
Ireland				
Dublin County	832	7.5	NA	NA

NOTE: NA means "not available."

Mobility for Metropolitan Areas

National rates of residential mobility can be misleading in that they probably mask considerable spatial variation in mobility within a country's borders. Chapter 6 showed that some older cities and metropolitan areas in the United States had residential mobility rates far below the national average, whereas some growing metropolitan areas had rates well above the average. Examining residential mobility for individual cities and metropolitan areas can provide better perspective on how, and perhaps why, nations vary in the propensity of their population to change their address.

One problem in doing so is that countries vary according to how they define cities and metropolitan areas. Most countries provide some information on mobility status for specific large metropolitan areas, and residential mobility rates for a one-year period in 1970 or 1971 compiled for selected large metropolitan areas of the United States, Great Britain, Japan, New Zealand, and Ireland are presented in Table 8.4.[12] Where possible, metropolitan areas were divided into a core city and a periphery. In general, each country's own definitions of city and metropolitan areas were used, so strict comparability is out of the question. Table 8.4 should be interpreted as heuristic rather than definitive.

These data suggest that some conclusions reached earlier about urban residential mobility have international applicability. In almost every case, the core city is shown to have somewhat higher rates of residential mobility than the remainder of the metropolitan area. Many cities may appeal to young persons and have housing stocks that attract persons who expect to have comparatively short durations of stay. The image drawn in Chapter 6 of young persons flowing into cities for purposes of education or to take their first job and then moving out to the suburbs for the family-building stage of their lives may apply to a wide variety of urban settings and may contribute the somewhat higher rates of housing turnover in many cities than in the suburban periphery.

Six of the seven British conurbations (London is the exception) had rates of residential mobility slightly below the national average. In contrast, the seven metropolitan areas of Japan had residential mobility rates above the national average. At the time the data were collected in 1970 or 1971 the British urban regions were growing comparatively slowly, whereas the Japanese urban regions were growing more rapidly. Perhaps, as concluded in Chapter 6, inmigration to Japanese urban areas contributed to their having residential mobility rates above the national average, and, in reverse fashion, perhaps the outmigration from British urban areas outside the London region contributed to their having mobility rates below the national average. Whether this speculative interpretation is true or not, the conclusion is that large urban regions do not universally have high rates of residential mobility compared with the rest of the nation.

---

[12]The U.S. data for metropolitan areas are from microdata files of March Current Population Surveys for 1968, 1969, 1970, and 1971. The four years were combined in order to increase the sample size. The other data are from the 1971 censuses of Great Britain and Ireland and the 1970 census of Japan.

The level of residential mobility in New York City is similar to—
or possibly lower than—that found in London or Tokyo. The core areas
of these metropolitan regions are shown to have annual rates of housing
turnover of 13.7 percent in New York, 14.4 percent in London, and 16.1
percent in Tokyo. Age standardization, if possible, would raise the rate
slightly for London and lower the rate for Tokyo. In each metropolitan
area, the core seems to have slightly more active turnover of housing
than the balance of the metropolitan area. For these three countries the
largest urban regions appear to be more similar in rates of residential
mobility than the national averages.

Several U.S. metropolitan areas (Dallas, Houston, San Francisco–
Oakland, Los Angeles, and Washington, D.C.) had residential mobility
rates in 1971 of 20 percent or higher, as did Sapporo, Japan. The two
largest metropolitan areas of New Zealand—Auckland and Wellington—had annual residential mobility rates of about 18 percent, slightly
above the national average. Among Ireland's 27 counties, the highest
residential mobility rate was in Dublin, where 7.5 percent of the population had moved in the 12 months preceding the 1971 census.

Differences among countries in rates of residential mobility are reduced somewhat by limiting comparison to the largest urban regions in
each country. Doing this shows that the high national rate of moving in
the United States derives partly from a number of medium-sized metropolitan areas that have been growing very rapidly and have a high
turnover of housing. The international data reinforce the conclusion of
Chapter 6 that urban areas do not uniformly have higher rates of population turnover than the national average. In the international data there
appears to be a tendency for the core areas of urban agglomerations to
have more turnover than the balance of the agglomeration.

Whether for individual metropolitan areas or for nations, most
moves cover what seem like short distances. It is not possible to ascertain exactly how much of the movers in the metropolitan areas identified in Table 8.4 were "local movers" who moved "short distances."
Each of the countries distinguishes between those moving within and
between local areas, but differing size, shape, and significance of localities within and among the countries makes precise comparisons impossible. For the U.S. metropolitan areas, the proportion of movers who had
stayed within a county or county equivalent varied from 53 percent to
78 percent—compared with a national average of 61 percent (see Table
2.5). For Japanese metropolitan areas the proportion of moves that were
"local" varied from 43 to 54 percent. The U.S. metropolitan areas seem
to have proportionately more local movers than the Japanese areas simply because the U.S. counties are larger than the Japanese localities (*shi,
ku, machi,* and *mura*). Table 8.4 simply offers one indicator of spatial
variation in housing turnover, and there is no accurate way of compar-

ing the areas shown in the table according to how much turnover resulted from short-distance versus long-distance moves.

Distance Moved

As with many micro models of household decision making, the comparisons featured previously look upon mobility in dichotomous terms—either a move occurs or it does not. There seems to be growing willingness to accept the residential mobility rate as a measure of the overall level of geographical mobility of national populations. But only a few countries produce such data, and the more common approach is for population registers to record only those moves that cross the borders of administrative areas or for censuses to restrict questions to persons who moved from one administrative area to another. Some procedures, to be discussed later, may be applicable for making inferences about the underlying propensity to move when movement is recorded for successively larger areas, like counties, states, and regions in the United States.

Perhaps a more direct approach would be to have information on actual distance moved and assess the propensity of different populations to make a move of a given distance. Although there appears to be no modern census that asked respondents to report distance moved and very few surveys ever ask for distance moved, distance can be computed between the locality of origin and the locality of destination by using the population centers of the locality of origin and destination. The population center is the point on which the locality would exactly balance if each resident of the area exerted the same downward force. It is not to be confused with the geographic center, which is the point on which the area would balance if it were uninhabited and nothing else affected balancing the area at a single point. Using this method, the Swedish Central Bureau of Statistics furnishes data on migration distances.[13] The same method was used to compute distances of intercounty moves in the United States over the 1975–76 interval, based on data from the Current Population Survey of March 1976.

The use of population centers tends to overstate the distance covered by moves between contiguous localities, for many of these moves are simply from one side of a boundary to the other, and few cover the distance between the population centers. This source of bias decreases

---

[13]Data are from Swedish Central Bureau of Statistics, *Internal Migration in Sweden* (Stockholm: Swedish Central Bureau of Statistics, 1976), p. 54.

FIGURE 8.2

Propensity of the Populations of the United States and Sweden to Move Specified Distances in One Year: Around 1975

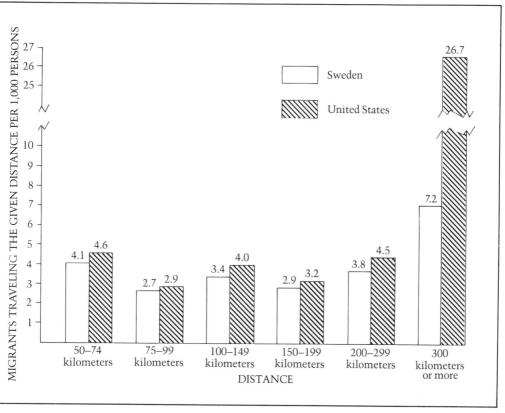

as the size of the areas gets smaller. The U.S. data were calculated in kilometers and are compared with the Swedish data in Figure 8.2. In computing U.S. migration distances, moves originating or terminating in Alaska or Hawaii were excluded. To facilitate comparison, moves under 50 kilometers were excluded because of the bias in estimating short-distance moves. The numbers of persons moving the various distances were divided by the total population (persons aged 1 and over for the United States, excluding Alaska and Hawaii) in order to express the results as rates.

The results may be interpreted as a series of migration rates, reflecting the propensity of the populations of the United States and Sweden to move given distances in one year. For example, out of every 1,000 persons in Sweden, 4.1 moved 50–74 kilometers over the one-year span compared with 4.6 in the United States. An additional 2.7 persons per 1,000 in Sweden moved 75–99 kilometers compared with 2.9 in the United States. At each successive distance, the percentage of population undertaking a move is greater in the United States than in Sweden, confirming notions of high migration propensities in the United States.

For distances under 300 kilometers, however, the differences seem quite small. The propensity to move 50 to 300 kilometers is only about 14 percent higher in the United States than in Sweden. These appear to be common migration distances in Sweden. For distances over 300 kilometers, the U.S. rate is understandably much higher than the Swedish rate—about 3.7 times higher. If one were to define migration as a residential change that covered a distance of at least 50 kilometers, one would conclude that the U.S. migration rate is about 90 percent greater than the Swedish rate, although a large part of the difference could be attributed to a higher rate of long-distance (over 300 kilometers) moves in the United States.

These results suggest that in comparing migration propensities among countries, there is a need to take into account common distances. Very rarely, however, do countries prepare and publish data on migration distances in a way that would allow comparison with the U.S. and Swedish data presented in Figure 8.2. This gap in migration information is unfortunate, and filling it need not be as expensive as one might think. With information from population registers, distance moved might be computed for only a sample of all the in-and-out moves recorded over a year's time. Similarly with censuses, migration distances might be computed for a sample of all persons moving between administrative areas. Surveys, too, might ask respondents to report distance moved. There is no evidence that respondents cannot give usable approximations to distance moved, and asking for distance of moves does not entail great expense for little or no coding is required. Only a few U.S. surveys have recorded distance moved. One was the Survey of Economic Opportunity, taken in 1967, which began a series of migration questions by asking if the respondent had ever lived more than 50 miles (about 80 kilometers) from the current residence.

Information on the distribution of migration distances in different countries would allow estimation of mean distance moved, the nature of migration distance-decay functions, or other measures of the propensity of different national populations to move internally. Such measures could be used as the dependent variable in multivariate approaches to explaining spatial mobility within different countries. Internal spatial mobility may be positively related to size of country, degree of urban primacy, other aspects of settlement structure, government policies, or other variables introduced to explain why countries differ in the rate or volume of internal geographical mobility. At the present time, testing such theories is impossible without information on migration distances for more countries.

The Implied Distance Moved

In the absence of data on migration distances, there are other approaches to comparing the internal spatial mobility of different countries. One possibility is simply to do what Ravenstein and Weber did 100 years ago. Limited to data on locality of birth, they inferred high migration rates in countries where the average size of localities was large and the percentage of population living outside their locality of birth was high. Ravenstein noted that information on place of birth was collected for counties in the United Kingdom and provinces in Holland. "Of 100 natives of Holland," he wrote, "as many as 90 live in their native province, whilst of 100 natives of the United Kingdom, only 75 live in their native county." Since the U.K. counties were larger than provinces in Holland, he concluded that "migration in Holland is going on at a far less active rate than in the United Kingdom."[14] A few years later, Weber made the same type of comparison:

> . . . Americans are more accustomed to migrate from State to State than are Europeans from county to county. The English are apparently the most mobile people of Europe, as regards internal migration at least; and yet the percentage of native Englishmen living outside their county of birth was in 1871 almost exactly equal to the percentage of native Americans living outside the State in which they were born—the percentages being 25.66 and 26.2 (1870) respectively.[15]

The apparent conclusion is that at that time Americans were more mobile than the English, who were more mobile than the Dutch.

This approach could obviously be extended with contemporary data on period rates of movement. More and more countries are reporting data on the number of persons moving between small administrative areas (such as parishes, communes, counties, and municipios) and the larger areas of which they are parts (provinces, states, or regions). Table 8.5 presents such data for 23 countries which measure migration over a one- or five-year interval and present such data for spatial units of suc-

---

[14]E. G. Ravenstein, "The Laws of Migration," *Journal of the Statistical Society* 48 (June 1885): 183.

[15]Adna Ferrin Weber, *The Growth of Cities in the Nineteenth Century* (Ithaca, NY: Cornell University Press, 1962 [1899]), pp. 250–251.

TABLE 8.5

Rates of Moving Between Administrative Areas of Varying Sizes, for Selected Countries: 1970 or 1971

	Administrative Areas			Persons Moving Between the Specified Areas per 1,000 Base Population
	Number	Average Size (km^2)	Radius (km)	
ONE-YEAR INTERVAL[a]				
Belgium				
communes	2,359	13	2.0	50.0
arrondissements	44	693	14.9	18.4
provinces	9	3,390	32.9	9.4
Bulgaria				
communes	1,258	88	5.3	12.9
districts	28	3,962	35.5	6.3
regions	7	15,847	71.0	3.9
Denmark				
municipalities	278	159	7.1	75.0
counties	16	2,756	29.6	43.6
Finland				
communes	518	651	14.4	52.8
lan	12	28,084	94.6	22.7
France				
communes	36,394	15	2.2	64.4
departments	95	5,753	42.8	30.9
regions	22	24,840	88.9	19.0
Great Britain				
local authority areas	1,230	198	7.9	54.8
regions	10	24,400	88.2	16.0
Hungary				
counties	25	3,721	34.4	61.4
regions	6	15,505	70.3	29.2
Japan				
shi, ku, machi, mura	3,364	111	5.9	73.2
prefectures	46	8,084	50.7	37.1
Netherlands				
municipalities	842	44	3.7	45.2
provinces	12	3,063	31.2	18.5
Norway				
kommuner	449	722	15.2	44.6
counties	20	16,211	71.9	28.6
regions	5	64,844	143.7	12.5
Sweden				
forsamlingar	2,570	175	7.5	80.8
kommuner	278	1,618	22.7	43.5
lan	24	18,741	77.3	21.5
Taiwan				
townships or precincts	361	98	5.6	67.8
counties or cities	21	1,676	23.1	39.2
United States				
counties	3,141	2,981	30.8	67.5
states	51	183,591	241.8	35.8
regions	4	2,340,792	863.4	19.1

TABLE 8.5 (continued)

	Administrative Areas			Persons Moving Between the Specified Areas per 1,000 Base Population
	Number	Average Size (km²)	Radius (km)	
FIVE-YEAR INTERVAL[b]				
Australia				
statistical areas	68	112,946	189.7	125.9
states	8	960,038	552.9	46.3
Austria				
gemeinden	2,327	36	3.4	76.3
bezirke	98	856	16.5	51.1
lander	9	9,317	54.5	24.8
Canada				
municipalities	4,586	2,175	26.3	194.3
provinces	12	831,349	514.5	45.7
Chile				
communes	314	2,362	27.4	182.7
provinces	25	29,671	97.2	77.6
Costa Rica				
cantons	79	644	14.3	176.6
provinces	7	7,272	48.1	80.6
Ecuador				
cities, rural parishes				
or cantons	945	290	9.6	129.1
provinces	21	13,034	64.4	72.6
El Salvador				
municipios	261	82	5.1	63.9
departamentos	14	1,528	22.1	39.1
Great Britain				
local authority areas	1,230	198	7.9	176.1
regions	10	24,400	88.2	51.0
Guatemala				
municipios	325	335	10.3	86.0
departamentos	22	4,950	39.7	49.4
Honduras				
municipios	282	397	11.2	117.0
departamentos	18	6,227	44.5	75.5
Japan				
shik, ku, machi, mura	3,364	111	5.9	206.0
prefectures	46	8,084	50.7	96.9
South Korea				
gu, si, gun	185	532	13.0	161.4
provinces	11	8,955	53.4	90.7
United States				
counties	3,141	2,981	30.8	182.8
states	51	183,591	241.8	92.6
divisions	9	1,040,352	575.6	67.0
regions	4	2,340,792	863.4	50.4

[a]Persons aged 1 and over.

[b]Persons aged 5 and over.

cessively larger size. The table shows the number and size of such areas and how the measured rate of migration decreases as the size of areas increases. These data are informative, but they are more suited to illustrating the difficulties of comparing internal spatial mobility across a wide variety of settings than they are at providing definitive answers. The 23 countries do not exhaust the number of countries for which such data are available.[16]

Ravenstein and Weber might have gone down the last column until they found two countries with similar migration rates, which would then be related to the average size of the migration-defining areas in the two countries (available from column 3). For example, the rate of movement between U.S. counties is similar to the rate of movement between French communes, but Ravenstein and Weber would have ranked the U.S. internal migration rate higher than the French rate because U.S. counties are, on average, larger than French communes. Such a ranking would be consistent with the direction of difference between the two countries in rates of residential mobility, as shown in Table 8.1.

Ravenstein and Weber might also have concluded that Britain still appears to have a higher rate of internal migration than the Netherlands. The percentage of population moving between local authority areas in Britain is shown to be higher than the percentage of population moving between municipalities in the Netherlands even though the British localities are, on average, larger than the Dutch localities.

More complex comparisons are also possible. For example, it is possible to compare Belgium and Bulgaria in two ways. First, using the Ravenstein-Weber approach, one sees that Belgian provinces are very roughly similar in size to Bulgarian districts, but the percentage of population moving between Belgian provinces is higher than that moving between Bulgarian districts; this difference implies a higher rate of internal migration for Belgium. Another approach is to infer migration over distances represented by differences in average size of successively larger areas. Belgian arrondissements and provinces have average radii of 14.9 and 32.9 kilometers, respectively, and in a year's time 9.0 percent of Belgium's population moves between arrondissements but within provinces, perhaps implying that 9.0 percent of the population migrates over a distance of 14.9 to 32.9 kilometers in a year. In Bulgaria, only 6.6 percent of the population appears to move a distance between

---

[16]The data are from official publications or from personal correspondence with statistical offices in the various countries. Data for France, however, are from Courgeau, "Les Migrations internes en France de 1954 à 1975," and represent his estimates of annual migration rates developed from the 1975 census question on residence in 1968. Data for Belgium, Bulgaria, Denmark, Finland, Hungary, the Netherlands, Norway, and Sweden are from population registers and, as in Table 8.1, have been adjusted to reflect movers. All other data are from censuses or national surveys.

5.3 and 35.5 kilometers, the difference between the average radii of communes and districts. The lower percentage of population moving over a wider distance in Bulgaria suggests a lower migration rate in Bulgaria than in Belgium over distances that appear to be fairly common in both countries.

Although Belgium's population appears to be more migratory than Bulgaria's, Belgium seems to have a low rate of internal migration in relation to most of the other Western European countries included in the table. Applying the Ravenstein-Weber approach or the alternative procedure of inferring migration distances, one concludes that Belgium's rate of internal migration is lower than rates in Denmark, Finland, France, Great Britain, the Netherlands, Norway, and Sweden. Either method suggests roughly similar rates of internal migration for the Scandinavian countries.

The Latin American countries shown in the table appear to have relatively high rates of internal migration. For example, Chile's communes are only slightly smaller than U.S. counties, but in a five-year period the percentage of population moving between these areas is the same in the two countries, implying that Chile's rate of internal migration is fairly close to the U.S. rate, which is high. The same approach suggests higher rates of migration in Chile, Costa Rica, Ecuador, Guatemala, Honduras, and South Korea than Austria, whose rate seems relatively low—lower than the British and Japanese rates of internal migration.

One could continue this process so as to rank all 23 countries and others with data on migration for geographical areas of successively larger size. Unanswered, of course, is the degree of difference, and at some point the rankings become less certain because of the variation that underlies the mean size of the various migration-defining areas. Although the table shows that U.S. counties or county equivalents average 2,981 square kilometers, the largest is 10,000 times the size of the smallest. Whether similar variability underlies some of the other spatial units is uncertain. The effect of such variability on inferring migration distances is unclear.

The most promising research to go beyond the ad hoc comparisons just described is by Courgeau whose work involves inferring distance-decay functions from average size of migration-defining areas for some countries.[17] Extending Courgeau's methods to more countries seems justified with the results produced so far, although work needs to be done on the stability of distance-decay functions over time. In regard to

---

[17]Daniel Courgeau, "Migrations et découpage du territoire," *Population* 28 (May–June 1973): 511–536; "L'Intensité des changements de categorie de communes," *Population* 30 (January–February 1975): 81–97; and "Comparison des migrations internes en France et aux États-Unis."

the last point, the association of migration and distance in the United States may have changed over the last 15 years or so, a time when intra-county moves have declined as a proportion of all moves, implying a change in the overall distance-decay function.

Recommendations for Improving International Comparability

Statistical bureaus can do many things to improve comparability of statistics on internal spatial mobility. First, countries with population registers could present statistics on movers as well as moves. This information would be useful not only to facilitate international comparisons but also to assess how much internal mobility is accounted for by a few people who move repeatedly.

Second, countries that rely on censuses and surveys instead of continuous population registration for data on internal spatial mobility could show more information on distance moved. Such information can be estimated from population centers of areas of origin and destination (the smaller the areas, the better the estimates). Calculating distance moved in this way is a fairly straightforward procedure and does not add to respondent burden. Alternatively, respondents could be asked to report the distance moved, for there is no evidence that respondents cannot or will not report such information, which is inexpensive to collect because it does not require extensive coding. Measuring internal migration according to distance moved would facilitate comparing the spatial mobility of different countries in many ways. One could compare the propensity to move beyond some minimum distance (presumably a distance that exceeds normal or usual commuting distances) or estimate the decline of migration with distances common in different countries.

Third, census or survey questions could greatly improve comparability by collecting information on the number of persons moving within localities. Obtaining such information does not require the coding of each change of usual residence. Inexpensive modifications can be made to existing census or survey questionnaires.

For example, many census questions on residence one or five years earlier begin by asking, "In what locality did you live one year (five years) ago?" and the respondent is asked to mark a circle or box for "this locality" or is given a line on which to write the name of the locality or country of residence one or five years earlier. The recommended alternative is to begin by asking the respondent, "Did you live in this residence (or at this address) on this date one year ago (five years ago)?"

These responses can be offered: (1) "Yes, this residence (address)," (2) "No, different house (address) in the same locality," and (3) "No, in a different locality (country)," with a line to write in the name of the locality or country of previous residence. These modifications add only a single line to census forms, do not appreciably add to respondent burden or processing costs, and generate data on moves within as well as between localities. The results would greatly facilitate international comparisons of data from fixed-period migration questions.

Duration-of-residence questions usually begin by asking, "How many years have you lived continuously in this locality?" or "When did you move to this locality?" For either version, respondents are given a number of categories for their response and then asked to name the locality or country of previous residence. To collect information on intralocality moves, the question can be restructured to begin asking about duration of residence in the current dwelling, or the traditional structure can be retained but a question added at the end to ask about duration in dwelling since moving to the locality.

These modifications to traditional fixed-period or duration-of-residence questions record the number of movers within local areas but do not require expensive coding. The current lack of information on the amount of movement within localities is a glaring statistical lacuna, for wherever the information is collected, the conclusion is that most geographical movement—as much as two thirds or three fourths of all moves—are within localities. Insofar as geographical mobility is concerned, the most unambiguous comparison now possible among countries is the probability of changing residence over a measured period of time. This "total" measure of mobility needs to be disaggregated by some measure of local and nonlocal moves and preferably by distance moved. International comparisons of the total amount of geographical mobility, its form, and who participates in it are areas of needed research which require the active participation of national statistical offices and international organizations.

Summary and Conclusion

Statistics presented in this chapter support the long-standing notion that the U.S. population exhibits considerable geographical mobility. The national average is high because (1) numerous growing metropolitan areas in the South and West compete with older areas for jobs and people and generate new migration streams whose termini are associated with extensive housing turnover; (2) a relatively large proportion of persons who move repeatedly seem to raise the U.S. rate and elevate estimates of moves per person in a lifetime above those of many other countries; and (3) various life-cycle stages, particularly the childbearing years, seem to generate more moves in the United States than in the other countries for which data were presented.

No single variable or characteristic can adequately account for the residential mobility differences among countries for which data were presented in this chapter. Size of country obviously puts constraints on the maximum distance of moves, but some comparatively small areas— for example, Hong Kong and Puerto Rico—have residential mobility rates almost as high as geographically large countries like the United States, Canada, and Australia. Many variables besides geographical size appear likely to influence the rate of residential mobility. For example, under some circumstances high personal income can positively affect national rates of residential mobility, allowing households to react to changes in needs and preferences over the life cycle; under other circumstances, however, low or unstable personal income may be associated with frequent moves and the inability to achieve housing commensurate with family requirements.

City size distributions and the patterning of settlements almost certainly affect national rates of geographical mobility. A settlement pattern dominated by high primacy ("all roads lead to Rome") probably negatively affects national rates of geographical mobility, whereas a scattered settlement pattern where metropolitan areas compete with each other to attract jobs and influence probably raises levels of moving. Levels of moving may be affected by national policies that favor either owning or renting or by local policies that, like rent control, may restrict residential changes. Multivariate testing of these possible explanations of differences among countries in residential mobility is currently impractical because of the small number of countries with comparable data.

The differences noted in the cross-sectional comparisons featured in this chapter are not necessarily permanent, and there is a clear need to document and account for changes in rates of internal geographical mobility. The data presented in the chapter were centered on the 1970–71 round of censuses, and complete data to update the comparisons to the 1980–81 censuses are not now available. Since 1970–71, however, the U.S. rate of residential mobility has fallen, as pointed out in Chapter 2. The rate for Britain and Japan fell by about 19 or 20 percent from 1970–71 to 1980–81—somewhat greater than the U.S. decline.[18] In New Zea-

[18]The British data are from Tim Devis, "People Changing Address: 1971 and 1981," *Population Trends* 32 (Summer 1983): 15–20. The Japanese data for 1980 are from Statistical Bureau, *1980 Population Census of Japan* vol. 4, pt. 1, div. 2 (Tokyo: Prime Minister's Office, 1984), pp. 32–33.

land, however, the residential mobility rate appears to have risen by about 26 percent from 1971 to 1981.[19] The five-year rate in Canada appears to have held steady between 1971 and 1981.[20] In France rates of moving within and between localities are reported to have dropped slightly between the 1975 and 1982 censuses.[21] By the late 1970s rates of moving between localities in Belgium and in the Netherlands were reported to be below rates recorded in the 1950s and 1960s.[22] For developed countries reports of declining rates of internal migration seem to be more common than reports of rising internal migration rates. For the United States the decline appeared to be greater for short-distance movement than for long-distance movement; whether similar changes have occurred elsewhere is not clear.

Several steps have been taken to facilitate comparability of general patterns of migration within countries. These actions have consisted mostly of guidelines for tabulations of census and survey data on internal migration and have been disseminated through conferences and publications of the United Nations and other organizations. But statistical bureaus of individual countries can do many things to facilitate comparison of the total volume of internal movement. They can make minor and relatively inexpensive modifications to census and survey questions so as to collect data on residential mobility—understood to mean measuring the likelihood of changing usual residence (dwelling) over a specified interval of time. They can differentiate "total" moves according to whether within or between localities and by distance. Countries with continuous population registration can disaggregate data for movers as well as moves. Longitudinal surveys, which follow the same persons over time, and data from population registration can be used to show how a country's current level of geographical mobility is due to a few persons moving repeatedly. Until these and other measures are taken, international comparisons of internal geographical mobility are likely to remain the stepchild of migration research.

There are many reasons for making such comparisons. Perhaps the most basic is simply the need to measure attachment to place and how

---

[19]The New Zealand data for 1981 are from Department of Statistics, *New Zealand Census of Population and Dwellings* 1981 vol. 2. Internal Migration (Wellington: Department of Statistics 1984).

[20]The 1981 data for Canada are from Statistics Canada, *1981 Census of Canada: Mobility Status* (Ottawa: Department of Statistics 1983).

[21]Daniel Courgeau, "Baisse de la mobilité residentielle," *Population et Societés*, no. 179 (Paris: Institut National d'Études Demographique, 1984).

[22]Michel Poulain and Brigitte Van Goethem, "Evolution de la mobilité interne de la population Belge de 1948 à 1979," *Population* 37 (March–April 1982): 319–340. R. F. van der Erf, "Internal Migration in the Netherlands: Measurement and Main Characteristics," in Henk ter Heide and Frans J. Willekens, eds., *Demographic Research and Spatial Policy: The Dutch Experience* (New York: Academic Press, 1984).

it influences and is influenced by commitments to organizations, associations, and relatives and other family members. In some countries, strong place commitment can restrict the operation of corporations accustomed to transferring employees when it is in the interest of corporations to do so. Strong place commitment can restrain national economic growth if workers are unwilling or unaccustomed to relocating to growing areas with industries that are internationally competitive. National policies regarding homeownership and home finance may unwittingly restrict the movement of workers and may work against programs to provide information on job opportunities or in other ways to increase worker mobility.

A high or an increasing level of mobility, however, may be associated with need for some types of social services that would otherwise be provided voluntarily by extended families. In-home care of elderly or dependent family members can be impractical if high levels of mobility geographically separate families, leading to demands for social provision of such services or other policies that may be needed more by high-mobility than low-mobility societies. The relationship of mobility and the scattering or concentration of family members is not commonly measured.

As birth rates approach replacement levels in many countries, population distribution policies are likely to receive more scrutiny by individual localities as well as national governments faced with deciding whether to enact "place" policies to increase economic opportunities in some areas or "worker" policies to increase mobility toward areas with growing employment opportunities. The international transferability of successful programs in these areas can depend very strongly on the level of geographical mobility in different countries. Better comparisons can mean better program planning and evaluation.

APPENDIX A:
SOURCES AND QUALITY OF DATA
ON INTERNAL MIGRATION

O NE PURPOSE of this appendix is to identify major publications which report data on internal migration, as measured by estimates of net intercensal migration, by census questions on residence five years earlier, and in Current Population Surveys. These major sources of data constitute the raw materials for most research on U.S. internal migration. The other purpose is to provide a brief overview of the general quality of census data on residence five years earlier, measured largely in terms of comparative rates of nonresponse. Also discussed is how the place-of-birth data can be affected by how the question is worded.

Sources of Data: Net Migration

As discussed in Chapter 1, the primary source of data on net migration for states over long periods of time is the University of Pennsylvania study which used the survival-rate method to estimate net migration by age, sex, race, and nativity (born in or born outside the United States) from 1870 to 1950. This series was expanded to include counties and updated to 1960 in Gladys K. Bowles and James D. Tarver, *Net Migration of the Population, 1950–60, by Age, Sex, and Color*, which was released in seven separately bound reports and distributed by the U.S. Government Printing Office in 1965. Volume 1 is in six parts (the Northeastern states, the North Central states, the South Atlantic states, the East South Central states, the West South Central states, and the Western states); volume 2 is a single report, "Analytical Groupings of Counties," which includes metropolitan-nonmetropolitan and other classifications of counties. The data were developed by a combination of residual and survival-rate methods.

Essentially the same methodology was used to estimate net migration at the county level for the 1960–70 decade, as reported in Gladys K. Bowles, Calvin L. Beale, and Everett S. Lee, *Net Migration of the Population, 1960–70, by Age, Sex, and Color*. Seven separate reports were published and distributed by the University of Georgia in 1975— parts 1–6, the Northeastern states, the North Central states, the South Atlantic states, the East South Central states, the West South Central states, and the Western states; and part 7, "Analytical Groupings of Counties." Chapter 5 draws upon net migration data from the University of Pennsylvania study and the two sets of estimates prepared by Bowles and her colleagues.

At the present time there is no standard reference for estimates of 1970–80 net migration by age, sex, and race for subnational geographical areas (states or counties). The problem with applying previously used methods is that the higher level of coverage in the 1980 census compared with the 1970 census prohibits strict application of previous methods, and there is now no satisfactory method for adjusting subnational areas for differential undercount in the two censuses. The Census Bureau has published three components of population change for states over the 1970–80 decade: net migration, natural increase, and "error of closure," which amounted to over 4.7 million persons for the nation as a whole. These estimates can be found in U.S. Bureau of the Census, "Estimates of the Population of States: 1970 to 1983," *Current Population Reports*, series P-25, no. 957 (Washington, DC: U.S. Government Printing Office, 1984). The "net migration" figure was used for the regional data included in Chapter 5.

"Current" estimates of net migration for states and counties are prepared annually by the Census Bureau and published in the P-25 and P-26 series of *Current Population Reports*. The post-1980 estimates of net migration for regions and divisions shown in Chapter 5 were aggregated from state data published in U.S. Bureau of the Census, "State Population Estimates by Age and Components of Change: 1980 to 1984," *Current Population Reports*, series P-25, no. 970 (Washington, DC: U.S. Government Printing Office, 1985).

Sources of Data:
Censuses and the Current Population Survey

Most of the 1940 census data in this monograph are from three special reports: *Internal Migration, 1935–40—Color and Sex of Migrants, Internal Migration, 1935–40—Age of Migrants,* and *Internal Migration, 1935–40—Social Characteristics of Migrants.* A fourth report, *Internal Migration, 1935–40—Economic Characteristics of Migrants,* was also published, as was a report on state of birth.

Data for 1955–60 migration are primarily from two special reports of the 1960 census: *Mobility for States and State Economic Areas* and *Lifetime and Recent Migration.* Other special reports included *State of Birth, Mobility for Metropolitan Areas,* and *Migration between State Economic Areas.*

Data for 1965–70 are from two special reports: *Mobility for States and the Nation* and *Lifetime and Recent Migration.* Other special reports on internal migration published in conjunction with the 1970 census included *State of Birth, Mobility for Metropolitan Areas,* and *Occupation and Residence in 1965.* After the census was completed, the Census Bureau developed a computer file which allocated nonresponse to the residence-five-years-ago question (see later section) and tabulated migration to and from counties by age, race, and a few other characteristics; this information was published in U.S. Bureau of the Census, "Gross Migration by County: 1965 to 1970," *Current Population Reports,* series P-25, no. 701 (Washington, DC: U.S. Government Printing Office, 1977).

Most of the 1975–80 migration data appearing in this monograph were developed from a computer file of intercounty movers. Published migration data from the 1980 census may be found in three reports in the "supplementary reports" series: *State of Residence in 1975 by State of Residence in 1980* (PC80-S1-9), *Residence in 1975 for States, by Age, Sex, Race, and Spanish Origin* (PC80-S1-16), and *Gross Migration for Counties: 1975 to 1980* (PC80-S1-17). The volume 2 series of reports included *Geographical Mobility for States and the Nation* and *Mobility for Metropolitan areas.*

Migration data from March Current Population Surveys are from microdata files or from the following published reports in the *Current Population Reports* series: "Mobility of the Population of the United States: March 1970 to March 1971" (P-20, no. 235), "Geographical Mobility: March 1975 to March 1976" (P-20, no. 305), "Geographical Mobility: March 1980 to March 1981" (P-20, no. 377), "Geographical Mobility: March 1981 to March 1982" (P-20, no. 384), "Geographical Mobility: March 1982 to March 1983" (P-20, no. 393), and "Geographical Mobility: March 1983 to March 1984" (P-20, no. 407).

Quality of Census Data on Internal Migration

The overall quality of census data can be a function of many things, including the wording of the questions and their placement on the census schedule, the procedures used in handling and processing the questionnaires, the quality of field personnel, and many other variables. At times quality can be a function of the sample size, for ever since the 1950 census, the migration questions, like many other census questions, have been asked of a sample of the population. In 1950 every fifth person was asked about residence one year earlier. In 1960 one household in four received a "long form" which contained the sample questions. In 1970 two long forms were distributed, one to 15 percent of households and another to a different 5 percent of households. The questions on residence five years earlier were on the 15 percent questionnaire. The 1970 census was the first to rely extensively on mail-out/mail-back procedures, whereby most urban households received questionnaires in the mail, filled them out, and mailed them back without being visited by a census enumerator.

In 1980 only one long form was used but a variable sampling ratio was employed. For most of the U.S. population about one household in six received the long form; for some types of areas with populations under 2,500, one household in two received the long form with the sample questions, including those on residence in 1975 and place of birth. For the nation as a whole, the long form was left at about 19 percent of housing units. The reason for using a variable sampling ratio and in effect "oversampling" in counties, incorporated places, or minor civil divisions with under 2,500 residents was to achieve acceptable quality of data on per capita income for use in General Revenue Sharing.

Budgetary considerations during the processing of the 1980 census led the Census Bureau to code the migration and place-of-work data for only one half of the questionnaires. These two sets of questions used the same coding materials and require extensive operations by trained coders, who have to look up many incomplete or inaccurate answers and write in codes with many digits. Such operations are comparatively expensive, and the Census Bureau decided to cut costs by coding only half of the information it requested of respondents on residence in 1975 and place of work.

One indicator of the quality of the residence-five-years-ago data is nonresponse and how it has changed over time, how it compares with other census questions, and how it varies geographically. The question on residence five years ago was not radically different in the censuses of 1940, 1960, 1970, and 1980,[1] but nonresponse probably doubled between 1940 and 1960, increased more than threefold between 1960 and 1970, and increased by about one third between 1970 and 1980. These changes mean that the nonresponse rate in 1980 was about eight times as great as in 1940.

Published reports of the 1940 census (cited above) show that 0.9 percent of the population aged 5 and over were in a category labeled "migration status not reported." The 1960 census processing procedures were slightly different, and persons who left the question blank were assigned a mobility status (same house as five years ago or different house) based on the question on the housing census on year moved into current house or apartment. Those who reported moving in after 1955 were assigned to the "same house" category, and all others were put in a category in the published reports labeled "moved, residence in 1955 not reported." This latter category represented 1.6 percent of all persons aged 5 and over in 1960.

In 1970 processing procedures similar to 1960 were followed, but persons in the category "moved, residence in 1965 not reported" represented 5.2 percent of the population aged 5 and over. This more-than-threefold increase seems to have been part of a very substantial increase in nonresponse rates between the 1960 and 1970 censuses for most census questions and not just the residence-five-years-ago questions. The considerable increase in nonresponse may be due partly to the shift to mail-out/mail-back procedures in 1970, to other collection and processing changes, to less cooperation on the part of the public at large, or to other factors that are difficult to quantify. Nonresponse to the residence-five-years ago question was highly visible in the published reports of the 1970 census because nonresponse to many other questions came to be allocated prior to publication.[2]

In 1980 nonresponse to the question on residence in 1975 was "completely" allocated. That is, procedures were again used to assign

---

[1] The questionnaires are reproduced in U.S. Bureau of the Census, *Twenty Censuses: Population and Housing Questions, 1790–1980* (Washington, DC: U.S. Government Printing Office, 1978).

[2] A summary of processing procedures and evaluations of many aspects of the 1970 census were published in U.S. Bureau of the Census, 1970 Census of Population and Housing, *Procedural History*, PHC(R)-1 (Washington, DC: U.S. Government Printing Office, 1976).

respondents to "same house" or "different house" in 1975 and 1980, but persons in the latter category were later allocated a place of previous residence (the procedures for doing so will be discussed shortly). About 8 percent of the U.S. population aged 5 and over were assigned a mobility status. In order to approximate a comparable figure for 1970, special tabulations were made from the 1970 files to determine how many persons were assigned to either "same house" or "different house," based on other census information. About 6.0 percent of all persons aged 5 and over were found to have been assigned to either "same house" or "different house." Hence, the increase in nonresponse to the residence-five-years-ago question was about one third—from 6.0 percent in 1970 to 8.0 percent in 1980—a rate of increase far below that between 1960 and 1970.

Comparative Levels of Nonresponse

Besides comparisons over time, two other evaluations of the geographical mobility data are useful—comparisons with other census questions and comparisons among geographical entities. Comparing nonresponse to different census questions is quite difficult, for obviously some questions call for more precise responses than others and the nonresponse to any census or survey question can depend on where it appears on the questionnaire. Appearing toward the end of the questionnaire or following questions that have very high nonresponse rates can adversely affect likelihood or quality of response. Such caveats should be borne in mind in interpreting Table A.1, which presents allocation rates for the migration questions and some some other questions included in the 1980 population census.[3]

This table suggests that nonresponse to the questions on residence or activity in 1975 is probably somewhat higher than average but not higher than some other questions. Low nonresponse rates characterize questions on age (which was allocated for 1.6 percent of the population), race (1.5 percent allocation rate), and household relationship (1.1 percent). Allocation rates were 8.0 percent for residence in 1975, between 5 and 6 percent for activity in 1975 (in armed forces, attending college,

---

[3]These data are from Tables C-1 and C-3 of U.S. Bureau of the Census, 1980 Census of Population, *General Social and Economic Characteristics: United States Summary,* PC80-1-C1 (Washington, DC: U.S. Government Printing Office, 1981). Table C-2 of this report shows for some questions the distribution of responses both before and after allocation, and this information was used for the state-of-birth data included in Chapter 2.

TABLE A.1

Allocation Rates for Migration Questions and Some Other Questions Asked in the 1980 Census

Characteristic	Percentage Allocated	Universe
Residence in 1975	8.0%	Persons aged 5 and over
Armed forces status in 1975	5.1	Persons aged 21 and over
College attendance in 1975	6.0	Persons aged 21 and over
Work status in 1975	5.3	Persons aged 21 and over
Place of birth	4.9	All persons
Age	1.6	All persons
Sex	0.7	All persons
Race	1.5	All persons
Household relationship	1.1	All persons
Language spoken at home	8.2	Persons aged 5 and over
School enrollment	4.5	Persons aged 3 and over
Labor force status	3.9	Persons aged 16 and over
Unemployment in 1979	15.9	Persons aged 16 and over
Weeks worked in 1979	9.4	Persons aged 16 and over who worked in 1979
Occupation	6.7	Employed persons aged 16 and over
Industry	6.7	Employed persons aged 16 and over
Individual income in 1979	11.5	Persons aged 15 and over
Household income in 1979	16.8	Households
Farm residence	7.4	Total rural population
Type of group quarters	13.1	Total persons in group quarters
Children ever born	6.0	Women aged 15 and over
Times married	5.5	Ever-married persons aged 15–54
Date of first marriage	9.7	Ever-married persons aged 15–54

or working at a job or business), and 4.9 percent for place of birth.[4] Somewhat higher nonresponse rates appear to characterize some other retrospective questions, such as date of first marriage (allocated for 9.7 percent of ever-married persons aged 15–54) and labor-force information

[4]The questions on activity status five years before the census can also be evaluated in terms of the degree to which the results are consistent with survey or other statistics on the distribution of the relevant populations five years earlier as working at a job or business, attending school, or being in the armed forces. One study compared the 1970 census questions on activity status in 1965 with what was reported in the April 1965 Current Population Survey and concluded that "the retrospective inquiry [1970 census] yielded reasonable approximations for most cohorts." Ann R. Miller, "Retrospective Data on Work Status in the 1970 Census of Population: An Attempt at Evaluation," *Journal of the American Statistical Association* 71 (June 1976): 286–292.

for 1979 (weeks worked in 1979 was allocated for 9.4 percent of persons aged 16 and over who worked in 1979, and periods of unemployment were allocated for 15.9 percent of persons aged 16 and over who worked in 1979). High allocation rates also characterize the questions on income in 1979, which was allocated for 11.5 percent of all persons aged 15 and over and 16.8 percent of all households. About 8.6 percent of workers aged 16 and over did not report place of work so that they could be classified as to whether they lived and worked in the same or different states; their nonresponse was not allocated.[5]

Another comparative view of nonresponse that is useful in evaluating migration data is geographical variability. Nonresponse to census questions in general tends to be higher in big cities than in rural areas, and the residence-five-years-ago question is no exception. About 9.6 percent of persons aged 5 and over in central cities had residence in 1975 allocated compared with 4.5 percent of farm residents. Suburbanites and residents of small towns had intermediate rates of allocation.

Since Chapters 3, 4, and 5 analyze migration data for states, it is important to ask how states vary in nonresponse to questions on residence five years earlier. Table A.2 shows nonresponse rates for each state to questions on residence five years earlier, as asked in the 1940, 1960, 1970, and 1980 censuses.

In 1980 allocation rates ranged from a low of 5.0 percent for Minnesota to 14.9 percent for the District of Columbia. Variability among states in this regard seems only partly attributable to differences in overall mobility status, rural-urban composition, or other compositional factors of states' population. One might expect high-mobility states to have high nonresponse rates to the residence-five-years ago question, and some do. Just over 13 percent of Alaska's population aged 5 and over did not report residence in 1975, and 10.7 percent of Florida's population similarly failed to respond. But some rural southern states without especially high population turnover also have high nonresponse rates: 12.8 percent of Louisiana's population and 10.5 percent of South Carolina's population did not answer the question on residence in 1975. Such variability might reflect many things, including the quality of Census Bureau field offices, population composition of the various states (like level of education), and simply attitudes of the public toward civic responsibilities in general and the federal government in particular.

Variability among the states in nonresponse to the residence-five-years-ago question may be decreasing somewhat. The coefficient of

---

[5]Table 292 in U.S. Bureau of the Census, 1980 Census of Population, *Detailed Population Characteristics: United States Summary, Section A: United States*, PC80-1-D1-A (Washington, DC: U.S. Government Printing Office, 1984).

TABLE A.2

Nonresponse to Five-Year Migration Questions in Censuses of 1940, 1960, 1970, and 1980, by State, for Persons Aged 5 and Over

	1935–40 Percentage with Migration Status Not Reported	1955–60 Percentage Moved, Residence in 1955 Not Reported	1965–70 Percentage Moved, Residence in 1965 Not Reported	1975–80 Migration Status or Previous Residence Allocated
United States	0.9%	1.6%	5.2%	8.0%
Alabama	1.1	0.7	4.6	7.7
Alaska	—	2.8	12.8	13.1
Arizona	1.4	2.2	7.1	9.3
Arkansas	1.3	0.6	5.2	7.1
California	1.0	2.1	5.6	9.4
Colorado	1.0	1.5	5.8	7.4
Connecticut	0.8	1.7	5.8	6.9
Delaware	1.0	2.1	7.2	8.0
District of Columbia	0.9	4.7	13.0	14.9
Florida	1.5	2.3	6.1	10.7
Georgia	1.1	1.1	5.9	9.2
Hawaii	—	1.0	6.1	8.1
Idaho	1.1	0.6	5.1	7.0
Illinois	0.8	2.4	5.3	8.0
Indiana	0.8	1.5	4.5	6.5
Iowa	1.3	1.0	3.2	5.1
Kansas	1.0	1.3	4.3	6.7
Kentucky	0.7	1.2	5.2	6.7
Louisiana	1.0	1.2	6.4	12.8
Maine	0.9	1.1	3.5	6.6
Maryland	1.5	2.0	6.2	7.6
Massachusetts	0.9	1.8	4.9	7.4
Michigan	0.6	1.3	4.5	6.0
Minnesota	1.0	1.0	4.1	5.0
Mississippi	1.4	0.6	5.3	8.3
Missouri	1.0	1.9	6.6	7.2
Montana	0.9	0.7	3.8	7.2
Nebraska	0.7	1.0	4.3	5.3
Nevada	1.6	1.9	9.7	9.8
New Hampshire	2.3	1.7	4.9	7.6
New Jersey	1.0	1.6	4.7	7.1
New Mexico	1.1	1.1	5.8	9.1
New York	0.8	1.9	4.8	8.4
North Carolina	1.3	1.2	5.4	8.8
North Dakota	1.2	0.6	3.0	5.3
Ohio	0.8	1.3	4.9	5.9
Oklahoma	1.4	1.8	5.3	7.2
Oregon	0.9	1.0	7.0	7.7
Pennsylvania	0.7	1.3	4.4	6.2
Rhode Island	0.7	2.2	6.5	6.9
South Carolina	0.7	1.1	5.6	10.5
South Dakota	1.0	0.6	3.6	5.9
Tennessee	1.2	1.3	6.0	8.4
Texas	0.8	1.6	5.0	10.0
Utah	0.7	0.9	5.6	6.4
Vermont	1.3	0.8	3.6	6.0
Virginia	0.9	1.4	5.7	8.4
Washington	0.9	1.1	6.0	7.4
West Virginia	1.0	1.1	3.9	6.7
Wisconsin	0.8	1.1	4.5	5.8
Wyoming	1.1	0.8	4.3	8.4

variation (the ratio of the standard deviation to the mean) was computed for the four columns of data in Table A.2. It was 0.30 in 1940, 0.50 in 1960, 0.35 in 1970, and 0.28 in 1980. These results suggest that since 1960 states have become slightly more alike in nonresponse to the residence-five-years-ago question even though nonresponse for most states rose.

Allocating Nonresponse

Persons in the 1980 census who did not report place of birth or residence in 1975 were assigned a response based on procedures similar to those developed for allocating nonresponse to other census questions. The usual procedures are to use as much information as is available for the person or household with no or incomplete information on birthplace or residence in 1975 and match the person missing such information with a person of otherwise similar characteristics.

The residence-in-1975 question had two parts. The first asked, "Did this person live in this house five years ago (April 1, 1975)?" and offered three circles to be filled in: "born April 1975 or later"; "Yes, this house"; and "No, different house." If the third circle was filled, the respondent was asked, "Where did this person live five years ago (April 1, 1975)?" followed by four lines (with circles for "yes" or "no" responses) for reporting "State, foreign country, Puerto Rico, Guam, etc."; county; "City, town, village, etc."; and "Inside the incorporated (legal) limits of that city, town, village, etc.?" The fourth line is intended to correct for the tendency of respondents to report a city as the place of previous residence when in fact they lived in its suburbs.

Responses for the two parts of the question were reviewed for consistency and changed if inconsistent. For example, a person who filled out the second part but not the first was assumed to have moved. If both parts of the question were left blank, householders who reported on the housing part of the questionnaire that they had moved in before 1975 were assigned to "same house." The year-moved-in question had already been allocated for nonresponse, using information on when the building was built and other characteristics. Then spouses and sons and daughters of the householder were assigned the mobility status of the householder or parent (if not the mother, then the father).

Persons who in this fashion were assigned to the "different house" category were next assigned to a place of previous residence. The general approach was to match the person not reporting with a previous person in the computer file who was of the same race, age group, armed forces status, educational level, type of current residence (central city, suburban, nonmetropolitan), and place of birth. Modifications were made for persons reporting some but not all of the requested information on place of previous residence; for example, some persons might simply report "United States" and others might report state but not county or city. Still other modifications were made for the Northeast in order to assign a specific county (borough) in New York City or the specific minor civil division.

Wording of Question and Effect on State-of-Birth Data

Comparisons of data from recent censuses on place of birth can be affected by differences in how the question is phrased on the questionnaire. A traditional issue is distinguishing between place of birth on an occurrence basis (location of hospital or other location of birth) and the usual residence of the respondent's mother when the respondent was born.

In 1950 the place-of-birth question may have emphasized reporting on an occurrence basis by asking, "What State (or foreign country) was he [the respondent] born in?" This question was followed by the instruction, "If born outside continental United States, enter name of territory, possession, or foreign country." In 1960 the question asked, "Where was this person born?" and gave much more detailed instructions on the questionnaire. "If born in hospital, give residence of mother, not location of hospital," was one instruction, which was followed by: "If born in the United States, write name of State. If born outside the United States, write name of country, U.S. possession, etc. Use international boundaries as now recognized by the U.S. Distinguish Northern Ireland from Ireland (Eire)."

In 1970 similar wording was used, but one change may have biased downward the number of persons reported as living outside their state of birth. In 1970 the basic question again asked, "Where was this person born?" and offered similar but slightly different instructions: "If born in hospital, give State or country where mother lived. If born outside U.S., see instruction sheet; distinguish Nothern Ireland from Ireland (Eire)." The big change, however, was that respondents were given the option of filling in a circle for "This State" rather than having to write their state of birth; persons not born in their state of residence at the time of the census were given a line on which to write "Name of State or foreign country; or Puerto Rico, Guam, etc." The option for reporting "This State" probably resulted in an overstatement of persons reporting that they were born in their state of current residence.[6]

In 1980 this option was removed, and the first part of the question reverted to phraseology similar to that used in 1950: "In what State or foreign country was this person born?" The instructions were: "Print the State where this person's mother was living when this person was born. Do not give the location of the hospital unless the mother's home and the hospital were in the same state."

These changes in the place-of-birth question probably overstate somewhat the increase between 1970 and 1980 in the percentage of population living outside their state of birth, as discussed in Chapter 2. And they probably overstate the amount of interstate migration in 1965–70 that was classified as returns to state of birth, as discussed in Chapter 4.

[6]J. Gregory Robinson, "Evaluation of Census Data on Place of Birth from the 1980 Content Reinterview Study" (forthcoming). Robinson's work was based on the Content Reinterview Study, which was a sample of persons who were asked a more detailed set of questions on place of birth on an occurrence basis (location of hospital) as well as mother's usual residence at the time of the respondent's birth, and the results were matched to 1980 census questionnaires. The study suggested that proxy respondents (persons who fill out census questionnaires for the entire household) may tend too readily to fill the circle for born in "this state" (the version used in 1970) when the birthplace of household members is uncertain.

APPENDIX B:
LIFETIME MOBILITY
AND CROSS-SECTIONAL DATA

FRANK AND ERNEST ®by Bob Thaves

SURE, THE AVERAGE PERSON MOVES ONLY ONCE EVERY SEVEN YEARS, ERNIE, BUT THAT'S HOUSE TO HOUSE!

© 1985 by NEA. Inc. THAVES 8-22

RESEARCHERS on geographical mobility are often asked to "translate" the cross-sectional data from censuses or surveys into individual terms—that is, to tell "what the data mean for an average person or family." Two common requests along these lines are useful for identifying some specific uses and manipulations of mobility statistics, some not-well-known audiences for information on geographical mobility, and some gaps in available statistics.

One of these requests is to fill in the blank in the sentence, "The average person (family) moves at least once every——years," with 5, 6, or 7 often suggested as the missing value. This type of request seems to come most often from corporations, from firms that contract with corporations to arrange employee transfers, and from moving companies whose primary business is with relocation of corporate executives. This approach to mobility is to conceptualize it as the average time spent in one location (or, alternatively, the time between moves), and a common purpose is to compare corporate executives and their families with the general population or to compare the frequency of moves by executives of different companies. An answer could be used as a response to a prospective employee who asks, "If I work for your company, how long can I expect to stay in one place?"

With the usual census data ("Where did you live on this date five years ago?") or Current Population Survey data ("Where did you live on this date one year ago?") there is no generally accepted way of saying that the average person or family in the population at large moves once every x years. Of course, it could be answered with life-history data collected on a continuing basis, as is done in countries with population registration that require each person or family head to register a change of residence from one locality to another.[1]

Such data might be collected retrospectively in a survey that asked each respondent to report every county or state lived in for some minimum period of time. The obvious problem with this approach is the difficulty of respondents' remembering where they lived many years earlier, and the problem is especially compounded for persons who have moved frequently. Some surveys have compromised and asked respondents where (city, county, and state) they lived at times of their lives considered significant—for example, where the respondent lived at age 16, at graduation from high school, where the respondent first took a full-time job after completing education, and so on. But no national survey in the United States has attempted to collect complete residence histories on a retrospective basis.[2] As a result, there is very little direct empirical basis for saying that an average American moves at least once every——years.

The Value of the Life Table

It is possible, however, to take a life table approach and estimate the number of moves a hypothetical cohort will make in its lifetime if it is subject to current age-specific probabilities of moving. The method for doing so is the same used in calculating other double-decrement life tables—for example, tables of expected working life, which show the number of years a person will spend working if present age-specific mortality and rates of labor force participation continue. The usefulness in the context of migration is not only to calculate the number of lifetime

---

[1]From time to time the United Nations surveys procedures for producing migration statistics from population registers. See United Nations, *Methodology and Evaluation of Population Registers and Similar Systems* (New York: United Nations, 1969). But even countries with registration systems that record moves between localities rarely develop measures of lifetime frequency of moving. Most simply report annual numbers of moves (not movers) between localities.

[2]A 1958 national sample conducted by the Census Bureau for the National Cancer Institute recorded up to five places (cities or counties) of previous residence. The results were reported in Henry S. Shryock, Jr., and Elizabeth A. Larmon, "Some Longitudinal Data on Internal Migration," *Demography* 2 (1965): 579–592; and Karl E. Taeuber, Leonard Chiazze, Jr., and William Haenszel, *Migration in the United States: An Analysis of Residence Histories* (Washington, DC: U.S. Government Printing Office, 1968).

moves but also to show what the changes in national mobility rates discussed in Chapter 2 mean in terms of an individual's expected moving.

The application to mobility rates was first illustrated by Wilber, who used an abridged life table and mobility data for broad age groups for the early 1960s.[3] Single-year-of-age data were first tabulated from Current Population Surveys conducted in the late 1960s and give a clearer view of the distribution of expected moving over the life cycle.[4] When using the one-year mobility rates from the CPS, one assumes that persons who were x years old at their last birthday were x + 0.5 years old at the time of the survey, and one year earlier—at the beginning of the migration interval—were x − 0.5 years old. Persons who moved during the interval were assumed to have moved at the mid-point of the interval and therefore were at exact age x at the time of moving.

To obtain the expected years with moves to be experienced by a life table cohort, rates of moving at age x (denoted R_x) were multiplied by l_x, which represents the life table population alive at exact age x. The sum of the values of $R_x l_x$ for each age x and for all later ages is the total expected years with moves during and after each age x; these values are analogous to the T_x values in an ordinary life table and have been denoted TM_x. The TM_x values are divided by L_{x-1}, which is the life-table population alive at the beginning of each of the age intervals from x − 0.5 to x + 0.5. This result expresses the expected years with moves per person at the given age and at all later ages; this value is analogous to the e_x column of an ordinary life table, which is the familiar measure of life expectancy at age x. The equivalent migration measure—migration expectancy at age x—has been denoted em_x in what follows.

These types of calculations were prepared in order to show mobility expectancy for all changes of residence and for the three components that have most commonly been measured in the Current Population Survey: moves within counties, moves between counties within a state, and moves between states. Since the mobility rates represent the probability of moving over a 12-month period rather than the actual number of moves, the calculations of mobility expectancy technically refer to years with moves rather than moves.

Calculations were prepared under three scenarios: one for 1966–71 annual rates of moving and a 1967 life table, another for 1982–83 rates of moving using the same 1967 life table, and a third using the 1982–83

[3]George W. Wilber, "Migration Expectancy in the United States," *Journal of the American Statistical Association* 58 (June 1963): 444–453.

[4]Larry Long, "New Estimates of Migration Expectancy in the United States," *Journal of the American Statistical Association* 68 (March 1973): 37–43.

rates of moving and a 1980 life table (the most recent one available at the time of writing).[5] These three sets of calculations are shown in Tables B.1, B.2, and B.3, respectively. The purpose behind these three scenarios was to compare the more recent data with the earlier findings and to show the effect that increasing life expectancy has on mobility expectancy. Increasing life expectancy causes mobility expectancy to go up simply because people live longer, and Tables B.2 and B.3 allow one to measure this effect.

An issue in making such calculations is how to treat movers from abroad. The mobility rates used for Tables B.1, B.2, and B.3 are based on the population at the survey dates, including movers from abroad because many were Americans returning from overseas. With the available data there is no way to separate them from others moving to the United States. Excluding all movers from abroad would clearly understate Americans' mobility expectancy, and the bias of including non-Americans is partially offset by the fact that computing rates in the way just described understates mobility by counting only the move back to the United States and not the move out of the country.

Table B.1 shows that 33.4 percent of 1-year-olds had moved in the last year (column 1), that the hypothetical cohort of 100,000 births would experience 1,267,280 years with moves before the last person died (column 2), and that the mean number of years with moves per person would be 12.93 (column 3). This last figure is the source for newspaper and magazine articles which say that the average American moves 13 times in a lifetime. At least this was the average for 1966–71.

Table B.2 uses the same life table values but the rates of moving in 1982–83. The average person is shown to expect only 10.33 moves in a lifetime (column 3). Hence, the 20 percent decline in the nation's residential mobility rate between the late 1960s and the early 1980s means that the average American will make about 2.6 fewer house-to-house moves (or, more precisely, 2.6 fewer years with moves).

Expected moves of each of the three types are down. The expected years with intracounty moves declined from 7.99 to 6.31. Expected years with moves between counties within a state changed hardly at all— from 2.19 to 2.05. Expected moves between states declined from 2.29 to 1.71.

The single-year-of-age detail is useful in answering many common types of questions. For example, a great many studies of internal migration have tediously observed that moving is concentrated in the "young-

---

[5]The 1980 life table values are from National Center for Health Statistics, *Vital Statistics of the United States, 1980,* vol. 2, sec. 6, Life Tables (Washington, DC: U.S. Government Printing Office, 1984).

TABLE B.1

One-Year Rates of Moving and Migration Expectancy, by Type of Move and Single Years of Age, According to Life Table Values for 1967 and Average Annual Rates of Moving Between 1966 and 1971

Age at Last Birthday	All Moves[a] Rate (Percentage Moving) R_x	Years with Moves[b] Total TM_x	Per Person em_x	Moves Within Counties Rate (Percentage Moving) R_x	Years with Moves[b] Total TM_x	Per Person em_x	Moves Between Counties Within a State Rate (Percentage Moving) R_x	Years with Moves[b] Total TM_x	Per Person em_x	Moves Between States Rate (Percentage Moving) R_x	Years with Moves[b] Total TM_x	Per Person em_x
1	33.4%	1,267,280	12.93	21.2%	783,345	7.99	5.4%	214,532	2.19	6.1%	224,181	2.29
2	30.0	1,234,655	12.64	19.0	762,666	7.81	5.0	209,233	2.15	5.3	218,254	2.23
3	27.7	1,205,358	12.35	17.1	744,099	7.62	4.6	204,319	2.10	5.4	213,064	2.18
4	24.8	1,178,340	12.08	15.2	727,444	7.46	4.3	199,824	2.05	4.7	207,836	2.13
5	22.8	1,154,191	11.84	14.0	712,607	7.31	3.9	195,610	2.00	4.2	203,277	2.09
6	21.2	1,131,953	11.62	13.0	698,928	7.18	3.5	191,842	1.97	4.2	199,160	2.04
7	19.5	1,111,285	11.42	12.1	686,294	7.05	3.1	188,414	1.94	3.7	195,113	2.00
8	17.9	1,092,332	11.23	11.1	674,515	6.93	3.0	185,369	1.90	3.4	191,548	1.97
9	17.1	1,074,879	11.05	10.4	663,700	6.82	2.8	182,461	1.87	3.5	188,248	1.94
10	16.7	1,058,213	10.88	10.3	653,577	6.72	2.7	179,708	1.85	3.3	184,874	1.90
11	15.0	1,042,007	10.72	9.3	643,589	6.62	2.6	177,124	1.82	2.8	181,662	1.87
12	14.7	1,027,436	10.57	9.3	634,576	6.53	2.3	174,632	1.80	2.7	178,940	1.84
13	14.8	1,013,178	10.43	9.3	625,543	6.44	2.5	172,407	1.77	2.6	176,325	1.82
14	13.7	998,824	10.29	8.8	616,515	6.35	2.2	169,932	1.75	2.4	173,802	1.79
15	14.2	985,500	10.15	9.2	608,018	6.26	2.4	167,810	1.73	2.2	171,443	1.77
16	13.5	971,740	10.02	8.9	599,061	6.18	2.1	165,481	1.70	2.2	169,310	1.75
17	14.4	958,631	9.89	9.7	590,443	6.09	2.1	163,448	1.68	2.2	167,157	1.73
18	21.1	944,699	9.76	13.8	581,072	6.00	3.4	161,373	1.66	3.4	165,065	1.71
19	29.2	924,383	9.56	17.8	567,755	5.87	5.1	158,145	1.64	5.5	161,745	1.67
20	36.9	896,140	9.28	22.1	550,517	5.70	6.4	153,180	1.59	7.1	156,478	1.62
21	44.2	860,478	8.92	24.6	529,194	5.49	7.5	146,988	1.53	9.0	149,650	1.55
22	48.8	817,916	8.49	26.2	505,457	5.25	8.9	139,758	1.45	9.9	140,937	1.46
23	48.0	770,963	8.01	26.5	480,270	4.99	8.1	131,129	1.36	10.5	131,440	1.37
24	44.3	724,837	7.54	25.7	454,809	4.73	7.6	123,345	1.29	8.6	121,361	1.26
25	40.9	682,330	7.11	24.2	430,112	4.48	6.7	116,084	1.21	7.7	113,071	1.18
26	36.6	643,133	6.71	21.6	406,872	4.25	6.2	109,606	1.15	7.1	105,703	1.10
27	33.7	608,084	6.35	20.2	386,192	4.04	5.5	103,663	1.09	6.7	98,949	1.03
28	32.1	575,876	6.03	19.2	366,890	3.84	5.6	98,427	1.03	6.1	92,534	0.97
29	29.3	545,192	5.71	17.4	348,575	3.65	5.1	93,077	0.97	5.7	86,679	0.91
30	27.0	517,269	5.43	16.0	331,985	3.48	4.9	88,228	0.93	5.0	81,226	0.85

TABLE B.1 (continued)

Age at Last Birthday	All Moves[a]			Moves Within Counties			Moves Between Counties Within a State			Moves Between States		
	Rate (Percentage Moving) R_x	Years with Moves[b] Total TM_x	Per Person em_x	Rate (Percentage Moving) R_x	Years with Moves[b] Total TM_x	Per Person em_x	Rate (Percentage Moving) R_x	Years with Moves[b] Total TM_x	Per Person em_x	Rate (Percentage Moving) R_x	Years with Moves[b] Total TM_x	Per Person em_x
31	24.7	491,535	5.17	14.8	316,733	3.33	4.5	83,549	0.88	4.3	76,455	0.80
32	23.2	468,046	4.93	13.5	302,626	3.19	4.1	79,323	0.84	4.4	72,355	0.76
33	22.2	446,007	4.70	13.1	289,769	3.05	3.7	75,414	0.79	4.4	68,160	0.72
34	19.9	424,941	4.49	11.8	277,349	2.93	3.2	71,936	0.76	4.0	63,952	0.68
35	19.6	406,075	4.30	11.3	266,223	2.82	3.3	68,878	0.73	4.0	60,172	0.64
36	18.5	387,551	4.11	11.1	255,533	2.71	3.1	65,808	0.70	3.7	56,397	0.60
37	17.3	370,087	3.93	10.2	245,100	2.60	3.0	62,878	0.67	3.2	52,913	0.56
38	18.1	353,807	3.77	11.0	235,495	2.51	3.2	59,996	0.64	3.2	49,947	0.53
39	15.3	336,793	3.60	9.3	225,194	2.40	2.4	57,002	0.61	2.6	46,904	0.50
40	15.5	322,505	3.45	9.5	216,493	2.32	2.4	54,801	0.58	2.7	44,431	0.48
41	13.7	308,053	3.31	8.6	207,666	2.23	2.3	52,537	0.56	2.4	41,895	0.45
42	13.4	295,334	3.18	9.0	199,716	2.15	1.9	50,371	0.54	2.0	39,697	0.43
43	12.9	282,935	3.06	8.4	191,356	2.07	2.2	48,590	0.52	1.9	37,832	0.41
44	12.4	270,995	2.94	8.1	183,611	1.99	1.9	46,528	0.51	2.0	36,101	0.39
45	12.6	259,556	2.83	8.1	176,149	1.92	2.0	44,737	0.49	2.1	34,266	0.37
46	11.3	248,024	2.72	7.5	168,747	1.85	2.0	42,887	0.47	1.5	32,331	0.35
47	11.2	237,725	2.62	7.5	161,910	1.78	1.7	41,073	0.45	1.8	30,921	0.34
48	11.5	227,555	2.52	7.7	155,120	1.72	1.8	39,484	0.44	1.8	29,326	0.32
49	10.7	217,162	2.42	7.3	148,208	1.65	1.8	37,809	0.42	1.3	27,748	0.31
50	11.0	207,584	2.33	7.4	141,663	1.59	1.8	36,209	0.40	1.6	26,549	0.30
51	9.9	197,804	2.23	6.8	135,106	1.52	1.3	34,593	0.39	1.6	25,145	0.28
52	9.6	189,043	2.15	6.5	129,085	1.47	1.7	33,473	0.38	1.2	23,746	0.27
53	9.3	180,595	2.07	6.3	123,374	1.42	1.4	31,938	0.37	1.4	22,728	0.26
54	9.6	172,482	2.00	6.5	117,906	1.37	1.6	30,654	0.35	1.4	21,553	0.25
55	10.1	164,198	1.92	6.8	112,316	1.31	1.7	29,317	0.34	1.4	20,355	0.24
56	9.0	155,652	1.84	6.1	106,542	1.26	1.7	27,890	0.33	1.0	19,183	0.23
57	8.6	148,066	1.77	6.1	101,415	1.21	1.3	26,521	0.32	1.0	18,308	0.22
58	9.5	140,923	1.71	6.5	96,312	1.17	1.5	25,405	0.31	1.2	17,505	0.21
59	9.4	133,152	1.64	6.3	90,961	1.12	1.8	24,184	0.30	1.1	16,501	0.20
60	8.4	125,599	1.57	5.7	85,881	1.07	1.5	22,749	0.28	1.1	15,632	0.20

Age at Last Birthday	All Moves[a]			Moves Within Counties			Moves Between Counties Within a State			Moves Between States		
	Rate (Percentage Moving) R_x	Years with Moves[b] Total TM_x	Per Person em_x	Rate (Percentage Moving) R_x	Years with Moves[b] Total TM_x	Per Person em_x	Rate (Percentage Moving) R_x	Years with Moves[b] Total TM_x	Per Person em_x	Rate (Percentage Moving) R_x	Years with Moves[b] Total TM_x	Per Person em_x
61	8.4	118,930	1.51	5.8	81,381	1.03	1.8	21,583	0.27	0.8	14,754	0.19
62	9.2	112,361	1.45	5.8	76,893	0.99	1.6	20,218	0.26	1.5	14,114	0.18
63	8.9	105,333	1.39	5.8	72,447	0.96	1.9	18,962	0.25	1.1	12,991	0.17
64	7.9	98,638	1.33	5.1	68,095	0.92	1.7	17,589	0.24	1.0	12,138	0.16
65	8.9	92,854	1.28	6.0	64,352	0.89	1.5	16,334	0.22	1.3	11,427	0.16
66	8.7	86,445	1.22	5.6	60,082	0.85	1.9	15,207	0.21	1.2	10,521	0.15
67	9.4	80,347	1.17	6.4	56,181	0.82	1.8	13,887	0.20	1.2	9,703	0.14
68	8.6	73,931	1.11	5.8	51,839	0.78	1.6	12,689	0.19	1.1	8,894	0.13
69	7.8	68,270	1.05	5.1	48,022	0.74	1.6	11,634	0.18	1.0	8,156	0.13
70	7.1	63,303	1.01	5.3	44,743	0.72	1.0	10,611	0.17	0.8	7,535	0.12
71	7.4	58,949	0.98	4.9	41,469	0.69	1.6	10,002	0.16	0.7	7,064	0.12
72	7.9	54,590	0.94	5.2	38,557	0.67	1.2	9,065	0.15	1.3	6,655	0.12
73	7.3	50,130	0.91	4.8	35,590	0.64	1.5	8,377	0.15	1.0	5,904	0.11
74	7.7	46,163	0.88	5.5	32,993	0.63	1.3	7,561	0.15	0.8	5,377	0.10
75+	8.9	42,224	0.84	6.4	30,162	0.60	1.5	6,882	0.14	1.0	4,967	0.10

NOTE: Rates of moving are from the March Current Population Surveys of 1966, 1967, 1968, 1969, 1970, and 1971.

[a]Includes movers from abroad.

[b]Expected years with moves at the given age and all later ages.

TABLE B.2

One-Year Rates of Moving and Migration Expectancy, by Type of Move and Single Years of Age, According to Life Table Values for 1967 and Rates of Moving Between March 1982 and March 1983

Age at Last Birthday	All Moves[a] Rate (Percentage Moving) R_x	Years with Moves[b] Total TM_x	Per Person em_x	Moves Within Counties Rate (Percentage Moving) R_x	Years with Moves[b] Total TM_x	Per Person em_x	Moves Between Counties Within a State Rate (Percentage Moving) R_x	Years with Moves[b] Total TM_x	Per Person em_x	Moves Between States Rate (Percentage Moving) R_x	Years with Moves[b] Total TM_x	Per Person em_x
1	28.9%	1,012,543	10.33	18.3%	618,132	6.31	5.1%	200,636	2.05	4.8%	167,177	1.71
2	26.8	984,315	10.08	16.8	600,203	6.14	4.8	195,648	2.00	4.8	162,513	1.66
3	22.8	958,177	9.82	15.2	583,768	5.98	3.5	190,960	1.96	3.9	157,798	1.62
4	22.1	935,905	9.60	14.3	568,948	5.83	3.7	187,499	1.92	3.6	154,030	1.58
5	20.7	914,357	9.38	13.5	555,044	5.70	2.8	183,884	1.89	3.6	150,532	1.54
6	19.0	894,174	9.18	11.9	541,909	5.56	3.8	181,112	1.86	2.7	147,007	1.51
7	19.3	875,641	9.00	12.2	530,353	5.45	3.7	177,442	1.82	2.8	144,368	1.48
8	13.2	856,855	8.81	8.6	518,496	5.33	2.3	173,869	1.79	1.9	141,627	1.46
9	12.4	843,972	8.68	8.0	510,150	5.25	2.3	171,636	1.76	1.9	139,747	1.44
10	13.2	831,949	8.56	7.8	502,401	5.17	2.5	169,400	1.74	2.5	137,931	1.42
11	12.7	819,130	8.43	8.1	494,864	5.09	2.4	166,982	1.72	1.8	135,490	1.39
12	12.9	806,781	8.30	8.7	486,990	5.01	2.4	164,612	1.69	1.5	133,695	1.38
13	10.9	794,219	8.18	7.1	478,583	4.93	1.5	162,274	1.67	2.0	132,202	1.36
14	11.1	783,670	8.07	6.9	471,704	4.86	2.2	160,840	1.66	1.8	130,282	1.34
15	10.8	772,852	7.96	7.1	465,023	4.79	1.9	158,733	1.64	1.6	128,509	1.32
16	9.9	762,362	7.86	6.4	458,160	4.72	1.5	156,932	1.62	1.8	126,943	1.31
17	12.4	752,718	7.77	8.2	451,917	4.66	2.1	155,471	1.60	1.8	125,216	1.29
18	18.3	740,702	7.65	10.5	444,008	4.59	4.2	153,469	1.59	2.7	123,493	1.28
19	23.7	723,008	7.48	14.4	433,828	4.49	4.9	149,387	1.54	3.9	120,924	1.25
20	29.4	700,064	7.25	17.7	419,876	4.35	6.1	144,696	1.50	4.9	117,136	1.21
21	32.5	671,656	6.96	20.0	402,817	4.18	6.3	138,843	1.44	5.6	112,425	1.17
22	36.9	640,321	6.65	20.8	383,579	3.98	8.3	132,818	1.38	6.7	107,005	1.11
23	37.1	604,796	6.29	21.7	363,531	3.78	8.1	124,799	1.30	6.7	100,532	1.04
24	37.0	569,104	5.92	23.3	342,640	3.57	7.6	117,017	1.22	5.4	94,116	0.98
25	34.5	533,574	5.56	21.7	320,275	3.34	6.4	109,732	1.14	5.4	88,948	0.93
26	32.2	500,487	5.22	20.7	299,514	3.13	6.3	103,592	1.08	4.5	83,735	0.87
27	31.0	469,682	4.91	17.3	279,653	2.92	7.0	97,597	1.02	5.8	79,462	0.83
28	29.6	440,032	4.60	18.6	263,120	2.75	5.7	90,923	0.95	4.5	73,920	0.83
29	25.3	411,791	4.32	15.5	245,366	2.57	4.5	85,515	0.90	4.6	69,617	0.77
30	23.3	387,694	4.07	13.8	230,547	2.42	4.6	81,218	0.85	4.1	65,198	0.73
31	21.4	365,461	3.84	12.7	217,416	2.28	4.6	76,833	0.81	3.7	61,266	0.68
32	20.9	345,151	3.63	13.3	205,386	2.16	3.5	72,505	0.76	3.6	57,793	0.61

Age												
35	18.3	290,365	3.07	10.9	173,026	1.83	3.8	61,337	0.65	2.9	48,094	0.51
36	15.9	273,096	2.90	9.5	162,740	1.73	3.5	57,759	0.61	2.3	45,386	0.48
37	14.0	258,145	2.74	8.0	153,763	1.63	3.2	54,493	0.58	2.2	43,208	0.46
38	13.2	244,981	2.61	8.1	146,217	1.56	2.4	51,529	0.55	2.1	41,175	0.44
39	11.9	232,641	2.48	6.5	138,593	1.48	2.6	49,300	0.53	2.3	39,237	0.42
40	11.1	221,532	2.37	6.6	132,496	1.42	2.3	46,906	0.50	2.0	37,066	0.40
41	10.5	211,214	2.27	5.5	126,354	1.36	2.2	44,726	0.48	2.3	35,223	0.38
42	12.3	201,490	2.17	6.9	121,246	1.31	3.1	42,682	0.46	1.9	33,039	0.36
43	10.0	190,138	2.06	5.9	114,869	1.24	1.8	39,808	0.43	1.8	31,233	0.34
44	10.8	180,922	1.96	6.8	109,418	1.19	1.8	38,121	0.41	1.8	29,547	0.32
45	9.5	170,985	1.86	5.7	103,208	1.12	1.8	36,438	0.40	1.6	27,864	0.30
46	8.2	162,277	1.78	4.2	97,952	1.07	1.9	34,752	0.38	1.7	26,413	0.29
47	8.2	154,850	1.70	5.3	94,137	1.04	1.5	33,047	0.36	1.3	24,830	0.27
48	9.8	147,437	1.63	4.8	89,330	0.99	2.6	31,662	0.35	2.2	23,689	0.26
49	8.6	138,627	1.54	5.7	84,988	0.95	1.6	29,344	0.33	1.4	21,666	0.24
50	7.6	130,897	1.47	4.2	79,919	0.90	1.7	27,950	0.31	1.3	20,441	0.23
51	7.0	124,114	1.40	4.1	76,193	0.86	1.5	26,442	0.30	1.4	19,269	0.22
52	8.6	117,928	1.34	5.6	72,591	0.83	1.8	25,111	0.29	1.2	18,016	0.20
53	7.3	110,369	1.27	4.7	67,691	0.78	1.0	23,554	0.27	1.4	16,990	0.19
54	6.5	104,042	1.20	3.8	63,604	0.74	1.4	22,689	0.26	1.1	15,733	0.18
55	6.7	98,432	1.15	4.3	60,322	0.71	1.4	21,468	0.25	0.8	14,779	0.17
56	5.7	92,761	1.10	3.0	56,707	0.67	1.6	20,263	0.24	0.9	14,141	0.17
57	5.4	87,977	1.05	3.1	54,183	0.65	1.3	18,907	0.23	0.9	13,350	0.16
58	6.2	83,469	1.01	3.4	51,592	0.63	1.5	17,842	0.22	1.2	12,604	0.15
59	6.4	78,418	0.97	4.0	48,810	0.60	1.5	16,634	0.20	0.8	11,652	0.14
60	5.2	73,292	0.92	2.7	45,602	0.57	1.3	15,417	0.19	1.1	10,989	0.14
61	5.6	69,165	0.88	3.5	43,468	0.55	1.2	14,368	0.18	0.8	10,114	0.13
62	6.0	64,767	0.84	3.9	40,764	0.53	1.2	13,395	0.17	0.6	9,465	0.12
63	5.7	60,168	0.79	3.8	37,745	0.50	0.9	12,447	0.16	1.0	9,009	0.12
64	6.2	55,855	0.75	3.7	34,894	0.47	1.3	11,752	0.16	1.0	8,242	0.11
65	4.7	51,322	0.71	2.5	32,189	0.44	1.5	10,800	0.15	0.6	7,518	0.10
66	5.1	47,924	0.68	2.8	30,397	0.43	0.7	9,717	0.14	1.2	7,107	0.10
67	5.3	44,348	0.64	3.3	28,451	0.41	0.8	9,201	0.13	0.8	6,273	0.09
68	5.1	40,780	0.61	2.9	26,235	0.39	1.5	8,637	0.13	0.5	5,709	0.09
69	4.1	37,443	0.58	2.3	24,294	0.38	1.4	7,628	0.12	0.4	5,360	0.08
70	5.0	34,849	0.56	3.1	22,845	0.37	1.0	6,751	0.11	0.8	5,131	0.08
71	4.1	31,801	0.53	2.6	20,935	0.35	0.8	6,164	0.10	0.6	4,617	0.08
72	5.8	29,393	0.51	3.1	19,425	0.34	2.3	5,674	0.10	0.4	4,250	0.07
73	4.6	26,090	0.47	3.0	17,679	0.32	1.2	4,345	0.08	0.5	4,022	0.07
74	4.1	23,606	0.45	3.2	16,079	0.31	0.6	3,713	0.07	0.3	3,769	0.07
75+	5.0	21,484	0.43	3.3	14,456	0.29	0.8	3,380	0.07	0.8	3,603	0.07

NOTE: Rates of moving are from the March 1983 Current Population Survey.

[a]Includes movers from abroad.

[b]Expected years with moves at the given age and all later ages.

TABLE B.3

One-Year Rates of Moving and Migration Expectancy, by Type of Move and Single Years of Age, According to Life Table Values for 1980 and Rates of Moving Between March 1982 and March 1983

Age at Last Birthday	All Moves[a] Rate (Percentage Moving) R_x	Years with Moves[b] Total TM_x	Years with Moves[b] Per Person em_x	Moves Within Counties Rate (Percentage Moving) R_x	Years with Moves[b] Total TM_x	Years with Moves[b] Per Person em_x	Moves Between Counties Within a State Rate (Percentage Moving) R_x	Years with Moves[b] Total TM_x	Years with Moves[b] Per Person em_x	Moves Between States Rate (Percentage Moving) R_x	Years with Moves[b] Total TM_x	Years with Moves[b] Per Person em_x
1	28.9%	1,039,637	10.52	18.3%	635,145	6.43	5.1%	205,853	2.08	4.8%	171,566	1.74
2	26.8	1,011,128	10.25	16.8	617,037	6.25	4.8	200,815	2.03	4.8	166,855	1.69
3	22.8	984,717	9.99	15.2	600,430	6.09	3.5	196,078	1.99	3.9	162,091	1.64
4	22.1	962,209	9.76	14.3	585,453	5.94	3.7	192,581	1.95	3.6	158,283	1.61
5	20.7	940,429	9.55	13.5	571,399	5.80	2.8	188,926	1.92	3.6	154,747	1.57
6	19.0	920,026	9.34	11.9	558,121	5.67	3.8	186,125	1.89	2.7	151,184	1.54
7	19.3	901,287	9.16	12.2	546,437	5.55	3.7	182,414	1.85	2.8	148,516	1.51
8	13.2	882,290	8.97	8.6	534,446	5.43	2.3	178,801	1.82	1.9	145,744	1.48
9	12.4	869,261	8.84	8.0	526,006	5.35	2.3	176,542	1.79	1.9	143,842	1.46
10	13.2	857,101	8.72	7.8	518,168	5.27	2.5	174,281	1.77	2.5	142,006	1.44
11	12.7	844,135	8.59	8.1	510,545	5.19	2.4	171,835	1.75	1.8	139,536	1.42
12	12.9	831,643	8.46	8.7	502,581	5.11	2.4	169,438	1.72	1.5	137,721	1.40
13	10.9	818,935	8.33	7.1	494,075	5.03	1.5	167,072	1.70	2.0	136,211	1.39
14	11.1	808,262	8.23	6.9	487,115	4.96	2.2	165,621	1.69	1.8	134,268	1.37
15	10.8	797,315	8.12	7.1	480,355	4.89	1.9	163,489	1.66	1.6	132,474	1.35
16	9.9	786,699	8.02	6.4	473,410	4.82	1.5	161,667	1.65	1.8	130,889	1.33
17	12.4	776,939	7.92	8.2	467,091	4.76	2.1	160,188	1.63	1.8	129,142	1.32
18	18.3	764,779	7.81	10.5	459,087	4.69	4.2	158,162	1.61	2.7	127,397	1.30
19	23.7	746,871	7.63	14.4	448,784	4.59	4.9	154,031	1.57	3.9	124,797	1.28
20	29.4	723,647	7.40	17.7	434,662	4.45	6.1	149,282	1.53	4.9	120,964	1.24
21	32.5	694,893	7.12	20.0	417,395	4.27	6.3	143,358	1.47	5.6	116,195	1.19
22	36.9	663,176	6.80	20.8	397,922	4.08	8.3	137,259	1.41	6.7	110,709	1.14
23	37.1	627,216	6.44	21.7	377,630	3.88	8.1	129,143	1.33	6.7	104,156	1.07
24	37.0	591,089	6.08	23.3	356,483	3.67	7.6	121,265	1.25	5.4	97,662	1.00
25	34.5	555,124	5.72	21.7	333,844	3.44	6.4	113,892	1.17	5.4	92,431	0.95
26	32.2	521,632	5.38	20.7	312,830	3.23	6.3	107,677	1.11	4.5	87,154	0.90
27	31.0	490,450	5.06	17.3	292,726	3.02	7.0	101,608	1.05	5.8	82,829	0.86
28	29.6	460,437	4.76	18.6	275,990	2.85	5.7	94,853	0.98	4.5	77,219	0.80
29	25.3	431,849	4.47	15.5	258,018	2.67	4.5	89,378	0.93	4.6	72,863	0.75
30	23.3	407,454	4.22	13.8	243,015	2.52	4.6	85,028	0.88	4.1	68,389	0.71
31	21.4	384,943	4.00	12.7	229,721	2.38	4.6	80,588	0.84	3.7	64,408	0.67
32	20.9	364,276	3.79	13.2	217,538	2.26	3.5	76,295	0.79	3.6	60,891	0.63

Age												
34	17.4	325,568	3.39	9.5	193,845	2.02	4.2	68,893	0.72	3.1	54,060	0.56
35	18.3	308,867	3.22	10.9	184,752	1.93	3.8	64,890	0.68	2.9	51,065	0.53
36	15.9	291,356	3.05	9.5	174,321	1.82	3.5	61,262	0.64	2.3	48,318	0.51
37	14.0	276,188	2.89	8.0	165,215	1.73	3.2	57,948	0.61	2.2	46,109	0.48
38	13.2	262,825	2.76	8.1	157,554	1.65	2.4	54,939	0.58	2.1	44,045	0.46
39	11.9	250,291	2.63	6.5	149,810	1.57	2.6	52,675	0.55	2.3	42,076	0.44
40	11.1	238,999	2.52	6.6	143,613	1.51	2.3	50,242	0.53	2.0	39,870	0.42
41	10.5	228,504	2.41	5.5	137,366	1.45	2.2	48,024	0.51	2.3	37,996	0.40
42	12.3	218,605	2.31	6.9	132,165	1.40	3.1	45,944	0.49	1.9	35,772	0.38
43	10.0	207,039	2.20	5.9	125,668	1.33	1.8	43,015	0.46	1.8	33,932	0.36
44	10.8	197,640	2.10	6.8	120,109	1.28	1.8	41,295	0.44	1.8	32,212	0.34
45	9.5	187,497	2.00	5.7	113,770	1.21	1.8	39,577	0.42	1.6	30,495	0.33
46	8.2	178,600	1.91	4.2	108,400	1.16	1.9	37,854	0.41	1.7	29,012	0.31
47	8.2	171,002	1.84	5.3	104,497	1.12	1.5	36,110	0.39	1.3	27,393	0.29
48	9.8	163,409	1.76	4.8	99,574	1.08	2.6	34,692	0.37	2.2	26,224	0.28
49	8.6	154,375	1.67	5.7	95,122	1.03	1.6	32,314	0.35	1.4	24,150	0.26
50	7.6	146,437	1.60	4.2	89,917	0.98	1.7	30,883	0.34	1.3	22,892	0.25
51	7.0	139,461	1.53	4.1	86,084	0.94	1.5	29,332	0.32	1.4	21,686	0.24
52	8.6	133,090	1.47	5.6	82,374	0.91	1.8	27,962	0.31	1.2	20,396	0.23
53	7.3	125,291	1.39	4.7	77,319	0.86	1.0	26,355	0.29	1.4	19,337	0.21
54	6.5	118,750	1.33	3.8	73,094	0.82	1.4	25,461	0.28	1.1	18,038	0.20
55	6.7	112,941	1.27	4.3	69,695	0.79	1.4	24,196	0.27	0.8	17,049	0.19
56	5.7	107,054	1.22	3.0	65,942	0.75	1.6	22,945	0.26	0.9	16,387	0.19
57	5.4	102,076	1.17	3.1	63,316	0.73	1.3	21,534	0.25	0.9	15,564	0.18
58	6.2	97,372	1.13	3.4	60,612	0.70	1.5	20,423	0.24	1.2	14,786	0.17
59	6.4	92,086	1.08	4.0	57,701	0.68	1.5	19,159	0.22	0.8	13,790	0.16
60	5.2	86,705	1.03	2.7	54,333	0.65	1.3	17,881	0.21	1.1	13,093	0.16
61	5.6	82,358	0.99	3.5	52,086	0.63	1.2	16,776	0.20	0.8	12,173	0.15
62	6.0	77,711	0.95	3.9	49,229	0.60	1.2	15,748	0.19	0.6	11,487	0.14
63	5.7	72,835	0.90	3.8	46,028	0.57	0.9	14,743	0.18	1.0	11,003	0.14
64	6.2	68,245	0.86	3.7	42,994	0.54	1.3	14,004	0.18	1.0	10,186	0.13
65	4.7	63,400	0.82	2.5	40,103	0.52	1.5	12,986	0.17	0.6	9,413	0.12
66	5.1	59,754	0.78	2.8	38,180	0.50	0.7	11,824	0.16	1.2	8,972	0.12
67	5.3	55,896	0.75	3.3	36,080	0.48	0.8	11,267	0.15	0.8	8,072	0.11
68	5.1	52,026	0.72	2.9	33,676	0.46	1.5	10,656	0.15	0.5	7,461	0.10
69	4.1	48,384	0.68	2.3	31,559	0.44	1.4	9,555	0.13	0.4	7,080	0.10
70	5.0	45,535	0.66	3.1	29,966	0.43	1.0	8,591	0.12	0.8	6,828	0.10
71	4.1	42,162	0.63	2.6	27,853	0.42	0.8	7,941	0.12	0.6	6,259	0.09
72	5.8	39,476	0.61	3.1	26,169	0.40	2.3	7,394	0.11	0.4	5,850	0.09
73	4.6	35,758	0.57	3.0	24,203	0.39	1.2	5,899	0.09	0.5	5,593	0.09
74	4.1	32,937	0.55	3.2	22,386	0.37	0.6	5,181	0.09	0.3	5,306	0.09
75+	5.0	30,502	0.53	3.3	20,524	0.36	0.8	4,799	0.08	0.8	5,115	0.09

NOTE: Rates of moving are from the March 1983 Current Population Survey.

[a]Includes movers from abroad.

[b]Expected years with moves at the given age and all later ages.

adult" years of life. If one were to define young adults as persons between ages 18 and 30, one can calculate how much of the cohort's moving occurs between these two ages by subtracting TM_{30} from TM_{18}. Dividing the result by TM_1 gives the proportion of the hypothetical cohort's moving that occurs after the eighteenth birthday and before the thirtieth. According to Table B.1, about one third (33.7 percent) of total residence changes occur at this age range. These young-adult years encompass about 31.8 percent of lifetime intracounty moving, 34.1 percent of lifetime movement between counties within a state, and 37.4 percent of interstate migration. This information quantifies the degree to which interstate migration is more compressed into the young-adult ages than is intracounty moving. The results suggest that the greater the distance of a move, the higher the concentration at the young-adult ages.

Mobility over other portions of the life cycle can also be quickly derived from the migration expectancy tables. For example, assume one wanted to know how much of a person's lifetime mobility occurs as a child moving with one's parents. If movement before a person's eighteenth birthday is taken to represent "childhood" moving, the answer is $(TM_1 - TM_{18})/TM_1$, or a little over one fourth of lifetime residential mobility, according to Table B.1.

The age by which one half of lifetime moving has been experienced can be found by locating the age when TM_1 has been reduced by one half. For total residential changes, the answer is just after one's twenty-sixth birthday (26.3 years, based on linear interpolation). One half of lifetime intracounty moving is experienced by age 26.7; one half of interstate migration is experienced slightly earlier—age 25.7, according to Table B.1.

The data from Chapter 2 indicated some changes in the distribution of geographical mobility over the life cycle. Some declines in residential mobility were evident after age 40 (see Figures 2.1 and 2.2), suggesting a decline in the proportion of lifetime mobility that occurs after age 40. The data in Tables B.1. and B.2 show that the 1966–71 rates of moving imply that 27.6 percent of lifetime intracounty moving occurs after age 40, whereas the 1982–83 rates imply that only 21.4 percent occurs after age 40.

Chapter 2 also reported that rates of interstate migration declined more for persons aged 18 to 30 than for older persons. Tables B.1 and B.2 show that these changes in cross-sectional age-specific rates of moving imply a decline from 37.4 to 34.8 percent in the proportion of lifetime interstate migration experienced between ages 18 and 30.

In terms of lifetime migration expectancy, declines in the cross-sectional rates of moving can be counterbalanced to some degree by increasing life expectancy brought about by mortality declines. To measure this effect, Table B.3 was constructed. Like Table B.2, it uses the 1982–83 rates of moving, but Table B.3 is based on a 1980 life table. The effect of increasing life expectancy between 1967 and 1980 was to raise the number of moves to be made by the hypothethical cohort from 1,012,543 to 1,039,637 or, on a per person basis, from 10.33 to 10.52 lifetime changes of residence.

Mobility Expectancy by Sex, Race, and Educational Level

The types of calculations presented in Tables B.1, B.2, and B.3 can be disaggregated by other relatively unchanging characteristics like sex, race, or educational attainment. Migration differentials by sex are small on a national basis. For women there has been a tendency for the typical mobility age profile (illustrated for both sexes in Figure 2.2) to be shifted slightly to the left of those of men. That is, the rapid increase in mobility that occurs in the late teens may begin somewhat earlier for women than for men, apparently because women still tend to marry slightly older men. Accordingly, the decline after the peak rate of moving begins slightly earlier for women. As a result, lifetime mobility is concentrated at a slightly younger age range for women than for men.

Mobility expectancy by race and educational level are highlighted in Table B.4 and summarize what cross-sectional national rates of moving have shown for the post–World War II period. Blacks typically have been found to have somewhat higher rates of moving within counties but whites have higher between-county rates. The 1966–71 rates of moving imply that a black person could expect 10.2 intracounty moves in a lifetime compared with 7.7 for whites. The cross-sectional rates for whites imply 2.3 moves between counties within a state (compared with 1.2 for blacks) and 2.4 moves between states (compared with 1.5 for blacks).

Though not shown in Table B.4, intracounty movement is less highly concentrated at ages 18–30 among blacks than among whites. The reason is that after age 30 or so rates of intracounty moving decline somewhat more rapidly for whites than for blacks, presumably reflecting, among other things, the greater residential stability that comes from higher rates of homeownership among whites. Since blacks are more likely to be renters and to be poor, they do not, on average, achieve the same residential stability that begins to characterize whites in their 30s.

TABLE B.4

Mobility Expectancy by Race and Years of School Completed: Annual Average, 1966–71

	All Moves[a]	Moves Within Counties	Moves Between Counties Within a State	Moves Between States
White, Aged 1 and Over	12.9	7.7	2.3	2.4
Black, Aged 1 and Over	13.1	10.2	1.2	1.5
Men Aged 25 and Over	7.3	4.5	1.3	1.2
Years of School				
Less than 8 Years	8.4	5.9	1.3	0.9
8 Years	7.6	5.1	1.4	0.9
9–11 Years	6.9	4.7	1.2	0.9
12 Years	6.5	4.1	1.2	1.0
13–15 Years	7.4	4.4	1.4	1.4
16 Years	7.7	3.8	1.5	1.9
17 or More Years	8.5	4.1	1.5	2.3

NOTES: One-year mobility rates were derived from microdata files of March Current Population Surveys of 1967, 1968, 1969, 1970, and 1971. Single-year-of-age data were used in calculating expectancy by race. A 1967 life table was used.

[a]Includes movement from abroad.

Mobility expectancy tables can also succinctly summarize the lifetime implications of the differentials by educational attainment, as discussed in Chapter 2. According to Table B.4, the most frequent movers over a lifetime are persons at the educational extremes. Based on the 1966–71 mobility rates, a 25-year-old man with less than eight years of school completed could expect 8.4 additional residential changes; if he had completed five or more years of college he could expect about the same future mobility—8.5 additional residential moves. The fewest additional changes of residence characterized those who had completed high school but had gone no further; they could expect 6.5 additional changes of residence. Underlying this U-shaped relationship between educational level and lifetime changes of residence are different patterns of short- and long-distance moving. The least-well-educated can expect more intracounty moves than the most highly educated, who can expect more interstate migration than those with little education. A 25-year-old man with less than a high school education can, in the context of life table calculations, expect to spend the rest of his life in his state of current residence. A 25-year-old man with five or more years of college can expect more than two additional moves between states. These values characterized the late 1960s, and less movement is implied by mobility rates of the early 1980s.

Finally, calculating mobility expectancy is a useful way of highlighting mobility among nations. Like the CPS, censuses or surveys in several countries ask if the respondent lived in the same or different house as a year earlier. Mobility expectancy calculations allow one to summarize in life-cycle terms the differences implied by annual rates of residential mobility. For example, in 1970 about 5 percent of the population of Ireland changed residence in one year, as did 19 percent of the U.S. population. In terms of mobility expectancy over the life cycle, these figures mean that an average American would make nearly as many moves by age 21 as the average resident of Ireland makes in an entire lifetime.[6]

Conclusion

If there is no official statistical basis for saying that the average person or family moves once every 5, 6, or 7 years, then why do these figures keep appearing in the popular press? The answer may involve an attempt to relate mobility expectancy and life expectancy. Life expectancy in 1967 was 70.5 years, and mobility expectancy was 12.93 years with moves; 70.5 divided by 12.93 is 5.45, deceptively suggesting that an average person might move about every five years in a lifetime. Life expectancy in 1980 was 74.5 years and mobility expectancy (Table B.3) was 10.52 years with moves; 74.5 divided by 10.52 yields 7.08, tempting one to conclude that the average person moves once every seven years.

One reason that this reasoning is misleading is that it ignores enormous variation by age in the propensity to move. In the late 1960s annual rates of moving reached 48 percent among persons in their early 20s, and a majority of persons at this age could reasonably anticipate moving at least once over a one- to two-year period. By age 50 only one person in 10 changes residence in a year, and saying that most 50-year-olds could anticipate moving within five to seven years is misleading (in the early 1980s annual residential mobility rates were below these levels at almost every age group). Another reason that it is misleading is that a few persons move repeatedly and inflate the mean.

Similar criticisms can be made about the life table calculation of mobility expectancy. The measure accurately describes the mobility of

---

[6]Larry Long and Celia Boertlein, "The Geographical Mobility of Americans: An International Comparison," *Current Population Reports*, series P-20, no. 64 (Washington, DC: U.S. Government Printing Office, 1975), p. 16.

the cohort, but converting it to a per person basis tells one nothing about how many persons fall below or exceed what looks like a lifetime quota of moves. Although the 1980 life table and the 1982–83 rates of moving imply 10.52 residence changes per person, there is at present no sound basis for saying what proportion of persons will experience one half as much moving, twice as much, or in other ways deviate from the mean. In time, longitudinal surveys should overcome this shortcoming.

Another shortcoming is the absence of local data on frequent movers or long-term residents. This gap in migration statistics could become more of an issue in future epidemiological studies of disease rates as well as court cases involving the potential toxic effect of radiation leaks, chemical dumps, or other environmental hazards.[7] Such uses of migration data shift attention toward questions of the distribution of local populations by their exposure to nonmigration for varying periods of time.

[7]Lincoln Polissar, "The Effect of Migration on Comparison of Disease Rates in Geographic Studies in the United States," *American Journal of Epidemiology* 111, no. 2 (1980): 175–182.

APPENDIX C:
HOW STATES RANK
ON VARIOUS MEASURES
OF MIGRATION

TABLE C.1

States, the District of Columbia, and Puerto Rico Ranked According to Rates of Outmigration: 1935–40, 1955–60, 1965–70, and 1975–80

1935–40		1955–60		1965–70		1975–80	
Area	Rate	Area	Rate	Area	Rate	Area	Rate
District of Columbia	28.3	Alaska	41.6	Alaska	39.7	Alaska	32.9
Nevada	20.7	District of Columbia	26.9	District of Columbia	24.6	District of Columbia	25.9
Wyoming	16.1	Nevada	26.1	Nevada	24.5	Hawaii	20.2
South Dakota	13.9	Wyoming	21.5	Wyoming	23.8	Nevada	19.9
Arizona	13.7	New Mexico	18.7	Hawaii	22.0	Wyoming	19.6
Oklahoma	13.6	Hawaii	16.4	New Mexico	21.5	Colorado	17.0
North Dakota	13.6	Idaho	16.3	North Dakota	18.6	Arizona	16.0
Idaho	12.8	Arizona	16.3	Idaho	18.1	Idaho	15.8
Nebraska	12.6	Colorado	15.4	Arizona	18.1	New Mexico	15.6
New Mexico	12.3	Kansas	15.4	Montana	17.5	Montana	15.0
Kansas	12.1	South Dakota	14.4	South Dakota	16.6	Delaware	14.9
Montana	11.0	Montana	14.2	Colorado	16.6	North Dakota	14.4
Colorado	11.0	Oklahoma	14.0	Kansas	15.2	New Hampshire	14.2
Arkansas	9.9	North Dakota	13.6	Virginia	14.0	South Dakota	13.9
Oregon	8.9	Nebraska	13.4	Utah	14.0	Kansas	13.3
Utah	8.7	Arkansas	13.3	Delaware	13.7	Virginia	13.1
Missouri	8.0	Oregon	13.0	Nebraska	13.4	Vermont	13.1
Vermont	7.5	West Virginia	12.9	Oklahoma	13.2	Nebraska	12.4
Washington	7.1	Virginia	12.4	New Hampshire	13.0	Maryland	12.3
Iowa	7.1	Washington	12.2	Florida	12.6	Florida	12.0
Florida	6.5	Vermont	12.0	West Virginia	12.5	Connecticut	11.7
New Hampshire	6.4	Delaware	11.6	Oregon	12.4	Utah	11.6
Tennessee	6.1	Utah	11.3	Arkansas	12.1	Oregon	11.0
Kentucky	5.7	Rhode Island	11.3	Rhode Island	11.7	New Jersey	10.9
Alabama	5.7	New Hampshire	11.1	Mississippi	11.7	Rhode Island	10.5
Georgia	5.6	Florida	11.1	Maine	11.6	Maine	10.3
Delaware	5.6	Mississippi	10.7	Vermont	11.5	Illinois	10.1

TABLE C.1 (continued)

Area	Rate	Area	Rate	Area	Rate	Area	Rate
West Virginia	5.6	Kentucky	10.7	Maryland	11.3	Oklahoma	10.1
Virginia	5.4	Tennessee	10.4	Washington	11.1	Arkansas	10.1
Minnesota	5.3	Maine	10.4	Alabama	10.9	New York	10.1
Texas	4.9	Missouri	10.3	South Carolina	10.7	Iowa	10.0
Mississippi	4.8	South Carolina	10.2	Georgia	10.4	Missouri	9.9
Illinois	4.8	Maryland	10.2	Iowa	10.3	Massachusetts	9.9
South Carolina	4.8	Georgia	9.8	Kentucky	10.3	Washington	9.9
Maryland	4.8	Iowa	9.8	Missouri	10.1	South Carolina	9.5
Indiana	4.7	Alabama	9.1	Connecticut	10.0	Mississippi	9.4
Maine	4.5	Indiana	9.0	Tennessee	9.9	Georgia	9.3
Rhode Island	4.3	Texas	8.7	Indiana	9.5	Indiana	9.1
New Jersey	4.3	North Carolina	8.6	New Jersey	9.5	Ohio	9.0
Louisiana	4.2	Illinois	8.5	Illinois	9.5	California	8.5
Wisconsin	4.2	Connecticut	7.9	North Carolina	9.1	North Carolina	8.4
Connecticut	4.1	Minnesota	7.7	Louisiana	9.0	Minnesota	8.4
Ohio	4.0	New Jersey	7.6	California	8.8	Tennessee	8.4
North Carolina	3.8	Massachusetts	7.5	Massachusetts	8.7	Kentucky	8.4
California	3.7	Ohio	7.5	Texas	8.5	West Virginia	8.4
Massachusetts	3.5	Louisana	7.3	Minnesota	8.4	Michigan	7.9
Pennsylvania	3.4	Michigan	7.3	Ohio	8.1	Alabama	7.7
New York	3.3	California	6.7	New York	7.9	Wisconsin	7.5
Michigan	3.3	New York	6.7	Wisconsin	7.4	Pennsylvania	7.4
Alaska	NA	Pennsylvania	6.6	Pennsylvania	7.1	Louisiana	7.4
Hawaii	NA	Wisconsin	6.6	Michigan	7.1	Texas	7.1
Puerto Rico	NA	Puerto Rico	6.5	Puerto Rico	6.2	Puerto Rico	6.8

NOTES: Outmigrants are persons aged 5 and over who were living in the specified area (state, District of Columbia, or Puerto Rico) five years before the census date but elsewhere in the United States at the census date. The outmigration rate is 100 times the number of outmigrants divided by the population of the area five years and over at the census date, minus the number of immigrants, plus the number of outmigrants. Persons who in 1940, 1960, or 1970 failed to report place of residence five years earlier were assigned a mobility status in accordance with the number who did report mobility status. NA means "not available."

313

TABLE C.2

States, the District of Columbia, and Puerto Rico Ranked According to Inmigration Rates: 1935–40, 1955–60, 1965–70, and 1975–80

1935–40		1955–60		1965–70		1975–80	
Area	Rate	Area	Rate	Area	Rate	Area	Rate
District of Columbia	33.4	Alaska	47.9	Alaska	44.7	Nevada	34.3
Nevada	27.5	Nevada	33.9	Nevada	30.6	Alaska	31.5
Arizona	21.4	Arizona	30.5	Arizona	25.4	Wyoming	29.5
Wyoming	17.3	Florida	28.8	Hawaii	25.1	Arizona	25.9
Oregon	16.3	New Mexico	24.5	Florida	23.5	Hawaii	22.8
Idaho	16.0	Hawaii	20.9	Colorado	21.4	Colorado	22.7
New Mexico	15.0	Wyoming	20.6	Wyoming	18.7	Florida	22.2
Florida	14.8	Colorado	20.0	Washington	18.1	Idaho	21.3
California	14.6	District of Columbia	19.8	District of Columbia	17.8	New Hampshire	19.4
Washington	12.5	California	16.8	New Mexico	17.4	New Mexico	19.3
Colorado	11.9	Delaware	16.5	New Hampshire	17.2	District of Columbia	19.1
Delaware	9.9	Idaho	15.7	Idaho	17.0	Oregon	18.6
Montana	9.4	Virginia	15.0	Delaware	16.9	Washington	18.5
Maryland	8.5	Washington	14.8	Virginia	16.7	Utah	18.0
New Hampshire	7.9	Maryland	14.3	Oregon	16.0	Virginia	16.1
Virginia	7.3	Oregon	13.5	Maryland	16.0	Montana	15.9
Utah	6.6	New Hampshire	13.4	Vermont	15.0	Vermont	15.2
Vermont	6.3	Utah	13.1	Oklahoma	14.1	Oklahoma	15.2
Kansas	6.2	Kansas	12.8	Utah	13.9	Delaware	14.6
Oklahoma	6.0	Montana	12.5	Kansas	13.7	Kansas	14.0
Arkansas	6.0	Oklahoma	11.8	Rhode Island	13.3	North Dakota	13.8
Connecticut	6.0	New Jersey	11.0	California	13.0	Texas	13.6
Missouri	5.8	Connecticut	10.8	Montana	13.0	California	13.2
Indiana	5.6	Vermont	10.6	Georgia	12.7	Arkansas	13.1
New Jersey	5.4	Rhode Island	10.5	Connecticut	12.4	Georgia	12.6
Michigan	5.1	Arkansas	10.1	New Jersey	11.9	South Carolina	12.4
Nebraska	4.9	Nebraska	9.9	South Carolina	11.7	Maryland	12.3

TABLE C.2 (continued)

State	Rate	State	Rate	State	Rate	State	Rate
South Dakota	4.9	Texas	9.6	Arkansas	11.5	South Dakota	11.8
Illinois	4.8	Georgia	9.6	North Dakota	11.1	Maine	11.7
Tennessee	4.8	South Dakota	9.5	Nebraska	11.1	Nebraska	11.6
Minnesota	4.7	Missouri	9.2	Texas	11.0	Tennessee	11.3
Louisiana	4.7	Maine	9.0	Missouri	10.7	Connecticut	11.1
Texas	4.7	South Carolina	9.0	Tennessee	10.2	Rhode Island	10.7
Iowa	4.7	Tennessee	8.5	North Carolina	10.0	North Carolina	10.6
Rhode Island	4.7	Indiana	8.4	South Dakota	9.9	Missouri	10.1
Georgia	4.6	North Dakota	8.3	Maine	9.8	Mississippi	9.9
West Virginia	4.1	Illinois	8.2	Massachusetts	9.5	New Jersey	9.9
South Carolina	4.0	Alabama	8.0	Mississippi	9.3	Kentucky	9.7
Ohio	4.0	Mississippi	7.8	Kentucky	9.0	Alabama	9.7
New York	3.8	Louisiana	7.8	Indiana	9.0	Louisiana	9.6
Maine	3.8	Kentucky	7.6	Alabama	8.8	West Virginia	9.1
Kentucky	3.7	Ohio	7.5	Illinois	8.7	Massachusetts	8.7
North Dakota	3.7	North Carolina	7.5	Louisiana	8.5	Iowa	8.6
Mississippi	3.5	Massachusetts	7.4	Minnesota	8.4	Minnesota	8.3
North Carolina	3.4	Minnesota	7.3	West Virginia	7.9	Indiana	8.2
Wisconsin	3.2	Iowa	6.6	Iowa	7.8	Illinois	7.8
Massachusetts	3.1	Wisconsin	6.5	Ohio	7.8	Wisconsin	7.3
Alabama	3.0	New York	6.2	Michigan	7.7	New York	6.5
Pennsylvania	2.4	Michigan	5.9	Wisconsin	7.7	Ohio	6.4
Alaska	NA	West Virginia	5.8	New York	7.3	Michigan	6.0
Hawaii	NA	Pennsylvania	4.5	Pennsylvania	6.9	Pennsylvania	5.9
Puerto Rico	NA	Puerto Rico	3.1	Puerto Rico	NA	Puerto Rico	5.3

NOTES: Inmigrants are persons who were living in the specified area (state, District of Columbia, or Puerto Rico) at the census date but not five years earlier and include movers from outside the United States. The immigration rate is 100 times the number of inmigrants (aged 5 and over) divided by the population aged five and over residing in the area at the census date. Persons who in 1940, 1960, or 1970 failed to report a place of residence five years earlier were assigned a mobility status in accordance with the number who did report mobility status. NA means "not available." Published data on inmigration for Puerto Rico for 1965–70 are in error.

TABLE C.3

States Ranked According to Percentage of Outmigrants Aged 5 and Over Who Were (1) Leaving Their State of Birth, (2) Returning to Their State of Birth, (3) Other U.S.-Born Interstate Migrants, and (4) Interstate Migrants Born Outside the United States: 1975–80

Persons Leaving State of Birth		Persons Returning to State of Birth		Repeat, Nonreturn Interstate Migrants[a]		Interstate Migrants Born Outside United States	
Pennsylvania	58.3%	Alaska	28.0%	Alaska	55.5%	New York	13.8%
New York	57.5	Nevada	28.0	Nevada	52.9	Hawaii	12.1
Ohio	51.5	Florida	27.0	Arizona	51.8	New Jersey	10.9
Iowa	51.1	Wyoming	25.8	Colorado	49.5	District of Columbia	9.6
West Virginia	50.7	Arizona	24.0	Wyoming	48.7	Rhode Island	7.8
Wisconsin	49.8	South Carolina	23.9	Hawaii	48.4	Connecticut	7.7
Michigan	49.3	North Carolina	23.5	Virginia	48.4	Massachusetts	7.4
Minnesota	49.3	Hawaii	23.4	Maryland	48.2	New Mexico	6.9
Illinois	48.3	Colorado	23.2	District of Columbia	45.8	California	6.8
Massachusetts	48.2	Oklahoma	23.0	Florida	45.3	Illinois	6.8
Indiana	45.8	New Mexico	22.7	New Hampshire	45.2	Florida	6.7
South Dakota	44.2	Oregon	22.1	Delaware	44.6	Texas	6.6
Alabama	44.1	Texas	22.1	Oregon	44.5	Maryland	6.5
Mississippi	43.5	Georgia	22.1	New Mexico	44.5	Virginia	5.7
Kentucky	43.4	Louisiana	22.0	Washington	44.4	Arizona	5.6
Missouri	43.2	Arkansas	21.8	Vermont	43.6	Washington	5.5
Rhode Island	42.2	Virginia	21.8	Idaho	43.0	Maine	5.4
Maine	40.9	Idaho	21.8	Montana	42.2	Nevada	5.2
New Jersey	40.6	New Hampshire	21.7	Utah	42.0	New Hampshire	5.2
Louisiana	40.5	Tennessee	21.7	South Carolina	41.4	Michigan	5.2
Nebraska	39.6	Washington	21.5	California	40.2	Delaware	5.1
Arkansas	39.0	Delaware	21.1	Connecticut	40.0	Alaska	5.0
Tennessee	38.0	Kansas	20.8	Georgia	39.7	Colorado	4.8
North Dakota	37.8	North Dakota	20.7	Kansas	39.4	Pennsylvania	4.7
Connecticut	37.1	Mississippi	20.5	Nebraska	39.0	Vermont	4.6
Kansas	35.9	Kentucky	20.2	North Carolina	38.8	Utah	4.4
Montana	35.6	California	19.9	Tennessee	37.9	Georgia	4.1
Oklahoma	35.2	Utah	19.4	Oklahoma	37.7	Wisconsin	4.1

TABLE C.3 (continued)

Persons Leaving State of Birth		Persons Returning To State of Birth		Repeat, Nonreturn Interstate Migrants[a]		Interstate Migrants Born Outside United States	
Texas	34.3%	Montana	19.0%	Maine	37.7%	South Carolina	4.1%
Utah	34.3	Vermont	18.7	North Dakota	37.6	Oklahoma	4.0
Georgia	34.2	Alabama	18.4	Texas	37.0	Kansas	3.9
North Carolina	33.8	Maryland	18.3	Arkansas	36.5	North Carolina	3.9
Vermont	33.1	Nebraska	17.8	Missouri	36.3	North Dakota	3.9
California	33.1	South Dakota	17.7	South Dakota	35.7	Oregon	3.8
Idaho	31.8	Indiana	17.6	Rhode Island	34.7	Louisiana	3.7
South Carolina	30.6	Missouri	17.2	Alabama	34.2	Kentucky	3.6
Oregon	29.5	West Virginia	17.0	New Jersey	34.1	Ohio	3.6
Delaware	29.3	Maine	16.0	Louisiana	33.8	Nebraska	3.6
District of Columbia	28.7	District of Columbia	15.9	Indiana	33.5	Idaho	3.4
Washington	28.5	Rhode Island	15.4	Mississippi	33.1	Minnesota	3.3
New Hampshire	27.9	Connecticut	15.2	Minnesota	32.8	Wyoming	3.3
Maryland	27.1	Iowa	15.1	Kentucky	32.7	Missouri	3.3
New Mexico	26.0	Minnesota	14.6	Massachusetts	31.7	Alabama	3.2
Virginia	24.0	Michigan	14.6	Wisconsin	31.7	Montana	3.2
Colorado	22.5	Illinois	14.6	Iowa	31.2	Indiana	3.1
Wyoming	22.3	Ohio	14.6	Michigan	30.9	Mississippi	2.9
Florida	21.1	New Jersey	14.4	Illinois	30.3	West Virginia	2.9
Arizona	18.6	Wisconsin	14.4	Ohio	30.3	Arkansas	2.6
Hawaii	16.1	Massachusetts	12.7	West Virginia	29.4	Iowa	2.6
Nevada	13.9	Pennsylvania	10.9	Pennsylvania	26.1	South Dakota	2.5
Alaska	11.4	New York	8.8	New York	19.9	Tennessee	2.4

[a]Interstate migrants who were born in the United States but were not moving to or from their state of birth.

TABLE C.4

States Ranked According to Percentage of Inmigrants Aged 5 and Over Who Were (1) Leaving Their State of Birth, (2) Returning to Their State of Birth, (3) Other U.S.-Born Interstate Migrants, (4) Interstate Migrants Born Outside the United States, and (5) Persons Living Outside the United States in 1975: 1975–80

Persons Leaving State of Birth		Persons Returning to State of Birth		Repeat, Nonreturn Interstate Migrants[a]		Interstate Migrants Born Outside United States		Migrants from Outside United States	
New Hampshire	48.8%	West Virginia	33.9%	Alaska	45.7%	New Jersey	10.5%	New York	41.8%
Wyoming	43.6	Pennsylvania	27.9	Nevada	42.1	Florida	9.2	California	35.2
Arizona	42.9	Alabama	26.4	Wyoming	41.9	Connecticut	7.0	Hawaii	25.8
Vermont	42.9	Iowa	26.2	Idaho	40.2	Hawaii	6.9	Illinois	22.6
Florida	42.6	Mississippi	25.4	Arizona	39.6	California	6.4	New Jersey	20.8
Nevada	41.1	Kentucky	25.3	Oregon	39.3	Maryland	6.2	Massachusetts	20.1
Delaware	39.6	Ohio	25.1	Colorado	39.2	Massachusetts	6.1	Texas	19.3
Colorado	39.6	South Dakota	23.9	New Mexico	38.9	Rhode Island	6.0	Rhode Island	17.9
Wisconsin	38.2	Minnesota	23.5	District of Columbia	38.8	District of Columbia	5.8	Connecticut	16.7
Alaska	37.9	Michigan	23.4	Virginia	38.6	Nevada	5.7	Maryland	15.2
North Dakota	37.8	Arkansas	23.3	Montana	38.5	New York	5.5	Michigan	15.0
Montana	37.6	Missouri	23.0	Washington	37.8	Texas	5.3	District of Columbia	14.8
Indiana	37.5	Indiana	22.6	Maryland	37.6	Virginia	5.2	Virginia	13.7
Kentucky	36.7	Wisconsin	22.4	Georgia	35.8	Washington	5.2	Pennsylvania	13.1
Idaho	36.7	Tennessee	22.0	Delaware	35.7	Pennsylvania	5.2	Washington	12.4
South Dakota	36.5	Louisiana	21.4	Nebraska	34.7	Alaska	5.0	Louisiana	11.9
North Carolina	36.3	North Dakota	21.3	South Carolina	34.5	Illinois	5.0	Minnesota	11.8
Maine	35.9	Maine	21.1	Hawaii	33.9	Arizona	4.9	Florida	11.7
South Carolina	35.9	Oklahoma	20.2	Arkansas	33.8	New Mexico	4.8	Utah	11.3
Oregon	35.8	Nebraska	19.7	Kansas	33.7	Vermont	4.3	Ohio	10.5
Georgia	35.7	North Carolina	19.4	Tennessee	33.7	New Hampshire	4.2	Kansas	10.0
Arkansas	35.7	Illinois	19.3	Vermont	33.7	Delaware	4.2	Oklahoma	9.6
Iowa	35.6	New York	19.0	North Carolina	33.3	Oregon	4.2	New Mexico	9.6
Tennessee	35.6	South Carolina	18.4	Oklahoma	32.8	Michigan	4.2	Wisconsin	9.2
New Jersey	35.4	Utah	18.3	Missouri	32.6	Maine	4.0	Colorado	9.1
Kansas	35.4	Massachusetts	17.8	New Hampshire	32.5	Colorado	4.0	Delaware	9.0
Utah	34.6	Kansas	17.7	Utah	32.0	Ohio	3.8	Nebraska	8.9
Missouri	34.4	Georgia	16.4	Mississippi	31.8	Utah	3.7	Oregon	8.9
Oklahoma	34.3	Montana	15.6	Louisiana	31.6	Louisiana	3.7	Georgia	8.6

318

TABLE C.4 (continued)

Persons Leaving State of Birth		Persons Returning to State of Birth		Repeat, Nonreturn Interstate Migrants[a]		Interstate Migrants Born Outside United States		Migrants from Outside United States	
Rhode Island	34.1%	Texas	14.7%	Connecticut	31.5%	South Carolina	3.7%	Alabama	8.2%
New Mexico	34.0	Rhode Island	14.5	South Dakota	31.3	Georgia	3.6	Nevada	8.0
Nebraska	33.8	Idaho	13.5	Florida	31.2	North Carolina	3.5	Arizona	8.0
Connecticut	33.6	Vermont	13.3	Alabama	31.2	Wisconsin	3.4	Iowa	7.9
West Virginia	33.6	New Mexico	12.7	Maine	31.1	Idaho	3.3	North Dakota	7.7
Minnesota	33.3	Washington	12.6	North Dakota	30.6	Indiana	3.2	Kentucky	7.7
Mississippi	33.3	New Jersey	12.1	Texas	29.9	Kansas	3.2	Maine	7.7
Ohio	32.2	Oregon	11.8	Indiana	29.1	Oklahoma	3.0	Indiana	7.6
Washington	32.0	Delaware	11.4	Minnesota	28.6	Alabama	3.0	Alaska	7.6
Michigan	31.5	Connecticut	11.2	Ohio	28.4	Nebraska	2.9	South Carolina	7.5
Louisiana	31.4	Virginia	11.2	Kentucky	27.7	North Dakota	2.8	North Carolina	7.5
Virginia	31.4	District of Columbia	11.1	Iowa	27.5	Minnesota	2.8	Missouri	7.2
Maryland	31.3	New Hampshire	9.7	Rhode Island	26.8	Mississippi	2.8	Mississippi	6.6
Alabama	31.2	Maryland	9.7	Wisconsin	25.9	Missouri	2.8	Idaho	6.3
Texas	30.8	California	8.6	Michigan	25.8	Tennessee	2.6	Tennessee	6.1
Pennsylvania	30.2	Wyoming	8.4	Massachusetts	25.8	South Dakota	2.5	South Dakota	5.9
Massachusetts	30.0	Illinois	8.1	Illinois	25.0	West Virginia	2.5	Vermont	5.8
District of Columbia	29.5	Hawaii	5.5	West Virginia	25.0	Montana	2.5	Montana	5.8
Hawaii	28.0	Florida	5.3	California	24.6	Kentucky	2.5	West Virginia	4.9
Illinois	27.4	Arizona	4.7	Pennsylvania	23.8	Iowa	2.5	Arkansas	4.9
California	25.2	Alaska	3.8	New Jersey	21.1	Arkansas	2.4	New Hampshire	4.7
New York	17.6	Nevada	3.2	New York	16.0	Wyoming	2.1	Wyoming	4.1

[a]Interstate migrants who were born in the United States but were not moving to or from their state of birth.

TABLE C.5

States Ranked According to "At Risk" Rates of Outmigration Among (1) Persons Leaving Their State of Birth, (2) Persons Returning to Their State of Birt. and (3) Others Making Repeat, Nonreturn Interstate Moves: 1975–80

Rate of Leaving State of Birth		Rate of Returning to State of Birth		Rate of Repeat, Nonreturn Inter- State Migration	
District of Columbia	193.9	Hawaii	179.5	Hawaii	371.9
Alaska	124.3	Alaska	137.9	Alaska	273.4
Nevada	124.1	North Dakota	123.5	North Dakota	224.2
Wyoming	102.9	Mississippi	97.6	District of Columbia	214.5
Idaho	98.4	North Carolina	96.8	Maine	187.4
Montana	91.9	South Carolina	94.3	South Dakota	185.2
Colorado	88.6	Kentucky	92.2	Virginia	179.8
Delaware	87.0	Wyoming	91.9	Nebraska	179.2
Arizona	86.0	South Dakota	91.6	Vermont	178.1
South Dakota	85.5	Louisiana	87.7	Wyoming	173.7
New York	83.3	Nebraska	82.0	Massachusetts	173.2
New Jersey	77.9	Georgia	81.3	Utah	173.2
Florida	76.9	New Mexico	81.2	South Carolina	163.3
New Mexico	76.8	Virginia	81.0	Rhode Island	162.7
New Hampshire	75.6	Kansas	80.4	North Carolina	159.8
Kansas	74.9	Utah	80.0	New Mexico	159.1
Connecticut	74.0	Arkansas	79.9	Montana	158.8
North Dakota	74.0	Maine	79.7	Mississippi	158.0
Oregon	71.1	Nevada	78.2	Colorado	157.2
Illinois	70.5	West Virginia	77.3	Iowa	153.5
Nebraska	69.4	Alabama	76.6	Kansas	152.2
Vermont	68.3	Vermont	76.4	New Hampshire	150.0
Massachusetts	65.8	District of Columbia	74.5	Kentucky	149.3
Iowa	65.2	Iowa	74.3	Delaware	147.9
Ohio	64.6	Colorado	73.8	Nevada	147.8
Rhode Island	63.2	Idaho	72.9	Connecticut	147.0
Maryland	62.0	Rhode Island	72.2	Georgia	146.1
California	61.8	New Hampshire	72.0	Idaho	144.2
Missouri	60.9	Tennessee	71.8	Maryland	142.3
Indiana	59.0	Montana	71.5	Alabama	142.1

TABLE C.5 *(continued)*

Rate of Leaving State of Birth		Rate of Returning to State of Birth		Rate of Repeat, Nonreturn Inter- state Migration	
Utah	57.8	Oklahoma	71.2	Arizona	139.0
Maine	56.7	Delaware	70.1	Pennsylvania	136.4
Washington	56.2	Massachusetts	69.3	New York	135.2
Arkansas	55.0	Texas	66.5	Louisiana	134.6
Minnesota	54.8	Arizona	64.4	Arkansas	133.5
Hawaii	54.8	Missouri	62.1	West Virginia	133.5
Oklahoma	54.5	Illinois	61.2	Missouri	131.3
Michigan	54.1	New York	60.2	Illinois	127.3
West Virginia	53.3	Indiana	59.0	Tennessee	125.7
Pennsylvania	52.5	Florida	57.4	Minnesota	125.2
Virginia	51.3	Pennsylvania	57.3	Wisconsin	123.8
Mississippi	51.3	Wisconsin	56.4	New Jersey	117.2
Wisconsin	47.8	Connecticut	55.8	Oklahoma	116.6
Kentucky	45.2	Minnesota	55.8	Indiana	112.5
Tennessee	43.4	Maryland	54.0	Texas	111.2
Georgia	43.3	Ohio	52.4	Ohio	109.0
Alabama	42.4	New Jersey	49.6	Michigan	102.0
South Carolina	39.0	Oregon	48.4	Washington	98.8
Louisiana	37.5	Michigan	48.2	Oregon	97.3
North Carolina	36.4	Washington	47.9	Florida	96.3
Texas	34.2	California	41.2	California	83.5

NOTES: Rates are expressed per 1,000 at risk. The universe is limited to persons aged 5 and over born in and living in the United States in 1975 and 1980. Repeat (nonreturn) interstate migrants are persons who were born in the United States and moved between states between 1975 and 1980 but not to or from their state of birth. The base for the rate of departure from state of birth is all persons born in state X and living in state X in 1975. The base for the rate of return outmigration and repeat (nonreturn) outmigration is the number of persons living in state X in 1975 and born in the United States but not in state X.

TABLE C.6

*States Ranked According to "At Risk" Rates of Inmigration Among
(1) Persons Leaving Their State of Birth, (2) Persons Returning to Their State of Birth
and (3) Others Making Repeat, Nonreturn Interstate Moves: 1975–80*

Rate of Leaving State of Birth		Rate of Returning to State of Birth		Rate of Repeat, Nonreturn Inter- state Migration	
Florida	6.6	California	116.5	Texas	32.4
California	5.8	Florida	109.0	Virginia	17.7
Texas	4.3	Utah	108.9	Washington	14.8
Arizona	2.1	Texas	108.9	New York	12.5
Virginia	1.9	Oregon	104.1	North Carolina	11.2
New Jersey	1.8	Washington	100.6	Ohio	11.1
Colorado	1.8	Louisiana	75.0	California	11.1
Illinois	1.8	Tennessee	72.7	Pennsylvania	10.5
Georgia	1.7	Michigan	72.7	Florida	9.7
Washington	1.7	North Carolina	71.6	Oregon	9.6
North Carolina	1.6	Arizona	71.3	Tennessee	9.2
Ohio	1.6	New Hampshire	68.3	Oklahoma	7.9
Pennsylvania	1.6	Delaware	67.3	South Carolina	6.9
New York	1.5	Maine	66.9	New Mexico	4.8
Tennessee	1.3	Ohio	66.3	Wisconsin	4.8
Michigan	1.3	Indiana	65.4	Utah	3.9
Oregon	1.2	Colorado	65.0	Arizona	3.9
Missouri	1.2	Georgia	64.9	Colorado	3.6
Indiana	1.2	Wisconsin	64.3	Georgia	3.5
Maryland	1.1	Minnesota	63.1	Illinois	3.4
Oklahoma	1.1	Virginia	62.0	Wyoming	2.8
Massachusetts	1.1	Maryland	61.9	Maryland	2.8
South Carolina	1.0	South Carolina	61.1	Missouri	2.3
Wisconsin	0.9	New Mexico	60.7	West Virginia	2.3
Kentucky	0.9	Missouri	58.2	New Jersey	2.2
Louisiana	0.9	Oklahoma	57.6	Michigan	2.1
Alabama	0.8	Connecticut	57.3	Massachusetts	1.9
Connecticut	0.8	Alabama	56.9	Indiana	1.9
Kansas	0.8	Massachusetts	56.1	Louisiana	1.8
Minnesota	0.8	New Jersey	56.1	Alabama	1.7
Nevada	0.8	Idaho	54.9	Nevada	1.6

TABLE C.6 *(continued)*

Rate of Leaving State of Birth		Rate of Returning to State of Birth		Rate of Repeat, Nonreturn Interstate Migration	
Arkansas	0.7	Wyoming	53.2	Kansas	1.6
Iowa	0.6	Kentucky	52.8	Connecticut	1.5
New Hampshire	0.6	Illinois	52.0	Arkansas	1.4
Utah	0.6	Pennsylvania	50.6	Kentucky	1.4
New Mexico	0.6	Hawaii	49.6	Rhode Island	1.4
Mississippi	0.6	Montana	47.1	North Dakota	1.4
Idaho	0.5	Arkansas	47.0	Minnesota	1.4
Nebraska	0.4	West Virginia	46.3	Vermont	1.3
Hawaii	0.4	New York	46.2	South Dakota	1.3
West Virginia	0.4	Nevada	45.6	Mississippi	1.1
Wyoming	0.4	Rhode Island	45.2	Idaho	1.1
Maine	0.3	Vermont	45.0	Hawaii	1.0
Alaska	0.3	Iowa	44.4	Iowa	1.0
Montana	0.3	Kansas	44.1	Nebraska	0.9
District of Columbia	0.3	Alaska	41.3	New Hampshire	0.8
Rhode Island	0.2	Mississippi	39.5	Alaska	0.8
Delaware	0.2	Nebraska	38.5	District of Columbia	0.7
North Dakota	0.2	South Dakota	35.8	Montana	0.7
Vermont	0.2	North Dakota	31.6	Maine	0.6
South Dakota	0.2	District of Columbia	21.2	Delaware	0.4

NOTES: Rates are expressed per 1,000 at risk. The universe is limited to persons aged 5 and over born in and living in the United States in 1975 and 1980. Repeat (nonreturn) interstate migrants are persons who were born in the United States and moved between states between 1975 and 1980 but not to or from their state of birth. The base for the inmigration rate to state X on the part of persons leaving their state of birth consists of all persons born in the United States (but not in state X) and living in their state of birth in 1975. The base for the return inmigration rate to state X is the number of persons born in state X and living outside state X in 1975 (but still in the United States). The base for the repeat inmigration rate to state X is all persons born in the United States but outside state X and were living in the United States in 1975 but not in their state of birth.

Bibliography

Adams, Arvil V., and Gilbert Nestel "Interregional Migration, Education, and Poverty in the Urban Ghetto: Another Look at Black-White Earnings Differentials." *Review of Economics and Statistics* 58 (May 1976):156–166.

Adams, J. S.; D. J. Caruso; E. A. Norstrand; and R. I. Palm "Intraurban Migration." *Annals of the Association of American Geographers* 63 (March 1973):152–155.

Adams, John S., and Kathleen A. Gilder "Household Location and Intra-Urban Migration." In D. T. Herbert and R. J. Johnston, eds., *Spatial Processes and Form.* London: Wiley, 1976, pp. 159–192.

Alba, Richard D., and Michael J. Batutis "Migration's Toll: Lessons from New York State." *American Demographics* (June 1985):38–42.

Alexander, James R. "Investment Strategies and the Problem of Outmigration." *Growth and Change* 9 (July 1978):14–21.

Allen, James P. "Changes in the American Propensity to Migrate." *Annals of the Association of American Geographers* 67 (December 1977):577–587.

Allen, Jeremiah "Information and Subsequent Migration: Further Analysis and Additional Evidence." *Southern Economic Journal* 45 (April 1979):1274–1284.

Alperovich, Gershon "The Cost of Living, Labor Market Opportunities and the Migration Decision: A Case of Misspecification? Comment." *Annals of Regional Science* 17 (March 1983):94–97.

——— "Economic Analysis of Intraurban Migration in Tel-Aviv." *Journal of Urban Economics* 14 (November 1983):280–292.

——— "Lagged Response in Intra-Urban Migration of Home Owners." *Regional Studies* 17 (May 1984):297–304.

Alperovich, Gershon; Joel Bergsman; and Christian Ehemann "An Econometric Model of Migration between U.S. Metropolitan Areas." *Urban Studies* 14 (June 1977):135–145.

Althaus, Paul G., and Joseph Schachter "Interstate Migration and the New Federalism." *Social Science Quarterly* 64 (March 1983):25–45.

Andrulis, John "Intra-Urban Workplace and Residential Mobility Under Uncertainty." *Journal of Urban Economics* 11 (January 1982):85–97.

Bach, Robert L., and Joel Smith "Community Satisfaction, Expectations of Moving and Migration." *Demography* 14 (May 1977):147–167.

Bachi, Roberto "Geostatistical Analysis of Internal Migrations." *Journal of Regional Science* 16 (April 1976):1–19.

Bacon, Lloyd "Poverty among Interregional Rural-to-Urban Migrants." *Rural Sociology* 36 (June 1971):125–140.

——— "Migration, Poverty, and the Rural South." *Social Forces* 51 (March 1973):348–355.

Balan, Jorge; Harley L. Browning; and Elizabeth Jelin *Men in a Developing Society: Geographic and Social Mobility in Monterrey, Mexico.* Austin: University of Texas Press, 1973.

Ballard, Kenneth P., and Gordon L. Clark "The Short-Run Dynamics of Inter-State Migration: A Space-Time Economic Adjustment Model of Inmigration to Fast Growing States." *Regional Studies* 15, no. 3 (1981):213–228.

Banfield, Edward C. *The Unheavenly City.* Boston: Little, Brown, 1968.

Barrett, Curtis L., and Helen Noble "Mothers' Anxieties Versus the Effects of Long Distance Move on Children." *Journal of Marriage and the Family* 35 (May 1973):181–188.

Barsby, Steve L., and Dennis R. Cox *Interstate Migration of the Elderly.* Lexington, MA: Heath, 1975.

Bartel, Ann P. "The Migration Decision: What Role Does Job Mobility Play?" *American Economic Review* 69 (December 1979):775–786.

Barth, Michael C. "Migration and Income Maintenance." *President's Commission on Income Maintenance Programs,* Technical Papers, Washington, DC: U.S. Government Printing Office, 1970, pp. 187–206.

Bartlett, Robin L.; William L. Henderson; Timothy I. Miller; and Charles Poulton-Callahan "Migration and the Distribution of Earnings in the South." *Growth and Change* 13 (April 1982):40–46.

Bass, Bernard M., and Ralph A. Alexander "Climate, Economy, and the Differential Migration of White and Nonwhite Workers." *Journal of Applied Psychology* 56, no. 6 (1972):518–521.

Beale, Calvin L. "Rural Depopulation in the United States: Some Demographic Consequences of Agricultural Adjustments." *Demography* 1, no. 1 (1964):264–272.

⸺ *The Revival of Population Growth in Nonmetropolitan America.* Economic Research Service, ERS-605. Washington, DC: U.S. Department of Agriculture, 1975.

⸺ "The Recent Shift of United States Population to Nonmetropolitan Areas, 1970–75." *International Regional Science Review* 2 (Winter 1977):113–122.

⸺ "Poughkeepsie's Complaint, or Defining Metropolitan Areas." *American Demographics* 6 (January 1984):29–31 and 46–48.

⸺, **and Glen V. Fuguitt** "The New Pattern of Nonmetropolitan Population Change." In Karl E. Taeuber, Larry L. Bumpass, and James A. Sweet, eds., *Social Demography.* New York: Academic Press, 1978, pp. 158–177.

Beguin, Hubert "The Effect of Urban Spatial Structure on Residential Mobility." *Annals of Regional Science* 16 (November 1982):16–35.

Behr, Michelle, and Patricia Gober "When a Residence Is Not a House: Examining Residence-Based Migration Definitions." *Professional Geographer* 34, no. 2 (1982):178–184.

Bellante, Don "The North-South Differential and the Migration of Heterogeneous Labor." *American Economic Review* 69 (March 1979):166–175.

Bible, Douglas S., and Lawrence A. Brown "A Spatial View of Intra-Urban Migration Search Behavior." *Socio-Economic Planning Science* 14 (1980):19–23.

Biggar, Jeanne C. *The Graying of the Sunbelt: A Look at the Impact of U.S. Elderly Migration.* Washington, DC: Population Reference Bureau, 1984.

Bilsborrow, Richard E., and John S. Akin "Data Availability Versus Data Needs for Analyzing the Determinants and Consequences of Internal Migration: An

Evaluation of U.S. Survey Data." *Review of Public Data Use* 10 (December 1982):261–284.

Billsborrow, Richard E., A. S. Oberai, and G. Standing *Migration Surveys in Low-Income Countries.* London: Croom Helm, 1984.

Black, Matthew "Migration of Young Labor Force Entrants." *Socio-Economic Planning Science* 17, no. 5–6 (1983):267–280.

Blackwood, Larry G., and Edwin H. Carpenter "The Importance of Anti-Urbanism in Determining Residential Preferences and Migration Patterns." *Rural Sociology* 43 (Spring 1978):31–47.

Boehm, Thomas P. "Inflation and Intra-Urban Residential Mobility." *Housing Finance Review* 3 (January 1984):19–37.

Bogue, Donald J. *Components of Population Change, 1940–50: Estimates of Net Migration and Natural Increase for Each Standard Metropolitan Statistical Area and State Economic Area.* Oxford, Ohio: Scripps Foundation for Research in Population Problems, Miami University, 1957.

———— **and Calvin L. Beale** *Economic Areas of the United States.* New York: Free Press, 1961.

Bogue, Donald J., and Margaret Jarman Hagood *Differential Migration in the Corn and Cotton Belts: A Pilot Study of the Selectivity of Intrastate Migration to Cities from Nonmetropolitan Areas.* Subregional Migration in the United States, 1935–40, vol. 2. Oxford, Ohio: Miami University, 1953.

Bogue, Donald J.; Henry S. Shryock, Jr.; and Siegfried A. Hoermann *Streams of Migration between Subregions: A Pilot Study of Migration Flows between Environments.* Subregional Migration in the United States, 1935–40, vol. 1. Oxford, Ohio: Miami University, 1957.

Bouvier, Leon F., and Edward E. Cahill "Demographic Factors Affecting the Educational Level of the South Atlantic States." *Review of Regional Studies* 5 (Fall 1975):70–83.

Bouvier, Leon F.; John J. Macisco; and Alvan Zarate "Toward A Framework for the Analysis of Differential Migration: The Case of Education." In Anthony H. Richmond and Daniel Kubat, eds. *Internal Migration: The New World and the Third World.* Beverly Hills, CA: Sage, 1976, pp. 24–36.

Bowles, Gladys K. "Contributions of Recent Metro/Nonmetro Migrants to the Nonmetro Population and Labor Force." *Agricultural Economics Research* 30 (October 1978):15–21.

————; **A. Lloyd Bacon; P. Neal Ritchey** *Poverty Dimensions of Rural-to-Urban Migration: A Statistical Report.* Department of Agriculture, Economic Research Service Statistical Bulletin no. 511. Washington, DC: U.S. Government Printing Office, 1973.

Bowles, Gladys K., and Calvin L. Beale "Commuting and Migration Status in Nonmetro Areas." *Agricultural Economics Research* 32 (July 1980):8–20.

————; **and Everett S. Lee** *Net Migration of the Population, 1960–70, by Age, Sex, and Color*, pts. 1–7. Athens: University of Georgia, 1975.

Bowles, Gladys K., and James D. Tarver *Net Migration of the Population, 1950–60, by Age, Sex, and Color*, vols. 1 and 2. Washington, DC: U.S. Government Printing Office, 1965.

Bowman, Mary Jean, and Robert G. Myers "Schooling, Experience, and Gains and Losses in Human Capital Through Migration." *Journal of the American Statistical Association* 62 (September 1967):875–898.

Brett, Jeanne M. "The Effect of Job Transfer on Employees and Their Families."

In C. L. Cooper and R. Payne, eds. *Current Concerns in Occupational Stress.* Chichester, England: Wiley, 1980, pp. 99–136.

—— "Job Transfer and Well-Being." *Journal of Applied Psychology* 67 (August 1982):450–463.

Brown, Alan A., and Egon Neuberger, eds. *Internal Migration: A Comparative Perspective.* New York: Academic Press, 1977.

Brown, David L. "Spatial Analysis of Post-1970 Work Force Migration in the United States." *Growth and Change* 12 (January 1981):9–20.

——, **and John M. Wardwell, eds.** *New Directions in Urban-Rural Migration: The Population Turnaround in Rural America.* New York: Academic Press, 1980.

Brown, H. James "Changes in Workplace and Residence Locations." *Journal of the American Institute of Planners* 41 (January 1975):32–39.

Brown, J. M. "The Structure of Motives for Moving: A Multidimensional Model of Residential Mobility." *Environment and Planning A* 15 (November 1983):1531–1544.

Brown, Lawrence A., and John Holmes "Intra-Urban Migrant Lifelines: A Spatial View." *Demography* 8 (February 1971):103–122.

Brown, Lawrence A.; Frank E. Horton; and Robert I. Wittick "Place Utility and the Normative Allocation of Intra-Urban Migrants." *Demography* 7 (May 1970):175–183.

Brown, Lawrence A., and David B. Longbrake "Migration Flows in Intra-Urban Space: Place Utility Considerations." *Annals of the Association of American Geographers* 60 (June 1970):368–384.

Brown, Lawrence A., and Eric G. Moore "The Intra-Urban Migration Process: A Perspective." *Geografiska Annaler* 52 (1970):1–13.

Browning, Harley L. "Migrant Selectivity and the Growth of Large Cities in Developing Societies." In National Academy of Sciences, *Rapid Population Growth: Consequences and Policy Implications.* Baltimore: Johns Hopkins University Press, 1971, pp. 273–314.

Brummel, Arden C. "A Model of Intraurban Mobility." *Economic Geography* 55 (October 1979):338–352.

—— "A Method of Measuring Residential Stress." *Geographical Analysis* 13 (July 1981):248–261.

Butler, E. W.; F. S. Chapin; G. C. Hemmens; E. J. Kaiser; M. A. Stegman; and S. F. Weiss *Moving Behavior and Residential Choice: A National Survey.* Washington, DC: Highway Research Board, 1969.

Butler, Edgar W., and Edward J. Kaiser "Prediction of Residential Movement and Spatial Allocation." *Urban Affairs Quarterly* 6 (June 1971):477–494.

Butler, Edgar W.; Ronald J. McAllister; and Edward J. Kaiser "The Effects of Voluntary and Involuntary Residential Mobility on Females and Males." *Journal of Marriage and the Family* 35 (May 1973):219–227.

Cadwallader, M. T. "Neighborhood Evaluation in Residential Mobility." *Environment and Planning A* 11 (April 1979):393–401.

—— "Structural-Equation Models of Migration: An Example from the Upper Midwest U.S.A." *Environment and Planning A* 17 (1985):101–113.

Cahill, Edward E. "Holding Power of the South." *Growth and Change* 7 (July 1976):39–42.

——, **and Urmil Saluja** "De-Population and Re-Population: A Demographic Analysis of Turn-Around Counties of the South." *Review of Regional Studies* 5 (Winter 1975):1–13.

Cahill, Edward E., and Leon F. Bouvier "The Effects of Migration on Educational Attainment in New England." *New England Journal of Business and Economics* 1 (Fall 1974):18–25.

Campbell, Rex R., and Lorraine Garkovich "Turnaround Migration as an Episode of Collective Behavior." *Rural Sociology* 49 (Spring 1984):89–105.

Campbell, Rex R., and Daniel M. Johnson "Propositions on Counterstream Migration." *Rural Sociology* 41 (Spring 1976):127–145.

_____; **and Gary Stangler** "Return Migration of Black People to the South." *Rural Sociology* 39 (Winter 1974):514–528.

_____ "Counterstream Migration of Black People to the South." *Review of Public Data Use* 3 (January 1975):13–21.

Caplow, Theodore "Incidence and Direction of Residential Mobility in a Minneapolis Sample." *Social Forces* 27 (May 1949):413–421.

Carpenter, Edwin H. "The Potential for Population Dispersal: A Closer Look at Residential Locational Preferences." *Rural Sociology* 42 (Fall 1977):352–370.

Castro, Luis J., and Andrei Rogers "Patterns of Family Migration: Two Methodological Approaches." *Environment and Planning A* 15 (February 1983):237–254.

_____ "What the Age Composition of Migrants Can Tell Us." *Population Bulletin of the United Nations*, no. 15 (1983):63–79.

Cebula, Richard J. "Interstate Migration and the Tiebout Hypothesis: An Analysis According to Race, Sex, and Age." *Journal of the American Statistical Association* 69 (December 1974):876–879.

_____ "Local Government Policies and Migration: An Analysis for SMSA's in the United States." *Public Choice* 19 (Fall 1974):85–93.

_____ "The Quality of Life and Migration of the Elderly." *Review of Regional Studies* 4 (Spring 1974):62–68.

_____ "Migration, Economic Opportunity, and the Quality of Life." *Annals of Regional Science* 9 (March 1975):127–133.

_____ "On the Impact of State and Local Government Policies on Human Migration: A Log-Linear Analysis." *Review of Regional Studies* 5 (Winter 1975):61–67.

_____ "Public Welfare and Nonwhite Migration: A Note." *Review of Business and Economic Research* 11 (Fall 1975):97–101.

_____ "A Note on Nonwhite Migration, Welfare Levels, and the Political Process." *Public Choice* 28 (Winter 1976):117–119.

_____ "An Analysis of Migration Patterns and Local Government Policy Toward Public Education in the United States." *Public Choice* 32 (Winter 1977):113–121.

_____ *The Determinants of Human Migration.* Lexington, MA: Lexington Books, 1979.

_____ "Geographic Mobility and the Cost of Living: An Explanatory Note." *Urban Studies* 17 (October 1980):353–355.

_____ "The Cost of Living, Labor Market Opportunities, and the Migration Decision: A Case of Misspecification?" *Annals of Regional Science* 15 (November 1981):73–79

_____ " 'Money Illusion' and Migration Decisions: An International Comparison of the United States and Canadian Experiences." *Regional Studies* 15, no. 4 (1981):241–246.

_____ "The Tiebout Hypothesis of Voting with One's Feet: A Look at the Most Recent Evidence." *Review of Regional Studies* 11 (Winter 1981):47–50.

—— "Real Earnings and Human Migration in the United States." *International Migration Review* 16 (Spring 1982):189–196.

——, and **Glenn Blomquist** "Government Policy and Migration: An Empirical Extension." *Review of Regional Studies* 6 (Winter 1976):70–75.

Cebula, Richard J., and Christopher Curran "Property Taxation and Human Migration." *American Journal of Economics and Sociology* 37 (January 1978):43–49.

Cebula, Richard J., and Margaret N. Davis "A Note on the Determinants of Inter-Metropolitan Migration." *Review of Regional Studies* 8 (Fall 1978):48–51.

Cebula, Richard J., and Robert M. Kohn "Public Policies and Migration Patterns in the United States." *Public Finance* 30, no. 2 (1975):186–196.

Cebula, Richard J.; Robert M. Kohn; and Richard C. Vedder "Some Determinants of Interstate Migration of Blacks, 1965–1970." *Western Economic Journal* 11 (December 1973):500–505.

Cebula, Richard J., and Richard K. Vedder "A Note on Migration, Economic Opportunity, and the Quality of Life." *Journal of Regional Science* 13 (August 1973):205–211.

—— "An Empirical Analysis of Income Expectations and Interstate Migration." *Review of Regional Studies* 5 (Spring 1975):19–28.

Chalmers, James A., and Michael J. Greenwood "The Regional Labor Market Adjustment Process: Determinants of Changes in Rates of Labor Force Participation, Unemployment, and Migration." *Annals of Regional Science* (March 1985):1–17.

Chevan, Albert "Family Growth, Household Density, and Moving." *Demography* 8 (November 1971):451–458.

——, and **Lucy Rose Fischer** "Retirement and Interstate Migration." *Social Forces* 57 (June 1979):1365–1380.

Chilton, R., and R. W. Poet "An Entropy Maximizing Approach to the Recovery of Detailed Migration Patterns from Aggregate Census Data." *Environment and Planning A* 5, no. 1 (1973):135–146.

Christenson, James A. "Value Orientations of Potential Migrants and Nonmigrants." *Rural Sociology* 44 (Summer 1979):331–344.

——; **Lorraine E. Garkovich; and Gregory S. Taylor** "Proruralism Values and Migration Behavior." *Population and Environment* 6 (Fall 1983):166–178.

Clark, Gordon L. "Dynamics of Labor Migration." *Annals of the Association of American Geographers* 72 (September 1982):297–313.

—— "Volatility in the Geographical Structure of Short-Run U.S. Interstate Migration." *Environment and Planning A* 14 (February 1982):147–167.

—— *Interregional Migration, National Policy, and Social Justice.* Totowa, NJ: Rowman & Allanheld, 1983.

——, and **Kenneth P. Ballard** "The Demand and Supply of Labor and Interstate Relative Wages: An Empirical Analysis." *Economic Geography* 56 (October 1980):95–112.

—— "Modeling Out-Migration from Depressed Regions: The Significance of Origin and Destination Characteristics." *Environment and Planning A* 12 (July 1980):799–812.

Clark, Gordon L., and J. Whiteman "Why Poor People Do Not Move: Job Search Behavior and Disequilibrium amongst Local Markets." *Environment and Planning A* 15 (June 1983):85–104.

Clark, W. A. V. "Measurement and Explanation in Intra-Urban Residential Mobility." *Tijdschrift voor Economische en Sociale Geografie* 61 (January–February 1970):49–57.

——— "Migration in Milwaukee." *Economic Geography* 52 (January 1976):48–60.

——— "Residential Mobility and Neighborhood Change: Some Implications for Racial Residential Segregation." *Urban Geography* 1 (April–June 1980):95–117.

——— "Recent Research on Migration and Mobility: A Review and Interpretation." *Progress in Planning* 18, pt. 1 (1982):1–56.

——— *Human Migration.* Scientific Geography Series, vol. 7. Beverly Hills, CA: Sage, 1986.

———, **and Martin Cadwallader** "Locational Stress and Residential Mobility." *Environment and Behavior* 5 (March 1973):29–41.

——— "Residential Preferences: An Alternate View of Intraurban Space." *Environment and Planning* 5 (November–December 1973):693–703.

Clark, W. A. V.; M. C. Deurloo; and F. M. Dieleman "Housing Consumption and Residential Mobility." *Annals of the Association of American Geographers* 74 (March 1984):29–43.

Clark, W. A. V., and J. O. Huff "Some Empirical Tests of Duration-of-Stay Effects in Intraurban Migration." *Environment and Planning A* 9 (December 1977):1357–1374.

——— "Sources of Spatial Variation in Residential Mobility Rates." *Urban Geography* 1 (July–September 1980):202–214.

———; **and J. E. Burt** "Calibrating a Model of the Decision to Move." *Environment and Planning A* 11 (June 1979):689–704.

Clark, W. A. V., and Eric G. Moore, eds. *Residential Mobility and Public Policy.* Beverly Hills, CA: Sage, 1980.

——— "Residential Mobility and Public Programs: Current Gaps between Theory and Practice." *Journal of Social Issues* 38, no. 3 (1982):35–50.

Clark, W. A. V., and June L. Onaka "Life Cycle and Housing Adjustment as Explanations of Residential Mobility." *Urban Studies* 20 (February 1983):47–57.

——— "An Empirical Test of a Joint Model of Residential Mobility and Housing Choice." *Environment and Planning A* 17 (July 1985):915–930.

Clark, W. A. V., and T. R. Smith "Housing Market Search Behavior and Expected Utility Theory: 2. The Process of Search." *Environment and Planning A* 14 (June 1982):717–737.

Clayton, Christopher "Interstate Population Migration Process and Structure in the United States, 1935 to 1970." *Professional Geographer* 29 (May 1977):177–181.

——— "The Structure of Interstate and Interregional Migration: 1965–1970." *Annals of Regional Science* 11 (March 1977):109–122.

Cloward, Richard A., and Frances Fox Piven "Migration, Politics, and Welfare." *Saturday Review*, November 16, 1968, pp. 31–35.

Coelen, Stephen P. "Structural Change in Models of Migration: Omission of Psychic Income." *Review of Regional Studies* 7 (Spring 1977):81–86.

Committee on National Urban Policy, National Research Council *Rethinking Urban Policy.* Washington, DC: National Academy of Sciences Press, 1983.

Congdon, Peter "A Model for the Interaction of Migration and Commuting." *Urban Studies* 20 (May 1983):185–195.

Cook, Annabel Kirschner, and John M. Wardwell "Population Policies and Public Opinion." *Social Science Quarterly* 58 (March 1978):683–691.

Courgeau, Daniel "Migrations et découpages du territoire." *Population* 28 (May–June 1973):511–536.

—— "Migrants et migrations." *Population* 28 (January–February 1973):95–128.

—— "L'Intensité de changements de categorie de commune." *Population* 30 (January–February 1975):81–97.

—— "Quantitative, Demographic, and Geographic Approaches to Internal Migration." *Environment and Planning A* 8 (May 1976):261–269.

—— *Analyse quantitative des migrations humaines.* Paris: Masson, 1980.

—— "Comparaison des migrations internes en France et aux États-Unis." *Population* 37 (November–December 1982):1184–1188.

—— "Premiers migrants, migrants secondaires et retours (France 1968–1975)." *Population* 37 (November–December 1982):1189–1193.

—— "Baisse de le mobilité résidentielle." *Population et Sociétés,* no. 179. Paris: Institut National d'Études Démographiques, 1984.

—— "Relations entre cycle de vie et migrations." *Population* 39 (May–June 1984):483–514.

Cronin, Francis J. "The Efficiency of Housing Search." *Southern Economic Journal* 48 (April 1982):1016–1030.

Crowley, Ronald W. "An Empirical Investigation of Some Local Public Costs of In-Migration to Cities." *Journal of Human Resources* 5 (Winter 1970):11–23.

Cutright, Phillips "Region, Migration, and the Earnings of Black and White Men." *Social Forces* 53 (December 1974):297–305.

DaVanzo, Julie "Differences between Return and Non-Return Migration: An Econometric Analysis." *International Migration Review* 10 (Spring 1976):13–27.

—— *Why Families Move: A Model of the Geographic Mobility of Married Couples.* Washington, DC: U.S. Department of Labor, 1977.

—— "New, Repeat, and Return Migration: Comment." *Southern Economic Journal* 44 (January 1978):680–684.

—— "Does Unemployment Affect Migration?—The Evidence from Microdata." *Review of Economics and Statistics* 60 (November 1978):504–514.

—— "Microeconomic Approaches to Studying Migration Decisions. In Gordon F. DeJong and Robert W. Gardner, eds. *Migration Decision Making: Multidisciplinary Approaches to Microlevel Studies in Developed and Developing Countries.* New York: Pergamon Press, 1981, pp. 90–129.

—— "Repeat Migration, Information Costs, and Location-Specific Capital." *Population and Environment* 4 (Spring 1981):45–73.

—— "Repeat Migration in the United States: Who Moves Back and Who Moves On?" *Review of Economics and Statistics* 65, no. 4 (1983):552–559.

——, **and Peter A. Morrison** "Return and Other Sequences of Migration in the United States." *Demography* 18 (February 1981):85–101.

Darroch, A. Gordon "Migrants in the Nineteenth Century: Fugitives or Families in Motion?" *Journal of Family History* 6 (Fall 1981):257–277.

DeJong, Gordon F. "Residential Preferences and Migration." *Demography* 14 (May 1977):169–178.

——, **and Zafar M. N. Ahmad** "Motivation for Migration of Welfare Clients." In Anthony H. Richmond and Daniel Kubat, eds. *Internal Migration: The New World and the Third World.* Beverly Hills, CA: Sage, 1976, pp. 266–282.

DeJong, Gordon F., and William L. Donnelly "Public Welfare and Migration." *Social Science Quarterly* 54 (September 1973):329–344.

DeJong, Gordon F., and Robert W. Gardner, eds. *Migration Decision Making.* New York: Pergamon Press, 1981.

DeJong, Gordon F., and Craig R. Humphrey "Selected Characteristics of Metropolitan-to-Nonmetropolitan Area Migrants: A Study of Population Redistribution in Pennsylvania." *Rural Sociology* 41 (Winter 1976):526–538.

DeJong, Gordon F., and Ralph R. Sell "Population Redistribution, Migration, and Residential Preferences." *Annals of the American Academy of Political and Social Sciences* 429 (January 1977):130–144.

Deaton, Brady J., and Kurt R. Anschel "Migration and Return Migration: A New Look at the Eastern Kentucky Migration Stream." *Southern Journal Of Agricultural Economics* 6 (July 1974):185–191.

Deaton, Brady J.; Larry C. Morgan; and Kurt R. Anschel "The Influence of Psychic Costs on Rural-Urban Migration." *American Journal of Agricultural Economics* 64 (May 1982):177–187.

Denslow, David A., Jr., and Peter J. Eaton "Migration and Intervening Opportunities." *Southern Economic Journal* 51 (October 1984):369–387.

Department of Statistics *Internal Migration.* New Zealand Census of Population and Dwellings: 1981, vol. 2. Wellington: 1984.

Devis, Tim "People Changing Address: 1971 and 1981." *Population Trends* 32 (Summer 1983):15–20.

Doling, J. "The Family Life Cycle and Housing Choice." *Urban Studies* 13 (February 1976):55–58.

Dorkoosh, Saeed Abedin "Destination Choice of Interstate Family Migrants to Selected Areas in California." *Annals of Regional Science* 16 (March 1982):57–74.

Downie, N. M. "A Comparison between Children Who Have Moved from School to School with Those Who Have Been in Continuous Residence of Various Factors on Adjustment." *Journal of Educational Psychology* 44 (January 1953):50–53.

Droettboom, Theodore; Ronald J. McAllister; Edward J. Kaiser; and Edgar W. Butler "Urban Violence and Residential Mobility." *Journal of the American Institute of Planners* 37 (September 1971):319–325.

Duncan, Greg J., and Sandra J. Newman "People as Planners: The Fulfillment of Residential Mobility Expectations." In Greg J. Duncan and James N. Morgan, eds. *Five Thousand American Families—Patterns of Economic Progress*, vol. 3. Ann Arbor: Institute for Social Research, University of Michigan, 1975, pp. 279–318.

———— "Expected and Actual Residential Mobility." *Journal of the American Institute of Planners* 42 (April 1976):174–186.

Duncan, R. Paul, and Carolyn Cummings Perucci "Dual Occupation Families and Migration." *American Sociological Review* 41 (April 1976):252–61.

Dunlevy, James A., and Don Bellante "Net Migration, Endogenous Incomes and the Speed of Adjustment to the North-South Differential." *Review of Economics and Statistics* 65 (February 1983):66–75.

Eagelstein, A. Solomon, and Yitzhak Berman "Long-Term Multivariate Prediction of Migration Patterns." *Social Indicators Research* 15 (1984):281–288.

Eldridge, Hope T. "A Cohort Approach to the Analysis of Migration Differentials." *Demography* 1 (1964):212–219.

———— "Primary, Secondary, and Return Migration in the United States, 1955–60." *Demography* 2 (1965):444–455.

————, **and Dorothy Swaine Thomas** *Demographic Analyses and Interrelations.* Population Redistritubion and Economic Growth, United States 1870–1950, vol. 3. Philadelphia: American Philosophical Society, 1964.

Engles, R. A., and Mary K. Healy "Measuring Interstate Migration Flows: An Origin-Destination Network Based on Internal Revenue Service Records." *Environment and Planning A* 13 (November 1981):1345–1360.

Evenson, James A., and Donald D. Rohdy "The Economic Effect of Age and Education on the Regional Flows of Black Human Capital." *Annals of Regional Science* 10 (November 1976):106–116.

Evers, Gerard H., and Anne van der Veen "A Simultaneous Non-Linear Model for Labour Migration and Commuting." *Regional Studies* 19 (June 1985):217–229.

Falaris, Evangelos M. "Migration and Regional Wages." *Southern Economic Journal* 48 (January 1982):670–686.

Farber, Stephen C. "A Directional Flow Migration Model." *Southern Economic Journal* 45 (July 1978):205–217.

—— "Post-Migration Earnings Profiles: An Application of Human Capital and Job Search Models." *Southern Economic Journal* 49 (January 1983):693–705.

Feder, Gershon "Alternative Opportunities and Migration: An Exposition." *Annals of Regional Science* 13 (November 1979):57–67.

—— "On the Relation between Origin Income and Migration." *Annals of Regional Science* 16 (July 1982):46–61.

Fein, Rashi "Educational Patterns in Southern Migration." *Southern Economic Journal* 32 (July 1965):106–124.

Fellin, Phillip, and Eugene Litwak "Neighborhood Cohesion under Conditions of Mobility." *American Sociological Review* 28 (June 1963):364–376.

Fernandez, Richard R., and Don A. Dillman "The Influence of Community Attachment on Geographic Mobility." *Rural Sociology* 44, no. 2 (1979):345–360.

Ferraro, Kenneth F. "Relocation Desires and Outcomes among the Elderly." *Research on Aging* 3 (June 1981):166–181.

Fields, Gary S. "Labor Force Migration, Unemployment and Job Turnover." *Review of Economics and Statistics* 57 (November 1976):407–415.

—— "Place-to-Place Migration: Some New Evidence." *Review of Economics and Statistics* 61 (February 1979):21–32.

Findley, Sally E. *Migration Survey Methodologies: A Review of Design Issues.* IUSSP Papers no. 20. Liège, Belgium: International Union for the Scientific Study of Population, 1982.

Fliegel, Frederick C.; Andrew J. Sofranko; and Nina Glasgow "Population Growth in Rural Areas and Sentiments of the New Migrants toward Further Growth." *Rural Sociology* 46 (Fall 1981):411–429.

Fligstein, Neil *Going North: Migration of Blacks and Whites from the South, 1900–1950.* New York: Academic Press, 1981.

—— "The Transformation of Southern Agriculture and the Migration of Blacks and Whites, 1930–1950." *International Migration Review* 17, no. 2 (1983):268–290.

Flowerdew, Robin "Search Strategies and Stopping Rules in Residential Mobility." Institute of British Geographers, *Transactions* 1, no. 1 (1976):47–57.

Fredland, Daniel R. *Residential Mobility and Home Purchase.* Lexington, MA: Lexington Books, 1974.

—— "A Model of Residential Change." *Journal of Regional Science* 15 (August 1975):199–208.

Freeman, Linton C., and Morris H. Sunshine "Race and Intra-Urban Migration." *Demography* 13 (November 1976):571–575.

Frey, William H. "Population Movement and City-Suburb Redistribution: An Analytic Framework." *Demography* 15 (November 1978):571–588.

—— "The Changing Impact of White Migration on the Population Composition of Origin and Destination Metropolitan Areas." *Demography* 16 (May 1979):219–237.

—— "Status Selective White Flight and Central City Population Change: A Comparative Analysis." *Journal of Regional Science* 20, no. 1 (1980):71–89.

—— "A Multiregional Population-Projection Framework That Incorporates Both Migration and Residential Mobility Streams: Application to Metropolitan City-Suburb Redistribution." *Environment and Planning A* 15 (December 1983):1613–1632.

—— "Lifecourse Migration of Metropolitan Whites and Blacks and the Structure of Demographic Change in Large Central Cities." *American Sociological Review* 49 (December 1984):803–827.

—— "Mover Destination Selectivity and the Changing Suburbanization of Metropolitan Whites and Blacks." *Demography* 22 (May 1985):223–243.

——, **and Frances H. Kobrin** "Changing Families and Changing Mobility: Their Impact on the Central City." *Demography* 19 (August 1982):261–277.

Fried, Marc "Deprivation and Migration: Dilemmas of Causal Interpretation." In Daniel P. Moynihan, ed. *On Understanding Poverty.* New York: Basic Books, 1968, pp. 111–159.

Fuchs, Roland J., and George J. Demko "The Postwar Mobility Transition in Eastern Europe." *Geographical Review* 68 (April 1978):171–182.

Gallaway, Lowell E. "The Effect of Geographic Labor Mobility on Income: A Brief Comment." *Journal of Human Resources* 4 (Winter 1969):103–109.

—— *Geographic Labor Mobility in the United States: 1957 to 1960.* Washington, DC: U.S. Government Printing Office, 1969.

——, **and Richard K. Vedder** "Mobility of Native Americans." *Journal of Economic History* 31 (September 1971):613–649.

Galle, Omer R., and Karl E. Taeuber "Metropolitan Migration and Intervening Opportunities." *American Sociological Review* 31 (February 1966):5–13.

Galle, Omer R., and Max W. Williams "Metropolitan Migration Efficiency." *Demography* 9 (November 1972):655–64.

Gallup Poll *Gallup Opinion Index*, no. 116, February 1975.

—— *Gallup Report*, no. 188, May 1981.

Garnick, Daniel H. "Shifting Patterns in the Growth of Metropolitan and Nonmetropolitan Areas." *Survey of Current Business* (May 1983):39–44.

—— "Shifting Balances in U.S. Metropolitan and Nonmetropolitan Area Growth." *International Regional Science Review* 9 (December 1984):257–273.

Gibson, John G. "The Intervening Opportunities Model of Migration: A Critique." *Socio-Economic Planning Sciences* 9 (1975):205–208.

Giles, Michael W.; Douglas S. Gatlin; and Everett F. Cataldo "The Impact of Busing on White Flight." *Social Science Quarterly* 55 (September 1974):493–501.

Ginsberg, Yoana, and Arza Churchman "Housing Satisfaction and Intention to Move: Their Explanatory Variables." *Socio-Economic Planning Science* 18, no. 6 (1984):425–431.

Glantz, Frederick B. "Migration and Economic Opportunity: The Case of the Poor." *New England Economic Review* (March–April 1973):14–19.

—— "The Determinants of the Intermetropolitan Migration of the Poor." *Annals of Regional Science* 9 (July 1975):25–39.

Gober-Meyers, Patricia "Interstate Migration and Economic Growth." *Environment and Planning A* 10 (November 1978):1241–1252.

—— "Migration Analysis: The Role of Geographic Scale." *Annals of Regional Science* 12 (November 1978):52–61.

Golant, Stephen M. "The Housing Tenure Adjustments of the Young and the Elderly: Policy Implications." *Urban Affairs Quarterly* 13 (September 1977):95–108.

——; **Gundars Rudzitis; and Sol Daiches** "Migration of the Elderly from U.S. Central Cities." *Growth and Change* 9 (October 1978):30–35.

Goldhaber, Marilyn K.; Peter S. Houts; and Renee DiSabella "Moving after the Crisis: A Prospective Study of Three Mile Island Area Population Mobility." *Environment and Behavior* 15 (January 1983):93–120.

Goldstein, Sidney "Repeated Migration as a Factor in High Mobility Rates." *American Sociological Review* 19 (October 1954):536–541.

—— "Migration and Occupational Mobility in Norristown, Pennsylvania." *American Sociological Review* 20 (August 1955):72–76.

—— *Patterns of Mobility, 1910–1950: A Method for Measuring Migration and Occupational Mobility in the Community.* Philadelphia: University of Pennsylvania Press, 1958.

—— "The Extent of Repeated Migration: An Analysis Based on the Danish Population Register." *Journal of the American Statistical Association* 59 (December 1964):1121–1132.

—— "Facets of Redistribution: Research Challenges and Opportunities." *Demography* 13 (November 1976):423–434.

——, **and Alice Goldstein** *Surveys of Migration in Developing Countries: A Methodological Review.* Honolulu: East-West Population Institute, 1981.

Goldstein, Sidney, and Kurt Mayer "Migration and the Journey to Work." *Social Forces* 42 (May 1964):472–481.

—— "Migration and Social Status Differentials in the Journey to Work." *Rural Sociology* 29 (September 1964):278–287.

—— "The Impact of Migration on the Socio-Economic Structure of Cities and Suburbs." *Sociology and Social Research* 50 (October 1965):5–23.

Golledge, Reginald G. "A Behavioral View of Mobility and Migration Research." *Professional Geographer* 32 (February 1980):14–21.

Goodman John L. "Local Residential Mobility and Family Housing Adjustments." In James N. Morgan, ed. *Five Thousand American Families—Patterns of Economic Progress,* vol. 2. Ann Arbor: Institute for Social Research, University of Michigan, 1974, pp. 79–105.

—— "Housing Consumption Disequilibrium and Local Residential Mobility." *Environment and Planning A* (December 1976):855–874.

—— "Reasons for Moves Out of and Into Large Cities." *Journal of the American Planning Association* 45 (October 1979):407–416.

—— "Linking Local Mobility Rates to Migration Rates: Repeat Movers and Place Effects." In W. A. V. Clark, ed. *Modelling Housing Market Search.* New York: St. Martin's Press, 1982, pp. 209–223.

——, **and Mary L. Streitwieser** "Explaining Racial Differences: A Study of City-to-Suburb Residential Mobility." *Urban Affairs Quarterly* 18 (March 1983):301–325.

Goodrich, Carter *Migration and Economic Opportunity.* Philadelphia: University of Pennsylvania Press, 1936.

Gordon, Ian "The Analysis of Motivation-Specific Migration Streams." *Environment and Planning A* 14 (January 1982):5–20.

_____, and Roger Vickerman "Opportunity, Preference and Constraint: An Approach to the Analysis of Metropolitan Migration." *Urban Studies* 19 (August 1982):247–261.

Gordon, Suzanne *Lonely in America*. New York: Simon & Schuster, 1975.

Goss, Ernst P., and Niles C. Schoening "Search Time, Unemployment, and the Migration Decision." *Journal of Human Resources* 19, no. 4 (1984):570–579.

Gramlich, Edward M., and Deborah S. Laren "Migration and Income Redistribution Responsibilities." *Journal of Human Resources* 19, no. 4 (1984):489–511.

Grant, E. Kenneth, and John Vanderkamp "The Effects of Migration on Income: A Micro Study with Canadian Data 1965–71." *Canadian Journal of Economics* 13, no. 3 (1980):371–406.

Graves, Philip E. "A Reexamination of Migration, Economic Opportunity, and the Quality of Life." *Journal of Regional Science* 16 (April 1976):107–112.

_____ "Income and Migration Revisited." *Journal of Human Resources* 14 (Winter 1979):112–121.

_____ "A Life-Cycle Empirical Analysis of Migration and Climate, by Race." *Journal of Urban Economics* 6 (April 1979):135–147.

_____ "Migration with a Composite Amenity: The Role of Rents." *Journal of Regional Science* 23, no. 4 (1983):541–546.

_____, and Peter D. Linneman "Household Migration: Theoretical and Empirical Results." *Journal of Urban Economics* 6 (July 1979):383–404.

Graves, Philip E.; Robert L. Sexton; and Thomas A. Knapp "A Multi-Disciplinary Interpretation of Migration: Amenity Capitalization in Both Land and Labor Markets." *Annals of Regional Science* 18 (July 1984):35–44.

Greenberg, Michael R., and Thomas D. Boswell "Neighborhood Deterioration as a Factor in Intraurban Migration: A Case Study in New York City." *Professional Geographer* 24 (February 1972):11–16.

Greenwood, Michael J. "Urban Economic Growth and Migration: Their Interaction." *Environment and Planning A* 5 (1973):92–112.

_____ "Research on Internal Migration in the United States: A Survey." *Journal of Economic Literature* 13 (June 1975):397–433.

_____ "Simultaneity Bias in Migration Models: An Empirical Examination." *Demography* 12 (August 1975):519–536.

_____ "A Simultaneous-Equations Model of Urban Growth and Migration." *Journal of the American Statistical Association* 70 (December 1975):797–810.

_____ "A Simultaneous-Equations Model of White and Nonwhite Migration and Urban Change." *Economic Inquiry* 14 (March 1976):1–15.

_____ *Migration and Economic Growth in the United States*. New York: Academic Press, 1981.

_____ "Human Migration: Theory, Models, and Empirical Studies." *Journal of Regional Science* 25, no. 4 (1985):521–544.

_____, and Patrick J. Gormely "A Comparison of the Determinants of White and Nonwhite Interstate Migration." *Demography* 8 (February 1971):141–155.

Greenwood, Michael J., and Gary L. Hunt "Migration and Interregional Employment Redistribution in the United States." *American Economic Review* 17 (December 1984):957–969.

Greenwood, Michael J., and Douglas Sweetland "The Determinants of Migration between Standard Metropolitan Statistical Areas." *Demography* 9 (November 1972):665–681.

Greer-Wooten, Bryn, and G. M. Gilmour "Distance and Directional Bias in Migration Patterns in Depreciating Metropolitan Areas." *Geographical Analysis* 14 (1972):92–97.

Grigg, D. B. "E. G. Ravenstein and the 'Laws of Migration.' " *Journal of Historical Geography* 3 (January 1977):41–54.

Grundy, E. M. D., and A. J. Fox "Migration During Early Married Life." *European Journal of Population* 1 (July 1985):237–263.

Gustavus, Susan O., and L. A. Brown "Place Attributes in a Migration Decision Context." *Environment and Planning A* 9 (May 1977):529–548.

Haenszel, William "Concept, Measurement, and Data in Migration Analysis." *Demography* 4, no. 1 (1967):253–261.

Hagerstrand, Torsten "Geographic Measurements of Migration: Swedish Data." In Jean Sutter, ed. *Human Displacements.* Paris: Hachette, 1962, pp. 61–83.

Hajj, Hatim "Internal Migration Models and Population Forecasts." Proceedings of the American Society of Civil Engineers, *Journal of the Urban Planning and Development Division* 101 (November 1975):201–215.

Hamilton, C. Horace "Population Pressure and Other Factors Affecting Net Rural-Urban Migration." In Joseph S. Spengler and Otis Dudley Duncan, eds. *Demographic Analysis: Selected Readings.* Glencoe, IL: Free Press, 1956, 419–424.

———— "Educational Selectivity of Net Migration from the South." *Social Forces* 38 (October 1959):33–42.

———— "The Negro Leaves the South." *Demography* 1 (1964):273–295.

———— "Continuity and Change in Southern Migration." In John C. McKinney and Edgar T. Thompson, eds. *The South in Continuity and Change.* Durham, NC: Duke University Press, 1965, pp. 53–78.

———— "Practical and Mathematical Considerations in the Formulation and Selection of Migration Rates." *Demography* 2 (1965):429–443.

Hansen, Niles M. "Migration Centers, Growth Centers and the Regional Commissions: An Analysis of Expected Future Lifetime Income Gains to Migrants from Lagging Regions." *Southern Economic Journal* 37 (April 1972):508–517.

———— "Does the South Have a Stake in Northern Urban Poverty?" *Southern Economic Journal* 45 (April 1979):1220–1224.

Hanushek, Eric A., and John M. Quigley "An Explicit Model of Intra-Metropolitan Mobility." *Land Economics* 54 (November 1978):411–429.

Harris, Richard J. "The Rewards of Migration for Income Change and Income Attainment: 1968–73." *Social Science Quarterly* 62 (June 1981):275–293.

Harris, Richard S., and Eric G. Moore "An Historical Approach to Mobility Research." *Professional Geographer* 32 (February 1980):22–29.

Hart, R. A. "Interregional Economic Migration: Some Theoretical Considerations (Part I)." *Journal of Regional Science* 15 (August 1975):127–138.

———— "Interregional Economic Migration: Some Theoretical Considerations (Part II)." *Journal of Regional Science* 15 (December 1975):289–305.

Haurin, Donald R. "The Regional Distribution of Population, Migration, and Climate." *Quarterly Journal of Economics* 95 (September 1980):293–308.

Hawley, Amos *Human Ecology: A Theory of Community Structure.* New York: Ronald Press, 1950.

———— *Urban Society: An Ecological Approach.* New York: Ronald Press, 1971.

Haynes, Kingsley E.; Dudley L. Poston, Jr.; and Paul Schnirring "Intermetropolitan Migration in High and Low Opportunity Areas: Indirect Tests of the Distance and Intervening Opportunities Hypotheses." *Economic Geography* 49 (January 1973):68–73.

Heaton, Tim B.; William B. Clifford; and Glenn V. Fuguitt "Temporal Shifts in the Determinants of Young and Elderly Migration in Nonmetropolitan Areas." *Social Forces* 60 (September 1981):41–60.

Heaton, Tim B.; Carl Frederickson; Glenn V. Fuguitt; and James J. Zuiches "Residential Preferences, Community Satisfaction, and the Intention to Move." *Demography* 16 (November 1979):565–573.

Herzog, Henry W., Jr., and David J. Bjordstad "Urbanization, Interregional Accessibility, and the Decision to Migrate." *Growth and Change* 13 (July 1982):21–25.

Herzog, Henry W., Jr.; Richard A. Hofler; and Alan M. Schlottmann "Life on the Frontier: Migrant Information, Earnings and Past Mobility." *Review of Economics and Statistics* 67 (August 1985):373–382.

Herzog, Henry W., and Alan M. Schlottmann "Labor Force Migration and Allocative Efficiency in the United States: The Roles of Information and Psychic Costs." *Economic Inquiry* 19 (July 1981):459–475.

———— "Moving Back vs. Moving On: The Concept of Home in the Decision to Remigrate." *Journal of Regional Science* 22, no. 1 (1982):73–82.

———— "Migrant Information, Job Search and the Remigration Decision." *Southern Economic Journal* 50 (July 1983):43–56.

———— "Labor Force Mobility in the United States: Migration, Unemployment, and Remigration." *International Regional Science Review* 9, no. 1 (1984):43–58.

————; and William R. Schriver "Regional Planning and Interstate Construction Worker Migration." *Growth and Change* 14 (April 1983):50–54.

Hill, C. Russell "Migrant-Nonmigrant Earnings Differentials in a Local Labor Market." *Industrial and Labor Relations Review* 28 (April 1975):411–423.

Hitt, Homer "Migration Between the South and Other Regions, 1949 to 1950." *Social Forces* 35 (October 1957):9–16.

Hodge, Ian "Employment Expectations and the Costs of Migration." *Journal of Rural Studies* 1, no. 1 (1985):45–57.

Holtmann, A. G. "Migration to the Suburbs, Human Capital, and City Income Tax Losses: A Case Study." *National Tax Journal* 21 (September 1968):326–331.

Hsieh, Chang-Tseh, and Ben-Chieh Liu "The Pursuance of Better Quality of Life." *American Journal of Economics and Sociology* 42 (October 1983):431–440.

Huff, James O. "Residential Mobility Patterns and Population Redistribution within the City." *Geographical Analysis* 11 (April 1979):134–148.

————, and W. A. V. Clark "Cumulative Stress and Cumulative Inertia: A Behavioral Model of the Decision to Move." *Environment and Planning A* 10 (October 1978):1101–1119.

Humphrey, Craig R.; Ralph R. Sell; John A. Krout; and R. Thomas Gillaspy "Net Migration Turnaround in Pennsylvania Nonmetropolitan Minor Civil Divisions, 1960–70." *Rural Sociology* 42 (Fall 1977):332–351.

Hunt, Gerald J., and Edgar W. Butler "Migration, Participation and Alienation." *Sociology and Social Research* 56 (July 1972):440–452.

Hunt, Janet C., and James B. Kau "Migration and Wage Growth: A Human Capital Approach." *Southern Economic Journal* 51 (January 1985):697–710.

Iden, George "Factors Affecting Earnings of Southern Migrants." *Industrial Relations* 13 (May 1974):177–189.

—— "Alternative Migration Strategies for the Southern Poor." *Review of Regional Studies* 5 (Spring 1975):29–36.

Inoki, Takenori, and Terukazu Suraga "Migration, Age, and Education: A Cross-Sectional Analysis of Geographical Labor Mobility in Japan." *Journal of Regional Science* 21, no. 4 (1981):507–517.

Isserman, Andrew M. "Economic-Demographic Modeling with Endogenously Determined Birth and Migration Rates: Theory and Prospects." *Environment and Planning A* 17 (1985):25–45.

——; **David A. Plane; and David B. McMillan** "Internal Migration in the United States: An Evaluation of Federal Data." *Review of Public Data Use* 10 (1982):285–311.

Isserman, Andrew M.; David A. Plane; Peter A. Rogerson; and Paul M. Beaumont "Forecasting Interstate Migration with Limited Data: A Demographic-Economic Approach." *Journal of the American Statistical Association* 80 (June 1985):277–285.

Izraeli, Oded, and An-Loh Lin "Recent Evidence on the Effect of Real Earnings on Net Migration." *Regional Studies* 18 (April 1984):113–120.

James, Franklin J., and John P. Blair "The Role of Labor Mobility in a National Urban Policy." *Journal of the American Planning Association* 49 (Summer 1983):307–315.

Johnson, Daniel Milo "Community Satisfaction of Black Return Migrants to a Southern Metropolis." *American Journal of Community Psychology* 3 (September 1975):251–259.

——, **and Rex R. Campbell** *Black Migration in America: A Social Demographic History.* Durham, NC: Duke University Press, 1981.

Johnson, Kenneth M., and Ross L. Purdy "Recent Nonmetropolitan Population Change in Fifty-Year Perspective." *Demography* 17 (February 1980):57–70.

Jones, C.; S. Gudjonsson; and J. Parry Lewis "A Two-Stage Model of Tenure Mobility." *Environment and Planning A* 10 (January 1978):81–92.

Jones, Colin "Residential Mobility: An Economic Model." *Scottish Journal of Political Economy* 28 (February 1981):62–75.

Jones, Stella B. "Geographic Mobility as Seen by the Wife and Mother." *Journal of Marriage and the Family* 35 (May 1973):210–218.

Kain, John F., and Joseph J. Persky "The North's Stake in Southern Rural Poverty." *President's National Advisory Commission on Rural Poverty.* Washington, DC: U.S. Government Printing Office, 1968, pp. 288–308.

Kain, John F., and Robert Schaefer "Income Maintenance, Migration, and Regional Growth." *Public Policy* 20 (Spring 1972):199–225.

Kalbach, Warren E.; George C. Myers; and John R. Walker "Metropolitan Area Mobility: A Comparative Analysis of Family Spatial Mobility in a Central City and Selected Suburbs." *Social Forces* 42 (March 1964):310–314.

Kaluzny, Richard L. "Determinants of Household Migration: A Comparative Study by Race and Poverty Level." *Review of Economics and Statistics* 57 (August 1975):269–274.

Kammeyer, Kenneth C. W., and McKee McClendon "Some Tests of, and Comments on, Lee's Theory of Migration." In Kenneth C. W. Kammeyer, ed. *Population Studies: Selected Essays and Research.* Chicago: Rand McNally, 1975, pp. 214–220.

Kantor, Mildred B. *Mobility and Mental Health.* Springfield, IL: Thomas, 1963.

—— "Internal Migration and Mental Illness." In Stanley C. Plog and Robert B. Edgerton, eds. *Changing Perspectives in Mental Illness*. New York: Holt, Rinehart & Winston, 1969, pp. 364–394.

Kasarda, John D. "Urban Change and Minority Opportunities." In Paul E. Peterson, ed. *The New Urban Reality*. Washington, DC: Brookings Institution, 1985, pp. 307–315.

Kasl, Stanislav V., and Ernest Harburg "Perceptions of the Neighborhood and the Desire to Move Out." *Journal of the American Institute of Planners* 38 (September 1972):318–324.

Kau, James B., and C. F. Sirmans "Migration and the Quality of Life." *Review of Regional Studies* 6 (Winter 1976):76–85.

—— "New, Repeat, and Return Migration: A Study of Migrant Types." *Southern Economic Journal* 43 (October 1976):1144–1148.

—— "The Influence of Information Cost and Uncertainty on Migration: A Comparison of Migrant Types." *Journal of Regional Science* 17 (April 1977):89–96.

—— "A Recursive Model of the Spatial Allocation of Migrants." *Journal of Regional Science* 19 (February 1979):47–56.

Kaun, David E. "Negro Migration and Unemployment." *Journal of Human Resources* 5 (Spring 1970):191–207.

Kee, Woo Sik "The Causes of Urban Poverty." *Journal of Human Resources* 4 (Winter 1969):93–99.

Keeley, Michael C. "The Effect of a Negative Income Tax on Migration." *Journal of Human Resources* 15 (Fall 1980):695–706.

Kendig, Hal L. "Housing Careers, Life Cyle and Residential Mobility: Implications for the Housing Market." *Urban Studies* 21 (1984):271–283.

Kennedy, Joseph *Report of the Superintendent of the Census for December 1, 1852*. Washington, DC: Robert Armstrong, Printer, 1853.

Keyes, Ralph *We, the Lonely People*. New York: Harper & Row, 1973.

Kiker, B. F., and Earle C. Traynham "Earnings Differentials among Nonmigrants, Return Migrants, and Nonreturn Migrants." *Growth and Change* 8 (April 1977):2–7.

Kim, Joochul "Factors Affecting Urban-to-Rural Migration." *Growth and Change* 14, no. 3 (1983):38–43.

Kirschenbaum, Alan "Patterns of Migration form Metropolitan to Nonmetropolitan Areas: Changing Ecological Factors Affecting Family Mobility." *Rural Sociology* 36 (September 1971):315–325.

—— "City-Suburban Destination Choices among Migrants to Metropolitan Areas." *Demography* 9 (May 1972):321–335.

——, and Albert I. Goldberg "Organizational Behavior, Career Orientations, and the Propensity to Move among Professionals." *Sociology of Work and Occupations* 3 (August 1976):357–372.

Kleiner, Morris M. "Evidence on Occupational Migration." *Growth and Change* 13 (July 1982):43–48.

—— "Metropolitan Migration and Labor Market Changes by Industry." *Annals of Regional Science* 18 (July 1984):11–24.

——; Robert S. Gray; and Karen Greene "Barriers to Labor Migration: The Case of Occupational Licensing." *Industrial Relations* 21 (Fall 1982):393–391.

Kleiner, Morris M., and William T. McWilliams, Jr. "Analysis of Alternative Labor-Force Population Migration Forecasting Models." *Annals of Regional Science* 11 (July 1977):74–85.

Kleiner, Robert J., and Seymour Parker "Migration and Mental Illness: A New Look." *American Sociological Review* 24 (October 1959):687–690.

———— "Goal Striving and Psychosomatic Symptoms in a Migrant and Non-Migrant Population. In Mildred B. Kantor, ed. *Mobility and Mental Health.* Springfield, IL: Thomas, 1963, pp. 78–85.

———— "Social-Psychological Aspects of Migration and Mental Disorder in a Negro Population." *American Behavioral Scientist* 13 (September–October 1969):104–125.

Kohn, Robert M.; Richard K. Vedder; and Richard J. Cebula "Determinants of Interstate Migration by Race, 1965–70." *Annals of Regional Science* 7 (June 1973):100–112.

Kono, Shigemi 1969. "Evaluation of the Japanese Population Register Data on Internal Migration." In International Union for the Scientific Study of Population, *International Population Conference, London, 1969*, London: IUSSP, 1971, pp. 2766–2775.

Kopf, Edward "Untarnishing the Dream: Mobility, Opportunity, and Order in Modern America." *Journal of Social History* 11 (1977):206–227.

Kosinski, Leszek A. "Education and Internal Migration." In Helmut V. Muhsam, ed. *Education and Population: Mutual Impacts.* Liège, Belgium: Ordina Editions, 1975, pp. 205–232.

Kottis, Athena "Impact of Migration on Housing in Urban Areas." *Annals of Regional Science* 5 (June 1971):117–124.

———— "Mobility and Human Capital Theory: The Education, Age, Race, and Income Characteristics of Migrants." *Annals of Regional Science* 6 (June 1972):41–60.

Kriesberg, Ellis M., and Daniel R. Vining "On the Contribution of Out-Migration to Changes in Net Migration: A Time-Series Confirmation of Beale's Cross-Sectional Results." *Annals of Regonal Science* 12 (November 1978):1–11.

Krumm, Ronald J. "Regional Labor Markets and the Household Migration Decision." *Journal of Regional Science* 23, no. 3 (1983):361–376.

———— "Household Tenure Choice and Migration." *Journal of Urban Economics* 16 (1984):259–271.

Kulldorff, Gunnar *Migration Probabilities.* Lund: C. W. K. Gleerup, 1955.

Kumar, Rishi "More on Nonwhite Migration, Welfare Levels, and the Political Process." *Public Choice* 32 (Winter 1977):151–154.

Kuznets, Simon; Ann Ratner Miller; and Richard A. Easterlin *Analyses of Economic Change.* Population Redistribution and Economic Growth, United States, 1870–1950, vol. 2. Philadelphia: American Philosophical Society, 1960.

Laber, Gene "Human Capital in Southern Migration." *Journal of Human Resources* 8 (Spring 1973):223–241.

Ladinsky, Jack "Geographic Mobility of Professional and Technical Manpower." *Journal of Human Resources* 2 (Fall 1967):475–494.

———— "Occupational Determinants of Geographic Mobility among Professional Workers." *American Sociological Review* 32 (April 1967):257–264.

Laird, William E., and Warren F. Mazek "City-Size Preferences and Migration." *Review of Regional Studies* 4, supplement (1974):18–26.

Land, Kenneth C. "Duration of Residence and Prospective Migration: Further Evidence." *Demography* 6 (May 1969):133–140.

Lansing, John B.; Charles Wade Clifton; and James N. Morgan *New Homes and Poor People: A Study of Chains of Moves.* Ann Arbor: Institute for Social Research, University of Michigan, 1969.

Lansing, John B., and Eva Mueller *The Geographic Mobility of Labor.* Ann Arbor: Institute for Social Research, University of Michigan, 1967.

Larson, David A., and Walton T. Wilford "A Note on Differential Net Migration and the Quality of Life." *Review of Economics and Statistics* 62 (February 1980):157–162.

Lawrence, Sheila M., and Jeffrey K. Smith "Projecting the Net Migration Rate of the School Age Population." *Socio-Economic Planning Sciences* 18, no. 1 (1984):1–14.

Lebergott, Stanley "Migration within the U.S., 1800–1960: Some New Estimates." *Journal of Economic History* 30 (December 1970):839–847.

Lee, Anne S. "Return Migration in the United States." *International Migration Review* 8 (Summer 1974):283–300.

——, **and Gladys K. Bowles** "Contributions of Rural Migrants to the Urban Occupational Structure." *Agricultural Economics Research* 26 (April 1974):25–32.

Lee, Everett S. "Migration and Mental Disease: New York State, 1949–51." In Milbank Memorial Fund, *Selected Studes of Migration Since World War II.* New York: Milbank Memorial Fund, 1958, pp. 141–152.

—— "The Turner Thesis Reexamined." *American Quarterly* 13 (Spring 1961):77–83.

—— "A Theory of Migration." *Demography* 3, no. 1 (1966):47–57.

—— "Migration in Relation to Education, Intellect, and Social Structure." *Population Index* 36 (October–December 1970):437–444.

——, **and Anne S. Lee** "Internal Migration Statistics for the United States." *Journal of the American Statistical Association* 55 (December 1960):664–697.

Lee, Everett S.; Ann Ratner Miller; Carol P. Brainerd; and Richard A. Easterlin *Methodological Considerations and Reference Tables.* Population Redistribution and Economic Growth, United States, 1870–1950, vol. 1. Philadelphia: American Philosophical Society, 1957.

Leslie, Gerald R., and Arthur H. Richardson "Life-Cycle, Career Pattern, and the Decision to Move." *American Sociological Review* 26 (December 1961):894–902.

Levine, Murray "Residential Change and School Adjustment." *Community Mental Health Journal* 2 (Spring 1966):61–69.

Levy, Mildred B., and Walter J. Wadycki "The Influence of Family and Friends on Geographic Labor Mobility: An International Comparison." *Review of Economics and Statistics* 55 (May 1973):198–203.

—— "What Is the Opportunity Cost of Moving? Reconsideration of the Effects of Distance on Migration." *Economic Development and Cultural Change* 22 (January 1974):198–214.

Lewis, G. J. *Human Migration.* New York: St. Martin's Press, 1982.

Lewis, W. Cris "The Role of Age in the Decision to Migrate." *Annals of Regional Science* 11 (November 1977):51–61.

Li, Wen Lang "A Note on Migration and Employment." *Demography* 13 (November 1976):565–570.

——, **and Sheron L. Randolph** "Return Migration and Status Attainment among Southern Blacks." *Rural Sociology* 47, no. 2 (1982):391–402.

Lianos, Theodore P. "The Migration Process and Time Lags." *Journal of Regional Science* 12 (December 1972):425–433.

Lichter, Daniel T. "Household Migration and the Labor Market Position of Married Women." *Social Science Research* 9 (March 1980):83–97.

—— "The Migration of Dual-Worker Families: Does the Wife's Job Matter?" *Social Science Quarterly* 63 (March 1982):48–57.

—— "Socioeconomic Returns to Migration among Married Women." *Social Forces* 62 (December 1983):487–503.

——; **Tim B. Heaton; and Glenn V. Fuguitt** "Trends in the Selectivity of Migration between Metropolitan and Nonmetropolitan Areas: 1955–1975." *Rural Sociology* 44 (Winter 1979):645–666.

Lieberson, Stanley "Generational Differences among Blacks in the North." *American Journal of Sociology* 79 (November 1973):550–565.

—— "A Reconsideration of Income Differences Found between Migrants and Northern-Born Blacks." *American Journal of Sociology* 83 (January 1978):940–966.

——, **and Christy A. Wilkinson** "A Comparison between Northern and Southern Blacks Residing in the North." *Demography* 13 (May 1976):199–224.

Lim, Jung Duk "Cost of Living, Labor Market Opportunities and the Migration Decision: A Case of Misspecification? A Comment." *Annals of Regional Science* 17 (November 1983):83–88.

Linneman, Peter "Migration and Job Change: A Multinomial Logit Approach." *Journal of Urban Economics* 14 (1983):263–279.

Litwak, Eugene "Geographic Mobility and Extended Family Cohesion." *American Sociological Review* 25 (June 1960):385–394.

Liu, Ben-Chieh "Differential Net Migration Rates and the Quality of Life." *Review of Economics and Statistics* 57 (August 1975):329–337.

Lloyd, Robert E. "Temporal Change in Revealed Migration Preferences." *Review of Regional Studies* 6 (Winter 1976):19–28.

Long, John F. "The Effects of College and Military Populations on Models of Interstate Migration." *Socio-Economic Planning Sciences* 17, no. 5–6 (1983):281–290.

Long, Larry H. "The Influence of Number and Ages of Children on Residential Mobility." *Demography* 9 (August 1972):371–382.

—— "Migration Differentials by Education and Occupation: Trends and Variations." *Demography* 10 (May 1973):243–258.

—— "New Estimates of Migration Expectancy in the United States." *Journal of the American Statistical Association* 68 (March 1973):37–43.

—— "Poverty Status and Receipt of Welfare among Migrants and Nonmigrants in Large Cities." *American Sociological Review* 39 (February 1974):46–56.

—— "Women's Labor Force Participation and the Residential Mobility of Families." *Social Forces* 52 (March 1974):342–348.

—— "Does Migration Interfere with Children's Progress in School?" *Sociology of Education* 48 (Summery 1975):369–381.

—— "How the Racial Composition of Cities Changes." *Land Economics* 51 (August 1975):258–267.

—— *Interregional Migration of the Poor: Some Recent Changes.* Washington, DC: U.S. Government Printing Office, 1978.

—— "Back to the Countryside and Back to the City in the Same Decade." In Shirley Bradway Laska and Daphne Spain, eds. *Back to the City: Issues in Neighborhood Renovation.* New York: Pergamon Press, 1980, pp. 61–76.

——, **and Celia G. Boertlein** *The Geographical Mobility of Americans: An International Comparison.* Washington, DC: U.S. Government Printing Office, 1976.

Long, Larry, and Diana DeAre *Migration to Nonmetropolitan Areas: Appraising the Trend and Reasons for Moving.* Washington, DC: U.S. Government Printing Office, 1980.

———. "The Suburbanization of Blacks." *American Demographics* (September 1981):16–21.

———. "Repopulating the Countryside: A 1980 Census Trend." *Science*, September 17, 1982, pp. 1111–1116.

———. "The Slowing of Urbanization in the United States." *Scientific American*, July 1983, pp. 33–41.

Long, Larry, and Paul C. Glick "Family Patterns in Suburban Areas: Recent Trends." In Barry Schwartz, ed. *The Changing Face of the Suburbs.* Chicago: University of Chicago Press, 1976, pp. 39–67.

Long, Larry, and Kristin A. Hansen "Trends in Return Migration to the South." *Demography* 12 (November 1975):601–614.

———. "Interdivisional Primary, Return, and Repeat Migration." *Review of Public Data Use* 5 (March 1977):3–10.

———. "Selectivity of Black Return Migration." *Rural Sociology* 42 (Fall 1977):317–331.

———. "Reasons for Interstate Migration: Jobs, Retirement, Climate, and Other Influences," *Current Population Reports*, series P-23, no. 81. Washington, DC: U.S. Government Printing Office, 1979.

Long, Larry, and Lynne R. Heltman "Migration and Income Differences between Black and White Men in the North." *American Journal of Sociology* 80 (May 1975):1391–1409.

Longino, Charles F. "Going Home: Aged Return Migration in the United States, 1965–1970." *Journal of Gerontology* 34, no. 5 (1979):736–745.

———, **and Jeanne C. Biggar** "The Impact of Retirement Migration on the South." *Gerontologist* 21, no. 3 (1981):283–290.

Lowry, Ira S. *Migration and Metropolitan Growth: Two Analytical Models.* San Francisco: Chandler, 1966.

Luloff, A. E. "Migration and the Utility of the Continuous Work History Sample (CWHS): A Comparative Note." *Review of Public Data Use* 7 (December 1979):62–65.

McAllister, Ronald J.; Edgar W. Butler; and Edward J. Kaiser "The Adaptation of Women to Residential Mobility." *Journal of Marriage and the Family* 35 (May 1973):197–204.

McAllister, Ronald J.; Edward J. Kaiser; and Edgar W. Butler "Residential Mobility of Blacks and Whites: A National Longitudinal Survey." *American Journal of Sociology* 77 (November 1971):445–456.

McAuley, William J., and Cheri L. Nutty "Residential Preferences and Moving Behavior: A Family Life-Cycle Analysis." *Journal of Marriage and the Family* 44 (May 1982):301–309.

McCarthy, Kevin F., and Peter A. Morrison "The Changing Demographic and Economic Structure of Nonmetropolitan Areas in the United States." *International Regional Science Review* 2 (Winter 1977):123–142.

McCraken, K. W. J. "Household Awareness Spaces and Intraurban Migration Search Behavior." *Professional Geographer* 27 (May 1975):166–170.

McHugh, Kevin "Explaining Migration Intentions and Destination Selection." *Professional Geographer* 36, no. 3 (1984):315–325.

McInnis, Marvin "Age, Education and Occupation Differentials in Interregional Migration: Some Evidence for Canada." *Demography* 8 (May 1971):195–204.

Macisco, John J., and Edward T. Pryor "A Reappraisal of Ravenstein's 'Laws' of Migration: A Review of Selected Studies of Internal Migration in the United States." *American Catholic Sociological Review* 24 (Fall 1963):211–221.

McKay, John, and James S. Whitelaw "The Role of Large Private and Government Organizations in Generating Flows of Inter-Regional Migrants: The Case of Australia." *Economic Geography* 53 (January 1977):28–44.

Mackett, R. L., and I. Johnson "Residential Search Behavior." *Tijdschrift voor Economische en Sociale Geografie* 76, no. 3 (1985):173–179.

McLeod, Karen D.; Jan R. Parker; and William J. Serow "Determinants of State-to-State Flows of Elderly Migrants." *Research on Aging* 6 (September 1984):372–383.

McNabb, Robert "A Socio-Economic Model of Migration." *Regional Studies* 13, no. 3 (1979):297–303.

McNeill, William H. "Human Migration in Historical Perspective." *Population and Development Review* 10 (March 1984):1–18.

————, **and Ruth S. Adams, eds.** *Human Migration: Patterns and Policies.* Bloomington: Indiana University Press, 1978.

MacRae, Duncan, Jr., and John R. Carlson "Collective Preferences as Predictors of Interstate Migration." *Social Indicators Research* 8 (1980):15–32.

Mahoney, Bette Silver "The Case for Migration." *New Generation* 50 (Summer 1968):6–10.

Mangalam, J. J. *Human Migration: A Guide to Migration Literature in English, 1955–62.* Lexington: University of Kentucky Press, 1968.

Mann, Philip A. "Residential Mobility as an Adaptive Experience." *Journal of Consulting and Clinical Psychology* 39 (August 1972):37–42.

Markham, William T.; Patrick O. Macken; Charles M. Bonjean; and Judy Corder "A Note on Sex, Geographic Mobility, and Career Advancement." *Social Forces* 61 (June 1983):1138–1146.

Marr, W. L.; D. J. McCready; and F. W. Millert "Canadian Interprovincial Migration and Education." *Canadian Studies in Population* 5 (1978):1–11.

Martin, Jack K., and Daniel T. Lichter "Geographic Mobility and Satisfaction with Life and Work." *Social Science Quarterly* 64 (September 1983):524–535.

Martin, Philip "Noneconomic Determinants of Nonmigration: A Comment." *Rural Sociology* 40 (Fall 1975):353–359.

Masnick, George S. "Employment Status and Retrospective and Prospective Migration in the United States." *Demography* 5, no. 1 (1968):79–85.

Masser, Ian "The Design of Spatial Systems for Internal Migration Analysis." *Regional Studies* 10, no. 1 (1976):39–52.

Masters, Stanley H. "Are Black Migrants from the South to Northern Cities Worse Off Than Blacks Already There?" *Journal of Human Resources* 7 (Fall 1972):411–423.

Mazek, Warren F. "Unemployment and the Efficacy of Migration: The Case of Laborers." *Journal of Regional Science* 9 (April 1969):101–107.

————, **and John Chang** "The Chicken or Egg Fowl-Up in Migration: Comment." *Southern Economic Journal* 39 (July 1974):133–139.

Mazek, Warren F., and William E. Laird "City-Size Preferences and Population Distribution: The Analytical Context." *Quarterly Review of Economics and Business* 14 (Spring 1974):113–121.

Mead, Arthur C. "A Simultaneous Equations Model of Migration and Economic Change in Nonmetropolitan Areas." *Journal of Regional Science* 22, no. 4 (1982):513–527.

Michaelson, William "Residential Mobility as a Dynamic Process: A Cross-Cultural Perspective." In Clare Ungerson and Valerie Karn, eds. *The Consumer Experience of Housing: Cross-National Perspectives.* Westmead, England: Gower, 1980, pp. 36–49.

Mickens, Alvin "Regional Defense Demand and Racial Response Differences in the Net Migration of Workers." *Quarterly Review of Economics and Business* 17 (Spring 1977):65–82.

Miller, Ann R. *Net Intercensal Migration to Large Urban Areas of the United States, 1930–40, 1940–50, 1950–60.* Philadelphia: Population Studies Center, University of Pennsylvania, 1964.

—— "Migration Differentials in Labor Force Participation: United States, 1960." *Demography* 3 (1966):58–67.

—— "The Migration of Employed Persons to and from Metropolitan Areas of the United States." *Journal of the American Statistical Association* 62 (December 1967):1418–1432.

—— "Note on Some Problems in Interpreting Data from the 1960 Census of Population: An Attempt at Evaluation." *Journal of the American Statistical Association* 71 (June 1976):286–292.

—— "Interstate Migrants in the United States: Some Social-Economic Differences by Type of Move." *Demography* 14 (February 1977):1–17.

Miller, Edward "A Note on the Role of Distance in Migration: Costs of Mobility versus Intervening Opportunities." *Journal of Regional Science* 12 (December 1972):475–478.

—— "The Flight of the Native Born." *Growth and Change* 4 (October 1973):10–15.

—— "Return and Nonreturn In-Migration." *Growth and Change* 4 (January 1973):3–9.

—— "Is Out-Migration Affected by Economic Considerations?" *Southern Economic Journal* 39 (January 1973):396–405.

Miller, Sheila J. "Family Life Cyle, Extended Family Orientations, and Economic Aspirations as Factors in the Propensity to Migrate." *Sociological Quarterly* 17 (Summer 1976):323–335.

Mills, K. E.; M. B. Percy; and L. W. Wilson "The Influence of Fiscal Incentives on Interregional Migration: Canada 1961–78." *Canadian Journal of Regional Science* 6 (Autumn 1983):207–229.

Milne, Dann "Migration and Income Opportunities for Blacks in the South." *Southern Economic Journal* 46 (January 1980):913–917.

Mincer, Jacob "Family Migration Decisions." *Journal of Political Economy* 86 (October 1978):749–773.

Moore, Eric G. "The Structure of Intra-Urban Movement Rates: An Ecological Model." *Urban Studies* 6 (February 1969):17–33.

—— "Comments on the Use of Ecological Models in the City." *Economic Geography* 47 (January 1971):73–85.

—— *Residential Mobility in the City.* Washington, DC: Association of American Geographers, 1972.

——, **and Richard S. Harris** "Residential Mobility and Public Policy." *Geographical Analysis* 11 (April 1979):175–183.

Morgan, Barrie S. " 'Why Families Move': A Reexamination." *Professional Geographer* 25 (May 1973):124–129.

Morgan, Celia "A Note on a Perennial Question in Migration Analysis." *Growth and Change* 5 (October 1974):43–47.

—— "An Analysis of Interregional Migration in Texas: 1965–1970." *Review of Regional Studies* 54 (Fall 1976):78–90.

—— "Is Out-Migration Affected by Economic Conditions? Comment." *Southern Economic Journal* 42 (April 1976):752–758.

Morgan, James N., and Edward H. Robb "The Impact of Age upon Interregional Migration." *Annals of Regional Science* 15 (November 1981):31–45.

Morris, Earl W. "Mobility, Fertility and Residential Crowding." *Sociology and Social Research* 61 (April 1977):363–379.

——; **Sue R. Crull; and Mary Winter** "Housing Norms, Housing Satisfaction, and the Propensity to Move." *Journal of Marriage and the Family* 38 (May 1976):309–321.

Morris, Earl W., and Mary Winter "A Theory of Family Housing Adjustment." *Journal of Marriage and the Family* 37 (February 1975):79–88.

Morrison, Peter A. "Duration of Residence and Prospective Migration: The Evaluation of a Stochastic Model." *Demography* 4, no. 2 (1967):553–561.

—— "Chronic Movers and the Future Redistribution of Population: A Longitudinal Analysis." *Demography* 8 (May 1971):171–184.

—— "Theoretical Issues in the Design of Population Mobility Models." *Environment and Planning A* 5 (1973):125–134.

—— "Urban Growth and Decline: San Jose and St. Louis in the 1960's." *Science*, August 30, 1974, pp. 757–762.

—— *Rural Renaissance in America?* Washington, DC: Population Reference Bureau, 1976.

—— "Migration and Rights of Access: New Public Concerns of the 1970's." In Mark Baldassare, ed. *Cities and Urban Living.* New York: Columbia University Press, 1983, pp. 197–211.

——, ed. *Population Movements: Their Forms and Functions in Urbanization and Development.* Liège, Belgium: International Union for the Scientific Study of Population, 1983.

——, **and Julie DaVanzo** "The Prism of Migration: Dissimilarities between Return and Onward Movers." *Social Science Quarterly* 67 (September 1986):1–13.

Mueller, Charles F. "Migration of the Unemployed: A Relocation Assistance Program." *Monthly Labor Review* 104 (April 1981):62–64.

—— *The Economics of Labor Migration.* New York: Academic Press, 1982.

Mueller, Eva, and Jane Lean "The Case Against Migration." *New Generation* 50 (Summer 1968):6–10.

Munick, Warren A., and Dennis Sullivan "Race, Age, and Family Status Differentials in Metropolitan Migration of Households." *Rural Sociology* 42 (Winter 1977):536–543.

Murdock, Steve H.; Banoo Parpia; Sean-Shong Hwang; and Rita R. Hamm "The Relative Effects of Economic and Noneconomic Factors on Age-Specific Migration, 1960–1980." *Rural Sociology* 49, no. 2 (1984):309–318.

Murphy, H. B. M. "Migration and the Major Mental Disorders: A Reappraisal." In Mildred B. Kantor, ed. *Mobility and Mental Health.* Springfield, IL: Thomas, 1965, pp. 5–29.

Muth, Richard F. "Migration: Chicken or Egg?" *Southern Economic Journal* 37 (January 1971):295–306.

Myers, Dowell "A New Perspective on Planning for More Balanced Metropolitan Growth." *Growth and Change* 9 (January 1978):8–13.

—— "Turnover and Filtering of Postwar Single-Family Houses." *Journal of the American Planning Association* 50 (Summer 1984):352–358.

Myers, George C.; Robert McGinnis; and George Masnick "The Duration of Residence Approach to a Dynamic Stochastic Model of Internal Migration: A Test of the Axiom of Cumulative Inertia." *Eugenics Quarterly* 14 (June 1967):121–126.

Nakosteen, Robert A., and Michael A. Zimmer "Migration and Income: The Question of Self Selection." *Southern Economic Journal* 46 (January 1980):840–851.

_____ "The Effects of Earnings of Interregional and Interindustry Migration." *Journal of Regional Science* 22, no. 3 (1982):325–341.

Nathanson, Constance A. "Moving Preferences and Plans among Urban Black Families." *Journal of the American Institute of Planners* 40 (September 1974):353–359.

Navratil, Frank J., and James J. Doyle "The Socioeconomic Determinants of Migration and the Level of Aggregation." *Southern Economic Journal* 43 (April 1977):1547–1559.

Neff, James Alan, and Robert J. Constantine "Community Dissatisfaction and Perceived Residential Alternatives: An Interactive Model of the Formulation of Migration Plans." *Journal of Population* 2 (Spring 1979):18–32.

Nelson, Kathryn P. "Recent Suburbanization of Blacks—How Much, Who, and Where." *Journal of the American Planning Association* 46 (July 1980):287–300.

Newman, Allen R. "A Test of the Okun-Richardson Model of Internal Migration." *Economic Development and Cultural Change* 29 (January 1981):295–307.

Newman, Robert J. "Industry Migration and Growth in the South." *Review of Economics and Statistics* 65 (February 1983):76–86.

Newman, Sandra J. "Objective and Subjective Determinants of Prospective Residential Mobility." *Social Indicators Research* 2 (June 1975):53–63.

_____ "Exploring Housing Adjustments of Older People." *Research on Aging* 3 (December 1981):417–427.

_____, **and Greg J. Duncan** "Residential Problems, Dissatisfaction, and Mobility." *Journal of the American Planning Association* 45 (April 1979):154–166.

Newman, Sandra J., and Michael S. Owen "Residential Displacement: Extent, Nature, and Effects." *Journal of Social Issues* 38, no. 3 (1982):135–148.

_____ *Residential Displacement in the U.S.: 1970–1977.* Ann Arbor: Survey Research Center, University of Michigan, 1982.

Nghiep, Nguyen huu; Henry W. Herzog, Jr.; and Alan M. Schlottmann "Earnings Expectations and the Role of Human Capital in the Migration Decision: An Empirical Analysis." *Review of Regional Studies* 11 (Winter 1981):38–46.

Niemi, Albert W. "Returns to Educated Blacks Resulting from Southern Out-migration." *Southern Economic Journal* 40 (October 1973):330–333.

Niemi, Beth "Geographic Immobility and Labor Force Immobility: A Study of Female Unemployment." In Cynthia B. Lloyd, ed. *Sex, Discrimination, and the Division of Labor.* New York: Columbia University Press, 1975, pp. 61–89.

Nijkamp, P. "Socio-Economic and Environmental Indicators as Determinants of Interregional Migration Flows." *Social Indicators Research* 3 (1976):101–110.

O'Loughlin, John, and Gunther Glebe "Intraurban Migration in West German Cities." *Geographical Review* 74 (January 1984):1–23.

Oberg, Sture, and Gosta Oscarsson "Regional Policy and Interregional Migration—Matching Jobs and Individuals in Local Labour Markets." *Regional Studies* 13, no. 1 (1979):1–14.

Okraku, Ishmael O. "The Family Life-Cycle and Residential Mobility in Puerto Rico." *Sociology and Social Research* 55 (April 1971):324–340.

Olson, Ruth A., and Avery M. Guest "Migration and City-Suburb Status Differences." *Urban Affairs Quarterly* 12 (June 1977):523–532.

Olsson, Gunnar "Distance and Human Interaction: A Migration Study." *Geografiska Annaler* 47B (1965):3–43.

Olvey, Lee D. "Regional Growth and Interregional Migration—Their Pattern of Interaction." *Review of Regional Studies* 2 (Winter 1972):139–163.

Onaka, J. L. "A Multiple-Attribute Housing Disequilibrium Model of Residential Mobility." *Environment and Planning A* 15 (June 1983):751–765.

————, **and W. A. V. Clark** "A Disaggregated Model of Residential Mobility and Housing Choice." *Geographical Analysis* 15 (October 1983):287–304.

Orbell, John M., and Toru Uno "A Theory of Neighborhood Problem Solving: Political Action vs. Residential Mobility." *American Political Science Review* 66 (June 1972):471–489.

Ornstein, Michael D., and G. Gordon Darroch "National Mobility Studies in Past Time: A Sampling Strategy." *Historical Methods* 11 (Fall 1978):152–161.

Pack, Janet Rothenberg "Determinants of Migration to Central Cities." *Journal of Regional Science* 13, no. 2 (1973):249–260.

Packard, Vance *A Nation of Strangers.* New York: McKay, 1972.

Parish, William L. "Internal Migration and Modernization: The European Case." *Economic Development and Cultural Change* 21 (July 1973):591–609.

Pederson, Frank A., and Eugene J. Sullivan "Relationships among Geographical Mobility, Parental Attitudes and Emotional Disturbances in Children." *American Journal of Orthopsychiatry* 34 (April 1964):575–80.

Perkinson, Leon "Are Migrants Universally Disadvantaged?" *Growth and Change* 11 (July 1980):17–25.

Persky, Joseph J., and John F. Kain "Migration, Employment, and Race in the Deep South." *Southern Economic Journal* 36 (January 1970):268–276.

Phipps, Alan G. "Residential Search and Choice of Displaced Households." *Socio-Economic Planning Sciences* 18, no. 1 (1984):25–35.

————, **and Jacquelyn E. Carter** "An Individual-Level Analysis of the Stress-Resistance Model of Household Mobility." *Geographical Analysis* 16 (April 1984):176–189.

Pickles, Andrew "Models of Movement: A Review of Alternative Methods." *Environment and Planning A* 12 (December 1980):1383–1404.

————, **and Richard Davies** "The Longitudinal Analysis of Housing Careers." *Journal of Regional Science* 25, no. 1 (1985):85–101.

Pickles, Andrew, and Peter Rogerson "Wage Distributions and Spatial Preferences in Competitive Job Search and Migration." *Regional Studies* 18 (April 1984):131–142.

Pickvance, C. G. "Life-Cycle, Housing Tenure and Intra-Urban Residential Mobility: A Causal Model." *Sociological Review* 21 (May 1973):279–297.

———— "Life-Cyle, Housing Tenure and Residential Mobility: A Path Analytic Approach." *Urban Studies* 11 (June 1974):171–188.

Pierson, George W. *The Moving American.* New York: Knopf, 1973.

Pitcher, Brian L.; William F. Stinner; and Michael B. Toney "Patterns of Migration Propensity for Black and White American Men: Evidence from a Cohort Analysis." *Research on Aging* 7 (March 1985):94–120.

Pittenger, Donald B. "A Typology of Age-Specific Net Migration Rate Distributions." *Journal of the American Institute of Planners* 40 (July 1974):278–283.

———. "On Making Flexible Projections of Age-Specific Net Migration." *Environment and Planning A* 10 (November 1978):1253–1272.

———. "On the Persistence of U.S. Net Migration Rates in the 20th Century." *Growth and Change* 12 (October 1981):43–49.

Plane, David A. "An Information Theoretic Approach to the Estimation of Migration Flows." *Journal of Regional Science* 22, no. 4 (1982):441–456.

———. "Migration Space: Doubly Constrained Gravity Model Mapping of Relative Interstate Migration." *Annals of the Association of American Geographers* 74 (June 1984):244–256.

———. "A Systematic Demographic Efficiency Analysis of U.S. Interstate Population Exchange, 1935–1980." *Economic Geography* 60 (October 1984):294–312.

———, **and Andrew M. Isserman** "U.S. Interstate Labor Force Migration: An Analysis of Trends, Net Exchanges, and Migration Subsystems." *Socio-Economic Planning Sciences* 17, no. 5–6 (1983):251–266.

Plane, D. A., and P. A. Rogerson "Economic-Demographic Models for Forecasting Interregional Migration." *Environment and Planning A* 17 (1985):185–198.

———; **and Allan Rosen** "The Cross-Regional Variation of In-Migration and Out-Migration." *Geographical Analysis* 16 (April 1984):162–175.

Ploch, Louis A. "The Reversal in Migration Patterns—Some Rural Development Consequences." *Rural Sociology* 43 (Summer 1978):293–303.

Pol, Louis "The Structural Correlates of Metropolitan Migration: 1970–1975." *Sociological Focus* 15 (April 1982):121–134.

Polachek, Solomon W., and Francis W. Horvath "A Life Cyle Approach to Migration: Analysis of the Perspicacious Peregrinator." In Ronald G. Ehrenberg, ed. *Research in Labor Economics.* Greenwich, CN: JAI Press, 1977, pp. 103–149.

Population Information Program "Migration, Population Growth, and Development." *Population Reports* 11 (September–October 1983):245–286.

Porell, Frank W. "The Effects of Generalized Relocation Costs Upon Intraurban Household Relocation." *Journal of Regional Science* 22, no. 1 (1982):33–55.

———. "Intermetropolitan Migration and Quality of Life." *Journal of Regional Science* 22, no. 2 (1982):137–158.

Poston, Dudley L., and Ralph White "Indigenous Labor Supply, Sustenance Organization, and Population Redistribution in Nonmetropolitan America: An Extension of the Ecological Theory of Migration." *Demography* 15 (November 1978):637–641.

Poulain, Michel, and Brigitte Van Goethem "Evolution de la mobilité interne de la population Belge de 1948 à 1979." *Population* 37 (March–April 1982):319–340.

Premus, Robert, and Robert Weinstein "Non-White Migration, Welfare Levels, and the Political Process: Some Additional Results." *Review of Regional Studies* 7 (Spring 1977):11–19.

President's Commission for a National Agenda for the Eighties *Urban America in the Eighties.* Washington, DC: U.S. Government Printing Office, 1980.

President's National Advisory Commission on Rural Poverty *Rural Poverty in the United States.* Washington, DC: U.S. Government Printing Office, 1968.

Price, Daniel O., and Melanie M. Sikes *Rural-Urban Migration Research in the United States.* Washington, DC: U.S. Government Printing Office, 1975.

Price, Michael L., and Daniel C. Clay "Structural Disturbances in Rural Communities: Some Repercussions of the Migration Turnaround in Michigan." *Rural Sociology* 45 (Winter 1980):591–607.

Pursell, Donald E. "Age and Educational Dimensions in Southern Migration Patterns, 1965–70." *Southern Economic Journal* 44 (July 1977):148–154.

Quigley, John M., and Daniel H. Weinberg "Intra-Urban Residential Mobility: A Review and Synthesis." *International Regional Science Review* 2 (Fall 1977):41–66.

Rabianski, Joseph "Real Earnings and Human Migration." *Journal of Human Resources* 6 (Spring 1971):185–192.

Rank, Mark R., and Paul R. Voss "Occupational Mobility and Attainment among Migrants Entering the Upper Great Lakes Region." *Rural Sociology* 47 (Fall 1982):512–528.

—— "Patterns of Rural Community Involvement: A Comparison of Residents and Recent Immigrants." *Rural Sociology* 47, no. 2 (1982):197–219.

Rapping, Leonard A. "Unionism, Migration, and the Male Nonwhite-White Unemployment Differential." *Southern Economic Journal* 32 (January 1966):317–329.

Ravenstein, E. G. "The Laws of Migration." *Journal of the Statistical Society* 48 (June 1885):167–227.

—— "The Laws of Migration." *Journal of the Royal Statistical Society* 52 (June 1889):241–301.

Raymond, Richard "Determinants of Non-White Migration during the 1950's." *American Journal of Economics and Sociology* 31 (January 1972):9–20.

Reaume, David M. "Migration and the Dynamic Stability of Regional Econometric Models." *Economic Inquiry* 21 (April 1983):281–292.

Rees, P.H. "The Measurement of Migration from Census Data and Other Sources." *Environment and Planning A* 9, no. 3 (1977):247–272.

—— "Multiregional Mathematical Demography: Themes and Issues." *Environment and Planning A* 15 (December 1983):1571–1583.

Regional Economic Analysis Division "Work Force Migration Patterns, 1960–73." *Survey of Current Business* 56 (October 1976):23–28.

Renas, Stephen M., and Rishi Kumar "The Cost of Living, Labor Market Opportunities, and the Migration Decision: Some Additional Evidence." *Annals of Regional Science* 15 (November 1981):74–79.

—— "Desirability of Climate and the Spatial Allocation of Migrants: A Statistical Inquiry." *Review of Regional Studies* 8 (Winter 1978):52–59.

—— "Climatic Conditions and Migration: An Econometric Inquiry." *Annals of Regional Science* 17 (March 1983):69–83.

Renshaw, Vernon "A Note on Lagged Response in the Decision to Migrate." *Journal of Regional Science* 14, no. 2 (1974):273–280.

——; **Howard Friedenberg; and Bruce Levine** "Work-Force Migration Patterns, 1970–76." *Survey of Current Business* 58 (February 1978):17–20.

Richter, Kerry "Nonmetropolitan Growth in the Late 1970s: The End of the Turnaround?" *Demography* 22 (May 1985):245–263.

Rieger, Jon H. "Geographic Mobility and the Occupational Attainment of Rural Youth: A Longitudinal Evaluation." *Rural Sociology* 37 (June 1972):189–207.

Rietveld, P. "Vacancies and Mobility in the Housing Market: An Exploratory Analysis." *Environment and Planning A* 16 (May 1984):673–687.

Riew, John "Migration and Public Policy." *Journal of Regional Science* 13 (April 1969):65–76.

352

Ritchey, P. Neal "Urban Poverty and Rural to Urban Migration." *Rural Sociology* 39 (Spring 1974):12–27.

———— "Explanations of Migration." In Alex Inkeles, ed. *Annual Review of Sociology.* Palo Alto, CA: Annual Reviews, 1976, pp. 363–404.

Rives, Norfleet W., and William J. Serow "Interstate Migration of the Elderly: Demographic Aspects." *Research on Aging* 3 (September 1981):259–278.

Roback, Jennifer "Exploitation in the Jim Crow South: The Market or the Law?" *Regulation* 7 (September–December 1984):37–43.

Robinson, J. Gregory "Evaluation of Census Data on Place of Birth from the 1980 Content Reinterview Study" (forthcoming).

Rogers, A.; R. Raquillet; and L. J. Castro "Model Migration Schedules and Their Applications." *Environment and Planning A* (May 1978):475–502.

Rogers, A.; F. Willekens; and J. Ledent "Migration and Settlement: A Multiregional Comparative Study." *Environment and Planning A* 15 (December 1983):1585–1612.

Rogers, Andrei *Regional Population Projection Models.* Beverly Hills, CA: Sage, 1985.

Rogerson, Peter, and David A. Plane "Monitoring Migration Trends." *American Demographics* 7 (February 1985):27–29, 47.

Roistacher, Elizabeth "Residential Mobility." In James N. Morgan, ed. *Five Thousand American Families—Patterns of Economic Progress*, vol. 2. Ann Arbor: Institute for Social Research, University of Michigan, 1974, pp. 41–78.

———— "Residential Mobility: Planners, Movers, and Multiple Movers." In G. J. Duncan and J. N. Morgan, eds. *Five Thousand American Families—Patterns of Economic Progress*, vol. 3. Ann Arbor: Institute for Social Research, University of Michigan, 1975, pp. 259–278.

Rones, Philip L. "Moving to the Sun: Regional Job Growth, 1968 to 1978." *Monthly Labor Review* 103 (March 1980):12–19.

Rose, Harold M. "Urban Black Migration and Social Stress: The Influence of Regional Differences in Patterns of Socialization." In Gary Gappert and Harold M. Rose, eds. *The Social Economy of Cities.* Beverly Hills, CA: Sage, 1975, pp. 301–333.

Roseman, Curtis C. "Migration as a Spatial and Temporal Process." *Annals of the Association of American Geographers* 61 (September 1971):589–598.

———— "Migration, the Journey to Work, and Household Characteristics: An Analysis Based on Non-Areal Aggregation." *Economic Geography* 47 (October 1971):467–474.

———— "Migration of Whites to Central Cities and Quality of Life." *Geographical Survey* 5 (January 1976):14–21.

———— *Changing Migration Patterns within the United States.* Washington, DC: Association of American Geographers, 1977.

———— "A Framework for the Study of Migration Destination Selection." *Population and Environment* 6 (Fall 1983):151–165.

———— "Labor Force Migration, Non-Labor Force Migration, and Non-Employment Reasons for Migration." *Socio-Economic Planning Sciences* 17, no. 5–6 (1983):303–312.

————, **and Prentice L. Knight III** "Residential Environment and Migration Behavior of Urban Blacks." *Professional Geographer* 27 (May 1975):160–165.

Ross, H. Laurence "Reasons for Moves to and from a Central City Area." *Social Forces* 40 (March 1962):261–263.

Rossi, Peter H. *Why Families Move.* Glencoe, IL: Free Press, 1955.

————, and Anne B. Shlay "Residential Mobility and Public Policy Issues: 'Why Families Move' Revisited." *Journal of Social Issues* 38, no. 3 (1982):21–34.

Rowland, D. T. *Internal Migration in Australia.* Cranberra: Australian Bureau of Statistics, 1979.

———— *Population and Educational Planning.* Canberra: Australian Government Publishing Service, 1983.

Russell, William R., and Alan R. Winger "Non-Money Income and Out-Migration in Lagging Regions." *Review of Regional Studies* 2 (Winter 1972):165–174.

Rust, Edgar *No Growth: Impacts on Metropolitan Areas.* Lexington, MA: Lexington Books, 1975.

Rutman, Gilbert L. "Migration and Economic Opportunities in West Virginia: A Statistical Analysis." *Rural Sociology* 35 (June 1970):206–217.

Sabagh, George; Maurice D. Van Arsdol, Jr.; and Edgar W. Butler "Some Determinants of Intrametropolitan Residential Mobility: Conceptual Considerations." *Social Forces* 48 (September 1969):88–98.

Saben, Samuel *Geographic Mobility and Employment Status, March 1962–March 1963.* Special Labor Force Report no. 44. Washington, DC: U.S. Department of Labor, 1964.

Sandefur, Gary D. "Variations in Interstate Migration of Men Across the Early Stages of the Life Cycle." *Demography* 22 (August 1985):353–366.

————, and Wilbur J. Scott "A Dynamic Analysis of Migration: An Assessment of the Effects of Age, Family and Career Variables." *Demography* 18 (August 1981):355–368.

Sandell, Steven "Women and the Economics of Family Migration." *Review of Economics and Statistics* 59 (November 1977):406–414.

Schachter, Joseph, and Paul G. Althaus "Neighborhood Quality and Climate as Factors in U.S. Net Migration Patterns, 1974–76." *American Journal of Economics and Sociology* 41 (October 1982):387–400.

Schlottmann, Alan M., and Henry W. Herzog, Jr. "Employment Status and the Decision to Migrate." *Review of Economics and Statistics* 63 (November 1981):590–598.

———— "Home Economic Conditions and the Decision to Migrate: New Evidence for the U.S. Labor Force." *Southern Economic Journal* 48 (April 1982):950–961.

———— "Career and Geographic Mobility Interactions: Implications for the Age Selectivity of Migration." *Journal of Human Resources* 19 (Winter 1984):72–86.

Schumaker, Sally Ann, and Daniel Stokols "Residential Mobility as a Social Issue and Research Topic." *Journal of Social Issues* 38, no. 3 (1982):1–19.

Schwab, Robert M. "Renovation and Mobility: An Application of the Theory of Rationing." *Southern Economic Journal* 52 (July 1985):203–215.

Schwartz, Aba "On Efficiency of Migration." *Journal of Human Resources* 6 (Spring 1971):193–205.

———— "Interpreting the Effect of Distance on Migration." *Journal of Political Economy* 81 (September–October 1973):1153–1169.

———— "Migration, Age, and Education." *Journal of Political Economy* 84 (August 1976):701–719.

Schwarzweller, Harry K. "Migration and the Changing Rural Scene." *Rural Sociology* 44 (Spring 1979):7–23.

Schwind, Paul J. "A General Field Theory of Migration: United States, 1955–60." *Economic Geography* 51 (January 1975):1–16.

Scott, Emmett J. *Negro Migration during the War.* New York: Arno Press, 1969 [1919].

Seek, N. H. "Adjusting Housing Consumption: Improve or Move." *Urban Studies* 20 (November 1983):455–469.

Sell, Ralph R. "A Research Note on the Demography of Occupational Relocations." *Social Forces* 80 (March 1982):859–865.

────── "Analyzing Migration Decisions: The First Step—Whose Decisions?" *Demography* 20 (August 1983):299–311.

──────, **and Gordon F. DeJong** "Toward a Motivational Theory of Migration Decision Making." *Journal of Population* 1 (Winter 1978):313–335.

Serow, William J. "Changes in the Composition of Migration for States: 1955–60 and 1965–70." *Review of Regional Studies* 5 (Fall 1975):12–28.

────── "The Role of the Military in Net Migration for States, 1965–1970." *Review of Public Data Use* 4 (May 1976):42–48.

────── "Return Migration of the Elderly in the USA: 1955–1960 and 1965–1970." *Journal of Gerontology* 33, no. 2 (1978):288–295.

────── "The Role of Long Distance Migration in the Rural Renaissance, in Gentrification, and in Growth of the Sunbelt." *Review of Regional Studies* 10 (Winter 1980):23–31.

──────; **Julia H. Martin; and Michael A. Spar** "Migration between State Economic Areas: Review of the Data and Some Initial Analyses." *Review of Public Data Use* 2 (July 1974):1–9.

Severy, Lawrence J. "Residential Migration and Crowding." *Journal of Population* 2 (Winter 1979):358–369.

Shafer, Daniel, and Niki Primo "The Determinants of Household Migration Into and Out of Distressed Neighborhoods." *Urban Studies* 22 (1985):339–347.

Shaw, R. Paul *Migration Theory and Fact.* Philadelphia: Regional Science Research Institute, 1975.

Shear, William B. "Urban Housing Rehabilitation and Move Decisions." *Southern Economic Journal* 49 (April 1983):1030–1052.

Shelley, Fred M., and Curtis C. Roseman "Migration Patterns Leading to Population Change in the Nonmetropolitan South." *Growth and Change* 9 (April 1978):14–23.

Shin, Eui Hang "Effects of Migration on the Educational Levels of the Black Resident Population at the Origin and Destination, 1955–60 and 1965–70." *Demography* 15 (February 1978):41–56.

────── "Trends and Variations in Efficiency of Black Interregional Migration Streams." *Sociology and Social Research* 62 (January 1978):228–245.

────── "Correlates of Intercounty Variations in Net Migration Rates of Blacks in the Deep South, 1960–70." *Rural Sociology* 44 (Spring 1979):39–55.

Short, John R. "The Intra-Urban Migration Process: Comments and Empirical Findings." *Tijdschrift voor Economische en Sociale Geografie* 68, no. 6 (1977):362–370.

────── "Residential Mobility." *Progress in Human Geography* 2 (October 1979):419–447.

Shryock, Henry S. *Population Mobility Within the United States.* Chicago: Community and Family Study Center, University of Chicago, 1964.

──────, **and Elizabeth A. Larmon** "Some Longitudinal Data on Internal Migration." *Demography* 2 (1965):579–592.

Shryock, Henry S., and Charles B. Nam "Educational Selectivity of Interregional Migration." *Social Forces* 43 (March 1965):299–310.

Shryock, Henry S.; Jacob Siegel; and Associates *The Methods and Materials of*

Demography, vols. 1 and 2. Washington, DC: U.S. Government Printing Office, 1971.

Siegel, Jay "Intrametropolitan Migration: A Simultaneous Model of Employment and Residential Location of White and Black Households." *Journal of Urban Economics* 2 (January 1975):29–47.

Silvers, Arthur L. "Probabilistic Income-Maximizing Behavior in Regional Migration." *International Regional Science Review* 2 (Fall 1977):29–40.

Simmons, James W. "Changing Residence in the City." *Geographical Review* 58 (October 1968):622–651.

Sjaastad, Larry A. "The Costs and Returns of Human Migration." *Journal of Political Economy* 70 (October 1962):80–93.

Slater, Paul B. "A Hierarchical Regionalization of State Economic Areas Based Upon Migration Flows." *Review of Public Data Use* 4 (November 1976):32–56.

—— "Origin and Destination Entropies of U.S. 1965–70 Age-Sex-Specific Intercounty Migration Flows." *Mathematical Social Sciences* 7 (1984):21–32.

—— "A Partial Hierarchical Regionalization of 3,140 U.S. Counties on the Basis of 1965–1970 Intercounty Migration." *Environment and Planning A* 16 (April 1984):545–550.

Sly, David F. "Migration and the Ecological Complex." *American Sociological Review* 37 (October 1972):615–628.

——, **and Jeffrey Tayman** "Ecological Approach to Migration Reexamined." *American Sociological Review* 42 (October 1977):783–795.

—— "Metropolitan Morphology and Population Mobility: The Theory of Ecological Expansion Reexamined." *American Journal of Sociology* 86 (July 1980):119–138.

Smith, Terence R. "Migration, Risk Aversion, and Regional Differentiation." *Journal of Regional Science* 19 (February 1979):31–45.

Snipes, Walter T. "Promotion and Moving." *Elementary School Journal* 65 (May 1965):429–433.

Sofranko, Andrew J., and Frederick C. Fligel "The Neglected Component of Rural Population Growth." *Growth and Change* 13 (April 1983):42–49.

Sommers, Paul M. "Analysis of Net Interstate Migration Revisited." *Social Science Quarterly* 62 (June 1981):294–302.

——, **and Daniel B. Suits** "Analysis of Net Interstate Migration." *Southern Economic Journal* 40 (October 1973):193–201.

Speare, Alden, Jr. "Home Ownership, Life Cycle Stage, and Residential Mobility." *Demography* 7 (November 1970):449–458.

—— "Residential Satisfaction as an Intervening Variable in Residential Mobility." *Demography* 11 (May 1974):173–188.

——; **Sidney Goldstein; and William Frey** *Residential Mobility, Migration and Metropolitan Change.* Cambridge, MA: Ballinger, 1975.

Speare, Alden, Jr.; Frances Kobrin; and Ward Kingkade "The Influence of Socioeconomic Bonds and Satisfaction on Interstate Migration." *Social Forces* 61 (December 1982):551–574.

Spitze, Glenna "Black Family Migration and Wives' Employment." *Journal of Marriage and the Family* 46, no. 4 (November 1984):781–790.

—— "The Effect of Family Migration on Wives' Employment: How Long Does It Last?" *Social Science Quarterly* 65 (March 1984):21–36.

Stahl, Konrad "A Note on the Microeconomics of Migration." *Journal of Urban Economics* 14 (1983):318–326.

Stapleton, Clare M. "Reformulation of the Family Life-Cycle Concept: Implications for Residential Mobility." *Environment and Planning A* 12 (October 1980):1103–1118.

Stapleton-Concord, Clare M. "Intraurban Residential Mobility of the Aged." *Geografiska Annaler* 66B, no. 2 (1984):99–109.

―――― "A Mover/Stayer Approach to Residential Mobility of the Aged." *Tijdschrift voor Economische en Sociale Geografie* 75, no. 4 (1984):249–262.

Statistical Bureau *1980 Population Census of Japan*, vol. 4, pt. 1, div. 2. Tokyo: Prime Minister's Office, 1984.

Statistics Canada *1981 Census of Canada: Mobility Status*. Ottawa: Statistics Canada, 1983.

Steinnes, Donald N. "Causality and Migration: A Statistical Resolution of the 'Chicken or Egg Fowl-Up.' " *Southern Economic Journal* 45 (July 1978):218–226.

Stevens, Joe B. "Satisfaction with Environment Change: An Empirical Analysis of Attitudes Toward Air Quality by Recent Interstate Migrants." *Journal of Environment Economics and Management* 11 (1984):264–281.

Stewert, Charles T., and Virginia Benson "Job Migration Linkages between Smaller SMSA's and Their Hinterlands." *Land Economics* 49 (November 1973):432–439.

Stillwell, J. C. H. 1978. "Interzonal Migration: Some Historical Tests of Spatial-Interaction Models." *Environment and Planning A* 10 (October):1187–1200.

Stinner, William F., and Gordon F. DeJong "Southern Negro Migration: Social Economic Components of an Ecological Model." *Demography* 6 (November 1969):455–471.

Stokols, Daniel, and Sally Ann Shumaker "The Psychological Context of Residential Mobility and Well-Being." *Journal of Social Issues* 38, no. 3 (1982):149–171.

―――― ; and John Martinez "Residential Mobility and Personal Well-Being." *Journal of Environmental Psychology* 3 (1983):5–19.

Stone, Leroy O. "On the Correlation between Metropolitan Area In- and Out-Migration by Occupation." *Journal of the American Statistical Association* 66 (December 1971):693–701.

Stouffer, Samuel A. "Intervening Opportunities and Competing Migrants." *Journal of Regional Science* 2 (1960):1–26.

Stubblefield, Robert L. "Children's Emotional Problems Aggravated by Family Moves." *American Journal of Orthopsychiatry* 25 (January 1955):120–126.

Sullenger, T. Earl "The Social Significance of Mobility: An Omaha Study." *American Journal of Sociology* 55 (May 1950):559–564.

Sundquist, James L. *Dispersing Population: What America Can Learn from Europe*. Washington, DC: Brookings Institution, 1975.

Suval, Elizabeth M., and C. Horace Hamilton "Some New Evidence on Educational Selectivity in Migration to and from the South." *Social Forces* 43 (May 1965):536–547.

Svart, Larry M. "Environmental Preference Migration: A Review." *Geographical Review* 66 (July 1976):314–330.

Swanson, Louis E., Jr.; A. E. Luloff; and Rex H. Warland "Factors Influencing Willingness to Move: An Examination of Nonmetropolitan Residents." *Rural Sociology* 44 (Winter 1979):719–735.

Swedish Central Bureau of Statistics *Internal Migration in Sweden*. Stockholm: Swedish Central Bureau of Statistics, 1976.

Swindell, Kenneth, and Robert G. Ford "Places, Migrants and Organization: Some Observations on Population Mobility." *Geografiska Annaler* 57B (1975):68–76.

Switzer, Robert E.; J. C. Hirschberg; Leila Myers; Elizabeth Gray; N. H. Evers; and Robert Forman "The Effect of Family Moves on Children." *Mental Hygiene* 45 (1961):528–536.

Tabuchi, Takatoshi "Time-Series Modeling of Gross Migration and Dynamic Equilibrium." *Journal of Regional Science* 25, no. 1 (1985):65–83.

Taeuber, Karl E. "Duration-of-Residence Analysis of Internal Migration in the United States." *Milbank Memorial Fund Quarterly* 39 (January 1961):116–131.

———— "Cohort Population Redistribution and the Urban Hierarchy." *Milbank Memoral Fund Quarterly* 43 (October 1965):450–462.

———— "Cohort Migration." *Demography* 3, no. 2 (1966):416–422.

———— "The Residential Redistribution of Farm-born Cohorts." *Rural Sociology* 32 (March 1967):20–36.

————; **Leonard Chiazze, Jr.; and William Haenszel** *Migration in the United States: An Analysis of Residence Histories.* Washington, DC: U.S. Government Printing Office, 1968.

Taeuber, Karl E., and Alma F. Taeuber "The Changing Character of Negro Migration." *American Journal of Sociology* 60 (January 1965):429–441.

Tarver, James D. "Differentials and Trends in Actual and Expected Distance of Movement of Interstate Migrants." *Rural Sociology* 36 (December 1971):563–571.

————, **and R. Douglas McLeod** "Trends in Distances Moved by Interstate Migrants." *Rural Sociology* 35 (December 1970):523–533.

———— "Trends in the Distance of Movement of Interstate Migrants." *Rural Sociology* 41 (Spring 1976):119–126.

Thernstrom, Stephan, and Peter R. Knights "Men in Motion: Some Data and Speculations about Urban Population Mobility in Nineteenth-Century America." In Tamara K. Hareven, ed. *Anonymous Americans: Explorations in Nineteenth-Century Social History.* Englewood Cliffs, NJ: Prentice-Hall, 1971, pp. 17–47.

Thibeault, Russell W.; Edward J. Kaiser; Edgar W. Butler; and Ronald J. McAllister "Accessibility Satisfaction, Income, and Residential Mobility." *Traffic Quarterly* 27 (April 1973):289–305.

Thomas, Dorothy S. *Research Memorandum on Migration Differentials.* New York: Social Science Research Council, 1938.

———— "Age and Economic Differentials in Interstate Migration." *Population Index* 24 (October 1958):313–325.

Thomlinson, Ralph "A Model for Migration Analysis." *Journal of the American Statistical Association* 56 (September 1961):675–686.

———— "The Determination of a Base Population for Computing Migration Rates." *Milbank Memorial Fund Quarterly* 40 (July 1962):356–366.

Thompson, Warren S. *Research Memorandum on Internal Migration in the Depression.* New York: Social Science Research Council, 1937.

Thorns, D. C. "Age Time and Calendar Time: Two Facets of the Residential Mobility Process." *Environment and Planning A* 17 (June 1985):829–844.

Thornthwaite, C. Warren *Internal Migration in the United States.* Philadelphia: University of Pennsylvania Press, 1934.

Tilly, Charles "Race and Migration to the American City." In James Q. Wilson, ed. *The Metropolitan Enigma.* Garden City, NY: Doubleday, 1970, pp. 144–169.

_____, **and C. Harold Brown** "On Uprooting, Kinship, and the Auspices of Migration." *International Journal of Comparative Sociology* 8 (September 1967):139–164.

Tocqueville, Alexis de *Democracy in America.* New York: Vintage Books, 1945 [1834].

Toney, Michael B. "The Simultaneous Examination of Economic and Social Factors in Destination Selection: Employing Objective and Subjective Measures." *Demography* 15 (May 1978):205–212.

Tooley, Kay "The Role of Geographic Mobility in Some Adjustment Problems of Children and Families." *Journal of the American Academy of Child Psychiatry* 9 (1970):366–378.

Tresch, Richard W. "State Governments and the Welfare System: An Econometric Analysis." *Southern Economic Journal* 42 (July 1975):33–43.

Tucker, C. Jack "Changing Patterns of Migration between Metropolitan and Nonmetropolitan Areas in the United States: Recent Evidence." *Demography* 13 (November 1976):435–443.

_____ "Age and Educational Dimensions of Recent U.S. Migration Reversal." *Growth and Change* 12 (April 1981):31–36.

_____ "City-Suburban Population Redistribution: What Data from the 1970s Reveal." *Urban Affairs Quarterly* 19 (June 1984):539–549.

Tweed, Dan L.; James W. Longest; Eugene H. Owen; and Patricia A. Dabbs "Labor Force Deconcentration in the United States: An Examination of the Relative Impacts of Intrasystemic and Intersystemic Movement." *Review of Public Data Use* 9 (July 1981):133–142.

United Nations *Methodology and Evaluation of Population Registers and Similar Systems.* New York: United Nations, 1969.

_____ *Methods of Measuring Internal Migration.* Manual 6. New York: United Nations, 1970.

_____ *Statistics of Internal Migration: A Technical Report.* Studies in Methods, series F, no. 23. New York: United Nations, 1978.

U.S. Bureau of the Census *Internal Migration, 1935–40—Color and Sex of Migrants.* Washington, DC: U.S. Government Printing Office, 1943.

_____ *State of Birth of the Native Population.* Washington, DC: U.S. Government Printing Office, 1944.

_____ *Internal Migration, 1935–40—Age of Migrants.* Washington, DC: U.S. Government Printing Office, 1946.

_____ *Internal Migration, 1935–40—Economic Characteristics of Migrants.* Washington, DC: U.S. Government Printing Office, 1946.

_____ *Internal Migration, 1935–40—Social Characteristics of Migrants.* Washington, DC: U.S. Government Printing Office, 1946.

_____ "Postwar Migration and Its Causes in the United States: August, 1945, to October, 1946." *Current Population Reports,* series P-20, no. 4. Washington, DC: U.S. Government Printing Office, 1947.

_____ *State of Birth,* P-E no. 4A. Washington, DC: U.S. Government Printing Office, 1953.

_____ *Population Mobility—States and State Economic Areas.* Washington, DC: U.S. Government Printing Office, 1956.

_____ *Population Mobility—Characteristics of Migrants,* P-E no. 4D. Washington, DC: U.S. Government Printing Office, 1957.

———— *Population Mobility—Farm-Nonfarm Movers*, P-E no. 4C. Washington, DC: U.S. Government Printing Office, 1957.

———— *Lifetime and Recent Migration*, PC(2)-2D. Washington, DC: U.S. Government Printing Office, 1963.

———— *Mobility for Metropolitan Areas*, PC(2)-2C. Washington, DC: U.S. Government Printing Office, 1963.

———— *Mobility for States and State Economic Areas*. Washington, DC: U.S. Government Printing Office, 1963.

———— *State of Birth*, PC(2)-2A. Washington, DC: U.S. Government Printing Office, 1963.

———— "Reasons for Moving: March 1962 to March 1963." *Current Population Reports*, series P-20, no. 154. Washington, DC: U.S. Government Printing Office, 1966.

———— *Migration between State Economic Areas*, PC(2)-2E. Washington, DC: U.S. Government Printing Office, 1967.

———— *Migration between State Economic Areas*, PC(2)-2E. Washington, DC: U.S. Government Printing Office, 1972.

———— "Mobility of the Population of the United States: March 1970 to March 1971." *Current Population Reports*, series P-20, no. 235. Washington, DC: U.S. Government Printing Office, 1972.

———— *Lifetime and Recent Migration*, PC (2)-2D. Washington, DC: U.S. Government Printing Office, 1973.

———— *Mobility for Metropolitan Areas*, PC2-2C. Washington, DC: U.S. Government Printing Office, 1973.

———— *Mobility for States and the Nation*, PC(2)-2B. Washington, DC: U.S. Government Printing Office, 1973.

———— *Occupation and Residence in 1965*, PC(2)-2E. Washington, DC: U.S. Government Printing Office, 1973.

———— *State of Birth*, PC(2)-2A. Washington, DC: U.S. Government Printing Office, 1973.

———— 1970 Census of Population and Housing. *Procedural History*, PHC (R)-1. Washington, DC: U.S. Government Printing Office, 1976.

———— "Geographical Mobility: March 1975 to March 1976." *Current Population Reports*, series P-20, no. 305. Washington, DC: U.S. Government Printing Office, 1977.

———— "Gross Migration by County: 1965 to 1970." *Current Population Reports*, series P-25, no. 701. Washington, DC: U.S. Government Printing Office, 1977.

———— *Twenty Censuses: Population and Housing Questions, 1790–1980*. Washington, DC: U.S. Government Printing Office, 1978.

———— 1980 Census of Population. *General Social and Economic Characteristics; United States Summary*, PC80-1-C1. Washington, DC: U.S. Government Printing Office, 1981.

———— 1979 Annual Housing Survey. *Housing Characteristics of Recent Movers*. Washington, DC: U.S. Government Printing Office, 1982.

———— 1980 Annual Housing Survey. *Housing Characteristics of Recent Movers*. Washington, DC: U.S. Government Printing Office, 1982.

———— *Nonpermanent Residents by States and Selected Counties and Incorporated Places: 1980*. PC80-S1-6. Washington, DC: U.S. Government Printing Office, 1982.

———— "Geographical Mobility: March 1980 to March 1981." *Current Popula-*

tion Reports, series P-20, no. 377. Washington, DC: U.S. Government Printing Office, 1983.

———— "Geographical Mobility: March 1981 to March 1982." *Current Population Reports*, series P-20, no. 384. Washington, DC: U.S. Government Printing Office, 1983.

———— 1981 Annual Housing Survey. *Housing Characteristics of Recent Movers.* Washington, DC: U.S. Government Printing Office, 1983.

———— *State of Residence in 1975 by State of Residence in 1980*, PC80-S1-9. Washington, DC: U.S. Government Printing Office, 1983.

———— 1980 Census of Population. *Detailed Population Characteristics: United States Summary, Section A; United States*, PC80-1-D1-A. Washington, DC: U.S. Government Printing Office, 1984.

———— "Estimates of the Population of States: 1970 to 1983." *Current Population Reports*, series P-25, no. 957. Washington, DC: U.S. Government Printing Office, 1984.

———— "Geographical Mobility: March 1982 to March 1983." *Current Population Reports*, series p-20, no. 393. Washington, DC: U.S. Government Printing Office, 1984.

———— *Gross Migration for Counties: 1975 to 1980*, PC80-S1-17. Washington, DC: U.S. Government Printing Office, 1984.

———— *Residence in 1975 for States by Age, Sex, Race, and Spanish Origin*, PC80-S1-17. Washington, DC: U.S. Government Printing Office, 1984.

———— *Geographical Mobility for States and the Nation*, PC80-2-2A. Washington, DC: U.S. Government Printing Office, 1985.

———— *Mobility for Metropolitan Areas*, PC80-2-2B. Washington, DC: U.S. Government Printing Office, 1985.

———— "Patterns of Metropolitan Area and County Population Growth: 1980 to 1984." *Current Population Reports*, series P-25, no. 976. Washington, DC: U.S. Government Printing Office, 1985.

———— "State Population Estimates by Age and Components of Change: 1980 to 1984." *Current Population Reports*, series P-25, no. 970. Washington, DC: U.S. Government Printing Office, 1985.

———— "Geographical Mobility: March 1983 to March 1984." *Current Population Reports*, series P-20, no. 407. Washington, DC: U.S. Government Printing Office, 1986.

U.S. Commission on Population Growth and the American Future *Population Distribution and Policy*, vol. 5. Washington, DC: U.S. Government Printing Office, 1972.

U.S. National Center for Health Statistics *Intellectual Development of Children by Demographic and Socioeconomic Factors.* Washington, DC: U.S. Government Printing Office, 1971.

———— *School Achievement of Children by Demographic and Socioeconomic Factors.* Washington, DC: U.S. Government Printing Office, 1971.

U.S. Office of Education *Pupil Mobility in Public Elementary and Secondary Schools during the 1968–69 School Year.* Washington, DC: U.S. Government Printing Office, 1971.

———— *Pupil Mobility in Public Elementary and Secondary Schools during the 1969–70 School Year.* Washington, DC: U.S. Government Printing Office, 1973.

Uhlenberg, Peter "Noneconomic Determinants of Nonmigration: Sociological

Considerations for Migration Theory." *Rural Sociology* 38 (Fall 1973):296–311.

Van Arsdol, Maurice D., Jr.; Georges Sabagh; and Edgar W. Butler "Retrospective and Subsequent Metropolitan Residential Mobility." *Demography* 5, no. 1 (1968):249–267.

Van Der Erf, R. F. "Internal Migration in the Netherlands: Measurement and Main Characteristics." In Henk ter Heide and Frans J. Willekens, eds. *Demographic Research and Spatial Policy: The Dutch Experience.* New York: Academic Press, 1984, pp. 47–68.

Vanderkamp, John "Migration Flows, Their Determinants and the Effects of Return Migration." *Journal of Political Economy* 79 (September–October 1971):1012–1031.

——— "Return Migration: Its Significance and Behavior." *Western Economic Journal* 10 (December 1972):460–465.

——— "The Role of Population Size in Migration Studies." *Canadian Journal of Economics* 9 (August 1976):508–517.

——— "The Gravity Model and Migration Behavior: An Economic Interpretaion." *Journal of Economic Studies* 4 (November 1977):89–102.

Varady, David A. "Residential Mobility in the Urban Homesteading Demonstration Neighborhoods." *American Planning Association Journal* 50 (Summer 1984):346–351.

Varady, David P. "White Moving Plans in a Racially Changing Middle-Class Community." *Journal of the American Institute of Planners* 40 (September 1974):360–370.

——— "Housing Problems and Mobility Plans among the Elderly." *Journal of the American Planning Association* 46 (July 1980):301–314.

——— "Determinants of Residential Mobility Decisions." *Journal of the American Planning Association* 49 (Spring 1983):184–199.

Villemez, Wayne J., and John D. Kasarda "The Impact of Regional Distination on Black Migrant Income." *Social Science Quarterly* 57 (March 1977):767–783.

Vining, Daniel R., Jr. "The Yule-Simon Model in Its Limiting Case as a Pure Migration Process." *Environment and Planning A* 16 (1984):1269–1278.

———, **and Thomas Kontuly** "Population Dispersal from Major Metropolitan Regions: An International Comparison." *International Regional Science Review* 3 (Fall 1978):49–73.

Vining, Daniel R., Jr., and Robert Pallone "Migration between Core and Peripheral Regions: A Description and Tentative Explanation of the Patterns in 22 Countries." *Geoforum* 13, no. 4 (1982):339–410.

———; **and David A. Plane** "Recent Migration Patterns in the Developed World: A Clarification of Some Differences between Our and IIASA's Findings." *Environment and Planning A* 13 (February 1981):243–250.

Vining, Daniel R., Jr., and A. Strauss "A Demonstration That the Current Deconcentration of Population in the United States Is a Clean Break with the Past." *Environment and Planning A* 9 (July 1977):751–758.

Voss, Paul R. "A Test of the 'Gangplank Syndrome' among Recent Migrants to the Upper Great Lakes Region." *Journal of the Development Society* 11 (Spring 1980):95–111.

Wadycki, Walter J. "Alternative Opportunities and Interstate Migration: Some Additional Results." *Review of Economics and Statistics* 56 (May 1974):254–257.

———— "A Note on Opportunity Costs and Migration Analysis." *Annals of Regional Science* 8 (February 1974):109–117.

———— "Stouffer's Model of Migration: A Comparison of Interstate and Metropolitan Flows." *Demography* 12 (February 1975):121–128.

———— "Alternative Opportunities and United States Interstate Migration: An Improved Econometric Specification." *Annals of Regional Science* 13 (November 1979):35–41.

———— "Single-Place Alternative Opportunities in an Economic Model of Migration." *Annals of Regional Science* 19 (July 1985):10–16.

Wardwell, John M. "Equilibrium and Change in Nonmetropolitan Growth." *Rural Sociology* 42 (Summer 1977):156–179.

————, **and C. Jack Gilchrist** "Improving the Utility of the Continuous Work History Sample (CWHS) for Analysis of Worker Mobility: The Case of Metropolitan Employment Deconcentration." *Review of Public Data Use* 7 (December 1979):54–61.

———— "Employment Deconcentration in the Nonmetropolitan Migration Turnaround." *Demography* 17 (May 1980):145–158.

Warnes, Anthony M. "Migration in Late Working Age and Early Retirement." *Socio-Economic Planning Sciences* 17, no. 5–6 (1983):291–302.

———— "Variations in the Propensity among Older Persons to Migrate: Evidence and Implications." *Journal of Applied Gerontology* 2 (1983):20–27.

Watkins, Alfred J. "Intermetropolitan Migration and the Rise of the Sunbelt." *Social Science Quarterly* 59 (December 1978):553–561.

Webber, M. J. "Life-Cycle Stages, Mobility, and Metropolitan Change: 1. Theoretical Issues." *Environment and Planning A* 15 (March 1983):293–306.

———— "Life-Cycle Stages, Mobility, and Metropolitan Change: 2. A Model of Migration." *Environment and Planning A* 15 (March 1983):307–317.

Weber, Adna Ferrin *The Growth of Cities in the Nineteenth Century.* Ithaca, NY: Cornell University Press, 1962 [1899].

Weinberg, Daniel H. "Toward a Simultaneous Model of Intraurban Household Mobility." *Explorations in Economic Research* 4 (Fall 1977):579–592.

———— "The Determinants of Intra-Urban Household Mobility." *Regional Science and Urban Economics* 9 (1979):219–246.

————, **and Reilly Atkinson** "Place Attachment and the Decision to Search for Housing." *Growth and Change* 10 (April 1979):22–29.

Weinberg, Daniel H.; Joseph Friedman; and Stephen K. Mayo "Intraurban Residential Mobility: The Role of Transactions Costs, Market Imperfections, and Household Disequilibrium." *Journal of Urban Economics* 9 (May 1981):332–349.

Weinstein, E. T. A. "The Movement of Owner-Occupier Households between Regions." *Regional Studies* 9 (1975):137–145.

Weisbrod, Glen, and Avis Vidal "Housing Search Barriers for Low-Income Renters." *Urban Affairs Quarterly* 16 (June 1981):465–482.

Weiss, Leonard, and Jeffrey G. Williamson "Black Education, Earnings, and Interregional Migration." *American Economic Review* 62 (June 1972):372–383.

Weissman, Myrna, and Eugene S. Paykel "Moving and Depression in Women." *Society* 9 (July–August 1972):24–28.

Wertheimer, Richard F. *The Monetary Rewards of Migration within the U.S.* Washington, DC: Urban Institute, 1970.

West, D. A.; J. R. Hamilton; and R. A. Loomis "A Conceptual Framework for Guiding Policy-Related Research on Migration." *Land Economis* 52 (February 1976):66–76.

White, Michael J. "Three Models of Net Metropolitan Migration." *Review of Regional Studies* 7 (Winter 1977):20–44.

White, Paul, and Robert Woods, eds. *The Geographical Impact of Migration.* London: Longman Group Limited, 1980.

White, Ralph B. "Family Size Composition Differentials between Central City–Suburb and Metropolitan-Nonmetropolitan Migration Streams." *Demography* 19 (February 1982):29–36.

White, Stephen E. "A Philosophical Dichotomy in Migration Reserach." *Professional Geographer* 32 (February 1980):6–13.

——— "The Influence of Urban Residential Preferences on Spatial Behavior." *Geographical Review* 71 (April 1981):177–187.

——— "Return Migration to Appalachian Kentucky: An Atypical Case of Nonmetropolitan Migration Reversal." *Rural Sociology* 48 (Fall 1983):471–491.

Wilber, George W. "Migration Expectancy in the United States." *Journal of the American Statistical Association* 58 (June 1963):444–453.

Willekens, Frans "Optimal Migration Policies. An Analytical Approach—Part I." *Regional Science and Urban Economics* 9 (1979):345–367.

Williams, James D. "The Nonchanging Determinants of Nonmetropolitan Migration." *Rural Sociology* 46 (Summer 1981):183–202.

———, **and David Byron McMillen** "Location-Specific Capital and Destination Selection among Migrants to Nonmetropolitan Areas." *Rural Sociology* 48 (Fall 1983):447–457.

Williams, James D., and Andrew J. Sofranko "Motivations for the Inmigration Component of Population Turnaround in Nonmetropolitan Areas." *Demography* 16 (May 1979):239–255.

Willis, Kenneth G. *Problems in Migration Analysis.* Westmead, England: Saxon House Books, 1974.

Wilson, Franklin D. "Cohort Size Effects and Migration." *International Migration Review* 17 (Autumn 1983):485–504.

——— "Migration and Occupational Mobility: A Research Note." *International Migration Review* 19, no. 2 (1985):278–292.

Winston, Stanford R. "The Relation of Educational Status to Interstate Mobility." *Social Forces* 8 (March 1930):380–385.

Wiseman, Robert F., and Curtis C. Roseman "A Typology of Elderly Migration Based on the Decision Making Process." *Economic Geography* 55 (October 1979):324–337.

Wolpert, Julian "Migration as an Adjustment to Environmental Stress." *Journal of Social Issues* 22 (October 1976):92–102.

Wrighton, Fred M., and Paul K. Gatons "Is Out-Migration Affected by Economic Conditions?: Comment." *Southern Economic Journal* 41 (October 1974):311–313.

Yapa, Lakshman; Mario Polese; and Julian Wolpert "Interdependencies of Commuting, Migration, and Job Site Relocation." *Economic Geography* 47 (January 1971):59–72.

Yee, William, and Maurice D. Van Arsdol, Jr. "Residential Mobility, Age, and the Life Cycle." *Journal of Gerontology* 32, no. 2 (1977):211–221.

Yezer, Anthony M., and Lawrence Thurston "Migration Patterns and Income Change: Implications for the Human Capital Approach to Migration." *Southern Economic Journal* 42 (April 1976):693–702.

Young, Geoffrey "The Choice of Dependent Variable for Cross-Section Studies of Migration." *Canadian Journal of Economics* 8 (February 1975):93–100.

Zelinsky, Wilbur "The Hypothesis of the Mobility Transition." *Geographical Review* 61 (April 1971):219–249.

────── "The Demographic Transition: Changing Patterns of Migration," In Institute of Life, *Population Science in the Service of Mankind* Liège, Belgium: International Union for the Scientific Study of Population, 1979, pp. 165–188.

────── "The Impasse in Migration Theory: A Sketch Map for Potential Escapees." In Peter A. Morrison, ed. *Population Movements: Their Forms and Functions in Urbanization and Development.* Liège, Belgium: International Union for the Scientific Study of Population, 1983, pp. 19–46.

Ziegler, Joseph A. "Interstate Black Migration: Comment and Further Evidence." *Economic Inquiry* 14 (September 1976):449–453.

Zimmer, Basil G. "Residential Mobility and Housing." *Land Economics* 49 (August 1973):344–350.

Zipf, George K. "The P1P2/D Hypothesis: On the Intercity Movement of Persons." *American Sociological Review* 11 (December 1946):677–686.

Zodgekar, A. V., and K. S. Seetharam "Interdivisional Migration Differentials by Education for Groups of Selected SMSA's, United States, 1960." *Demography* 9 (November 1972):683–699.

Zuiches, James J., and David L. Brown "The Changing Character of the Non-metropolitan Population, 1950–75." In Thomas R. Ford, ed. *Rural U.S.A.: Persistence and Change.* Ames: Iowa State University, 1978, pp. 55–72.

Zuiches, James J., and Edwin H. Carpenter "Residential Preferences and Rural Development Policy." *Rural Development Perspectives* (November 1978):12–17.

Zuiches, James J., and Glenn V. Fuguitt "Public Attitudes on Population Distribution Policies." *Growth and Change* 7 (April 1976):28–33.

Zuiches, James J., and Jon Rieger "Size of Place Preferences and Life Cycle Migration: A Cohort Comparison." *Rural Sociology* 43 (Winter 1978):618–633.

Name Index

Subject Index

Boldface numbers refer to figures and tables.

A

abroad, migrants from, 74–75; interstate outmigration rates for, **316–317**; life table approach to migration expectancy and, 298; repeat, **108**, 110–111; volume of, **49**, 50, **51**; *see also* foreign-born migrants

administrative areas: comparison of international rates of migration between, 273, **274–275**, 276–277

age of migrants: international comparisons, 258–259, 262–266, **263, 264**; interregional migration and, 138–139; interstate inmigration rates and, 88, 91, 92; interstate migration volume and, 30–31, 37–40, **39**, 42–45, **43**, 55, **55**; interstate net migration rate and, **93–96**, 97; interstate outmigration rates and, 88–89, **90**, 91–92, **93–96**, 96–97; life table approach to migration expectancy and, 298, **299–305**, 306; net migration for metropolitan and nonmetropolitan territory by, 200, **201**; poverty status of female-headed families according to, 166, **167**, 168; primary, 130–131, **131, 132**, 133; reasons for moving and, 237–238, **239**, 240–241, **241, 242–243**, 243–244, **245**, 247; -reason-specific interstate migration rates, 240–241, **241, 242–243**, 243–244; repeat, 130–131, **131, 132**, 133; return, 130–131, **131, 132**, 133; short-distance moving volume and, 53, **54–55**, 55

age question: allocation rate for, 288, **289**

age standardization: interstate migration by fixed-period data and, 32–33, **33**; interstate migration by state-of-birth and, 31; return and repeat interstate migration, **104**, 105

Alabama: efficiency of migration from, **78, 80, 81**; efficiency of migration to, **82**; foreign-born inmigrant percentage for, **319**; foreign-born outmigrant percentage for, **317**; inmigrant from abroad percentage for, **319**; immigration rates for, **315**; net migration for, **78, 80, 81, 82**; nonresponse in, 291; outmigration rates for, **69**, 72, 117, **312, 313**; primary at-risk inmigration rate for, **322**; primary at-risk outmigration rate for, **321**; primary inmigration percentage for, **112, 319**; primary outmigration percentage for, **316**; primary outmigration rate for, 117; repeat at-risk inmigration rate for, **322**; repeat at-risk outmigration rate for, **320**; repeat inmigration percentage for, **319**; repeat outmigration percentage for, **317**; return at-risk inmigration rate for, **322**; return at-risk outmigration rate for, **320**; return inmigration percentage for, **112**, 115, **318**; return outmigration percentage for, **317**; *see also* East South Central division

Alaska, 30; efficiency of migration from, **82**; efficiency of migration to, **79, 80**; foreign-born inmigrant percentage for, **318**; foreign-born outmigrant percentage for, **316**; inmigrant from abroad percentage for, **319**; immigration rates for, **70, 71**, 73–74, **118, 314, 315**; native population of, 74; net migration for, **79, 80, 82**; nonresponse in, 290, **291**; outmigration rates for, **68, 69**, 73, 117,